D042904S

FRANK HARRIS

A BIOGRAPHY

by Philippa Pullar

SIMON AND SCHUSTER
NEW YORK

Designed by Irving Perkins
Manufactured in the United States of America

1 2 3 4 5 6 7 8 9 10

Library of Congress Cataloging in Publication Data
Pullar, Philippa
Frank Harris.

Bibliography: p. 419
Includes index.
1. Harris, Frank, 1856–1931—Biography.
PR4759.H37Z735   828'.9'1209 [B]   75–23352
ISBN 0–671–22091–8

AUTHOR'S NOTE

Harris, being the journalist that he was, often abbreviated his letters, writing, especially to Nellie, in a kind of shorthand. For ease of reading I have for the most part rendered this back into ordinary English.

Contents

Preface

SINCE Frank Harris' death in 1931 there have been a number of biographies written about him. Of these the first was *Frank Harris* by Elmer Gertz and A. I. Tobin, 1931, a book that still has value as source material. Hugh Kingsmill's *Frank Harris*, in 1932, is unique as an autobiographical and personal memoir; Samuel Roth's *The Private Life of Frank Harris*, 1931, and E. M. Root's *Frank Harris*, 1947, are works by disciples; *Frank Harris* by Vincent Brome, 1959, despite circumstantial evidence to the contrary, relies mainly on printed sources.

I have attempted to locate primary source material either from surviving relations of Harris or through collections of unpublished letters, records, and diaries. I have traveled across England, Ireland and America and have examined thousands of letters and papers—most of which are in America, the three major collections being at the University of Texas at Austin, the Library of Congress, Washington (under the capacious files of Elmer Gertz), and the New York Public Library.

A biographer is faced by a dilemma when he sits down before his material. He must extract for the body of his work the facts, and he must resurrect the spirit of his subject. With the second he is confronted with a difficulty. Even the most straightforward people have a private and a public or social self. The private self sometimes goes undetected by contemporaries—who see only the social performance—and is revealed when the subject is alone, particularly when depressed. In this condition he will often resort to long letters in which he tries to share his melancholy. When he is with people the melancholy evaporates in the warmth of gaiety and vitality. Gaiety and vitality, which belong essentially to the tension of the moment, are largely invisible to the biographer since unlike wit they are not captured on paper. To repair this deficiency one must rely on eyewitness accounts, and here I have used several which have not been available to previous biographers.

In the case of Frank Harris the letters and papers not only reveal his private side, which hitherto has passed unnoticed, but they provide a key for deciphering his autobiography—a work notorious for its inaccuracies. When one learns that the volumes were dictated between 1921 and 1927 to a series of secretaries most of whom were in love with Harris (who was by then impotent), all of whom he hoped to titillate, it becomes clear that most of the sexual scenes are fantasy, a requiem for lost youth and virility. Nor is the autobiography helped by its author's tone, which is earnest and without humor, making much of the writing delightfully (if unintentionally) comic. In fact, Harris found writing extremely difficult. He wanted to think great thoughts, feel great feelings, write great writings, of the passion of the soul, joy and sorrow. But as he told Arnold Bennett on December 29, 1910, it seemed that he had no pictorial faculty. "There is a page of mine before me," he wrote. "I've written it a dozen times. It's all wrong, it does not give me the impression I want to give . . . I hate it." He tried too hard, peppering his passages with genitals and embraces—and often the results were ridiculous.

Harris' prime motive for writing *My Life and Loves* was to make money. It was also to be a document demonstrating to the world how misunderstood and wronged he had been. Neither project was successful.

To make money Harris believed that he must be sensational. Success, he thought, could be won by offering to his readers what he called a freedom of speech such as Chaucer had enjoyed. In this he was stimulated by a genuine frustration of censorship and by what he referred to as the castration of the Anglo-Saxon tongue. He meant, he said, to liberate the English language. He reinforced his bawdiness by adding to it another sort of sensation: the incorporation of stories about those friends and contemporaries with whom he was disenchanted. To achieve his revenge he employed a technique of which toward the end of his life he became increasingly fond—balancing the light with the shade, which meant simply repeating the salacious rumors that at one time or another had circulated the smoking rooms: these rumors, which almost always contained a substantial grain of truth, nearly always ended up with the victim's sexual debility or disease leading to a nasty death, and always to Harris' being denounced more than ever.

Certainly many of his anecdotes were inaccurate. All his life he had a fine talent for telling a story. Gradually a tale would seem a little flat, he would embellish it, help his audience by inserting himself in the role of hero, so that it was *he* who hunted the Indians, advised the world's most important men, deflowered the tenderest virgins. In his autobiography there is hardly a country he had not visited, a historic event he had not witnessed. His fantasies eclipsed reality, but he genuinely believed his words were true. With his childhood, however, much genuinely *is* true. There was little here about which he wished to boast. He had never wanted to speak about his origins either from the rostrum or at evening parties. Indeed he took care to present his background as something of a mystery, and so his statements are uncontaminated by repetition and adjustment.

Ironically, with his autobiography he castrated his own life. His fear, paranoia and disappointment obliterated everything but his posturing in more and more fabulous scenes. His fantasies rose superior to self-interest, flew independent of copyright. However tall his stories, they were brought down at every frontier—then pirated.

It is tempting for us to feel ourselves more worthy, sympathetic and serious than Harris; to be disappointed with the facts of his life since they do not support the notion of him as the anti-puritan hero that he longed to be. In this biography I have tried to show Harris as someone more human and complicated than either a hero or a villain. He was a man whose ambitions exceeded his talent and his energy. This is a condition that at one time or another has afflicted most of us and calls for the kind of understanding that we would wish for ourselves.

Finally, this is a biography and not a work of literary criticism. I have used Harris' papers and books for their autobiographical interest.

Here I lie dead at last at rest
With a crucifix upon my breast
And candles burning at head and feet
And I cannot see the flowers so sweet
I cannot smell and I cannot weep
And I cannot wake and I cannot sleep.
For I who laughed and loved am dead,
And laid out on my cold white bed,
With my jaw tied up lest it give offence
And my eyelids closed with a couple of pence.
But for all I am blind I know the tread
Of the friends that crowded round my bed
And I know what they meant by the words they said.
The woman I loved for her golden hair
Who was just as false as she was fair
Cried till her eyes were no longer blue
And said she was sorry, and meant it too.
The girl I wronged had a kindly word
And kissed and forgave me and hoped I heard
And said "after all if the truth were confessed"
That I was "better by far than all the rest."
And the man I helped tho' he takes my place
Cried like a child and kissed my face
And said tho' I passed as a cynic 'mongst men
I had a heart of gold and a brilliant pen,
The strength of seven and the wit of ten
And they would never look on my like again,
And altho' they are only hysterical fools
Fit for asylums and for schools
And I hated death and loved to live
And had lived a life that was sensitive,
It is well worth while to lie here at rest
With a crucifix upon my breast
And candles burning at my head
To hear the kindly things they said.
And yet it makes one long to live
To make amends and to forgive
And yet I'm glad to lie here dead
And rest these tired hands and head
When these poor hands have had to do
Work that they never could get through
In sixty weeks of sixty years
When they might work for these poor dears
Who now can do no more than cry—
It seems a senseless thing to die!

FRANK HARRIS

CHAPTER 1

Family Origins

JAMES Thomas Harris was born in Galway on February 14, 1856, according to both the 1871 census for Ruabon, Denbighshire, and the 1875 one for Lawrence, Kansas. Galway in the 1850s was a most run-down city. With its gloomy atmosphere, its beggars and old dark houses it startled travelers, one and all, by its singular Spanish atmosphere; its singular dirt, collected from the narrow, ill-paved streets but once each year, was also startling. There was hardly a footpath, and the wise traveler stepped out from his train to the new railway station, whose platform gave immediately into the Great Southern Hotel, and arrived fresh in his rooms without suffering stickiness or robbery in the streets.

Not so Mr. and Mrs. Hall,[1] who, while making their itinerary of Ireland, traveled intrepidly through Galway's streets peering down every alley. They remarked upon the numerous crumbling houses, the richly carved doorways, the coats of arms of long-dead merchants; past broad entrance stairs they found glimpses of mysterious courtyards and sliding observation wickets. More curious still were the outskirts. Outside the city gates, settled on the marshes looking over the bay, with its wild gray lights, its purple mountains, was the village of Claddagh—a separate community with its own elected king, superstitions and laws

[1] Samuel Carter and Anna Maria Hall, *Handbooks for Ireland*, 2 vols. (1853), and *Ireland, Scenery, Character, etc.*, 3 vols. (1841–43).

—whose living was fishing. The women wore scarlet petticoats, wonderful handwoven patterned shawls and flat fish baskets on their heads
carrying ling, cockles, mussels and scallops. They had their own marriage ceremony, reputed to be one of capture, which was sealed with a
carved ring made like a heart held by two hands.

On the other side of the city, toward the east, lay Bohermore—a
long, wide lane lined on either side by miserable thatched cabins. This
was the main road into the city, leading down past two duck ponds
into the wide, grassy Eyre Square, where fairs and cattle markets took
place. It was one of these small cabins that Thomas Harris had rented
for his family. The Griffith Valuation of Ireland[2] shows that he rented a
house, a yard and a small garden covering in all an area of eleven
square rods, poles or perches.

There has been so much speculation about the Harrisian origins
that it is necessary to establish the facts once and for all. James
Thomas Harris was the fourth of five children: Vernon, William and
Annetta were older, Chrissie was younger. In 1856 their father,
Thomas Vernon Harris, was engaged as steward on H.M.S. *Amphi-
trite*.[3] She was a small revenue cruiser of 30 tons, based on Galway,
whose job it was to patrol the bays, inlets and river mouths. Thomas
Harris was a remarkable sailor with a nasty temper; a small, mean,
domineering and puritanical man, full of energy, known to be partial
to a jar or two, but silent and unable to express himself. His photograph shows a fleshy nose and large ears—both features inherited by
his third son—narrowed, angry eyes, a luxurious beard striped down
the middle, half black, half white, and thin, scraggy hair scraped back
against the salt winds. His was, and had been always, a hard life. He had
joined the Coast Guard in 1833, aged nineteen, and worked his way
up through the ranks on board the *Skylark*, a boat of 160 tons based on
the South Wales coast, from First Class Boy and Ordinary Mariner to
Steward. Himself one of seven children,[4] he had been born on November 10, 1814, to David and Martha Harries[5] at Gilfachgoch, Fishguard,
Pembrokeshire, and was baptized into the Church of England on June
10, 1815.[6] The fact that he was the only child who was suggests that

[2] Griffith Valuation of Ireland: Co. Galway, 1855.
[3] Admiralty Records, 1822–59: ADM 175 24; ADM 119 14; ADM 119 15; ADM 119 8.
[4] Hannah, John, James, Mary, Martha and Amelia.
[5] The family name is spelled variously throughout the records as Harry, Harries and
Harris.
[6] No. 69 in Bishop's Transcripts, Fishguard.

after his birth the Harrieses became disillusioned with the established church and severed connections, moving to some nonconformist faith. All his life Thomas Harris was to hold austere puritanical views on religion, attended Baptist services, and was described later in life as a fervent member of the Plymouth Brethren.

Gilfachgoch is a small holding, still existing in 1972, comprising five acres of poor marshy land, arable and pasture. The house was mean, the pigsty meaner, the whole tucked under the mountain, protected from the worst gales, commanding a fine prospect of Fishguard built high up above the crescent-shaped bay with its marvelous fragrant air and seals. The family may be traced from the Land Tax Returns to have occupied Gilfachgoch from 1809, when it belonged to Thomas Harries, who died a merchant, intestate, in 1811, leaving goods and chattels worth under £300. His progeny pursued a life that was common to many—a practical mixture of farming and seafaring.[7] A hard life but one that worked: the land would be set to provide food and shelter, and the men and boys went to sea. Often the income was further supplemented by smuggling. Silks and satins, tobacco, brandy and wines came in little vessels on muffled oars under curious-shaped headlands where wild goats still grazed among the blue corn cockles. South Wales was a country pockmarked with caves and secret places; narrow paths climbed from the slate-pebbled beaches up perpendicular cliffs whirling with gulls and guillemots.

The grand epoch of smuggling that lasted from 1700 to 1850 had just ended. Nevertheless this was not immediately obvious to the authorities, and coast guards manned all possible points. They were a most unpopular breed. The more prosperous a country, the more the smuggling trade roared and the more the revenue men were detested. Local papers ironically reported incidents of innocent parties of fishermen, picnicking on hilltops, interfered with by revenue men waving cutlasses and pistols. It was a nice thing, said the local papers, when men could not even ignite a bonfire from which to light their pipes without being roughly ordered to extinguish it—why, one poor devil had even been shot in the thigh. The south was notorious. Lists of con-

---

[7] Keith Harries claims that he is related to Frank Harris and that they belong to the Harries family of Letterston and Tre-coon. Frank visited Keith Harries' grandfather in Monmouthshire sometime before the 1914–18 war wearing a pinstriped suit and sporting a massive gold watch chain. The family has a coat of arms: twin boars of Glyndwr surrounded by holly; the motto was changed in the nineteenth century to Y Gwir yn Erbyn y Byd—The truth shall prevail against the Word.

fiscated articles that had lain in Her Majesty's Custom House at peak times make most interesting reading. At Rochester baskets of eggs, prunes, dutch drops, eau de cologne, cheese and sugar were impounded; at Ramsgate the booty included boats, oars, anchors, rope, yards of silk lace, ass carts, harness, muslin caps, umbrellas, petticoats, reticules, chocolate, baskets of fish, cushions, garters, bonnets and fifty-five pounds of feathers. A ton and a half of tobacco turned up in a hay-stack, and two trunks of silk handkerchiefs in Fleet Prison; it was all very bewildering. Punishment for armed smugglers was death by the gallows, but often they evaded the law. At Deal the crowd unseated the mayor and his constables, who were at table in the act of trying a band of armed smugglers, and retired with the prisoners in a cascade of ink; at Dover they removed the roof of the jail, extracted the prisoners and vanished.

The remedy against all this lawlessness and illicit trafficking was thought to be a number of men-of-war stationed at principal ports, commanding fast revenue cutters to patrol the coasts, sneaking up behind the loaded boats, into the creeks, beaches and underground caves. There was also a land force, housed in specially constructed barracks. Often these were isolated and inaccessible, furniture and belongings having to be lowered down cliffs by rope. Every coast-guard station was equipped with bulletproof shutters, every man with a mixture of tomahawks, coal shovels, gravel spits, sword sticks and darkened lanterns.

Ireland was the most detested posting of all. Far from home, friends and relations, it was bad for families and promotion. In the 1850s, still bearing the scars of the 1846 famine, the population was struggling to subsist, to find shelter and raise crops with which to pay the rent, rather than dallying with cream jugs, silks and satins. In lusher waters the revenue man's payroll was substantially subsidized by a scale of prize money raised on each convicted smuggler and his contraband; in Ireland there was little opportunity, and the main job was to arrest the illegal distilling of poteen. With so little incentive the service was notoriously incompetent and the men apathetic. Officers were constantly changing and the crews kept their ships neither smart nor efficient.

This, then, was the unpromising prospect that confronted Thomas Vernon Harris, steward of H.M.S. *Skylark,* his new son and his equally new bride in 1846. That October two happy events had taken place.

On October 19 Vernon James Herbert had been born at Gilfachgoch; he had escaped illegitimacy by the skin of his gums, for on October 8 his parents were married at the Haverfordwest Register Office. The facts that neither the bridegroom's nor the bride's father signed the register and that both were elevated from their various professions of mariner and Baptist minister to gentlemen suggest that neither was present and that the marriage had not received their blessing. Anne Thomas had been born in 1816, at Waterholmes Farm, Molleston, Pembrokeshire. She was one of eleven children,[8] the daughter of Martha and James Hughes Thomas, who had been appointed minister of Molleston Church one year before. He was known both as Thomas of Waterholmes and the Apostle of Pembrokeshire, a designation he had earned, the Baptist Union Handbook tells us, by earnestly and diligently carrying the Gospel into those parts of the county where it had not before been preached. Indeed, it was due to his diligence that many Baptist churches in Pembrokeshire owe their formation and chapels their erection. Not only was the Apostle a devout gentleman but he was also a practical one and not above viewing his income with a knowing eye, as well he might, for all the time he was in Molleston, the faithful Handbook tells us, his toil was "well-nigh gratuitous"; in none of these years did his income from his church defray the keep of his horse. In 1834 he sought fresher pastures and on August 27 wrote to his "Beloved Brethren" in Trowbridge, Wiltshire, that while it was his prayer to be directed by all events "and as far as I am acquainted with His mind and feel a wish to do His will," the salary proposed of £110 per annum "is certainly below what I expected and which I fear will not be sufficient . . . yet I feel a degree of confidence in you as faithful and affectionate people. There has not any notice been taken of the expense of our removing which I think will not be overlooked or neglected by the Church. I must request that you will engage a House. Mrs. Thomas thinks the house in which the Wesleyan Minister lives will do for the present. Some of our female friends will see that this is managed in proper time. I should wish to know the size of the rooms. You will lose no time in writing to me as I shall not bestir myself about the sale until I hear from you. May the God of peace sanctify you wholly is the sincere wish of Yours in all truth J. H. Thomas."

But the God of peace evidently did not move His people to be

---

[8] Joseph, Benjamin, William, Alfred, Herbert, John, Martha, Eliza, Elizabeth and Daniel (Baptist Register of Baptisms, Molleston, Pembrokeshire).

quite faithful or affectionate enough to support the Thomas family. Soon Thomas became Home Missionary for the coast borders of Pembrokeshire, moved in 1840 for two years to Liverpool and then trundled all the way back again to Pembrokeshire, Milford, where in October 1861 his "robust frame" showed "manifest marks of advancing age and approaching decay," and he died having preached 7,292 sermons and having baptized 711 persons.

Less is known about his daughter Anne. She is said to have had a marvelously sweet disposition and to have been too good for her mean little husband. From the Haverfordwest Register Office she had gone to Gilfachgoch, where eleven days after her marriage her son had been born. From Gilfachgoch she disappears silently from view, presumably out into the Atlantic and into the rain that drives across those western mountains like iron bars. About five years later her second son, William Arnold Horace, was born, at sea.[9] It is probable that she was in the process of removing house, since this was the conventional way in which the Royal Navy transported households—by gunboat—road conditions being so bad. All the furniture was packed on the upper deck, and the only shelter was a tarpaulin. There was no accommodation, and depending on the weather and the destination, the journey might last for several days. Belongings were constantly damaged or lost and there was no compensation. This, with the total lack of comfort, would have been a frightful experience for the most robust lady; for Anne Harris, who was to die eight years later from consumption, it must have been appalling. Two years later she bore Annetta Clare, and then in 1856 there was James Thomas.

[9] Verbal evidence of Mrs. T. K. Harris, Canton, Ohio, daughter-in-law of William Arnold Horace.

CHAPTER 2

Life Without Father

THE picture of James's (or Jim's or Joe's as he was variously known) childhood is a cold and bleak one. He grew independent from an early age, but he never actually grew up. There is no one more egocentric than an insecure, unloved child, and there was no one more egocentric than Harris himself at full age. His egocentricity had developed, stunting his emotional growth. Always his aims in life were the same as those in childhood. Always he was insecure, vain and uneasy, fearing loneliness and being alone, longing for love and praise; it was for this that he was aggressively competitive, wanting always to win and be on top. He needed an applauding audience to whom he could perform. He rebelled against the unjust, puritanical authority of his father, and because he himself was unloved he was unloving. Never at any time was he able to love anyone in the proper sense; he admired women, was obsessed by them, lusted after them, idealized them, but he never loved them.

Nowhere is there a record of the boy's birth or baptism into the Church of Ireland. Official Irish registers start in 1861, yet before this the country should have been one of the best documented in the world, with its censuses, land surveys and church registers; but as all who have worked among the records know, most material relating to years before 1920 was burned during the "troubles." However, parish registers for Galway do exist. Not a Harris is registered between 1850 and

1860. This suggests that Thomas and Anne Harris adopted the prime Baptist principle: infants should not be baptized into the Christian church. Faith, it was argued, was a conscious act requiring intelligence and should not be undertaken on another's behalf. Children should be at an age to profess it for themselves. Independently the Baptists had their own ceremony of total immersion in a river or pool of running water and met under various ministers in chapels and private houses to break bread, recite hymns and prayers. Springing as they did from the English Reformation, nonconformists were made of Puritan stock. Many of their aims, as one reads them in the theological pages, seem sickening: all those divine patiences, heavenly serenities, majestic meeknesses, all that righteousness they sought, manifested itself all too often in bigotry, philistinism, earnestness and a horror of beauty and sensual pleasure. There is no doubt, however, that the resulting sublimation often produced a strange concentration of energy passing into the next generation like an electric current. William and Jim Harris both received this benefit—together with the earnestness. At no time in his life, either as James or as Frank, did Harris possess a grain of humor; wit, yes; humor, no. Humor is that magic carpet upon which one may fly up and, detached, look down upon the world. Without it one is submerged and limited. For most of his life James-Frank spent his time fighting his two parts: there was the deeply melancholy one who would sink down to the marrow of his body, struggling to rise up and escape into the sparkling, vociferous fellow who could captivate audiences and build up his resources on their congratulations.

Soon after the birth of his younger son, Thomas Harris received promotion. June 1856 found him in command of four mariners, five boys and H.M.S. *Bantry*, a cruiser of 39 tons. The family, which was notorious for its seasickness, faced once more the disagreeable removal boat, and set sail for Kerry, whose coast shot out like tongues into the roaring sea. It is certain that they must have gone to Cahirciveen. Valentia Harbour was then a base for the revenue men, and there is no other port in South Kerry that would have been deep enough to draw in the Indiaman on which Jim's Uncle James came to visit them. Kerry was at this time a backward county with poor roads, three main towns and a swirling, dangerous coast. Cahirciveen was, and still is, a gray town straggling down a long dirty street moving with donkey carts and women selling fish on corners. Here the boy's first memory is a long, dark room up which he toddles, supporting his frail mother like a walking stick while she teaches him to recite hymns; next, his Uncle James bounces him on his boot. There is his mother again, cold and dead,[1] followed not by grief but by gloom and a terrible silence as all the reassuring household routine is halted. A change of scene, and a red-moustached man is in bed with the children's nurse, on whom Jim subsequently promises to "tell" unless she sprinkles his bread with sugar.

Once again Thomas Harris received promotion, and on December 29, 1860, he became Acting Second Master of H.M.S. *Racer*. This time the family removed to Kingstown (now Dun Laoghaire), near to Dublin. Here James—not yet five—is apparently so precocious at arithmetic that he is in the top form, and spends his time dropping his slate pencil in order to fiddle about among the girls' legs. The picture emerges of a bright child who longs for praise and affection, whose childhood is spent over both northern and southern Ireland shuffling from one lodging house to another under the protection of his brother Vernon.

In Galway, where Vernon returned in 1863 to read agriculture at Queen's College, James ran wild; in Belfast he peered under his old Methodist landlord's bed and discovered colored medical plates of pudenda; in Carrickfergus, where Vernon worked as a bank clerk and all the family once more lived together, he examined the developing breasts of his sisters, and dived from the pier and swam, having learned the rudiments of swimming from a book belonging to Vernon. In Armagh—Vernon's next bank appointment—a boy introduced him to masturbation, and he learned with astonishment that a *Roman Catholic* could be a normal human being and could even be an agreeable companion. Here is proof that Thomas Harris had been active in passing on his bigotry. Much later, in the pages of *Vanity Fair*, Harris describes one of the worst memories of his childhood in the north of Ireland, having to learn by heart and repeat the shorter catechism of the Presbyterian Church "with its brainless, hair-splitting, mean low tone and harsh insistence on mere puerilities." He hated the whole of it.

---

[1] I hoped that since no record of Mrs. Harris' death has as yet been unearthed, her grave might be discovered in Cahirciveen Protestant graveyard. That, in high summer, was a vain hope. The ground has to be seen to be believed. Twisted trees, brambles and nettles are as high as an elephant's eye, not to mention the dumps of rejected bedsprings, frying pans and other unsavory rubbish. After disentangling the undergrowth and debris, several mid-nineteenth-century graves were indeed discovered, most of which have eroded headstones and are yawning to the skies, since, an Irish friend explained with relish, French tourists had carried off the skulls with which to make lampshades. The whereabouts of poor Mrs. Harris still remains a subject for speculation.

In all it was a restless life, rootless, with no continuity and no friends—except for his masturbating Roman Catholic—since he was forever changing schools. By the age of twelve James was a self-conscious, insecure, uneasy boy and small for his age. He longed for people to like and admire him and took great trouble with his clothes, dressing himself carefully in shirts and ties purchased for him by Vernon and three suits—"one in black with an Eton jacket for best and a tall hat, and the others in tweeds"—washed carefully and brushed his hair to regulation smoothness. When at evening parties he was invited to recite, he would pout and plead that he did not want to, in order to be pressed. He recalled in *My Life and Loves*: "I was always wondering how I looked and watching to see if people liked me. I used to try and speak with the accent used by the 'best people' and, on coming into the room, I prepared my entrance. Someone . . . said I had an energetic profile, so I always sought to show my profile. . . . I often used to think that no one cared for me really and I would weep over my unloved loneliness."

He was full of self-pity, unloved and unloving. For there was no one either for whom he really cared. The two people he claims to have liked best were Vernon and his youngest sister, Chrissie. They were both sweet-natured and took after their mother rather than their father. James did not have much time with Chrissie, whom he describes as two years younger than he, pretty and clever, with dark curls and large hazel eyes. She died, it is said,[2] killed by a drunken doctor, probably between 1869 and 1871. Vernon was at this time a sort of father figure and hero to James; he was kind and he flattered him. William, on the other hand, being near to him in age, was a rival whom he actually disliked and fought. Moreover, William could recite and act better than James, and worst of all, he was taller—height being a subject about which James-Frank was always touchy, reaching, without shoes, only five feet five inches. For Annetta, too, he had little time. She was affected, putting on airs and graces, objecting, for example, to being called Annie, after her mother; this she pronounced common and preferred to be known as Nita, which was, she said, the stylish French way of pronouncing Annie.

Most of all he disliked his father. The news that his ship was approaching port sickened him with fear. Thomas Harris was a man

[2] Notes given by Gwladys Price Williams to Elmer Gertz.

who ruled by punishment and instilled his religion by fear, a stern, narrow, little bigot, with no time for children or childish ways—"a get all, give nought, a mean stingy hound," his son described him many years later in a letter. He was keen on duty, sought to humiliate and never, never praised—probably, he confided later, because he did not know how to communicate his emotions. James has a list of grievances against him. Once, he claims, he caught him on the boat listening to the sailors telling dirty stories, and for this his father beat him with a strap. When he had been drinking, he would, in his cups, put the boy to various antics. Once he is supposed to have forced him to swim, spluttering, round and round the boat under the nose of a Lord of the Admiralty, and once sent him racing up the rigging against a ship's boy. "The memory of my fear," wrote his son fifty years later, "made me see that he was always asking me to do too much, and I hated him who could get drunk and shame me and make me run races up the rigging with the cabin boys who were grown men and could beat me."

In Armagh, he grumbled, his father sent him to bed at nine instead of the eleven and twelve o'clocks to which he was used with Vernon. Every evening he liked to take a stroll with the boy directly after school. These promenades were frightful for James, who found that every time he opened his mouth some word or story would fall out with which his father found fault. "So I walked beside him silently taking heed as to what I should say in answer to his simplest question. There was no companionship!" Before he had perfected his technique, however, there descended the name of James Stephens, who in March 1867 had led the unsuccessful Fenian rising against British rule. Harris tells us that it was his Roman Catholic friend from the Royal School of Armagh who had initiated him into the mysteries surrounding James Stephens and his cause—subjects that immediately appealed to his imagination along with all the banshees, fairy queens and heroes which he claimed lived in his head. There was little, however, to appeal to his father, who was horrified—perhaps understandably, since one of the main targets of the Fenians seems to have been Her Majesty's Coast Guard Stations. (In February 1867 they had seized the station at Cahirciveen and in March had overcome one in the Cork area, burning down the police barracks.)

These revolutionary sympathies must be squashed in his son, and at once. He must be sent away to school in England.

CHAPTER 3

Ruabon Grammar School

RUABON Grammar School, Denbighshire, must have seemed ideal to Thomas Harris. Situated within easy reach of Liverpool, it was a church foundation under the headmastership of the Reverend A. L. Taylor, M.A., and the patronage of Sir Watkin Williams Wynn of Wynnstay. The industrial revolution was just beginning to smother the surrounding countryside with small coalpits, brickyards, ironworks and stone quarries, but for the most part the small village itself lay unchanged, dominated by Wynnstay Park lying magnificently behind its walls. From the gardens, with their beautiful terraces, conservatories, obelisks and towers, observations of the most scientific sort were reported carefully in the *Wrexham Advertiser*. The ranges of barometer were noted, the temperature of water and of the earth one foot below the ground; the couplings of thrushes, woodpeckers, crows and pigeons were spotted, the blooming of primroses and alders. On June 4, 1870, readers were astonished by the hatching of a monster pheasant with three legs and three feet. On Sir Watkin Williams Wynn's birthday the church bells rang out, a flag flew from the steeple and all the tenants were entertained to lunch; many a good toast was honored, many a good glass raised to "Sir Watkin's foxhounds" and to "The coal and iron trade of Ruabon." Upon Miss Williams Wynn's birthday, scholars of the National School were treated to roast beef and plum pudding while Lady Williams Wynn opened a soup kitchen wherein benefactors dished out soup and rolls of flannel.

Since Ruabon was such a small community the grammar school participated in the village entertainments. The Working Men's Association Evening was reported each year by the friendly *Wrexham Advertiser*. There would be the Reverend H. Humphreys' rendering of "The Merry Fairy Elves" and "The Nightingale's Trill," Mrs. Williams' glee "Haste Thee Nymph" and Mr. Copland with "The Rose Will Cease to Blow." Miss Bellis and party would deliver "Rock Me to Sleep, Mother," Mr. W. Jones had the audience much amused at "My Complaints," while the reading of "How to Raise the Wind" was admired. Besides performing at the Working Men's soirees, the grammar school, according to the *Wrexham Advertiser*, sang in church and performed plays. The sports day and prizegiving was a major event of the year. The Williams Wynn family would attend, there would be expeditions to the park, rich teas of cake, and afterward buns and nuts would be distributed in the gardens.

The Reverend A. L. Taylor adopted the line of most schoolmasters of that time. He was slow to praise and quick to punish. According to an 1869 report under the Endowed Schools Act he had raised the school from a very low condition into a popular boarding and day school, "chiefly but not exclusively for professional men's sons. The fee for parishioners for the general course is only £4 per annum. Hence the school contains some day boys of a lower class, but they and the six free boys named by the Vicar under the terms of former Vicar Robinson's will seldom learn anything but the English subjects and a little Latin." The fee for boarding was £35 and the boys were housed in a large stone residence, just outside the village, the home of the Reverend A. L. Taylor, Mrs. Taylor and their six children. The 1871 census records twenty boarders, including James, whose ages ranged from eleven to seventeen, born mostly in the surrounding counties—Lancashire, Shropshire and Merioneth—but with two boys from London, one from Dublin and one from county Down.

James was at the grammar school for about two and a half years, arriving near the beginning of 1869 before his thirteenth birthday, small for his age, measuring under five feet. The school was for him the worst sort of nightmare. He was not liked and felt lonely and isolated. He was good at lessons, particularly arithmetic, and in spite of being shortsighted was keen on sport and by 1870 was playing for the first cricket eleven on the strength of his bowling. The *Wrexham Advertiser* reports a match against Hadodybych, for which James is going in tenth and scoring 13 not out. He was not, however, a sportsman and tells how just before a cricket match, in front of the rival team, he threw a cricket ball at the head of Jones, the captain, who was apparently a nasty bully and who had beaten him up. For this he was sent to Coventry; no one, neither the upper nor the lower boys, would speak to him.

The school seems to have been, like most contemporary establishments, a prison of discomfort, fagging, fighting, bullying and stupidity. Indeed, James's account differs from other nineteenth-century school stories only in that he lubricates the classrooms and dormitories liberally with tales of "frigging" and semen. A hundred years later it is not his facts that are questionable—it is perfectly accepted that wherever adolescents are contained there will always be masturbation, just as in segregated schools there will always be homosexual affairs—it is his tone in relating these pursuits. He tries so hard to make his effect that he often overpaints, turning his nudes into ludicrous peep shows. We are all lined up at the keyhole peering at the older boys kicking, beating, burning the trousers off the smaller fellows, and jumping into bed with them. James claims that he himself was not a popular bed-fellow—he caught the semen in a boy's nightshirt, so that the fellow went off muttering darkly, never to return. As for masturbation, he says, he allowed himself this treat only on Sundays, since he discovered that the practice spoiled his performance at the high jump. Here we have the Victorian notion that "self-abuse" was debilitating and could cause madness. One little boy, Harris tells us, had worn a hole in his pocket the better to abuse himself. None of the masters noticed that he grew gradually paler, cried in corners and was shaken for a quarter of an hour at a time by unaccountable tremblings, until at last he was removed by his parents.

That summer James returned to Ireland for the holidays, spending them in Ballybay, county Monaghan, where Vernon had been appointed by the bank and where his father and Nita now lived. Here, he says, he learned from his sister the rudiments of seduction by flattery—how to win the confidence of girls by admiring their teeth, their eyes, their hats, how to assure each that she was unique, the only girl in the world. With this policy of flattery and devotion the kissing would follow automatically, Nita assured him. From Vernon he learned the principles of fighting, and on his return to school arranged a full-scale fight against Jones, his cricket-ball enemy, which he won in spite of his inferior size, reducing Jones to a battered, bleeding wreck. This helped him, he said; people liked him better after the fight.

That summer something else had happened. On his arrival at Ruabon he had been deeply religious. His father had done his work well. The word of God must be obeyed—believe not and eternal damnation and torture would follow. Then some boy pointed out that the Bible stories he so earnestly believed were nothing more than fairy tales. How on earth could a man get down a whale's throat? Plainly it was balderdash. In a flash the fabric of his belief lay ruined. He refused to be confirmed. His loss of faith was at first a frightening and painful experience, and for a while he felt more alone and isolated than ever. He foraged continually for books to convince him and for biblical smutty stories with which he nightly regaled the boys in the bedroom.

Now that he had no faith, James argued, he had no prohibitions, he could enjoy all the sexual adventure he could get, since there was nothing to forbid it. Clearly, he told Upton Sinclair fifty years later, he was a highly sexed boy, whose mind and body were tormented with sex, from the age of thirteen to twenty. In puberty all women tempted him. His eyes were like fingers probing and feeling. His own accounts dilute his virility. For he did have a virility. Even when he was impotent he still had the air of a stallion. He exuded sex, Leo Rosten said, when he met him in New York in 1928—he was so swarthy, so highly charged, so male. Behind his autobiographical sex scenes lies a complicated network of facts. He was impotent at the time of writing; many performances therefore are fabricated from a nostalgic randiness, many are simply an old man's fantasy. He was dictating to (and he hoped titillating) a series of young secretaries, many of whom were in love with him and with all of whom he was having affairs. He believed that he was going to liberate the Anglo-Saxon tongue from the prison into which the puritans had locked it and bring back free speech, with the result that his pages are peppered with genitals defined by every name under the sun, often with ridiculous, and boring, results.

His sexual debut, he claims, was made when, aged almost five, he dropped the slate pencil in the arithmetic class in order to crawl among the girls' legs and touch them. Here one feels is fantasy. All his life Harris admitted to a fascination for legs. A margin of thigh glimpsed, shining like alabaster, under the rucked-up skirts of a young girl and his mouth would parch, his voice falter. What more delightful notion to such a man of sixty-five than to crawl in a fragrant forest of pubescent limbs? The next adventure, aged thirteen, was with a girl to whom he refers as "E," whom he encountered behind a piano where they were both singing alto, in preparation for a church festival. This is almost certainly not fantasy (he describes how years later she saw him again when he was working for the *Fortnightly Review*). Voyeurs once more, we are treated to a nice scene: "E" standing on a chair listening to the organist explaining the new plainchant while James, his "heart-pulse" throbbing in his throat, scrabbles about up her skirts researching into the technicalities of the female genitalia. Another succulent scene takes place in the Reverend Ebenezer Edward's rustic summer house, whither he had been gratefully invited after rescuing the Edward boy from some bully. James was quick to spot the slim ankles of Lucille, the French governess, and before the turn of the page he is practicing his rudiments of seduction. He flatters her in French, copies out poems, and soon, breathless with kissing, works his way under her clothes. Here we come to another instance of Harris' Victorianism. It was widely held that nocturnal emissions were as debilitating as self-abuse[1]—though less sinful; their occurrence was recognized in the medical profession as spermatorrhea, against which all kinds of spiked contraptions and electric alarms were worn. Most nights James found himself dreaming of the yielding Lucille and had a wet dream; the next morning his performance over the high jump suffered. Then, he says, he happened upon a small piece of whipcord.

> That night I tied up Tommy and gave myself to thoughts of Lucille's private parts: as soon as my sex stood and grew stiff, the whipcord hurt dreadfully and I had to apply cold water at once to reduce my unruly member to ordinary proportions. I returned to bed and went to sleep: I had a short sweet dream of Lucille's beauties, but then awoke in agony. I got up quickly and sat on the cold marble slab of the washstand. That acted more quickly than

---

[1] Harris in the preface to the second volume of *My Life and Loves* repeats the story of Balzac, who came in one day with a long face. "What's the matter?" someone—he thought it was Gautier—asked. "Matter enough," Balzac replied, "another masterpiece lost to French literature." "What do you mean?" asked Gautier. "I had a wet dream last night," Balzac replied.

even the cold water. . . . The cord was effective, did all I wanted: after this experience I wore it regularly and within a week was again able to walk under the bar and afterwards jump it, able to pull myself up with one hand till my chin was above the bar. I had conquered temptation and once more was captain of my body.

The captain was determined to idealize his feelings of lust. He held the theory, which he spent some time developing, that the awakening of desire awoke also an appreciation of nature. His life became enriched, ennobled, transfigured, he says; he began to live an enchanted life. So melodramatic does he make his arousal that it seems as though Mother Nature herself had stumbled upon and raped him. At all times of the night and day glimpses would come that would ravish him with delight "and turned my being into a hymn of praise and joy."

He offers us two accounts of this phenomenon. The first is in Volume I of *My Life and Loves.* He had never noticed the beauties of nature, he said; whenever he had come across descriptions of scenery in books he had always skipped them. Now, in full sunshine, on a bridge spanning the river Dee,[2] his eyes were unsealed: "On my right the river made a long curve, swirling deep under a wooded height, leaving a little tawny sandbank half bare opposite to me: on my left both banks, thickly wooded, drew together and passed round a curve out of sight. . . . And when I left the place and came out again and looked at the adjoining cornfields, golden against the green of the hedgerows and scattered trees, the colours took on a charm I had never noticed before."

The second comes in Volume II. He had, he says, been invited to Wynnstay for luncheon and afterward to wander with Lady Williams Wynn among her flower beds. They walked between two herbaceous borders. "For the first time I saw the glory of their colouring, and the exquisite fragility of the blossoms: my senses were ravished and my eyes were flooded with tears." No doubt they were. What Harris fails to make clear is that his visit to Wynnstay Park must have been one of the school treats, an outing with buns. The lovely gardens and park so securely tamed would certainly have appealed to him. He cared extremely for scenery provided that it was arranged in such a way that he could comfortably conduct his party to a spectacular point of view whence he could show off the ravishing sights and give tongue to re-

[2] Hesketh Pearson claimed that this revelation of nature was pinched from Hazlitt, who actually used the same river Dee for his purpose.

citation. For him the country was always a place to visit and admire rather than for work and relaxation. He was essentially a man of cities. His favorite places in the world, he once said, were the green strip of Roehampton, lying between Kingston and Putney, and the Riviera, between Cannes and Monte Carlo, both situations carefully controlled and suburban, with all the sophisticated comforts of good hotels in the vicinity, operas and theaters. The wild parts of Wales and Ireland, whence he originated, with their soft airs, winds rushing through the heather, nostalgic peat-smokes and fuchsia hedges winding with roses were not so much scenery as a damp background from which to escape.

One other story from the wild hills of Rhyl is revealing. During the short Christmas holidays, he explains, his father, who encouraged independence, sent him seven pounds and advised him to pass Christmas in lodgings in a neighboring town. So to Rhyl, he claims, he went, there to witness the train crash that took place and to kiss Gertrude Hannaford, who refused however to allow him to indulge in his favorite scrabbling. "You'll make me couple 'dirty' with 'Gertie' if you go on using it so often," he had to rebuke her. One evening there was an earthquake. "An explosion," cried James, and together they ran, vaulting over the railway fence—not without experiencing a delightful skirmish among Gertie's skirts, conveniently allowing the hero to advance. "My right hand stopped on her sex and began to touch it." "Open-eyed," they watched workmen pulling charred remains from the Irish express, which had crashed into a freight train loaded with oil barrels and had caught fire. "Slowly I returned to my lodgings only to find myself the hero of the house when I told the story next morning." The fact is that there was an appalling accident: at Abergele the Irish mail train en route to Holyhead ran into a freight train loaded with casks of petrol, caught fire immediately and thirty-three people were burned to death; but this happened on August 20, 1868, when James would have been in Ireland, and not during the Christmas holidays. He would have heard about it—perhaps from people who had witnessed the disaster—taken the story, embroidered in some sex with his colored wool, and fifty years later he was there on the night—eyes and hands busy.[3]

[3] He admits this himself in *My Life and Loves*: "As I came to maturity I found that my memory . . . began to colour incidents dramatically. For example I had been told a story by someone, it lay dormant in me for years; suddenly some striking fact called back the tale and I told it as if I had been present and it was fulfilled with dramatic effects, far beyond the first narration."

During his time at Ruabon James endured frightful claustropho-
bia. The rigid discipline, the stupid punishments imposed by Doctor
Taylor were all to much like the regimen imposed by his father.
Soon he had read all the books in the library and life at school seemed
stale, flat and unprofitable. He was a caged bird, said he—how was he
going to escape? Would his father recommend him for a nomination
in the navy, which must be done before his fourteenth birthday, in
1870? He wrote a careful and flattering letter. To this his father replied with biblical exhortations, followed by silence. February 14 came
and went without James's name being sent up for nomination. This, his
father explained later, was purely for the good of his son. His own experience had been so intolerable that he knew the navy was no career
for the boy. To get on in the British navy one had to be either well
born or well off. James was neither. For a youth without position or
money the only possible roads up were servility or silence. James was
incapable of either. He was so impulsive and quick-tempered that some
officer would take an instant dislike to him, and then in some port
where the officer was powerful James would be court-martialed and
dismissed, ruined. Unfortunately his father was so well versed in his
own course of silence that he failed to communicate these reasons to
his son, who sat fretfully thumbing his way through papers describing
the diamond fields of South Africa. Determined, he said, to escape, he
selected America, with its great plains, buffalo, Indians, cattle and
cowboys, on account of the cheaper passage, and set himself to mathematics with the view to winning the second prize of ten pounds
(awarded toward the purchase of books) in the mathematical scholarship exam, which was held in the summer. He worked, he tells us, as
he had never worked before. He soaped the stairs, so that "Shaddy,"
his housemaster, who had given him a hundred lines to learn, fell
down and hurt his hip,[4] he was kissed by the mathematics master and
he delighted various members of the local gentry, including the Williams Wynns and Lucille, by his interpretation of Shylock. And then at
last the assembly was gathered in the schoolroom to learn the results of

[4] Hugh Kingsmill adds in his *Frank Harris* that, after the stair-soaping episode, Harris
had told him that he fled in panic to the maids' bedroom and sought shelter with the
cook. "I was very small for my age." The cook (Maria Evans, according to the census) just
laughed and took him in her arms. The next night he ran in again, pretending more fear,
and got into bed with one of the housemaids (either Sarah Davies or Mary Jane Edwards),
who were younger and prettier than the cook, but he forgot to play the baby and they all
pushed him out of the room.

the examination, which were announced in person by a Cambridge professor. Harris remembers receiving the check and then pretending outraged disappointment at not receiving the first prize. Never again, he complained to an embarrassed school, would he enter, his father should be the first to hear of his failure, and by noon the next day he was in Liverpool with fifteen pounds in his pocket, ready to embark for America.

What emerges from the *Wrexham Advertiser* is that although the gist of Harris' story is more or less right, there are confusions. He did win prizes, but in 1870, and he did not leave the school until April or May 1871.[5] If there was a midsummer exam that year it was not reported by the *Wrexham Advertiser*. The event of the year was the annual prizegiving, which took place on Tuesday, December 20, 1870, in the presence of a large company that included even the Reverend Humphreys of "Merry Fairy Elves" fame. The report reveals marvelously the whole scale of earnestness and duty that rang round the establishment.

> Great interest was manifested by the visitors in the large collection of drawings exhibited, the work of the scholars during the past half year. They included water-colour, crayon, and pencil studies of landscape, mechanical, and other subjects, and showed the teaching in this department to be of high-class order. The mechanical drawings especially were pronounced to be of a very superior class; and the other studies also reflected the greatest credit on the school.
>
> In opening the proceedings, the headmaster, the Rev. A. L. Taylor, M.A., said he much regretted than another Christmas had come round and they were not honoured with the presence of Sir Watkin and Lady Williams Wynn, for they always much appreciated their attendance; and if Sir Watkin had been able to be present this year it would have been the twelfth Christmas on which he had kindly come to give away his handsome presents to the boys of the school. However, in his unavoidable absence, the Hon. Mr. Kenyon, of Gredlington, had kindly consented to take his place, and he begged to introduce that gentleman to the school. (Cheers.)

---

[5] The *Wrexham Advertiser*, January 2, 1869, carries a short account of the Mathematics Scholarship, December 2, 1868. The examiners were Rev. E. B. Smith, Caius College, Cambridge, and R. B. Bagnall Wilde, Esq., B.A., Caius College, Cambridge. The mathematics prize was awarded to W. M. Gordon. Harris is not mentioned.

Several boys then recited a portion of the "Merchant of Venice" in a very creditable manner, after which the Rev. E. B. Smith (Oxon), examiner of the school, read his report, and it appeared from the result of his examination that the elementary subjects taught, such as Geography, English, History, Grammar, English Composition, and Latin, were in a most satisfactory condition throughout the school. Many of the pupils were especially referred to by the examiner, and amongst them Mr. E. L. Jones, he stated, highly distinguished himself, he having obtained an average of 85 per cent. on all his papers. In a like manner Messrs. Harris, Caroes (2), W. Hughes, Taylor, C. Edwards, James, Smith, George, Miller, Lloyd Smith, Findlater, Grimshaw, R. G. Evans, Green, T. Jones, Negus, and several others were very favourably noticed. . . . It may be remarked that of the pupils of the school, Messrs. Caroe and Harris obtained a second-class certificate in the Oxford Local Examination at Midsummer. . . .

At the conclusion of the interesting ceremony, the Hon. Mr. Kenyon said that he was called upon to say a few words instead of the gentleman—he alluded to Sir Watkin—whom they would much rather have seen that day as president, and whose worth they all appreciated. The fact of the matter, however, was that Sir Watkin, who was a very loyal subject, had been asked to meet some members of the royal family in the north, and, of course, could not refuse. Lady Williams Wynn, he was sorry to say, was unwell in London. It would be superfluous on his part to dwell at any length upon the nature of the education received at that school, but the recitation from Shakespeare given by the boys, and the satisfactory report Mr. Smith had read, showed that the education there given was placed upon a good and solid basis, and if the scholars would but make the most of their time they would never have cause to regret it in after years. The question of education had lately been brought prominently before the public. . . . He strongly recommended parents to recognise the importance of sending their children to school as early as possible, and to keep them there as long as they could. . . .

The Rev. T. E. Laurence, senior curate of Ruabon, then made a few observations, containing excellent advice and counsel to the boys, and remarks on the importance of the work which those had to carry out who prepared them for the battle of life, and who specially enabled them to benefit their fellow-men.

Mr. Edward Peel (High Sheriff of Flintshire) then addressed the boys and pointed out to them that prizes were not things to be gained in a day or a half-year, but were a proof that the holders of them had listened from early years to the advice of their parents, and afterwards to that of their tutors. He said as a rule it was not the geniuses who took the victory, but the steady plodding boys who day by day faithfully performed their allotted work and gradually improved themselves. This fact was daily illustrated by innumerable instances around them. Speaking to those who were not fortunate enough to be prize-takers, he said that the man of moderate abilities often gained in a few years a more substantial reward than he who perhaps, blessed with better abilities, did not through lack of perseverance put them out to the best of his power. He urged the boys to have a settled purpose in life and to exercise all their powers to perfect themselves in the professions they should choose, and above all things he exhorted them never to lose sight in years to come of the great moral and religious truths which he was sure they received at their masters' hands.

The Rev. T. E. Laurence proposed, and the Rev. H. Humphreys seconded, a vote of thanks to the Hon. G. T. Kenyon for presiding. . . . Mr. J. F. James proposed three cheers for Sir Watkin for giving the prizes, and the call was heartily responded to, Lady Williams Wynn, Mr. Taylor, and the ladies present being similarly honoured.

The last event to be recorded by the *Wrexham Advertiser* before James set sail for America occurred on April 20, 1871, and was the Annual Athletic Sports, which "came off" in the presence of a great number of people. The prizes comprised "silver cups, pencils, knives, etc." The highest prize was a silver cup presented by a Mr. Bagnall Wilde, "which was keenly contested by R. Taylor (the headmaster's son) and J. Harrie[s?] and won by the latter." Certainly there is no record of any J. Harrie being at the grammar school at this time; it is likely that this is a misprint, or illegible writing by the reporter; it is also likely that it was the silver cup that provided the funds James required to reach America.

He claims that on the night that he arrived in Liverpool, Albery's comedy *The Two Roses*[6] was playing. In spite of his loss of faith he had not lost the fear of his father. The theater, he had been told again and again, was "an open door to hell." He bought a ticket and for the

---

[6] *The Two Roses* opened at the Royal Alexander Theatre on May 29, 1871, according to the *Liverpool Daily Post*, and played for 18 nights.

next four hours came many times to the verge of surrendering it. Fear, he said, came over him like a vapor. What if his father was right? But he did not give up his ticket, and the moment the curtain rose he fell in love with the heroine. How lovely she was, how affectionate and true! What noble feelings she engendered in Harris that evening! Self-abuse was nearly impossible from that night forth. Forty years later he told Hugh Kingsmill that he had been so deeply impressed by this lovely, affectionate, true heroine that for her sake he remained chaste for three years. Probably he did, but the fact that he continued virginal was more likely due to lack of opportunity than to moral strength. The next years were to be physically hard ones for Harris.

CHAPTER 4

A Little Irish Immigrant . . .

EIGHTEEN years later, when Harris was Conservative candidate for South Hackney, he gave biographical details to the Hackney *Mercury*. Throwing off the shackles of school life, he said, he went to Canada, then soon passed to the United States. Elsewhere he claimed that he made his first Atlantic crossing on the S.S. *Scotia*, which was known as the "ladies' ship," since it was held to be a miracle of comfort. In fact it was frightful—a little ship of 5,000 tons that rolled and pitched in bad weather. Everything about her was rough; no consideration was paid to the weak and ailing, no food given on deck except by the doctor's orders. It was the doctor who, Harris claimed, took him under his wing—after some trouble over the boy's lack of bedding in which to sleep on his plot of deck—and into his cabin, where there was a wealth of Macaulay. At once James was reciting from memory the essay on Warren Hastings, a performance that the doctor required him to repeat in the first cabin. A hat was passed round, a collection made and Harris was the possessor of a first-class ticket.

His boat trip would not be complete without a girl to kiss or an opportunity for him to exercise his literary technique in body exploration. This time the girl is called Jessie, and under the canvas coverings of the lifeboats, Harris assures us, "my right hand was busy. . . . I had got my fingers to her warm flesh between the stockings and the draw-

3 8

ers and was wild with desire, soon mouth to mouth I touched her sex. What a gorgeous afternoon we had." One more half-remembered conquest mixed with fantasy to linger over, to provide relief for its jaded author languishing in the hot stickiness of the Catskill Mountains—polishing warm marble bottoms, breasts like apples, smooth thighs, soft hair, resuscitating caressing fingers—like young eyes satisfying curiosity.

With Harris' tone, his embellishments, his penetrations, it is all too easy to lose the truth. To travel to America had required a great deal of courage; he arrived in a raw, tough country without money or friends. According to him, he walked the mean streets of New York, between the horse carts, until he arrived in Central Park, where he shacked up with some kind "Irish folks" who lived in a wooden house complete with outhouse, poteen, bucket and cow, where he was as welcome "as the flowers in May." To get money, he claimed, he worked as a bootblack and then on the river bed, in a caisson, building Brooklyn Bridge—a dangerous and painful job and one that is likely to have been endured by another, since its description first makes its appearance in *The Bomb*, which was written in 1907, after he had come back from a trip across America interviewing a series of people from New York, Chicago and Salt Lake City. At the invitation of a satisfied bootblacked customer he continued to Chicago[1] to work as night clerk in the customer's Fremont Hotel, where through his sharpness and dexterity he rose to bookkeeper and manager of the billiard room. He interviewed a prostitute, who flabbergasted him by saying she had had a baby because she wanted one, and a hobo, who first tried to rob him and then administered some useful advice about stealing rides on freight trains, boxcars and on tops of coal wagons. For love interest he brought to his reception desk a wonderful Spanish lady complete with shrugs, contemptuous nods and black mantilla. Her quiet question "Any letters for us?" had James dumbfounded and enthralled—in spite of her beaked nose. The magic of her glance, the proud grace of her carriage threw him into a fit of fever. It was not until he saw her in evening dress that he stripped her with his green imagination. "Would she ever kiss me? What was she like undressed? My imagination was still untutored. I could picture her breasts better than her sex and I made up my mind to examine the next girl I was lucky enough to see naked more precisely."

[1] He claims that he witnessed the Great Fire, which happened in October 1871.

One of the tragedies surrounding Harris and his writing is that to compensate for his disappointments, failures and old age he must always be elevating his past—apart from his childhood—and himself. The bare tale of his survival in America would have been remarkable enough; instead he had to embroider it, make it fabulous. Conceived through his lips, rising from his pages comes Harris the hero, Harris the god in all his guises: Harris of mercy, Harris of grace, showing the brightness of his face, a god of all trades and for all seasons. There a rain god bestowing on the earth and various maidens the goodness of his semen, here from the great prairies Harris the Hercules of strength and courage, all wiry frame and bronzed muscles. At the age of fifteen, he told Hugh Kingsmill, he examined himself in a mirror and saw that he was ugly; from that moment on, said he, he put all thought of his appearance from his head. This he certainly did not do. He was obsessed with himself and with his looks. In the middle of a talk with Kingsmill a few days after this revelation he jumped up, pulled out his ears at right angles to illustrate their size, tapped his nose ruefully and dropped his arms to their full length: "Look, Lunn, gorilla arms."[2]

Arthur Leonard Ross and other good friends have rushed indignantly to defend Harris against accusations that he never was a cowboy. He could ride, they pointed out, and see how authentic *On the Trail* was. *On the Trail* was a series of articles that he wrote for *Vanity Fair* under the title of "The Odyssey of the Great Trail," starting on January 1, 1908, after he had returned from the American expedition, quite a part of which had involved traveling across the prairies—in the observation car of a railway train. He admitted to his third wife, Nellie, that at the time of writing he found the American part particularly confusing, since he was muddled by the Life, his novel. Thomas Bell, who was Harris' secretary for about six years at the turn of the century, explains in an unpublished work, "Oscar Wilde Without Whitewash," that he had a number of small details wrong that would be impossible for any true cowboy. Bell recognizes in his scenes set in Texas and the Mexican border (whither Harris claimed he had ridden in search of his Mexican lady) some of the minor incidents that he himself had once told

[2] After the publication of his first book in 1919, *The Will to Love*, Kingsmill dropped the Lunn from his surname. This was for two reasons, one practical, the other personal. There was already a surfeit of Lunn authors, his two brothers Brian and Arnold and his father Sir Henry; it marked the growing antipathy he felt toward his father, choosing to adopt instead his mother's name. Harris knew him while he was called Lunn and always referred to him by that name.

Harris "of my life on the border when I worked in Devil's River country for old man Campbell of Del Rio, and when I took charge of Mackerrow's place . . . in Kinney County after Mac had been murdered by ambush by Mexicans. And that bit about the doctor saving the wounded cowboy who had lost so much blood, by injecting salt water into his veins, why, damn his impudence, he got that not from any cowboy experience—I surely need not tell you that the use of such salt water injections was absolutely unknown in Texas, if known anywhere at all, in 1871—but from my telling him how Dr. Rosanoff, of Nice, saved the life of my little daughter in that way in 1903. I am positive, quite positive that Harris never was in South West Texas or old Mexico in his youth."

What apparently had happened, according to Bell, was that James had taken the hobo's advice and had stolen some rides on the freight trains, arriving from Chicago to spend the winter of 1871 in Denver. It was not a good time. Insufficient in clothes and money, he lived that winter by watching for a wagon carrying fuel, running after it to its destination and there asking for the job of unloading. "For that he would get half a dollar, or at least twenty-five cents, and he was able to live another day." Thomas Bell continued that when he worked for Harris he was suffering from asthma and proposed to join his brother, Albert Turner, in his cattle business in Montezuma Valley, western Colorado, on account of the delightful climate. For this he was treated to some invective from Harris. "For God's sake, Tom, don't be crazy. Winter short! Climate delightful! Don't talk such nonsense to me. I've been through it. I know. Never, never in my life have I suffered as I did in Denver in the winter of '71. Oh, what a frightful time I had! Don't dream of it, man."

Sometime in 1872 James arrived in Lawrence, Kansas, according to him, on a hot, blazing day. An old gray-haired man sat opposite him on the train, moving restlessly, mopping his face, removing his vest and going at last to refresh himself on the observation platform. He left behind him on the seat two books: poetry of William Morris and Swinburne. Harris picked up and at once responded to the Swinburne; by the time the gray-haired man had returned he knew half the volume by heart and had his eyes full of tears. The gray-haired man, anyway in retrospect, was suitably impressed. "I've never heard of such a thing in my life," he cried. "Fancy a cowboy who learns Swinburne by merely reading him. It's astounding."

Probably the main reason that James went to Lawrence was that his brother William was there. They met, Harris recalls, in the Eldridge House. William was not impressed with James's looks. He was as yellow as a guinea, and although he had grown, he looked ill, very ill. William, on the other hand, was the picture of health and better looking than his brother had remembered. With his height of five foot ten, his fine figure, his jet-black beard, straight, thin nose, long hazel eyes and black lashes he might have stood as a model for a Greek god if it were not, Harris added, that his forehead was too narrow and his eyes too close. William had arrived in America in 1870; to him it was the greatest country in the world, providing opportunities for any young man who was willing to work. He was his father's son; earnestly Christian, he had been baptized into the Baptist Church, wherein, his younger brother observed, he had swallowed all the idiocies of that incredible creed. With a fair tenor voice he led the choir, he was a teetotaler, a nonsmoker and determined to be chaste. Although his goodness was a trifle poxed by his weakness for masturbation, we are told, he was, all in all, a most upright citizen.

He was, with his puritanical attitude, his earnest application, just the type to fit well into the austere pioneering society. Lawrence was a patriotic place and as puritanical as anything Thomas Harris might wish. It was a newly gathered community, strictly formal, divided into groups round various churches, united in a spirit of stern sincerity, a horror of sham and pretense, a contempt for riches and prosperity as against moral laws. There were many New Englanders, the Puritan strain having been intensified by border warfare, crop failures and epidemics of church revivals and prohibition. To be a free trader was an unpardonable sin; equally, one should never tolerate a liberal idea. Tolerance was the most deadly sin of all. To be a democrat or a liberal was to be an enemy of good government; to be tolerant was to be a traitor. There were very few traitors just then in Lawrence, which was a rugged-individual town, substantially rebuilt after the sacking and plundering that had taken place twelve years before during the Civil War. Now there were fine modern banks and offices, and the new Union Pacific Railroad passed nearby.

One of Lawrence's finest patriots is Kate Stephens, brave, whimsical and endearing. She recalls marvelously the agricultural life in which she was brought up. She loved Lawrence and for this one can excuse the soppy poems with which she began her book *Life at Laurel Town, Kansas.*

> A little city, a meet human nest,
> Lies snug on teeming lands of Central West;
> Its houses broadly parked with neighbours stand
> Mid shrub and blossom, in a friendly band
> And midst bud-haunted maples, trees so tall
> They seem like rows of pillars or a wall
> To lift the wide and open, sparkling sky
> By winter's sun-dogs, of July's red eye.

Another she ended:

> Thou art a Land of Futures place apart—
> A little city of state-building Hearts.

From this "little city" the flat, wide clay lands rolled westward, the wide sky converted into a bowl shutting in a thick melancholy that brooded over the state and its wooded virgin lands. In spring the country was lush with brightening tree trunks and a musical stirring of leaves and doves. In June there was wild grape blossom, blue grass and yellow oxalis, the river turned to silver ribbon, and there were rainbows in the early morning; August saw thick invasions of grasshoppers; September, tuberoses. Kate Stephens' father's farm was unusual for its undulations. There was an amber stream known as "brewery brook," and primeval forest stretched away to the north with wild geraniums and columbines, windflowers, purple violets, black-walnut trees, sycamores with satin bark, skating water bugs and frogs.

As recorded by Kate Stephens, the land had been successfully tamed, hacked from the wild and the Indians. It was a settled life, moving rhythmically round the seasons, fat with ruminating cattle, bulging black piglets and bright-plumaged Spanish pheasants that laid translucent eggs. The farm workers came from the north of Europe, stunted and brawny; even their faces were muscular. One was a pied piper called Neilson, remarkable for his love of animals. He would hug the horses and pigs till they squealed and with a pipe go down by the north meadow piping, followed by the horses, the mules, the cows and the sheep. There was a small hybrid terrier called John. Everyone in

Lawrence knew John, just as everyone in Lawrence knew everyone else's business. And what a day it was when some poor Texan steers escaped from their cattle car as they passed close by on the railroad, herded and shunted across the interior to the meat markets, terrified by the clattering, hungry and thirsty. Kate Stephens remembers them rampaging, and the sleek black Kansas cattle startled up from nosing their golden pumpkins and crunching their red-corn breakfasts. Never before had they seen such scalawags.

This was a society nourished by Wilkie Collins, George Eliot, Victor Hugo and Charles Reade. What a day it was again when the news came that Charles Dickens was dead, that his pen had fallen. How could the sun shine, the birds sing? And then, what music Kate Stephens could remember. Lawrence was a far cry from Ruabon and the Working Men's Association, and yet not so far. Here they sang "Scots Wha' Ha' wi' Wallace Bled," "Bonnie Doon" and "Mary's Dream" interspersed with American melodies, Irish folk songs, Chopin nocturnes and Wagner operas. Local newspapers carried the intelligence of sows and Texan herds, ox-yoke factories, cabbages and prairie grass; instructions for prairie-breaking, planting hedges, re-carpeting the Methodist Hall and making batter potpie. They reported skittishly the latest lawn amusement, kissing croquet, during which a lady might move her ball six inches every time she favored her gentleman opponent with a caress.

In strict formality ladies called upon one another, driving out wearing light-colored silks, full floating skirts—soft grays, blues, greens and lavenders, with never a foot to be seen. In summer there were diaphanous llama-lace shawls, white or black, pinned to the dress at the shoulder, and for colder weather velvet and paisley cloaks. Light-colored kid covered the hands, the left always carrying a card case made from ivory, mother-of-pearl or silver, and upon the head a bonnet. Sometimes in summer the heat was so intense that the ladies were driven out of doors for their meetings; sometimes redheaded woodpeckers set up such a drumming as to inconvenience the chatterings, the pleasantries, the exchange of embroidery patterns, cookery recipes and household remedies. Meals were substantial. Kate Stephens describes a delicious tea enjoyed with Judge Welch: damask linen spread about with cold meats, sour conserves, hot steaming biscuits, boiled custards flavored with almonds, flecked with white of egg and currant jelly, floating islands, and in the center a shining silver tea service. She tells also the story of how once a wrapped box the shape and size of a coffin arrived at the Eldridge House addressed to a certain Ephraim Quat. All the good people gathered round perplexed; a body, they calculated, would in that high temperature soon become malodorous. The situation was intolerable. At length, after much discussion, no less a person than Lord Denman accompanied the coffin to the cemetery and there interred it with the last rites of the church. A day or so later a lusty young farmer drove up: Ephraim Quat. He was expecting, he said, a box filled with new fittings for his farm machinery. Red-faced, the good people were obliged to hurry to the cemetery and disinter the box, which came up as sweet as new-mown hay.

In the spring, beside the advertisements for hyacinths, were notices for entertainments taking place in Liberty Hall, a most splendid place situated at the northeast corner of Winthrop and Massachusetts streets. There were religious services, children's sociables and comic operas performed by the Chapman sisters, Blanch, Ella and Belle—the *Daily Kansas Tribune* was quite taken with Miss Ella, "the most genuine little artiste that ever graced the operatic stage." There were minstrel troupes, complete with brass bands and bones. There was first-class fun and farce. "If you don't feel well, and don't digest well, and don't enjoy yourself, and don't want to get right, and laugh and strain your buttons and grow fat and banish the devils, why, don't go," giggled the *Daily Kansas Tribune*. All in all, Liberty Hall was a hive of marvelous things. In 1874 Martino, the Far-Famed California Illusionist, his Famous Talking Lion and Instantaneous Growth of Flowers in the Air manifested themselves. "They were all wonderful to say the least," sighed the *Daily Kansas Tribune*, "the little ones were nearly crazed with excitement and the adults wonder-stricken too with the enchanted pavilion and the child sleeping in the air." Meanwhile, down on the ground floor, James had rented a storeroom complete with an expensive chest for storing ice through the summer and an elaborate system of pulleys and chains.

The two Harris brothers were prepared to set their hands to anything that would make them a bit of money. They worked hard and remarkably. Their energy was astonishing. James himself claims that he was a bouncer at a casino, a waiter at the Eldridge House, worked in the box office of Liberty Hall from two to seven and, on the side, did a lively business in billboards, promoting many of the wonderful entertainments at Liberty Hall. By May 15, 1873, Douglas County Records[3] show that he had built up enough reserves to buy and sell land; three weeks later W. A. H. Harris[4] appears in real estate. From there on, the grantor-grantee index shows evidence of a brisk turnover, and the firm of Harris and Harris was established. The index records numerous transactions taking place up to the year 1892, by which time James's place had been taken by Vernon and it had become a family concern— William's and Vernon's wives, Emma and Mary, also participating. The transactions start modestly in small lots on streets like Louisiana, New York, Vermont and Pennsylvania, expanding gradually to include whole blocks of the rapidly developing Lawrence. With his money William bought books and studied for the law, educating himself and working his way "manfully," as his obituary said. In between he kept the butcher's stall that belonged to his younger brother. It was in the meat trade that Harris the Cowboy[5] was born and James's knowledge of cattle was acquired. To store his beasts in good heart he would have husbanded them. He would have learned which animal was the leader and how to goad him up when he fell in the foul cattle trucks, bringing the rest down with him. Finally, he would have driven them to the slaughter. To protect farmers from Texas fever, which was carried by ticks, a law had been passed in 1871 making it illegal for Texan cattle to be driven through Kansas, east of a certain line. In spite of this the *Daily Kansas Tribune* was constantly reporting accidents occurring as butchers drove their beef through the streets. On August

---

[3] May 15, 1873: Harris, James T., to Helen Farwell, deed, "land in addition 12 N. Lawrence" (Register of Deeds Office, grantor-grantee index of Douglas County, Kansas, Vol. 9, p. 268).

[4] June 9, 1873: Harris, W. A. H., *et al.* to John Dean, deed, W½ of NE¼ of Sec. 14. T. 15, R. 20. (ibid., Vol. 9, p. 343).

[5] There were often cases of Indian attacks reported in the papers. On November 13, 1874, the *Daily Kansas Tribune* reported the massacre of Captain Short and his surveying party. They had traveled with a yoke of oxen and wagons, their cattle had got away as a result of an Indian scare, men trying to return to camp were cut off by six Indians, one made a successful dodge and was followed by six redskins until after dark. "The Indians have by tradition, and personal experience, learned and are convinced that upon whatsoever part, plot or piece of prairie, bottom or timber the white man takes sight through those sphynx-like tubes, sets little wooden stakes and plants those little stones, parcelling out the land into little squares—from that time those acres cease to be grazing ground for buffalo, elk, deer and all ruminant game. They know the encroaching survey narrows the limits of their hunting grounds. They believe that the surveyor is sure to be followed by the pioneer with team, wagon, plow and ax. They feel that year by year their hunting domain of green grass is disappearing before the greed and push of the white man and his arts of civilization and they foresee the day of doom for their wild race, unless they succeed in stemming the encroaching tide. The surveyor is the usher of the settler. Hence the compass, chain, pins and corner stones are regarded by them as tools of robbers, and surveyors and chainmen death-deserving oppressors."

16, 1874, Mrs. Crew, her baby carriage and nurse were all obliged to step into the ditch to avoid a poor enraged Texas cow newly separated from her calf. Unfortunately, Mrs. Crew failed to make the ditch in time and was severely gored.

The butcher's business, one way and another, ran the brothers into trouble and provided ample opportunity for William to practice his newly acquired knowledge. In September 1873 Andrew Terry, the proprietor of Liberty Hall, sued James for $20 rent owed for the ground-floor storeroom and for $300 damages.[6] By September of the following year the business was finished. There had been an unfortunate scene on April 1, when William was obliged to appear in the police courts "before his Honor, Judge Smith" for summarily ejecting Dr. Hartmann from his butcher stall on March 28.

> Mr. Harris conducted the case ably in his own defense [reported the *Daily Kansas Tribune*]. It transpired in evidence that Mr. Harris kept a meat market belonging to his brother; that he owed Dr. Hartmann an old balance on account; that on Saturday Dr. Hartmann called for a veal roast and soup bone, amounting to fifty-five cents, and desired them charged to him on account. Harris demurred, as he was not authorised to make accounts, or do that kind of business. Thereupon Hartmann flew into profane extravagance of speech in giving his opinion of a man that wouldn't pay his debts. A lady and gentleman were also present, and Mr. Harris exclaimed that he would like to have the Doctor leave, and even opened the door to make the way plain. The Doctor continued abusive, and Mr. Harris led him to the door and pushed him out into the street. It developed that the lady was annoyed and Dr. Hartmann had the will to cut Harris's heart out, but had left his pocket knife at home. Though Harris argued ably, and quoted profusely, to show that he was only exercising the reserved rights of a citizen and storekeeper, attorney Fischer held the case down to ordinance, and Judge Smith found him guilty and annexed a fine of five dollars and costs. Mr. H. intimated that he should take an appeal.

There was more trouble to come, this time with the butcher's equipment of icebox and pulleys. When he gave up the business, James sold all the gear to Andrew Terry for $155. Terry did not pay. Once

[6] State of Kansas, Douglas County, District Court Records.

more William was obliged to exercise his legal expertise, and the Harrises were awarded $47. At the same time James sold goods, wares, merchandise and grain, amounting to a total of $125, to W. J. Barker, a merchant from Denver. The amount was still outstanding on August 26, 1875, when again William brought an action, with John K. Rankin, the banker, standing surety for costs of action; but of Mr. Barker there was no trace, not a good, chattel, stock or interest of his to be found.

The main reason for James's selling his butcher's equipment was that he wished to enroll at the university and needed money. On January 24, 1874, the *Daily Kansas Tribune* had announced that one of the most instructive and entertaining lectures of the season was to take place the following Thursday at the Free Congregational Church, delivered by Professor Smith of the university. Tickets were thirty-five cents and the subject was "Culture as a Creed"—a subject to which James would have responded violently, and there is no doubt that he was deeply influenced by the lecture. From that Thursday on, Professor Byron Smith became his hero, culture his creed, and his whole outlook changed. He would put away material things, sell his business and become once more a student. The lecture was the foundation on which he built himself. It is likely that he changed some of the message, adapted it and made it his own, but there is no doubt that it contained the seeds of his beliefs. In his first volume of short stories, *Elder Conklin and Other Stories*, which he wrote about seventeen years later, he included "Gulmore, the Boss," a tale of university plot and intrigue. Byron Smith appears as Professor Roberts. "He gave a lecture on Culture as a Creed . . . which made some folks mad. The other professors are Christian and, of course, all the preachers took it up. He compared Buddha with Christ, said . . . that Shakespeare was the Old Testament of the English-speaking peoples. . . . He said too, that Shakespeare was inspired in a far higher sense than St. Paul, who was thin and hard, a logic-loving bigot." To go with his new outlook he gave himself a new identity. He is listed in the Ninth Annual Catalogue of the Officers and Students of the University of Kansas, 1874–75, under "Collegiate Department, Select Course," as James F. Harris, Tenby, Wales. (Tenby was where his father and sister were living at the time.) He took his father's address but discarded his name, Thomas, and with it, he believed, the narrowness and bigotry. It seems too trite to be true that he chose the name Frank because that is what he was intending to be

—ingenuous, outspoken, unreserved—but it seems that this was exactly so. He was going to be Frank by name, frank by nature. Not that his colleagues seem to have been aware of the transformation; his contemporaries all remembered him as Jim, although some did complain of his loud mouth.

In so small a society as Lawrence the university was closely involved with ordinary life. The newspapers eagerly reported its annual functions and the antics of some of the more unruly students, "some of our fast young men," who were often getting up to jolly pranks, a favorite one being to steal chickens and turkeys from people's chicken houses and roast and eat them. Kate Stephens remembers another occasion: the chancellor beaming round at the end of a hard year's work, the United States Army playing a Strauss waltz, the tables groaning with iced tea—"the prince of potables," as the *Daily Kansas Tribune* called it—when suddenly, much to the dismay of all who were gathered together, the university skeleton descended through a hole in the ceiling. She remembers, too, a day when Ned Bancroft and "Jim Galway," as she calls Harris in *Life at Laurel Town*, strolled into an African church just as the parson was giving out the last hymn and locked the doors. No one, intent as the congregation was upon singing, noticed. Jim and Ned sat giggling under a hedge waiting for the hymn to finish, and then there was a commotion, a great rattling of locks as people tried to escape. Elder Johnson climbed on a chair to jump out of the window, and one boosted another onto the window ledges and climbed down the outer walls, while Harris and Bancroft peered through the hedge roaring with laughter.

Elmer Gertz and A. I. Tobin, when they were researching their biography of Harris,[7] around 1928, collected a mixed bag of memories. Neither Harris brother was popular, they claim—people were suspicious of them, though no one could quite remember why. "My impression is there was something disreputable about their characters but what it was I haven't the slightest idea," one lady wrote helpfully. Martha Hallowell recalls that William had given her an unpleasant half hour at a revival meeting, until her brother-in-law asked him to stop molesting her. H. S. Tremper said that his relations with Jim Harris were never cordial—from the first he disliked his aggressive egotism and his insistence on airing his half-baked notions of religious and political

---

[7] Elmer Gertz and A. I. Tobin, *Frank Harris.*

affairs. E. B. Tucker said that William was tried before the First Baptist Church for crooked dealings, made his own defense and got free, while James failed to pass his examination in natural history before Professor Snow; he asked his neighbor to write him a description of a blue jay, Snow discovered, and that was the end of the exam. Benjamin J. H. Horton told Elmer Gertz that William had been regarded as rotten; he did not know why though, since the worst thing he could see that he did was to "get religion" and talk at revival meetings.

It should be taken into account that the Harris brothers' contemporaries were being invited by Mr. Gertz to deliver their memories shortly after the publication in 1929 of *The Lies and Libels of Frank Harris*, a work edited by Kate Stephens, wherein she and Smith's septuagenarian brother and sister, Gerrit and Mary Caldwell Smith, had gallantly hobbled to defend Byron against Harris' accusations that he had died young on account of wet dreams.[8] Many of them, respectable, elderly puritans that they were, may have been therefore somewhat prejudiced. One lady described Jim's studying as "philosophizing" and "speculation," another regarded him as a loafer who liked to read, but a third wrote, "I remember Jim Harris having the reputation of being a brilliant though erratic student," and Hannah Oliver stated: "James Harris was a brilliant youth, with a remarkable power of absorbing knowledge. He was a great reader and an eloquent, fascinating talker. He was self-confident and sometimes showed an extraordinary youth's lack of respect for the opinion of others, and this I think, won him some dislike." A university paper, the *Observer of Nature*, records that he was heard in chapel, speaking, rendering a bass solo, and was encored. He delivered one of the most thoughtfully prepared orations of the term. Already he was haranguing the school system and was trying out his left-wing views, which would have been most unpalatable to Lawrence. According to him, reported the *Observer of Nature*, the withholding of just and due equivalent for what one obtains is taught by every school, legalized by long custom, justi-

<hr/>

[8] *The Lies and Libels of Frank Harris* was published in 1929 at some expense for its editors—"towards a thousand dollars"—but Kate Stephens had kept a sharp tongue and had not lost her whimsical sense of humor, particularly over her title, which she imagined might have sounded unfortunate to the Harrisian supporters, whom she called "the Frankforters." "Do pardon this joke, my machine is a bit skittish this morning," she wrote to "the turtle doves" Elmer Gertz and his wife Caretta. Frank, she told them, was a sort of literary saxophone; his bits on Smith in *My Life and Loves* were the hallucinations of a paranoiac. He had made a silly recital, childish and senile: what a rancid old satyr had fancied he had done and said. Over all an inferiority complex was clearly indicated.

fied by special statute and is the selfsame fraud for which thieves are hunted. "Mr. Harris as an advocate of communism looks forward to the time when all men shall have one creed, self-control, and one God, a perfect and symmetrical development of the whole man."

As for William, the person who seems to have disliked him most of all was James. He did not pay his debts, he claimed, in spite of the money he was supposed to have lent him. Selfish, that was what he was. Years later Annetta, his sister, is supposed to have told him that many times William had written to his father asking for money, saying it was for James, since he was studying and could not earn. As a matter of fact, the evidence as reported in the local newspapers shows William to have been respected and successful. In 1875 he was reported as making a fine speech at Black Jack to celebrate the Fourth of July. "Everything common to outdoor sport had been provided: swings, croquet, ball space, quoit grounds, and everything of that kind"—including lemonade. Dinner was served from liberally covered tables that claimed "illustrious attention" from the diners. At two o'clock order was called, the band played and "Mr. W. A. H. Harris of Lawrence was introduced. Mr. Harris talked for about twenty minutes. He has a forcible manner, a good delivery, and his effort called out the warmest expressions of gratification from the audience." By 1879 he was an attorney listed in the city directory and a member of the executive committee of the State Temperance Union. Over the next six years his reputation strengthened, but his health weakened. By 1885 he was married, with two sons, the owner of a small farm worth three thousand dollars, four apple trees, four pear trees, four cherry trees, two horses and a cow; 1886 and he was judge at a divorce suit, which was followed by the family's progress to the north, where they spent the rest of the summer. On January 26, 1887, William died; all three newspapers carried obituaries, the most extensive being that from the *Lawrence Daily Journal*, January 30, 1887.

W. A. H. Harris died at his residence in this city on the 26th inst. and his remains were deposited in the receiving vault by Oak Hill cemetery yesterday after brief religious services conducted by Revs. Marvin, Cordley and Stote at the house, which services were attended by the members of the bar headed by Judge Benson, and by a large number of our citizens. It is the intention of Mrs. Harris to take his remains in to his [her] old home at Canton, Ohio, for final interment.

Mr. Harris was foreign born. He came to this country in 1870, at the age of sixteen, and settled in the same year at Lawrence, where he soon after commenced the practice of law. He worked his way manfully, bought books, and read books, keeping himself well versed in all pertaining to his profession and when ill health compelled him to cease practice, he stood near the head of his profession and commanded a very lucrative business. He took a prominent part in the temperance work, was secretary of the Kansas State Temperance Union during all the years preceding the adoption of the prohibition amendment, and as an executive officer and by almost unparalleled ability as an orator did probably as much as any one man to bring about the change of public sentiment in Kansas that made the amendment possible. His natural abilities were of very high order, and his varied learning and extensive knowledge of the world supplemented by his wonderful social qualities, made him a power among men.

His father is a retired English gentleman living in London. His brother James is editor of the *London Fortnightly* at a salary of ten thousand a year. Another brother Vernon H.,[9] and his only sister, Mrs. Williams,[10] live in Lawrence and are well known to our citizens.

Mr. Harris was ill over two years and was a great sufferer

[9] Little is known about Vernon. He was a weak failure, and according to Harris, he tried to shoot himself in New York. "Still a failure you see, Joe, could not even kill myself though I tried," he is supposed to have told him—to which his brother rejoined that he was now called Frank. He had, Frank observed, only the veneer of a gentleman; he was as selfish as William but without his power of work; he had overestimated him wildly as a boy, believing him to be well read. He had manners and a good temper, but that was about all. In Lawrence, Kate Stephens remembers, he boarded at a small farm south of the town, and was supposed to have tried to cut his throat while drunk. In 1880 he lived with William on the west side of Mississippi Street; by 1882 he was dealing in real estate in the firm of Harris and Harris; by 1883 had qualified as a lawyer; was married around 1888; and before 1892 had moved to Micco, Brevard County, Florida. Years later Mrs. T. K. Harris remembers meeting one of his sons—a rather rough, loutish youth, she recalled.

[10] Annetta had married Henry Price-Williams, captain in the 3rd Battalion, King's Light Infantry, Shropshire Regiment, on January 25, 1882. After their marriage he was elected an honorary member of the Tenby fire brigade and she continued as principal of the "kindergarten, preparatory and advanced school" that she had opened in May 1878 at St. Clare's House, Esplanade, Tenby, assisted by "efficient foreign and English masters and governesses." She had two sons, Vernon and John Frank, and sometime after 1884 they arrived in Lawrence, leaving after William's death for Florida, where they had an orange grove on the Miami River, according to John Frank's wife (Mrs. Jane Price-Williams); two girls were also born—Florence and Gwladys. Henry Price-Williams left some time before 1908 for Cuba, where he died; Annetta sold the orange grove and moved to Miami. She died of tuberculosis in 1910 in Waynesville, North Carolina.

during the last six months, but he bore it all without a murmur or complaint and died in perfect peace.

This notice would be far from complete without prominent mention of his accomplished, heroic, devoted wife, to whom he was united in marriage April 15, 1879, at Canton, Ohio. She was the daughter of J. G. Keith, an old and prominent citizen of the last named city, was carefully and brilliantly educated and in all respects worthy and well qualified to adorn any circle in life. After four years of a happy wedded life, Mr. Harris was taken ill and his disease soon developed into the dread consumption. Since which time during the long months and years that followed, she cared for him as few invalids have been cared for, seldom leaving his bed side, but persistently, continually, bravely, seeking to win him back to health and life. She took him to the lakes, to the seaside, again and again, never for one moment resigning him to the care of less tender hands and when all hope of final recovery was gone, brought him back to his elegant home in Lawrence and watched and cared for him until finally he slipped from her grasp and left her widowed and sorrowing. The sympathy of the entire community is hers, and whether she decides to remain in Lawrence or to return to her old home in Ohio, her wifely devotion and sterling qualities will long be the theme of all who have known her.

According to himself, Frank's time at the university was a dazzling one. Kate Stephens describes him introducing his performances like a ringmaster in spangled tights, cracking his whip as each success gallops in. He is the boy hero, star of political speeches, academic business and love affairs. He makes love frequently; never has he had it so good or so often. In that rigid society, he would have us believe, he could sweep horizontal at the merest touch a crowd of sighing matrons and virgins, penetrate them to the hilt and leave them sobbing for more. It is likely that most of his "loves" were the nightmare women who rave in the minds of lonely men, soft women marvelously acquiescent, silent as marble, but acquiescent; that most of the female bodies he saw or touched were veiled firmly in muslin, unyieldingly vertical. There is a fine and convincing description of one of these heroines in "A Modern Idyll": she was mouth-watering "as she leaned back in the cushions in her cool white dress which was so thin and soft and well fitting that her form could be seen through it almost as clear as water." Now, fifty years later, with a wave of his pen he could summon his fantasies, draw Kate, Rose, Sophy, Lorna down from the clouds, thrust aside their long swaying skirts, kiss them, caress them, ravish them most luxuriously. Even the seducer himself straightens up after one orgy of thrusting, plunging and unlimited orgasm, which ends with a sheet of blood over the bed, and pauses before a matron whom he is about to "plough" and scatter in a storm of squeals and tears: "I meant to write nothing but the truth in these pages; yet now I am conscious that my memory has played a trick on me: it is an artist in what painters call foreshortening; events that is, which took months to happen, it crushes together into days, passing so to speak, from mountain top to mountain top of feeling, and so the effect of passion is heightened by the partial elimination of time. I can do nothing more than warn my readers that in reality some of the love passages I shall describe were separated by weeks and sometimes by months, that the nuggets of gold were occasional 'finds' in a desert."

Shimmering always like a mirage through the sands of 1874 was his infatuation for Byron Caldwell Smith, whom, according to Frank, he had confounded with his brilliance and with whom he had formed a close and poetic relation that was the envy of Lawrence. Smith was twenty-five years old. With his lustrous brown eyes, his olive-tinted skin, luxurious brown side-whiskers and moustaches surrounding a carefully shaved cleft chin, he was a remarkable and a romantic figure. In the sunlight, Kate Stephens said, his hair took on a golden light. He had studied in Europe—Heidelberg, Berlin, Munich, Vienna and Athens. In 1872 he became Instructor of Greek at the University of Kansas, and in 1873 was made Professor of Greek Languages and Literature. He was the youngest and most brilliant member of the faculty. There is no doubt that he inspired many of his students, a fact which is amply endorsed by his obituaries in the May 23, 1877, number of the *Kansas Collegiate*. J. A. Wickersham wrote: "The name of Professor Smith brings to my mind a picture of true, earnest manhood, of noble striving and grand accomplishment. That student who has been in his classes and seen the glow of his eye, felt the magnetism of his presence and kindly sympathy, and whose own heart has warmed up as it caught the reflection of the master's enthusiasm, cannot refrain from an expression of sorrow when he sees the blight that has withered the life of his ideal man."

He was sympathetic, learned, and exerted a magnetic influence over his students, winning their confidence by his rare dialectic skill and his frequent visits to their societies. He encouraged them, yet allowed the less talented to see their limitations, so that they accomplished always the best results and did not overstretch themselves and dilute their work. In the classroom his movements were nervous and energetic; during exercises of Greek translation his whole frame seemed to vibrate. "The feelings which I experienced at his recital of an old Greek song in praise of Harmodius and Aristogiton shall not soon be forgotten," wrote Andrew Atchison. "As he ran through the measures it seemed as if a living Burns was breathing melody on the chords of the Greek tongue." He would invite his students home and ask them to express their opinions, but these were no rambling conversations and no one was allowed to be silent—each must think vigorously and form a conclusion as a result of the discussion. In religion he was a skeptic, but allowed Christ the foremost place in history as a reformer.

According to Frank, he met Smith, not at his lecture "Culture as a Creed" but on the occasion of Senator Ingalls' speech (which took place after he had enrolled at the university on October 21, 1874), at which he astounded everyone by his eloquence. "To think of you as a cowboy is impossible," Smith is supposed to have exclaimed, in words remarkably similar to those of the gray-haired man on the train. "Fancy a cowboy knowing books of Virgil and Swinburne by heart, it's absurd: you must give your brains a chance and study." On learning that this brilliant cowboy had no money he offered to pay the fee himself. "I won't take your money," Frank cried (tears burning). "Every herring should hang by its own head these democratic days." From that moment, in memory, Frank bounds like a goat from mountaintop to mountaintop. There is no limit to the fantasies, the gods and demigods with whom he is best friends, no end to his marvelous sentiments. "This man has chosen and called you very much as Jesus called his disciples," he told himself: "Come, I will make you fishers of men! Already I was dedicated heart and soul to the new gospel"—and to this sunlit god who bestowed upon him liberally Latin and Greek-English dictionaries and translations of *Das Kapital*.

Smith was one of Harris' first heroes, one of many, whom he was to revere and admire all his life. His heroes were his fathers, whose direction he could follow, on whom he modeled himself, with whom he filled himself and identified. The love affairs he offers us with his crew of Roses, Kates, Sophies, Lornas, matrons and virgins are mostly made of dreams. The love affair with Smith was real, or rather his obsession was. Kate Stephens remembers how during the year 1874–75 he hung around the classroom during the Professor's open hours, how he would wait in the corridors to walk home with him and how when the Greek society met at Judge Stephens' law office he would attend. He would often form part of Smith's discussion groups. Kate grudg- ingly admits, as an aside, that for a short time they lodged together in the same boardinghouse. It was a small, plain stone house, with all the rooms leading onto an outside veranda, set in a city lot south of the Baptist church. The landlady, Mrs. Gregory, was strong and able. Other lodgers consisted of a professor of German and mechanical engi- neering, said to be a political refugee from Poland, his wife, who was a typical German *frau*, an English graduate of Cambridge who had fallen on evil days and was obliged to increase his income by coaching students in Latin, Greek and mathematics, his daughter who kept a kindergarten, a physicist at the university, and several young men in- cluding "Jim Harris." There was nothing more, said Kate Stephens, and homeric laughter was the only emotion that his claims excited in her.

Frank, however, thought otherwise. "Our relation was really rather like that of a small, practical husband with some wise and in- finitely learned Aspasia," he announces conjugally. Then it seems that they were all girls together, he, Plato, Smith and Sophocles, and one year had expanded to five. "Ah! how much it was worthwhile spending five years of hard labour to enter in their intimacy and make them sister-spirits of one's soul"—all gods and girls together watching the poor humans fumbling about in the university below.

In fact, Frank, hanging round the classrooms and corridors to catch a glimpse or a word from his god, was likely to have had a bad time: a small idealistic ex-butcher with a large inferiority complex among mostly hostile people and arrogant professors. Looking back, he finds it necessary to correct the image of Professor Kellogg, an emi- nently respectable and puritanical clergyman. The correction was one he was fond of making and one for which he had a special label, calling it "painting in the shade," which consisted invariably of revelations of sexual weakness or debility. In Professor Kellogg's case he is dis- covered kissing a pretty maid—entirely against her will; soon Harris is acting as mediator, although the idea of an old professor and clergy- man trying to win a young girl by force made him roar with laughter.

" 'Oh, Rose,' I said, 'Professor Smith has been telling me of your trouble but you ought not to be angry: for you are so pretty that no wonder a man wants to kiss you: you must blame your lovely eyes and mouth.' " At which pretty words Rose is mightily delighted; she simpers off and the day has been saved for the record—by Harris.

The wise and infinitely learned Aspasia was, meanwhile, having a spot of bother below the belt. "Almost in the beginning I had serious disquietude," the small practical husband tells us in his most confidential manner, drawing his chair closer and leaning forward. "Every little while Smith was ill and had to keep to his bed for a day or two." At last he was able to make his diagnosis. Nocturnal emissions. Happily he had up his sleeve his remedy: whipcord. The unfortunate scholar was trussed up, and with a suitably frank air the "husband" tells us that the wet dreams were caused by a passionate love affair Smith had enjoyed in Athens with the lady with whom he worked orally—at Greek conversation, so as to acquire fluency.[11] On his return to the United States his passionate dreams got the better of him. He became weakened and exhausted. The matter was not improved by the kissing sessions American custom allowed him upon his betrothal to the delicious Miss Stephens. A day or two spent in the company of his love and all the good that Harris had managed with his whipcord was undone.

To extract the full comedy, as well as the tragedy, of this ridiculous scene, it is necessary to know a little about the love affair between Kate Stephens and Byron Caldwell Smith. It was romantic and unconsummated. Kate Stephens was at the university for five years, from 1871. She was nineteen, with an oval face, ash-brown hair, and large gray-green eyes, when she first met and fell in love with Smith. He was the teacher of advanced classes of Greek, she very often was the only pupil. They would walk hand in hand through her father's woods and fields. In 1875 Smith, suffering from undiagnosed renal neuralgia, left for Philadelphia with the hope that the climate might be more auspicious for his health. His many letters[12] came back to her in Lawrence pessimistic, redolent with nostalgia, river-skirted roads and set-

[11] The rumor that Smith had had an affair with a Greek girl was put about in 1875 by D. B. English, who agreed to take charge of Smith's post at the university while he was in Philadelphia for health reasons. English, treacherously seeking to secure the post for himself, broadcast the story. Smith was peremptorily dismissed from the university in the summer of 1875.

[12] Published first in 1919 as *The Professor's Love-Life: Letters of Ronsby Maldclewith;* then in 1930 as *The Love-Life of Byron Caldwell Smith* (New York, Antigone Press).

ting suns, lyrical and fresh, illuminating his invalid love. "We shall never be happy," he wrote on January 13. "I told you so once, but you would not believe it, Kate, and I let myself be dazed into half accepting what your dearest heart prophesied—it was what my own so longed for." Uncertain, weak, often in pain, he wrote on: "How my memory treasures every sweet stray moment of our past—handclasp, kiss and heart-beat, the passion of those dear unfathomable eyes, the rustle of garments, the gliding step and lingering farewells! It seems I could not forget those things underground. Oh, Katherine, yes, I *must* see you again—die in your arms or live in your embrace." On March 25 he wrote again: "I have heard the philosopher Emerson lecture, and a famous quartette play, and seen a much-talked-of gallery of engravings and mezzotints. Alas! how the devotee of literature and arts has become something else. Art and literature are no longer the supreme objects of my desire. I know a sweet girl, who may see these lines, whose lips have more eloquence than the great philosopher, more enchantment than the songs of Schubert, sweeter lines than an angel of Toschi's. . . ."

Frank has his own account of the end of Byron Smith and his own university career. He was expelled, he says, because of a reversal in religious policy; rebelling righteously, he kicked down a door before prayers, whereupon "by an unanimous vote of the Faculty I was expelled from the University and free to turn my attention to law." This he studied in the office of Barker and Sommerfeld between visits to Philadelphia to see Smith, who was calling him thither more and more frequently. They met at the railway station, the reunion shaken by Smith's wretched little cough, unallayed in spite of his continually sucking lozenges. He was a sorry sight. With the help of a lump of ice the struggle was resumed against the dread nocturnal emissions, while Frank became a reporter on a Philadelphia journal, working hand in glove with Smith interviewing Walt Whitman and Emerson, until he was obliged to return to his billboard business and his law exam. And a tricky exam it was too, he tells us, but in spite of all the traps and loopholes, he sailed through triumphantly and was admitted to the bar.

Soon he became a partner in the same firm of Barker and Sommerfeld, owing to the unfortunate decease of Mr. Barker from an attack of hiccups. His income was so large he ate in the Eldridge House and slept in the office only to satisfy his lechery—which he did often, driving out Lily or Rose in his buggy, enjoying them "anytime, anywhere."

Poor Smith was meanwhile deteriorating; he "had got a bad wetting one night and caught a severe cold." Doctors were urging him to go to the mountain air of Denver. He would stop and see Frank on the way. And what a shocking sight he was again, great eyes burning like lamps in his face, doomed. He urged Frank to throw up the law, hurry to Europe and make himself a real scholar. " 'I'm finished, Frank,' he declared, 'but I'd regret life less if I knew that you would take up the work I once hoped to accomplish—won't you?' I couldn't resist his appeal. 'All right,' I said, after choking down my tears. [Frank's emotional scenes were always damp ones.] 'Give me a few months and I'll go round the world first and then to Germany to study.' He drew me to him and kissed me on the forehead: I felt it as a sort of consecration."

This scene, together with Emerson's advice to the scholars of Dartmouth College,[13] which Frank came upon one day in the library, was the reason he gives for suddenly leaving Lawrence. "I must," he cried to the astonished librarian, "the ground burns under my feet—if I don't go now, I shall never go."

Transformed suddenly into a Lady Williams Wynn, he bestows dresses, little hats, books and chinchilla capes upon his crew of lovelorn ladies shortly to be left weeping behind, takes a black one with him as far as Frisco, then boards his steamer alone, sets his eyes on the Golden Gate and moves out in his imagination into the Great Pacific.

Nature possibly dropped a stitch or two when she knitted Frank Harris, Kate Stephens rejoins acidly. In *The Lies and Libels of Frank Harris* she and Gerrit and Mary Caldwell Smith claim that he won no honors at all at the university. "He was merely a little Irish immigrant, clad in a senescent corduroy jacket and atrocious swagger . . . not good humoured, not radiating a natural sweetness, as many of Irish blood, but scolding and gibing." His memory was diseased, they said; furthermore, sometimes on the page he assumed two personalities, as if one was not enough for his ego; often he interrupted himself, breaking into his own conversations. His speech at Ingalls' meeting, his solitary visits to Smith's rooms, his staying at the Eldridge House—all this was nonsense. There was no gift of a translation of *Das Kapital*, since no translation existed until the eighties, and Barker did not die until 1912, and not from hiccups. As for the expulsion episode, it was probably a tiny incident when "one morning during chapel exercises two students

[13] Contained in "Literary Ethics," delivered at Dartmouth College, July 24, 1838.

asked the door-keeper, who sat in a chair with his hand on the knob of the chapel-door holding it closed, to let them out. The boy-monitor hesitated, in a trice the group brushed by him and flung the door from his grasp. Frank seized this bravado and made himself the solo performer in a drama. . . . His letter to the Faculty and his intimation that he talked with Judge Stephens, his report of an offer of Judge Stephens to bring action against the Faculty, the whole tale is libellous fiction, diabolical blah." Honors at the university indeed! What he did was to loaf about for a few months essaying a course known as "select." Moreover, Frank paid no visits to Philadelphia. He slunk away one day like a dog with its tail between its legs.

The truth lies somewhere between these two lines. He did pass his law exam. On Friday, June 25, 1875, the *Republican Daily Journal* reported: "Mr. James T. Harris, student at law, will be examined for admission to the bar next Monday at the Court-house. Judge Stevens [*sic*], Justice Chadwick and Esquire Foote are to conduct the examination." Four days later the paper reported that the exam had been successful; J. T. Harris was duly admitted to the Douglas County bar, having creditably passed an examination lasting six hours. At this point Tobin and Gertz claim that Frank passed by way of Columbus, Ohio, where a former colleague, Ned Bancroft, was working on the railway and in a position to obtain for Harris a free pass to Philadelphia, where he hoped to collect some money from Smith. Certainly around this time he wrote to Smith—a fact that annoyed Kate Stephens extremely. She, too, suggested that it was because Harris required money to return to England; he had only to say that he needed money for studying to move, immediately, Professor Smith's heart. Anyway, Smith replied to the letter; its contents were apparently gratifying, and Harris went around showing them to everyone. Evidently certain "commonsense men of business in the street" feared that it smacked of more than the eye could see and hurried along to Kate Stephens' father. Kate was astounded by the rumors and wrote at once to Byron Smith her unreserved opinion of "Jim Harris"—which could not, in fact, have been all that informed, since elsewhere she tells us proudly that she hardly knew him while he was at Lawrence and had spent only one afternoon in his company.[14]

[14] Harris had apparently issued from ambush and joined her uninvited. "When we had left the sidewalks of the town, we came to a path running by the river, where floods were swirling in little back-sets and gleaming up through the pale green of overhanging

What she fails to report is that by the late summer and autumn of 1875, the roles had been reversed. Now it was she who was depressed and pessimistic. The invalid love affair was getting her down and she was writing complaining letters to Smith. On November 2 he had tried to cheer her melancholy.

> I snatch an interval of leisure in this evening of election returns . . . to write you, sweet, not a lecture for your sad-hearted letter, but if possible a word of cheer. It will be hard to send sunshine and breezes to your soul, when I could not, with all my kisses and chiding and chatter, keep you from drooping while I was there.
>
> What terrible foreboding oppresses your soul? I can not divine it. It seems some terrible premonition. You say you were not born for happiness. Oh how you make my heart ache with such cruel forecast! . . .
>
> You must be happy. The decree has gone forth. It is my life's work, and failure in it I can not brook. If I can not make you happy and contented, I had better never been born. . . . Do you not know our love will be one long sweet dream and worship of love?— . . . You *must* not be sad, sweet heart, and all aweary of existence with the warm heaven of love impending over you. It is wicked, do you know?

Katherine, however, would not be appeased, and in her next letter, besides picking past quarrels, passing on trivial gossip and complaining of the shortness of Smith's letters, she complains also of Harris. She was jealous of anyone who claimed the frail attentions of Smith; she wanted them all for herself. Smith replied on November 9:[15]

---

willows. At this point Frank pulled from the breast pocket of his coat a photograph of the *carte de visite* size. He held it towards me and told me that it was of his sweetheart in England, to see whom he was sick even to tears, unbearably heartsick, that only the other night, when we had that terrific storm, he was suffering unutterable longings and he opened his window and laid his head on the outer sill and let the rain beat upon him and drench him, so great—there he drew a long breath through clenched teeth—was his pain. After he had unburdened his soul of his love story, meanwhile holding in his hand the card showing a sweet young face of a refined southern type, he turned back and I went on alone."

[15] This letter is almost certainly the reason why Harris took the rumors of Smith's Greek love affair and embroidered them so astonishingly. He must have read the letter in typescript with Kate Stephens in the summer of 1915 (see p. 328) and been deeply hurt and shocked. All the idealizing built up over the previous forty years had been exploded in a few seconds. From then on he began making references to Smith's sexual weaknesses in letters to Kate Stephens—much to her horror—and death by nocturnal emission was the final solution.

If my letters are short, Katherine, yours are not long, and yet you have the more time. Somehow I find it unaccountably difficult to write you long letters. In the first place there is little gossip from Philadelphia, for we have so small acquaintance. . . . So it comes that my only resort—that a most unfortunate and poor one—is to lecture you as you call it. . . . But I must offer what reason I can for my writing the letter to Harris. You saw it of course and will therefore be able to judge the value of my plea.

You know I have no confidence in or respect for the moral character of the man and could not therefore dream of making him a confidential friend. He has, however, been so persistently kind to me, and seemed to build so much upon my good opinion, and besides wrote me so ardent and eloquent a letter, that I could not find it in my heart to answer in terms not somewhat touched with warmth. But I was careful to express only that enthusiasm for humanity which is natural to me, and goes out to every one who appeals to it—without meaning to establish relations of personal confidence. Doubtless he understood me in a personal sense. I wished only to benefit him by pointing out that the only foundation of friendship which I recognize is that of personal honor and devotion to great and worthy aims. I overdid the matter and felt that I had before your letter brought it home to me with so much force.

Two years later Smith was dead.[16] Kate Stephens was so devastated that she never really recovered. She lived a solitary and learned life, waxing old and whimsical in memories consecrated to her virginal love. The disgruntlements, jealousies, disagreements and bad emotions were all swept away in the final tragedy. Harris steaming with effort to produce uncastrated language, with images of his red-hot organ massaging grateful Kansas ladies and the professor trussed up like a roast, was frightful to her. In 1929 she and Gerrit and Mary Caldwell Smith, all of them in their seventies and outraged, were obliged to gird up their crabbed fingers and raise their pens in a paper defense of their dear departed lover and brother. They make an awful scene, these poor septuagenarians scrambling about after Harris from one mountaintop to another, wreathed in the fogs of fantasy, dissecting his "nuggets of gold," which on close inspection appear to them to be more like heaps of ordure. *The Lies and Libels of Frank Harris* is

---

[16] Byron Smith died of consumption at Boulder, Colorado, May 5, 1877.

understandably prejudiced; it is invaluable when it comes to understanding Harris. It is the code by which we may decipher his fantasies,
his maneuvers to put himself in the superior position, and understand them for what they are: compensations for his disappointments,
isolation and failure. It does not make him more likable—on the contrary, one knows how noisy, tiresome and untidy he must have seemed
to his contemporaries—but it makes him more understandable.

CHAPTER 5

The Hero as Harris

FRANK arrived in Tenby earlier in 1875 than Byron Smith's November letter would lead us to believe. On August 17 he is announced in the visitors' list of the *Tenby Observer* as freshly arrived from Philadelphia and staying at 2 Olive Buildings. His journey was described in the October 26 issue of the *Kansas Collegiate;* it seems that Ned Bancroft had failed to come up with a pass and that Frank had resorted once more to his tricks. "James F. Harris, the young man of infinite capabilities and a thundering bass voice, was last heard from in Philadelphia, at which place he had arrived on his way to England. He described his journey as a succession of forced marches, midnight rides on the cow catcher and perilous passages over the car tracks. After Jimmie has enjoyed a few days' deck work on the Atlantic his experiences as a cheap traveller will surely be complete."

Annetta and her father were newly established in Tenby. Captain Harris had retired some five years before, as the result of a bad accident, according to Frank, falling into a dry dock and receiving injuries that caused him to go deaf and his beard to turn half white, half black. For a little they had made their home in Carrick on Shannon—yet another bank appointment of Vernon's, no doubt—but upon the latter's departure to America they removed to Tenby and prepared for Annetta to start her kindergarten. With its wide sandy beaches, scattered with green seaweed-covered rocks, curled shells, microscopic dragons and fossil hunters, Tenby was a quiet and peaceful watering place, a home for displaced gentlefolk. Every curving bay, promontory and point moved with a retired captain; every seat and old wall held a colonel taking his daily air as befitted an officer and a gentleman.

Inside the town itself there were arches and towers, neat, pretty walks and benches in the surrounding rock. It exuded a placid tedium, a gentle society that draped itself regularly in ecru satins, blue velvets and embroideries to rotate sedately at various balls and ceremonies. To Thomas Harris, retired from the gales of the Atlantic and the discomforts of lodging houses, the town with its sheltered seas must have seemed a haven of calm and comfort. There was little but the health-giving breezes to ruffle the air. The retired colonels and captains tended their greenhouses, their late peas, and gazed upon cottage gardens full of fat turnips, pines and vines, sweet peas and ribbon grass. The occasional shark was sighted, the occasional complaint lodged against those who husbanded pigs in the middle of the town.

All was well on the week of Frank's battered arrival. The promenade band had been playing "Charlie," the Tenby School Feast had been digested and two people had escaped certain death while bathing. According to an advertisement in the *Tenby Observer* some years later, 2 Olive Buildings, which was described by Harris as "a little house in a side-street," was very little indeed. There were apparently only two bedrooms, with three beds, and one sitting room. No sooner had Frank appeared and squeezed in with his father and sister than two weeks later the *Tenby Observer* announced the arrival from Columbus, Ohio, of E. Bancroft II, Esq., who had thrown up his job on the railway to taste the delights of Europe and of 2 Olive Buildings. Ned Bancroft had been in love with Kate Stephens before her romance with Byron Smith. He was a tall, strong fellow, with a pale face, and gray eyes, kind and intelligent. Harris however tells us that he was never entirely sympathetic toward him—probably because he was more successful with women—and could not account for their companionship except that he, Harris, was full of human, unreflecting kindness.

About a month after Bancroft's appearance at Tenby the two young men departed for Paris. There they made an ill-matched pair, totally opposed to each other. Ned had sophisticated tastes, while Frank describes himself as being careless of dress and food, intent only on acquiring knowledge. His first impressions of Paris give him nice opportunity for melodrama. Who could evoke the deathless fascination of the mere name, of that first view for the young student who had read and thought? Certainly not Harris himself, who was, he said, in a fever of wonder, his eyes full of tears, his mouth so full of poetry that words were not able to describe what he saw.

They were able however to describe the demise of Ned Bancroft. Ned and he lodged with a portly, pleasant lady called Marguerite, who kept a wine-shop restaurant. Frank threw himself into an orgy of learning. He read incessantly, he told the Hackney *Mercury* years later, and heard such lectures as seemed really worth hearing. To us he divulges that the first five days were spent learning all the verbs, then he read with a dictionary Hugo's *Hernani* in eighteen hours and went to the Comédie Française to see the play acted by Sarah Bernhardt. After the second act he could catch every word, and when he came out he understood everything that was said to him. He concluded his course by swallowing breathlessly *Madame Bovary* and never had any trouble with the French language again. It has been confirmed often that he was a fine linguist and spoke fluent French and German. His course must have been astonishingly effective; he was in Paris barely four months and was able the following autumn to secure the position of French tutor—not English, as he claims—at Brighton College.

Ned Bancroft meanwhile preferred orgies of another sort. He would hurry off to dine at smart restaurants. In one of these, while with Frank, he spotted a splendid-looking brunette dining with two men. Soon he was exchanging looks and signs with her. Frank, one imagines, was most irritated by all this and announced his intention of going home. Ned agreed that he too desired to go—home to the brunette's place. It was not long before she and Ned departed, leaving her two former companions ominously doubled up on the pavement with laughter. Her rooms were lovely, he told Frank, much satisfied on his return, the sanitary arrangements were those of a queen, there was no cause for worry. Alas! in spite of the imposing drainage Ned had contracted gonorrhea, and Harris tells us he was obliged to foot the bills. The convalescence was highly expensive. What with the new rooms in a gayer part of the city, drives to the Bois, visits to the Opéra, the Café Anglais and the Trois Frères, he began to run out of money. Declaring later to the Hackney *Mercury* that he had required to recover his health, he set out once more for Tenby, arriving there around January 27, 1876, with every aspect of ague, whose symptoms, he is at pains to assure us, had nothing at all to do with sexual indulgence; his breakdown in health came from his passionate desire to learn. He never again mentions poor Ned Bancroft, who had apparently exasperated more than his nerves and never recovered his health. Byron Smith heard of his death in January 1877, a few months before his own.

Back in Tenby everything was the same. There was the occasional Urban Sanitary Authority's meeting, plans for new seats and lamps for the Esplanade. A roaring black sea monster with a head full of holes, eyes like an ox and a body forty-five feet in length was sighted several thousand miles to the north of Bell Rock by a crew of fishermen hauling in their haddock nets. It came up to blow only a few yards from their boat and helped itself to several haddocks. Hardly less frightful was the "favourite comedy" *Used-Up,* which was performed by the local amateur theatrical association. It is of interest since it illustrates the low quality of stuff generally available for the entertainment of retired gentlemen and their ladies. As reported by the *Tenby Observer,* it has a plot of the most muddled sort. The curtains rise upon Ironbrace, a blacksmith, examining a balcony at Sir Charles Coldstream's and chatting to James the footman and Mary Wurzel. He reveals that "some fine gentleman" has run off with his wife and he wishes to pound him to jelly. Scene 2 introduces Sir Charles Coldstream, Sir Adonis Leech, and the Honorable Tom Savill on seats in the drawing room. Sir Charles is a fashionable fellow of thirty-three, with a town house, three country houses and a box on the Isle of Man, who has *used up* existence. What an awful bore everything is—Egypt is a desert, the Pyramids humbug, Naples a wretched smoky mountain, Germany nothing but women with thick ankles. What he needs, his friends say, is to be married. The widow Lady Clutterbuck is announced, come to solicit subscriptions for her kindergarten. Sir Charles is pleased to offer her his hand, and drops off to sleep on the sofa. Ironbrace enters from the balcony and discovers Lady Clutterbuck to be his errant wife and prepares an attack against Sir Charles. They wrestle. The balcony and both men crash into the river below. Scene 3 takes the audience into Farmer Wurzel's kitchen. In come Joe the ploughboy, who is Sir Charles Coldstream in disguise. Farmer Wurzel exits, saying Joe is too late for dinner, and enters again with the intelligence that Sir Charles Coldstream is drowned. Mary and Joe rush out, Ironbrace rushes in imploring Farmer Wurzel to hide him since he is about to be arrested for Sir Charles's murder. A trapdoor opens revealing a dungeon and Ironbrace vanishes. In come a lawyer, Savill, Leech, Mary and Joe, and Coldstream's will is read. The property is to be divided between Leech and Savill, who hurry out to inspect the boundaries. Joe raises his pen and adds a codicil leaving everything to Mary. His disguise is apprehended and the police are called. He is accused of the murder of Ironbrace. He too vanishes into the dungeon. All ends happily ever after. Sir Charles marries Mary, and the play is followed by the comic song "I'm So Volatile."

Frank spent about six months in Tenby. According to him, his life there seems to have been as precarious as Sir Charles Coldstream's. He was near to death most of the time. No sooner were his nerves repaired and he was accompanying his father on long walks under the gray-green cliffs than he got wet and went down with lumbago. The "pleasant local" doctor prescribed for him belladonna for massaging into the afflicted area—a standard remedy for muscular disorders—and a second black draught for swallowing. Unfortunately the maid, Lizzie (whom Frank had already brought to a couple of dozen orgasms at one sitting), got the medicine bottles muddled up. Here the author cannot resist an opportunity for melodrama. He rattles up the curtain on the sick-room scene complete with a noble young life being snatched from the jaws of death, burning candles and sobbing relations. He knows no limit and asks us to believe that he quaffed sixty grains of belladonna. "I'm afraid there's no hope, Nita," he cried, "the doctor told me there was enough to kill a dozen men . . . but you've always been good to me, dear, and death is nothing." The doctor invaded the brave scene with his stomach pump, and then the patient sank into unconsciousness; colored lights and the doctor floated above him and the stern, unloving father sat, worried, beside him, all night perched stiffly on the edge of the brass bed. From that moment, Harris said, he grew to like and admire him, and it was at that moment that his father promised him an allowance of £100 a year to continue his studies. This is unlikely, since Frank did not resume his studies until the beginning of 1878; instead he went off and secured for himself the position of tutor of French at Brighton College, at a salary of £30 per term.[1]

[1] Twenty-three years later, when Captain Harris died, in December 1899, it was Frank who was his executor, and it was Frank who inherited his property and effects. No one else was mentioned. Mr. Alwyn Williams, of the Rhondda Borough Council, writes, on May 15, 1974, that Captain Harries' address was 66 Pontypridd Road, Porth, he died on December 22, 1899, and was buried at Trealaw Cemetery on December 29, 1899, in Grave No. H993. The owner of the grave space was Mr. Frank Harries, c/o G. C. Silk, Corrington Square, Russell Square, London W.C.

Securing the post at Brighton College gives him an occasion to drop two names. He asserts that on the recommendation of Taine he took over as master of English from Grant Allen, author of *The Woman Who Did*, who had left the college in 1871. The fact that Frank's name does not appear as the French tutor on the prospectus announcing the winter term 1876 suggests that this appointment was a last-minute affair. With his impatience, his noisy earnestness, his lack of humor and his facility to take offense, Frank was unpopular with the other masters. Only he and Herr Piper, who taught German, were without degrees. He was isolated and boycotted, he says, mainly because he refused to give witness that one of the boys had been seen at the skating rink with a girl friend. He was unhappy, unheard, frustrated and restless, finding most people at best dull, at worst fools. He was wasting time again. He planned great things, he wanted to accomplish them, but without money how could he begin, and when and where?

At this time Carlyle was one of Harris' main influences; he had replaced Byron Smith as idol. For Harris a reverence for Great Men was essential, filling the vacuum of his parentless childhood and his loss of religion and providing a working plan for all his life. He had read Carlyle's *Heroes and Hero Worship* in America. His own heroes adhered faithfully to the text: they were in turn men of action, poets, deities, both pagan and Christian, and men of letters. It was logical to suppose that, having admired and molded himself thoroughly on such company, he too would be great. The hero as Harris: man of action, man of letters, prophet, poet and divinity all under the same skin—the portable hero. Since Carlyle was his mentor, it was from Carlyle that he sought advice. One Sunday morning in January 1877 Frank went to him for the interview over which years later a furore was to rage—half an hour, which, according to him, was the first of four meetings taking place on the Embankment, during which Carlyle, Harris claimed, confessed to him his impotence.[2]

2 "Talks with Carlyle" was published in the *English Review* in February 1911. One of its strongest attackers was Alexander Carlyle, who stated firmly that Harris had visited Carlyle for half an hour and half an hour only, therefore it was an impossibility for Carlyle to have passed on intimate details. Furthermore, he produced a trump card: he had in his possession a letter that Harris had himself written to Carlyle from Germany in 1878 in which there was no mention of these other meetings. Harris replied in the August number of the *English Review*. "I may point out . . . that Mr. A. Carlyle's own temper really explains the reserve of my letter. I only met Carlyle once in his own house in 1877. I preferred to meet him outside. I should not have alluded to this if Mr. A. Carlyle had not made it necessary. But the same person who probably informed him that my first interview with Carlyle only lasted half an hour instead of the whole afternoon, might also

FRANK HARRIS

Knowing Harris it would be perfectly within the bounds of possibility for him to come up from Brighton of a Sunday morning and wait about on the Embankment for Carlyle to emerge. In the windy and self-conscious letter that Harris wrote to Carlyle two years later, in December 1878, he reminds him how he called with a note to solicit an interview. The conversation as recalled in the letter seems pompous but sound. Harris was "not to proclaim opinions, offensive to the majority of men, rashly and defiantly, but rather in silence and study to wait till my nonage was past. You hinted also that the best sign of maturity was moderation." Largely through his own fault and tone Harris has now been discredited, the truth lost. The facts are that Carlyle had been impressed by Harris; he wrote a letter[3] recommending him to Froude, stating that he expected great things of him. He did communicate to Harris some form of weakness (a point that was omitted by Alexander Carlyle), for in the letter from Germany Harris writes, "knowing by your silence of late years and by what you yourself told me about your bodily weakness that we can look for no more from your pen, I would not trouble you Sir, if I knew of any other help, but so it must be." And though the end of the interview is idealized—as melodramatic, as damp as usual—it does seem that Carlyle was moved; he had met someone displaying as strong a paranoia as his own. "When we parted you clasped the hand of the stranger in sympathy and brotherhood and bade Good Speed—the tears that then sprang into my eyes assure me that you also felt—no longer were you to me a voice, an abstraction but a living Man in the brotherhood of woe and duty."

---

have told him that she tried to persuade Carlyle not to see me at all, telling him that he was not well enough to see me. Under these circumstances I naturally preferred to meet Carlyle outside his house and did so meet him four times. . . . Now when I wrote to Carlyle two years later I naturally avoided speaking of these outside meetings for fear of making unpleasantness or at least of putting up the back of the Scotch attendants or relations against me who like Mr. A. Carlyle thought it their duty to keep everybody from getting 'wind' of the great man whom they guarded like a gaoler and bored to extinction. . . . Love and admiring sympathy are keys that unlock all hearts, far more reticent hearts even than that of Thomas Carlyle. But is it credible, one may ask, that an old and famous man should speak of his intimate affairs to a young man and a stranger? I can only say that it is often a stranger and often a young man in which such a man confides. . . . I plainly say in my article that I regarded Carlyle's remorse as exaggerated. It was perhaps because I showed him that I thought so, that he spoke freely to me. The interest of his bodily weakness to me is not an interest of scandal but of psychology."

[3] Debunkers are quick to scoff at this, suggesting that the letter existed only in Harris' mind; but while the letter itself has not yet turned up, one from Froude has, which refers to Carlyle's letter (see pp. 81–82).

It seems most unlikely that Carlyle should have confided intima-
cies to Harris on the Embankment, yet there is in existence a letter
from Charles Jescal, to whom Harris, thinking of taking out an action
against Alexander Carlyle, wrote while the storm was raging over
"Talks with Carlyle." Jescal remembered quite well, he said, having
him to dinner in the private dining room of the Garrick Club sometime in 1887. The guests included Sir Richard Quain, Fletcher Moulton and the Honorable C. N. Laurence; of the conversation he had no
recollection, but he certainly did remember Harris saying—it might
well have been on that occasion—that Carlyle had admitted to him his
impotence. He was, he said, prepared to swear to this in a court of law.
Another letter exists from J. Grigor, the proofreader of the *Saturday
Review*, who remembered Harris remarking to him that he had it from
the lips of Richard Quain that Mrs. Carlyle died *virgo intacta.*

It is now generally accepted that the Carlyle marriage was unsatisfactory, with all signs pointing to general neurosis and sexual frustration, and that from the moment his wife died Carlyle suffered remorse.
But with his tone Harris turns his account into farce and gives us a picture of Sir Richard Quain, a man of outstanding integrity, heaving the
elderly and erudite Mrs. Carlyle about like a sack of coals. One evening,
Sir Richard Quain is supposed to have revealed, Mrs. Carlyle was lying
on her sofa in great pain. Quain begged her to go to the bedroom and
he would examine her. Upstairs the door was locked and there was
no answer. Next time he paid an evening visit he was horrified to find
Mrs. Carlyle again on the sofa, iller and paler than ever. She was a
naughty, obstinate creature, and she was to think of Quain only as a
doctor. Half lifting her, half helping her, he got her to her room. After
ten minutes of preparation she was lying on the bed with a woolly
white shawl over her head and face. Quain thought this an absurd
affectation for an old married woman, and with one toss threw her
dress over her head, pulled her legs apart, dragged her to the edge of
the bed, and, inserting the speculum, met an object. "Why you're
virgo intacta," he cried. Mrs. Carlyle is supposed to have pulled the
shawl from her head and said, "What did you expect?" Mrs. Carlyle's,
alias Quain's, alias Harris' account of the marriage night is no better.
Carlyle, after the marriage, had been strange, nervous and irritable, his
bride was supposed to have confided to Quain—he had not kissed her
all day. Mrs. Carlyle undressed and got into bed, Carlyle got in beside
her, and the bride expected him to take her in his arms. Nothing of

the sort; he lay there "jiggling like." "I knew what she meant," Sir Richard Quain told Harris gravely in the private dining room of the Garrick Club. "The poor devil in a blue funk was frigging himself."

In Brighton, Harris tells us, he was rescued by Mrs. Newton, the wife of the vice-president of the college. She was apparently a social lady— one of the leaders of Brighton society—and through her, it seems, he attended some literary evenings, or at least this is a likely interpretation of his announcement that on her advice he taught literature to a class of young ladies. It was probably at one of these soirées that he met Florence Ruth Adams, one of the "loves" not to be recorded in his *Life*—or not unless there is a ghost of her in Molly, the daughter of a doctor's widow, living next door in Tenby. Molly, not pretty, was tall and slight and three if not four years older than Frank, but she was intelligent and witty, widely read, and knew French and German. He believed himself to be in love, they were engaged, but she had underrated his brains and his strength of will, and though she had a hundred pounds a year, this was "wholly inadequate," and the engagement was broken off during the belladonna convalescence. Florence was in fact four years older than Frank. In 1877 she was twenty-five, the only daughter of the newly widowed Ruth Adams, she had five brothers, about a thousand pounds and a grand piano, which had been left to her by her father, a retired maltster from Ware in Hertfordshire. To judge from their early death rate they were a sickly family. They lived at 13 Montpellier Terrace, one of the fashionable parts of Brighton. It was a well furnished house with pictures, books, linen and liquors, a cook, a housemaid and a nursemaid for the young children, Neale aged ten and Guy aged twelve. Frank, lonely and isolated at the college, no doubt found 13 Montpellier Terrace to be the home he had never had. No doubt there were charming evenings, Florence playing her piano, singing a little, Frank reciting poetry, astonishing the household with his voice, with wild tales of Indians, the prairie, Paris and Philadelphia, with his plans for the future, the great things he could accomplish if only he had the money. . . . In his autobiography he glosses over his time in Brighton, without even a romance or an orgasm. Indeed, the only sexual reference he makes comes later when, discussing chastity, he says that it was in Brighton that he first noticed a deterioration in his muscular performance, finding it difficult to have two embraces in succession. It is in 1877 that he passes from reality into total fantasy, galloping off in his imagination to Moscow to become a war correspondent and join Skobeleff at Plevna and the battlefields of the Russo-Turkish War.[4] That this was impossible is shown by the dates. Action at Plevna lasted intermittently from July 30 to December 10. During this time Harris was still teaching at the college. It is true that there were eight weeks or so summer holiday, but with communications as they were, it would hardly be possible to travel from Moscow, down to Plevna in Turkey and back again via Constantinople in the time. Certainly he went to Moscow —or he told the Hackney *Mercury* so—but not until a few years later. The fact is that the Russo-Turkish War was a subject of adventure and interest not only for the national newspapers but for school debates; at the beginning of the winter term Brighton College held a debate "that in the present war our sympathies should be with the Turks." Central Asia was seen as a training ground for soldiers, Russia regarded the war as a crusade, vast regions and lands should be conquered for civilization. Skobeleff was a romantic and popular hero (and one who was likely to capture the imagination of Harris), a scholarly general, a fine figure dressed always in white, galloping on a white horse, inspiring his men by incredible braveries—or insensitivities, whichever way one looks at them. "My little doves, try once more, my eagles, another hill my doves," and his doves, his eagles would advance to a redoubt that could not by any circumstance be taken, and cheering they would go to their death. This was the stuff for Harris. Bands played, drums rolled, the air was full of smoke and thundered with guns, horses and men were shattered, and then after the battle Skobeleff, his staff and his "war correspondent" walked back together (Skobeleff naturally confiding amatory secrets the while). There by the road were a number of Turkish soldiers who had been dumped by their comrades. Was there anything they would like? asked Skobeleff. All asked for food, recorded the "war correspondent," but one, his head bandaged, asked also for a cigarette. Skobeleff gave him his own. The Turk undid the knot of his bandage and began to unwind the dirty linen that covered his head. As the last fold dropped, half the man's jaw fell on his chest, whereupon the man smiled, replaced his jaw, wound up the

[4] It is worth noting that this incident with Skobeleff starts Volume II of the *Life.* Harris had been disappointed and angry at the reception of Volume I. He reacted by being newly determined to be as sensational as possible. The spectacle was the thing. Everyone who could be was going to be brought in to be painted as black as possible—that would show them.

bandage again and inserted his cigarette. "Fine men," said Skobeleff, "great soldiers."

Much of this comes from books that were published after Skobeleff's death in 1882: *Skobeleff and the Slavonic Cause,* by Madame Novikov, and especially *Reminiscences of General Skobeleff,* by his friend Nemirovitch Danchenko, who gives us the funeral scene where the crowd stands round, some silent, some with tears, and as they stand whispers run from one person to another of Skobeleff's death and the scandalous manner in which he passed his last moments. Harris, true to his wish to shock, be superior and make his hero human—which, unable to use humor, he does by some immoral turn—entertains us to the full with seamy gossip, which he had, he said, straight from the mouth of some Russian officer whom he met at the Russian Embassy. The general had entertained a number of junior officers to dinner. Afterward it was suggested that everyone should adjourn to a brothel; each picked his girl and disappeared into a bedroom. At midnight there was a mad shrieking, Skobeleff's girl was yelling, "The General is dead." There then ensured a frightful to-do of extracting special permits in the middle of the night so that the body might be transported back to its rooms and respectability.

In reality, Brighton College during the winter term 1877 was no more palatable than it had been before; Frank was more frustrated and impatient than ever. He decided, he says, that the majority of boys he was teaching were fools with whom he was not going to bother. The headmaster, the Reverend Mr. Bigg, put him on notice, a warning that Harris, unable to stomach criticism, would have found deeply cutting. Pinned publicly on the bulletin board in the sixth form was a report of Harris' work, stating that while some scholars displayed great improvement, the majority showed none at all. Harris tells us he immediately handed in his notice, to be taken up whenever the headmaster wished. The Reverend Mr. Bigg seems to have welcomed this at the end of the winter term. Harris received his term's salary and it was announced in the Brighton College magazine in February 1878 that Monsieur P. Carré had succeeded him as French tutor.

From Brighton Frank made his way, in the steps of Byron Smith, to Heidelberg, a town that he found most beautiful, with its wooded hills, ruined castle and river on which he would row. He registered in the Philology Department and fell upon the German language as avidly as he had fallen upon the French. He worked, he said, night and day, limiting both sleep and exercise. In less than three months he claimed to speak German fluently, to have read Lessing, Schiller, Heine's *Lieder* and all the ordinary novels. He had shaved off his moustache, entered the gymnasium, and, as Kingsmill said, he had put Professor Fischer right on the origin of Shakespeare. He had become a member of the Anglo-American Literary Society and was selected as one of two people to go to Mark Twain, when he came to Heidelberg, to ask him to address them. Twain was friendly, promised to speak and offered them cigars. Harris was soon telling him how much he liked Bret Harte, another of his literary heroes. Twain, however, had a great deal of bad things to say: Bret Harte was a disgrace to literature, dishonest, and had cheated his publisher. Harris was horrified. That a man cheated publishers was immaterial—in any case writers were insufficiently paid —but what he had written "was throned on my admiration for ever." Twain, however, believed that a man should be, above everything, honest; anyway, a writer did not need to write unless he wanted to— he could make shoes or do manual labor. Here was heresy to Harris, who was hurt to the soul, refused to go to the meeting and dismissed Twain thereafter.

He spent the long vacation that summer at Fluelen on the Lake of Lucerne, he tells us, reading and rereading, discovering and interpreting Shakespeare. He walked in the mountains about the lake and twice crossed the St. Gotthard Pass. He told Kingsmill, however, that he retired to Fluelen "in order to recover from circumcision in four letters, but it doesn't suit his romantic spirit to put things so plainly in his Autobiography."[5] What he failed to disclose to anyone, plainly or otherwise, was that on October 17, 1878, he was married to Florence. The *Kansas Collegiate* carried the following announcement on November 30: "James T. Harris the brilliant and talented young man whose name was once on our catalogue, and whose face is remembered by many of the present students was married on October 17 in charming Paris, to Miss Florence Adams of Brighton, England. After his marriage Mr. Harris resumed his studies at Heidelberg, Germany." The fact that a short announcement appeared in the *Brighton Times* requesting that no cards be sent and that neither Ruth Adams, nor Thomas Harris, nor indeed any member of the family, was present at the wedding, which took place at the British Embassy with the consent of the ambassador, suggests that this was an unapproved elopement.

[5] Kingsmill to Hesketh Pearson, April 5, 1926.

Their married life cannot have got off to a good start. There was apparently a brawl in the street and Frank knocked down a fellow student who pushed him roughly off the pavement. He was convicted of "a rude assault in the street" and was sentenced to six weeks in the student prison and dismissed from the university. His friends, he said, and presumably his unfortunate bride, brought him all sorts of delicacies. His meals were feasts. He would let down a rope from his window and draw up bottles of wine. On his release the couple repaired to Göttingen, lodging at 1C Nicolaus Berger Weg, and Frank registered at the university. His life there he describes as all work. He sprinted, he said, a couple of hours a day to keep himself fit and applied himself to a strict regimen. In fact, it must have been a difficult time. He was still insecure and uncertain of the future, he dreaded that he might not be able to make a decent living. Florence's health was almost certainly not good. As we know from the letter he wrote that December to Carlyle, he was working on a novel and finding the writing of it difficult. When he was not writing he would make schemes for the future and then, on rereading them, lose his temper. All this he confided to Carlyle in his verbose style of many commas, which he claimed came through the German influence. He announced that he had decided upon working with his pen. He saw himself a martyr, "a volunteer in the ranks to fight for what seems to me the best course." He had enough to live on in a modest way (no doubt due to his marriage to Florence), he knew his faults of bombast and weakness, but he found them difficult to correct. Was it Celtic vanity with its characteristic love of loud words? He was working on philology and history and in his spare time sketched plans and contemplated the future, and then he would be discouraged by his impotence and confine his projects to the fire. For the last three years he had been writing his novel. Was it any good? Only Carlyle could tell him. He had sent an outline sketch along and he wanted, he said, to discover all the faults; what he really wanted was reassurance and praise.

> You will at once see, nor would I even if able to, disguise, that no *Man* wrote this sketch. The liquor is still fermenting, throwing off many bubbles and is in a state of much greater commotion than a good liquor could be, yet you will be able to tell me, how to help the fermentation so as to bring it to a more speedy termination and you will be able to predict—what, if cleared and settled, the worth of the draught will be. Is there, do you think, the possibility

of a strong generous wine which maketh glad the heart, can come out of the muddy liquid? If your answer is favourable you will comfort me, which help I need; if unfavourable I must still work for this is appointed to me.

Aged eighty-three, Carlyle was three years from death. So far as we know, no record exists of any comment either on the novel or the quality of the draft. But, as appointed, Harris' life continued, reading and listening to music by Bach and Wagner, Mozart and Beethoven. On two occasions, he tells us, he even went to balls, presumably to please Florence, since he himself detested dancing, mainly because he was bad at it, rapidly becoming giddy. His time at Heidelberg and Göttingen, he tells us, was a chaste one. This is ironic just at the hour when he had secured a bride. Before leaving Brighton, he says, he submitted himself to be circumcised. For this he gives two reasons: one, that he feared his sexual powers were lessening and hoped that circumcision would enable him to continue making love much longer; the other, that he would be less likely to contract venereal disease— which, according to Kingsmill, he had done already. The operation was apparently most painful, particularly the aftereffects, and although he does introduce a little dalliance into *My Life and Loves* at this time, it is mostly of a mild sort and the unions are often unconsummated. Another reason for chastity may have been that having secured Florence and married her—not to mention her thousand pounds—he may not have found her so desirable. Frank was always one to be stimulated by a chase. What is probably nearest the truth is that she was often too low in health for much activity. In any event, chastity, Harris discovered, sounding again refrains of the Victorian neurosis, chastity enabled him to work longer hours than he had ever worked. He read Schopenhauer, Kant, Hume, Pascal, Joubert and Goethe and found fault in the usual way with the professor delivering the lectures.

About June, Florence became seriously ill. She returned to Sussex, to stay at 22 York Road, Hove, and was nursed by Ann Tinsley. She died on August 27. According to her death certificate she had had phthisis for three months—a wasting disease of the lungs—embolism for two hours, and exhaustion. It is curious that she was not staying at 13 Montpellier Terrace, though her mother was present at her death. Whether or not her husband was with her is not known, although we do know that he left Göttingen around the middle of August. He was, in any case, the main benefactor in her will, receiving five hundred pounds, while her two elder brothers, Herbert and Thomas, each received two hundred, Archibald, Guy and Neale nineteen pounds, nineteen shillings, and her nurse, Ann Tinsley, ten pounds.

On leaving Göttingen and his regular life, Frank looked for the stimulus of big cities, theaters and art galleries. He went first to Berlin, then the itinerary of his travels becomes muddled. He visited Venice, Florence and Athens, he told the Hackney *Mercury*, "acquiring in Athens the spirit of Greek literature and art." In Italy, he tells us, he learned Italian, bought a small collection of Visconti armor and was told by Lamperti that he had a great career before him, singing. Without training he could, he claimed, sing two notes lower than ever were written. "Your patrimony is in your throat," Lamperti said, assuring him that his dislike for the piano came from his exceptional ear. It was a sin not to cultivate his voice. "But," said Harris ominously, "I had more important things to cultivate."

Into his memories of Europe he throws his usual batch of rich and distinguished persons whom he advises and impresses, his catch of girls whom he kisses and seduces. One of these was apparently a strip dancer; she must have been the perfect companion for Frank—a born flatterer. Every week she found a new compliment, a new trait to praise. But after six weeks he was tired of her. She was too nice. In Athens not only did he acquire the spirit of Greek art, embedding in his mind forever the curved white marbles of pagan men and women imposed against deep blue sky, but he took himself on a tour with two other students. His account appears in the *Saturday Review*, March 30, 1895. Harris relates that early in October 1880, wandering through Greece, sometimes on foot, sometimes on horse, lodging sometimes at monasteries, they arrived at Thebes. They met Schliemann, who told them that a young Greek had newly excavated the grave of the "Sacred Band," who had died at the Battle of Chaeronea in 338 B.C. They pushed on and were duly fascinated and moved by the Greek's details and by the grave itself, filled with two layers of warriors packed in like sardines. Thirty years later, in his autobiography, it is Harris himself who, having brilliantly interpreted Plutarch's text, unearths 297 skeletons, complete with spears, spear wounds, broken backs, ribs and heads. From Greece, it seems, he moved to Munich, where he lodged at Briennerstrasse, as Elmer Gertz discovered, from January 17 to May 18, 1881. He gives no number, but Wagner and his wife had lodged at 80/1

Briennerstrasse during October and November of the preceding year. No doubt the neighborhood was full of the stories that later he was able to turn to his own account for his portrait of Wagner, and that stimulated Ernest Newman, Wagner's biographer, to join the band and spend a great deal of energy writing ironic articles in the *Sunday Times* (June 1924) disproving Harris.

According to the Hackney *Mercury*, Harris then went to Moscow, where he spent some time studying Russian literature and Russian peasants, and returned by way of Vienna to England. His student days, and presumably his five hundred pounds, were finished.

CHAPTER 6

Literary and Political Beginnings

BEFORE he was to emerge fully in London and on the literary scene, Frank tells us that he disappeared to Ireland, visiting again Dublin, Galway and Kerry, where he saw his mother's grave. He found the weather rainy, the land impoverished and the Catholic Church ruling the waves of morality. With his many-labeled suitcases he stopped for a while in Ballinasloe, where he had an experience with which, afterward, he used to regale Kingsmill. Astonished by the sheer loveliness of the innkeeper's daughter Molly (that name again), he would take her on excursions in jaunting cars, and before long was trying out his seduction techniques. Ofter he would kiss her and tell her how much he loved her. To his surprise she believed him. He would not want to be marrying her, she pointed out, it would be shame he would be feeling over there in Paris, Vienna and London (she had been reading the labels). But the kissing did not stop. She was delighted to appear in his bedroom, wrapped in a red shawl, delighted to enter the bed, but she was not delighted to be rid of her virginity. "You could not care for me much or you wouldn't deny me," was Harris' rejoinder, his behavior apparently like that of a spoiled little boy deprived of grabbing a cake. It should be explained that he believed going to bed with him could do no harm. On the contrary, it was a noble and enriching experience, not unlike visiting Chartres Cathedral. He would steer the lady, as he would through any fine building, exhibiting the sights. He acted on the misunderstanding that his syringe would remove any chance of pregnancy; and since pregnancy was no part of the noble and enriching experience, he dismissed it. It was himself, not children, in whom he was interested. Reproduction bore no relation to the sexual act. Pleasure without inconvenience was the net result for him and he could only imagine it was the net result for his partners. As for the inhibitions enveloping promiscuity, he waved them away as he would the buzzing of a bluebottle—tiresome conventions made for fools. He himself felt no immorality, therefore there was no immorality. *Quod erat demonstrandum.* So at first he smiled at Molly's refusal, but not even an introduction to the magic syringe could make any difference. "How could I go to church? I confess every month, sure it's a mortal sin," and she would change the subject, urging Frank to tell her of Paris, the French clothes, and, sighing with pleasure, she would long to travel herself. But Frank was not pleased with what he called the insane belief of the Irish in the necessity of chastity; he felt impatient to be about "his life's work" once more. He was, he explained, under a vow to develop every faculty he had at any cost; of knowledge and wisdom he was the lover and priest. At this point he seems to have had a hallucination: we have a vision of the poor consumptive Smith with a flaming torch rushing in from land and sea to light up Harris, who waits like an arena for the Olympic games to begin.

Thus kindled, he departed from the Virgin Molly, traveled to London and made his way almost directly to Froude—who was taking the airs at Salcombe in Devon—carrying a letter of recommendation from Carlyle. Margaret Froude remembers him stopping the night, although she herself was away at the time. Froude was apparently impressed by Carlyle's recommendation: "an extraordinary letter" he is supposed to have called it. "It's very astonishing Carlyle asks me to help you in your literary ambitions," Harris makes him exclaim forty years later. "He says he expects more considerable things from you than anyone he has met since parting from Emerson." And on his return to London he promised that he would give a party for Harris to which he would invite those literary figures who could help him. They parted, not before Frank had handed to him a small bound book with a few dozen poems—chiefly sonnets—inscribed therein in his best copperplate hand.

Carlyle's letter to Froude and the apparent lack of proof of its existence has provoked stiff comments. "No trace of this letter remains and it is difficult to believe that even in his eighty-fourth year Carlyle would have committed himself quite so extravagantly," Vincent Brome wrote in his *Frank Harris*. But a letter does exist, dated by the National Register of Archives November 11, 1882, written from Onslow Gardens by Froude—presumably on his return to London—to T. H. S. Escott of the *Fortnightly Review*.

> This will be given to you by a Mr. Harris who is certainly a *remarkable* man, though what his powers are and what the limits of them I have yet to learn. He struck *Carlyle* as he strikes me. He is original a rare quality in these days and he has force—but he has written nothing (printed nothing) so far as I know. He may be a great acquisition. He may be unable to convey into words the stuff that is in him. I cannot say—but he wishes to make the experiment and I think it will be worth your while to try him. It can do you no harm to let him send you a paper to look at. It will certainly do you none to talk to him for ten minutes.
>
> You will perhaps be as much puzzled by him as I am, still as an Editor you would be sorry to miss the chance of encouraging a person who may turn out something exceptional and I therefore send him to you. I thought of introducing him to Longman. But that *Magazine* looks so unpromising that I would rather see him try his chance in higher quarters.

Escott, however, was not, it seems, as helpful as Froude had been. Having established himself at 1 Gower Place, Endsleigh Gardens,[1] Frank tells us that he made his way punctually at nine o'clock to the offices of the *Fortnightly,* which he discovered, to his surprise, to be a sort of shop in the publishing house of Chapman and Hall. Mr. Chapman arrived at about ten-thirty. He was past the prime of life, Frank noted maliciously, with thinning hair and a tendency to stoutness. He was apparently impressed by Harris' "references" but said the matter rested with Escott, a good-looking, well dressed fellow, remarkable for his lack of originality. There was nothing, said Escott, nothing. Harris, however, remained undaunted. He would return every day and be on hand should they require a proofreader, an article verified, should they require anything. . . . And so every morning he returned

[1] *Spectator* list of contributors, 1883.

and was sitting there when Chapman and Escott came in. Chapman would be embarrassed and acknowledge his bow, but Escott would pretend not to see him. At one stage Chapman suggested that it was pointless for Harris to keep appearing like that. Harris just smiled.

Meanwhile, he says, in a railway compartment he had met A. R. Cluer, who had suggested that he should try the *Spectator*. The editor, Richard Hutton, was apparently astonished by Harris, who, undeterred by the information that there were already too many writers, announced that there was always room at the top and there were subjects about which he could write better than anyone. He departed, apparently, carrying a book by Freeman on America and one on the Russian war. His strategy, he says, was clear. To win Hutton he must know him. He went round to the British Museum and got out all his books. From these he discovered that Hutton was a religious man who would recognize Freeman as a rude, cocksure fellow. He wrote the best stuff he could on the Russian war, said he, then an honest but contemptuous piece on Freeman. He ended his paper, he says, "as Malebranche saw all things in God, so Mr. Freeman sees all things in the stout, broad-bottomed Teuton."

One of his friends, he claims, was at this time John Verschoyle, the young, blond, gray-eyed curate of Marylebone Church. He appeared at 1 Gower Place just as Frank (said he) was finishing his articles. He was at once asked to read them, their author requiring as always praise and reassurance. "I wanted your criticism," he insisted. "Please point out any faults; I'm more at home in German than in English." And Verschoyle—to his indignation—did. Indeed, he was obliged to give Frank an English lesson. It had taken him years to learn German; it took him twice as long to cleanse his brain of all traces of the tongue. At length the papers were dispatched, and there was silence.

That year Harris mingled with a most melancholy crew of poets. There was poor Philip Marston, blind and pessimistic, with, it seemed, the touch of death upon him—everyone around him had died like flies: his two sisters, his future wife, Mary Nesbit, his friends Oliver Madox Brown, Rossetti, and James Thomson, who had been taken with a seizure and carried from his very rooms to the hospital. There was Philip Marston's father, Westland, who had fallen upon bad times; Amy Levy, who later committed suicide; Miss Mary Robinson and

Francis Adams. All brothers and sisters in gloom together. Here we have the first exposure from Harris himself of his own Celtic melancholy, which often lay as heavy as the moist malodorous fogs and with which he fought all his life. Here he idealizes it and makes it the essence of poetry and the poets he knew. "The sheer pathos of their unhappy pale and immitigable sufferings" had, it seemed, a Christlike quality. Life was a tragedy, laughter was an undesirable prop—like a merino dressing gown, as he wrote in the *Evening News* a year later—that played no part in this production. He saw himself an outcast, a sad prophet, traveling down the granite path of duty; he saw his unhappy band as martyrs suffering for the good of everyone. Everything was difficult, worrying, painful; the patches where things got better were small. Miss Mary Robinson and her sister seem to have had a few sparks of humor; this was not what Frank needed. Neither of them got on well with him, he said; he could not understand their lack of sympathy. As for Miss Mary Robinson—once she made the mistake of laughing at something he said; he was chilled to the bone.

There is no doubt that Harris cared deeply about the inequality, squalor and poverty that was everywhere. He joined the Social Democratic Federation and was soon lecturing and speaking publicly at open-air meetings in Hyde and other parks. These meetings are recalled by Henry Mayers Hyndman in *The Record of an Adventurous Life*—although he puts the date at 1881. Some of the speaking was really excellent, he remembers, and Harris was one of "the most effective of our out-door orators," doing good service in helping the intellectual development of James McDonald and others. Frank at this time was shopping around politically and was viewed by several people with some suspicion. Charles Finger, in a letter dated February 5, 1923 (to an unknown correspondent), recalled Harris as a member of the Social Democratic Federation; he recalled also that he broke into the anarchist group and once gave a lecture on the subject in a basement somewhere in north London. Prince Kropotkin sent in a warning, said Charles Finger, against dealing with and trusting a "man of mystery." Like Annie Besant, he broke into every group, or tried to; and, like her, finding each impossible to capture, he left for another.

Harris explained his political views to the Hackney *Mercury*.[2] While he is being cautious, elevating himself, and diplomatically pre-

---

[2] July 6, 1889.

senting to a right-wing party left-wing beginnings—which could have been embarrassing—his words sound true.

> When I entered into English life [he puts the date at 1884] I was absolutely ignorant of practical English politics, conscious only that Liberals and Conservatives alike paid but scant attention to the improvement of the social condition of the lower classes of the people, the only object in home-politics which seemed to me at all worth striving for. I presided over a branch of the Social Democratic Federation simply and solely because it gave me the opportunity of promulgating my own views of politics and society. From the very beginning the leaders of the Social Democratic Movement combated my peculiar opinions. . . . I began to realize that I was out of sympathy with the aims and methods of that society almost as soon as I joined it.

He was constantly speaking and debating, he continued, and rapidly his ideas grew clearer and more definite. Soon he came to see that progress must be gradual, that it was impossible for Parliament to limit by law the working day to eight hours: "Exposed to foreign competition as we in Great Britain are, such a law if passed would only ruin hundreds of our manufacturers and throw many thousands of workmen out of employment." He resigned from the Social Democratic Federation.

The literary scene, meanwhile, began to seem more satisfactory. The reply from the *Spectator,* Harris said, had been a long time coming, but now the post brought a letter, containing the proofs, and, at the same time, the invitation to Froude's dinner. Froude's party, which, we are told, was given in honor of Frank and his poems, was not a success. Chenery, the editor of the *Times,* was there, Austin Dobson, Longman and countless other literary figures. The poems were fine, it was generally agreed; everyone drank to their author and wished him luck in the charming way of English bonhomie. It was delightful. As the party rose to withdraw for coffee Harris stopped in the hall to fetch from his overcoat his latest sonnet lest he should be called upon to read. On reaching the drawing room door he found it nearly closed and a man's shoulder leaning upon it. Someone was reading his poetry. Not wishing to push the door rudely, Harris waited outside and overheard a weak voice give the opinion that his sonnet was not bad, indeed it showed a good form of verse and genuine feeling, but there was no new cadence, no new singing quality. This for Harris was mortifying. He went, he said, hot and cold. He was neither a poet nor a genius, just a trained imitator! It was a real disappointment. At Gower Place, he said, he reread all his poems, then burned them.

Prospects on the *Spectator* front were better. Hutton, he said, was delighted with the articles and the writing, simple yet rhythmic. Of a Russian article at this time there is no trace, but Harris' 2,500-word notice of E. A. Freeman's book *Some Impressions of the United States* appeared on July 7, 1883, entitled "Mr. Freeman on the American." His style is not so flowery as that which bloomed in Göttingen, but it is still well peppered with commas. The piece is a lecture from Harris on the differences between the Americans and the English, while Freeman had set out to show "the essential oneness of the two branches of the English folk." He does not end on his note of Malebranche and broad-bottomed Teutons, which had obviously so tickled him, but he does have a passage somewhere in the middle that is vaguely similar: "Well, as we, too, see the limitless expanse of ether as a mere blue dome, we must not judge Mr. Freeman harshly, who sees the American as a flaxen-haired, broad-built, phlegmatic Teuton." The following week Mr. Freeman found it necessary to review his reviewer. The critic, he complained, had made no attempt to give any account of the general contents of the book, he made him say things that he had not said and made him leave unsaid things that he had said. Sometimes the critic made him say things the exact opposite to what he had written, and at one point he had put words into inverted commas that Mr. Freeman could not find between his pages. This point his reviewer when replying conceded: it was, he said, "a lapsus calami."

What Frank had done was to take the book and make it an avenue down which to parade his own views and knowledge. He had a quick brain, could extract what he needed, digest it, then develop it. Unfortunately what he needed was often not contained precisely in the original writing. Because he was impatient he did not revise the text, but on his own composition he worked painstakingly, correcting and rephrasing. Once he had formed an idea it became fact. As Kingsmill said, the furnishings of Harris' mind—as he himself called them—contained some stationary pieces as well as the floating bric-a-brac. He assimilated knowledge easily and then lost it equally easily.

Hutton, however, seems to have been delighted with Harris' paper. During the next five months Frank wrote ten more pieces. Four were sketches—of the builder of the Suez Canal, a statesman, a novelist and journalist, and a scientist; two were obituaries—of Ivan Tourgenief[3] and Hendrik Conscience; and four were reviews.[4] His last piece, on Coleridge, appeared on December 29, and according to the 1884 list of contributors he wrote nothing more for the magazine. Later he claimed that the pieces he wrote for the *Spectator* were political. This is true in the sense that he lost no opportunity to advance his hopes of equality, democracy and liberty for all countries, becoming during the course of his articles more and more radical.

During the autumn of 1883 Harris was also doing work for the *Fortnightly*. He claims that as soon as his piece on Freeman was printed Chapman began sending books to him for opinions and even Escott gave him a German volume to read, an Italian article to correct, and soon half the *Fortnightly* itself. The real break came in November. The topic for the day was, as Harris says, housing the poor. Every year more and more country people were squeezing into the cities; the overcrowding and general conditions were appalling. The serious magazines carried articles by various landlords, politicians and financial experts reporting the exploitation and profiteering that was going on in the "rookeries"—the nuisances of foul drains, neglected water butts and cisterns, the tiny fixed windows and rickety staircases—and proposals to arrest the evil. Lord Salisbury in a paper in the *National Review*[5] advocated huge structures built in the air, as had been erected in Paris and Vienna.

The *Fortnightly* was to run a series of articles on landlords, the first of whom would be Lord Salisbury himself; the article would review precisely what he was doing about his own poor on his estates. The well known war correspondent Archibald Forbes was to acquire the material and write the first articles and Joseph Chamberlain would conclude the series. The articles would have to be written in a digni-

---

[3] Tourgenief was not available in translation then and would have been read probably in French. It was unusual to be well read in Russian literature at this time.

[4] From the *Spectator* list of contributors, 1883: July 28, article, "M. Ferdinand de Lesseps"; August 4, article, "M. Challemel-Lacour"; August 25, article, "Jules Claretie"; September 8, obituary, "Ivan Tourgenief"; September 22, review, "John Bull et Son Ile"—*John Bull et Son Ile*, by Max O'Rell; October 20, obituary, "Hendrik Conscience"; November 17, review, "Russian Literature"—*Studies in Russian Literature*, by Charles Edward Turner; December 1, article, "Sir William Siemens"; December 20, review, "The Expansion of England"—*The Expansion of England: Two Courses of Lectures*, by J. R. Seeley, M.A.; December 29, review, "Coleridge as Thinker and Critic"—*Lectures and Notes in Shakspere*, by S. T. Coleridge, now first collected by T. Ashe.

[5] "Labourers and Artisans' Dwellings" (November 1883).

fied style to suit the character of the *Fortnightly,* Chamberlain wrote to Escott on November 2, and should be signed, or they would be described as anonymous slanders. "Since I saw you I have been looking at Lord Salisbury's article and at a number of papers on the subject. I am now able to promise you an article for the December number." And he thought, he said, that he saw his way to trump Lord Salisbury's best cards.

Forbes hurried off to Hatfield alone—although next time it was planned he should take Harris with him—and returned with horrible tales of feculent filth dripping from dining room ceilings into the plates at mealtimes. He had, he said in a report to Escott, "hit hard and *true.*" All in all the report was sensational, so sensational that it was proposed that Harris should go down to Hatfield and check the facts. He dispatched his report, sparsely punctuated this time, on the same day that Chamberlain had agreed to write the concluding article, in his haste dating it October 2 instead of November.

> I went down to Hatfield to spend ten hours with the best guide possible examining Lord S's property—In Forbes statement I find nothing but exaggeration in many cases he is altogether mistaken in others Lord S. can scarcely be held responsible—the truth is— that I saw 70 cottages all containing either 4 or 5 rooms the rent usually being 3/– . . . almost all these have been built within the last 10 years—& they do Lord S. credit as they are so well built that to speak of it as a profitable investment would be absurd—I saw besides about 15 cottages in the same class in course of erection destined to take the place of the old cottages which Forbes speaks of—& correctly—as condemned. These condemned cottages are as a rule uninhabited—that is, the people who were in them, have been gradually rehoused in new & good dwellings—In some of the condemned cottages people are still living—but only till the new dwellings are ready to receive them—that this is a favour can be seen in the fact that of 3 cases—2—paid—as very old servants of the family—a merely nominal rent 5d per year—This is not too much to say that whenever you see a very good cottage in Hatfield it is sure to be Lord Sy's & whenever you see a bad one, it certainly does not belong to him—There can be no doubt that his cottages are infinitely better than those of his neighbours & let at a far lower rent—not only is he well spoken of by his tenants, but also *all* other labourers are most anxious to get into his cottages. He can only be blamed for not building more & more rapidly, as *some*

few of his labourers have to seek lodging in the town: but to this reproach he could well answer that he has done much, is still doing much & that he improves as rapidly as his means allow.

Both Escott and Chamberlain were horrified. "I agree that in view of Harris's report you must give up the Hatfield article," Chamberlain wrote to Escott, and then in another dispatch written on the same day, November 16, "You have had a narrow escape. Damn all sensational writing, say I! On the whole I am inclined to give up the idea altogether—its realization is too risky under the circumstances."

Hitherto, because of lack of evidence surrounding Harris' early days in London, it has been convenient for his biographers and debunkers to take for their text a novel by Frederic Carrel, *The Adventures of John Johns.* Carrel was American, a contributor to the *Fortnightly Review* during the years 1893 and 1894,[6] when Harris was editor. During that time he would have had fair opportunity to observe him and dislike what he saw. His first book, *The City,* was an exposure of the "most inhuman of all vices, gambling as practiced in the most demoralizing and ruinous of all 'hells' the City." He was against commerce, the stock exchange and ambition. There is no doubt that Harris in the 1890s was ambitious and had around him the aura of success, both financial and otherwise. Carrel clearly read, marked, and learned; what he inwardly digested he found unpalatable. He presented a one-sided recognizable caricature that was much appreciated by some of Harris' more malicious friends. "The sketch of Frank Harris in John Johns is superb," Oscar Wilde wrote to Robbie Ross in 1897. Carrel collected the rumors and speculations as to Harris' origins and painted him as the figure of mystery that members of the Social Democratic Federation had found—a figure of mystery in 1883, and in 1897 one of some unpopularity. He is physically below medium height, strongly built and muscular, with a long, dark moustache, snub nose, deep voice, earnest expression; he is quick to strike certain attitudes, to adopt different airs—quiet pathos, for example, or indignation—quick to ventilate unexpected views that startle. The main feature in this portrait is the eyes—keen black eyes of extraordinary expression and penetration. Since in reality Harris carried a certain reputation with women, Carrel found it convenient for his plot to make Harris use a

[6] "The College of France" (January–June 1893); "English and French Manners" (January–June 1894).

woman to gain his place as editor of the *Evening News*: to wit, by seducing the owner's wife. Here the character is too calculating. Harris
was not a businessman; he was spontaneous, emotional, uneasy, untidy
and impatient, but never calculating. It has been argued that two ladies
were possible candidates for the bedroom scene, Lady Folkestone and
Mrs. Kennard. This is unlikely, not because it would have been beyond Harris but simply because he would not at this stage have met
either of them. He had not yet the entrée into society. His debut did
not come until he was inside the offices of the *Evening News*. It is unlikely also that Carrel knew Harris in 1883, or any time before 1893
when he first contributed to the *Fortnightly*. In a letter written to Nellie
Harris, on March 29, 1932, A. R. Cluer refuted the whole thing vigorously. "The story told about Frank Harris and the *Evening News* is a
cruel and baseless calumny and the invention in the States of some
spiteful and unscrupulous liar who could not have been in England in
1883 and could not have known anything about the *Evening News* of
that date. I who first knew your husband in 1880 can assure you that
this is a vile and lying libel."

Harris' own account relates that both Escott and Chamberlain were
so grateful at the lucky escape they had had that Escott gladly gave
Harris a letter recommending him for the editorship of the *Evening
News*. Thus furnished, he called upon Lord Folkestone, who was, together with Coleridge Kennard, the paper's chief financier. Folkestone
was a tallish man, slight, bald, with a pointed goatee and kind hazel
eyes. As they walked round the *Evening News* buildings he told Frank
that they were losing £40,000 a year. Harris' qualifications were fine,
but could he make the paper pay? Harris made up his mind to tell the
truth: the recommendation did not apply to that job at all, he had not
the slightest idea how to make a daily paper pay, he had absolutely no
experience. What was needed was a businessman, not a man of letters.
Could he have a month's trial to gain experience? He won Lord Folkestone, but next he had to win Kennard, a fussy little man, anxious to
keep the paper Conservative. Advertisements were increasing, but the
circulation, which should be increased from 6,000 a day to 50,000,
would not budge. How could it be done? It was agreed that Harris
should have his month's trial. He sacked staff, made improvements,
and when the month was up, he said, he was able to show that he had
increased the efficiency of the *Evening News* staff and had saved a great

deal of money. He had at the age of twenty-seven become the editor of the *Evening News.*

Dates and figures were never, in spite of his school facility for mathematics, Frank's strong point, and he told the Hackney *Mercury* that he had the editorship in 1885, which suggests that his trial lasted one year rather than one month—a more convincing span of time in which to make radical changes. He explains also how he abandoned his left-wing policies in favor of the Conservative party.

> I began to see . . . that if one wished to effect any real good, one would have to be enrolled in one or other of the recognized bodies. Between Liberals and Conservatives my choice was easy. Conservatives had passed the first effective Factory Act, and about this very time Lord Salisbury wrote upon the need of re-housing the poor in our great cities. Furthermore, I was always a firm believer in the future of our Empire, a partisan of Imperial Federation long before the Imperial Federation League came into existence. And so when in the beginning of 1885 the Editorship of the Conservative *Evening News* was offered to me I was eager to accept it. Here, I thought, the opportunity offers itself to me to put forward my opinions in such a way that they must be listened to and judged on their merits. I soon found however, that the task of Editor was not what I had fancied it to be.[7]

[7] *Mercury,* July 6, 1889.

CHAPTER 7

Money and the
London Evening News

HAD Harris arrived in London twenty years earlier he might have been unable to break his way in. England was still an aristocracy—as he himself pointed out in his Freeman piece—while America was a democracy. Until now England and the aristocracy had been more or less an exclusive stronghold, upholding certain conventions and dignities; there was a place for everyone and everyone was in his place—orderly, and on the whole safe. During the second half of the century the voice of earned money was gradually being heard, aristocracy was giving way to plutocracy. "Qui dit noble en Angleterre dit riche," wrote Max O'Rell in *John Bull et Son Ile*, and expressed surprise at the vulgarity and presumption of the nouveaux riches. Distinguished foreigners, actors and even men of trade—provided they were rich enough—were being invited into the salon.[1] Yet the general attitude to foreigners still inclined to be "What a pity"—that they were foreign. The majority of English had

---

[1] There had been a time when actors and actresses had been viewed with the utmost suspicion. "In the old days," Lady Dorothy Nevill (who was very much a member of the old order) said, "they were closely observed when encountered in the street, as though any minute they might invert themselves and continue the journey on their hands."

no facility in foreign tongues. Lady Dorothy Nevill, who was essentially snobbish and Conservative, took a great interest in democracy and Henry Hyndman. She describes marvelously in *My Own Times* not only the change from mid-Victorian aristocracy but some insular traveling scenes. One traveler, she says, arrived in Calais and was astonished to find even very young children jabbering in French. Another sat down in a restaurant and ordered his dish by drawing a fine mushroom; the waiter nodded and returned immediately with a splendid umbrella. In spite of railways and steamships, traveling to foreign parts remained something of an adventure, and travelers were treated a little like lions, especially those to and from America, which in its turn was treated rather like a curious zoo. On February 2, 1884, the *Evening News* reviewed "a delightful little book," *Don't,* which was "a very droll glimpse of the society code at present in force in America." "Perhaps we ought to say," said the *Evening News*, "it shows us how, in the amazing fast rising society spread over the huge territory of the United States the desire to behave properly is as yet in advance of the acquisition of the needful knowledge of what good behaviour is." One is warned not to munch apples on the promenade, not to take off one's gloves to shake hands, not to say "O my" or "O Cracky"; not to call potatoes "pertaters," position "persition," windows "winders," horse "hoss." Not to spit bones onto plates, or, when drinking, to "elevate the glass as if you were going to stand it inverted on your nose." An accomplished American gentleman should not drop egg and grease on his coat, or drink from his saucer, or spit into the fireplace—or even upon the sidewalk—but go to the gutter for the purpose. Above all things, he must not blow his nose with his fingers. On July 22, 1884, the *Evening News* reported that at a New York dinner party tiny gilded dustpans were used as menu cards, with the bill of fare painted in blue letters inside the pan and the guest's name on the handle.

From the outside, London salons must have seemed scintillating; from the inside, many were very dull indeed. Although conversation was cultivated as a social accomplishment—like playing the pianoforte —there should be anecdote without argument, nothing strenuous or irksome. Ladies often contributed nothing, Lady Dorothy Nevill said, except to nod, beck and wreathe smiles, but "never one little word."

Poor Isidore de Lara, who wrote the famous "Garden of Sleep," shared many egocentricities with Harris and became his friend and supporter, remembers giving recitals before beautiful women and distinguished men. He was an agile social climber and dropper of names and in 1886 was lampooned by *Punch*. The first verse went:

> Successful? Rather! I should say I was!
> I had to struggle hard at first because
> To gain a reputation I allow
> One must eat dirt! But there! I've done it now.

And the last:

> And though my songs may possibly make you sick
> The ladies like them, and they buy my music
> Farewell, farewell! Here take this brace of grouse
> Sent by the Duke. I'm off to Squallborough House.

In *Many Tales of Many Cities* he conjures up his memories florally and sees his titled ladies and gentlemen planted out like so many flowerpots. There was Lady Walter Campbell "radiant as the richest red roses in May," the Duchess of Leinster most beautiful of pink carnations, Gladys, Countess of Lonsdale as tall and graceful as a lily, Miss Creswell exquisite as a violet, Miss Dorie Davis, Lady Randolph Churchill and Mrs. Plowden bestowing on the stalls of Steinway Hall the appearance of a parterre of flowers, staked up no doubt by their distinguished escorts—Danish ministers, equerries and dukes. And as, years later, he wandered through the streets of London he would pause, arrested by the sight of some house in which he had met some important personage—Lord Wolseley, perhaps, just off to take command of the Egyptian campaign, Lady Blanche Hozier, Madame de Falbe, at whose brilliant parties he sang to the fame, fashion and beauty of England—and he would pass on in his memories, alert, nodding here and there, bowing to the right and the left. "Bon soir, Excellence." "Bon soir, Monsieur de Lara," replies the French ambassador.

In spite of the many beautiful blooms, de Lara never liked singing in drawing rooms; "most of the people invited to hear music in private houses would much prefer to hear the music . . . of their own voices," he observed acidly. Once he discovered a Hungarian singer slumped in a state of distress at the piano; she could not sing in a room where there was such a noise—and sure enough, when she began, the talking and laughing continued greater than ever. She sang on, tears in her eyes. De Lara assured her, comfortingly, that when he performed he would command silence. He did not. He struck some notes, the noise continued. So he gave the soirée a nice harangue. Ill-bred philistines, they were, vulgar vandals, had they no respect for the most beautiful of all arts? He gathered strength and shouted for a quarter of an hour, his indignation whipping on his eloquence. Not a soul took any notice. Two or three men standing by the piano just looked round, thinking he was mad. So, offering his arm to the Hungarian artiste, they left, with difficulty thrusting their way through the noisy throng. Some hostesses, he said, Mrs. Jeune and Lady Warwick for two, did insist that guests should behave themselves properly, but once the Prince of Wales had talked so loudly to Count Herbert von Bismarck all the way through de Lara's recital that he had had to exercise all his self-restraint not to cause a scandal.

His were sentimental songs, rendered, he liked to think, passionately and poetically. Once he was delivering "Mine Today." "Come what you will you are mine today while the woodbirds sing and the world is grey," he warbled, and then noticed a peer of the realm signaling to a young lady to leave the room. The gentleman was not ill, his hostess informed him later; he had insisted that his fiancée leave— de Lara's singing he thought too passionate to be modest. "The Garden of Sleep" sold hundreds of thousands of copies. Heartbroken ladies would ask him to sing it in small boudoirs to their dying husbands.

> On the grass of the cliff, at the edge of the steep,
> God planted a Garden, a Garden of Sleep,
> Neath the blue of the sky, in the green of the Corn
> It is there that the regal red poppies are born,

he would croon to the fading spouse. On one occasion he was met by an enchanting young lady all dressed in white with a pink sash round her waist. They toyed with strawberries and cream and talked of romance, the lovely girl gazing with her blue eyes into Isidore's. Would he sing "The Garden of Sleep"? Of course he would. But in came a tall military man—the girl's lover. She had dreamed of being near him while de Lara sang. So de Lara with a sunken heart serenaded the certain rustlings that went on behind the curtain.

For an outsider, entry into society was made possible by money and by wit. With money one could eat at restaurants, one could purchase houses and land and the aristocratic pursuits of hunting, shooting and fishing. What hours were spent galloping over the country, what ditches, bullfinches and poorhouse drains were cleared; what necks and backs broken, buttocks peppered with shot. What a proportion of a gentleman's life was spent creeping about deer forests, grouse moors, bogs and sedge, what splashing, what mud, what salmon and minnow, wet and dry flies. Beaters rattled, hooves thundered, game pockets bulged and lunch boxes emptied; the coverts of England echoed with "By Gads!" and "My dear Sirs!"; "Good sport!" was the cry. What Lady Dorothy Nevill and her order felt was great distress at the genuine impoverishment and loss of dignity that was suffered when men occupied themselves solely with paper wealth and material benefits; it was a distress that had nothing to do with arrogance or lack of compassion for the horrible conditions endured by the poor. "To eat and drink and sleep," she said, "to be exposed to darkness and the light, to pace round in the mill of habit and turn thought merely into an implement of money making, is but a poor existence." No questions were asked as to how a multimillionaire had accumulated his wealth; provided he had accumulated it in large enough quantities, he was accepted. Yet these nouveaux riches seemed to possess no spontaneous expression of joy, no art or knowledge of living—they were weighed down by anxiety and the peculiar kind of sadness that is connected with wealth of this sort.

The aristocracy and upper classes may have been excessively occupied with pleasure, but many of them really cared about their land and their people. There were some, of course, who cared for little but themselves. Harris was to lament the incredible boorishness and stupidity of people who seemed actually proud of their ignorance and insularity. Once he had heard a millionaire—ennobled for his wealth—boast that he had in his house only two books, one of them the "Guide Book," the Bible, which he never opened, the other a checkbook. Many memories covering these years support Harris. One such collection, *Edwardian Hey-days*, comes from George Cornwallis-West, who became Lady Randolph Churchill's second husband. He tells of a contemporary of his who eventually became head of one of the largest business establishments in the country, who got through Eton only because of his father's influence. When he left he wrote to his tutor asking to be recommended to his wife; not one letter in the word "wife" was given correctly—he spelled it "yph." Another tale, of appalling manners, is recounted in a waggish tone. He and Colonel

Claude Lowther, "an amusing member of the Garrick Club," visited a play, *In Dahomey,* acted by black actors. Of course, said Cornwallis-West, he and his friend were bored stiff. In the middle of the second act the amusing Colonel Lowther struck up a political argument. Two ladies directly in front of them shushed them violently. "My dear George," wagged the colonel, "we mustn't talk, we're annoying the relations of the actors."

In more gentle circles the power of the word reigned supreme. To secure votes politicians relied upon rhetoric and oratory, although cunning was beginning to be an ingredient in the mixture. Writing was no longer the miracle it had once been, but writers of newspapers, pamphlets, poems and books were a real force; the best seller of the day would be the clubman's talking point. Yet language, as Harris was to complain, was castrated, and at the bottom end of the scale literature was of very poor quality indeed. Lady Dorothy Nevill quotes some ridiculous passages from the romantic novelettes that one imagines young ladies read lying on chaises longues. They were sentimental and badly written, filled with extraordinary statements: "All of a sudden the girl continued to sit on the sand gazing on the briny deep, on whose heaving bosom the tall ships went merrily by, freighted—ah! who can tell with how much joy and sorrow, and pine and lumber, and emigrants, and hopes, and salt fish?" Another author, speaking of fire, wrote, "A horse entirely consumed made its escape, uttering horrible cries!" And, quoted Lady Dorothy, an unfortunate traveler "after being perforated with innumerable bullets by bandits, and thrown into a lime-kiln, where he was burnt to a cinder, had strength and resolution enough to drag himself to a neighbouring village, and lodge an information before a magistrate!" She has a lyrical piece on modern newspapers, freighted with merchandise, which bound the world, circling, into their columns. Cities boom, steamships dock, corn blades glitter, wheat rustles and lightning flashes from thought. Markets hum, from a thousand hills the cattle low; the poet sings, "and with his song the low wind comes fresh and sweet over old meadows."

Before Harris could sing he had to make the newspaper pay. He found the apathy in the office of the *Evening News* to be appalling. The previous editor, he tells us, had never entered the machine room at all. Therein he discovered a dismal scene. Even the best machine was a dreadful rattling old thing and took an hour to make the stereo plates; the head machinist, Macdonald, claimed that he was the only one able to make the tin-pot contraption work at all. Harris' crew seemed to him a sulky pessimistic lot—it was almost impossible, they said, to make a Conservative newspaper pay.

His visits to the machine room were not welcome, and soon he was hit in the face by a workman measuring six feet. Gradually Harris managed to win round a Mr. Tibbett, who told him the position. Macdonald, he said, was no good, neither were twelve Scotsmen with him. Would Tibbett and four good men be able to do the work? Tibbett was not enthusiastic, but after much coaxing he agreed. Macdonald and his gang were discharged. An hour later a dreadful commotion broke out in the machine room. Everyone called Tibbett names and Tibbett knocked everyone down, the police were called, and Tibbett was arrested for assault. It all ended happily, however; the machines worked better than they had ever done and soon were casting plates in twelve minutes instead of one hour.

The next improvement came through the young newspaper boys. One morning an infernal din set up from the outer office, where the boys would assemble to wait for the first edition. All the boys were noisy and discontented. One, aged about twelve, pushed the contents bill into Harris' face, told him it was bloody awful and asked how he was expected to sell papers like that. Now, the *Daily Telegraph* really had something—a sensational bill full of slaughter in Egypt. The subeditor defended his quiet bill. The *Evening News,* he said, was a Conservative paper; it did not shout. From that moment Harris said he knew what the public wanted. Not thought, but sensation, and sensation was what they were going to have. His next passage has often been quoted: "I had begun to edit the paper with the best in me at twenty-eight: I went back in my life and when I edited it as a boy of fourteen I began to succeed; my obsessions then were kissing and fighting: when I got one or other or both of these interests into every column, the circulation of the paper increased steadily."

Frank disliked getting up early; once he took a column[2] to complain about an article in the *Lancet* that recommended rising at five o'clock, and later he spent a greal deal of his day in bed writing. But now, he said, every morning he rose at seven with breakfast and the papers—he could hardly rise earlier, he pointed out, since the milk did not come before then. He would take sensational accounts from the

[2] "Sleep No More," February 9, 1884.

daily papers—particularly the *Telegraph*—and improve them, add bits from other pages—French, Italian, Spanish and German papers too—and before nine would have the *Evening News* together and selling. Through the agency of the twelve-year-old boy's brother he was able to apprehend the special news releases arriving at four in the morning at the *Daily Telegraph* offices. On receipt of an especially juicy piece, there would be a tremendous bustle at the office. Once a compositor eager to save time jumped into the letter lift and was saved from plunging down five stories only by his friends, who clung to the ropes, receiving for their pains badly bleeding fingers. That time the *Evening News* was out on the streets five minutes before the special edition of the *Daily Telegraph*.

During 1884 Harris learned and practiced nearly every journalistic trick in the trade. On the front page in the right-hand column he would write each day an essay on diverse subjects including impropriety, food, bullying, anxiety, hypocrisy and drains, or he would report some scandal, some case of injustice, or some interview with a person of special "human interest," as he would put it. His presence is first mentioned on January 25 in a piece entitled "A Grey World." He is attacking Mr. Barnum's famous white elephant. Black was black, white was white, and Mr. Barnum had introduced a wretched scaly brute, no bigger than a horse, and had persuaded everyone that it was a snowy-white, earthshaking creature. "There is no hope that we shall ever behold a real white elephant at all," he assured his readers. "No such thing exists. They are the Mrs. Harrises of natural history . . . purely imaginary." That white elephant assumed quite an importance in the pages of the *Evening News*. An invitation was extended to visit the elephant at the zoo and meet the Burmese priests who had arrived to pay it homage; the *Evening News* declined to accept.

At the end of February the announcement came that Lord Garmoyle and the actress Miss Fortescue had broken off their engagement. Within ten minutes Harris had discovered Miss Fortescue's address and hurried round to interview her. She was a golden-haired girl, who blamed Lord Garmoyle's father. He was a dreadful prude who spoke of Sunday as the Sabbath and believed, like Captain Harris, the stage to be the antechamber of hell. Certainly he did not want his son to marry an actress, who seemed little better to him than the whore of Babylon. Into Harris' hands Miss Fortescue put certain letters, and on February 27 two columns appeared on the front page entitled "Beauty and the

Peer" (by "one who knows"). A few days later Miss Fortescue received a thousand pounds' damages. People were startled that a Conservative newspaper should attack a Conservative peer. Most startled of all was Coleridge Kennard, who, from Brighton, urged that Harris should stop publishing the "obscene story." Lord Folkestone, however, apparently supported Harris. He did not care for Earl Cairns, Garmoyle's father. The affair was, said Harris, a journalistic triumph and doubled the circulation of the paper. By Derby Day, which fell that year on May 30, *Life* was quoted on the front page.

> The *Evening News* performed something like a journalistic feat yesterday. In all the editions (the first being published at 8 a.m.) it gave the complete card of Epsom Races, so that the buyers of the paper saved 5½d. The circulation reached 100,000 copies. New machinery is about to be put up and the *Evening News* will apparently soon rival the New York *Morning News*, in point of enterprise and circulation. The same paper seems to be remarkably well informed about the Euston case.[3]

To this piece a note was added by the *Evening News*: "We are much obliged for our contemporary's kind remarks, but, as we like to be perfectly frank, we may state that our exact circulation on Derby Day was 76,693."

His columns during 1884 show not only a remarkable picture of Harris himself but a remarkable picture of the London of Mr. and Mrs. Charles Pooter. To complete the spectacle, George and Weedon Grossmith give a very funny portrait of Harris in *The Diary of a Nobody*. As Mr. Hardfur Huttle, "a very clever writer," he holds forth at dinner, astonishing all the respectable ladies and gentlemen by his unorthodox ways and extreme tactlessness.

> I shall never forget the effect the words, "happy medium," had upon him [Mr. Charles Pooter told his diary]. He was brilliant and most daring in his interpretation of the words. He positively alarmed me. He said something like the following: "Happy medium, indeed. Do you know . . . the happy medium means respectability, and respectability means insipidness? Does it not, Mr. Pooter?"
> I was so taken aback by being personally appealed to, that I

[3] Friday, May 30, interview with the Countess of Euston ("What Lady Euston Told the Representative of the *Evening News*").

could only bow apologetically, and say I feared I was not competent to offer an opinion. Carrie was about to say something; but she was interrupted, for which I was rather pleased, for she is not clever [enough] to discuss a subject with a man like Mr. Huttle.

He continued, with an amazing eloquence that made his unwelcome opinions positively convincing: "The happy medium is nothing more or less than a vulgar half-measure. A man who loves champagne and, finding a pint too little, fears to face a whole bottle and has recourse to an imperial pint, will never build a Brooklyn Bridge or an Eiffel Tower. No, he is half-hearted, he is a half-measure—respectable—in fact, a happy medium, and will spend the rest of his days in a suburban villa with a stucco-column portico, resembling a four-post bedstead."

We all laughed.

"That sort of thing," continued Mr. Huttle, "belongs to a soft man, with a soft beard, with a soft head, with a made tie that hooks on."[4]

From the columns it emerges that Harris, although he cared deeply about poverty and injustice, by no means advocated equality. In many ways he was as reactionary as a Conservative newspaper could wish. Ability, he believed, was an inherited quality that could not be instilled by education. Progress must come, but gradually, and for some of the changes already visible he did not care too much. At first his pieces are written very much by a man of letters—his material is drawn either from his education or from recent books and articles. A book on political economy by the Liberal Émile de Lavelaye gives him an article, "Free Trade a Free Fight" (January 15), and an opportunity to attack the Liberal policy in a manner befitting a Conservative newspaper. "The Art of Borrowing" (January 16) discusses the subject of credit and opens with an anecdote on Goldsmith, who meets a creditor. "My dear Sir," said the poet after much parleying, "you and I are in exactly the same position—you are anxious to be paid, I am anxious to pay you; and we are both disappointed." He continues by saying the practice of using that which does not belong to us is a mark by which the nineteenth century will be distinguished. Making profit by lending money, the Greek philosophers had argued, was an unnatural offense. Money could not increase and multiply like animals.

[4] Mr. Charles Pooter was of course exactly this soft man: he had a soft beard and his tie hooked on.

During the following months Walt Whitman, Herodotus, Dr. Johnson, Carlyle, Pepys, Balzac and Byron, among many others, lend a hand to Harris' articles on many subjects, particularly against the middle classes, hypocrisy and pretension, appearing under such titles as "Constancy," "Consistency," "Moon Lore," "The Marriage Markets of Belgravia," "Mrs. Gladstone's Cotton-wool," "Paterfamilias," "Manners Make the Man," "Superior Persons," "Cheap Dinners," "Avarice," "Conversation," "Humble Pie" and "Snobs."

On January 23 we have "Brummagemism"—against the belief that a showy sham can always get the better of a sober reality. There is the vulgar millionaire who desires the entrée into society but is worried by society's attitude toward the nouveaux riches; at dinner he talks loudly about his titled friends, yet provided Mr. Brummagem has a large bank balance and Mrs. Brummagem entertains well, he would be accepted. "There are patent faults in the narrow exclusiveness of an old aristocracy, but these are multiplied enormously when the door of the *salon* is opened, not to personal worth, but only to the clink of money bags." Brummagemism pervaded all grades of society, homes and goods: the flimsy stucco-ornamented suburban mansion in which the well-to-do tradesman's wife was "at home" substituting cheap champagne for "wholesome beer"; the shoddy cloth with which the Brummagem trader was destroying the character of English commerce; the press, the pulpit, the walls of the academy—even philanthropists who howled with indignation at the nakedness of the natives in Borrioboola Gha were guilty, giving no thought to their countrymen starving at their doors.

"Radicalism and Science" (January 22) discussed the doctrine of "hereditary genius" and education. Education was not a magic wand and could not perform miracles. Heredity supplied the character and the ability. Surely the political lesson to be learned from Darwin was that one should look for ability among children of professional and upper classes. Education appears again on February 4 in "I Can't Do It." The pressures of compulsory education proved to be too great for many children. What were the lady members of school boards about? They should be providing motherly feeling and insight. As it was, many children were weak, sickly little things, ill fed, ill clothed; some with overtaxed brains were dying, raving of their school work, or committing suicide.

Harris the hostesses' friend appears in "Reception Day" (February 4). The institution of a reception day at all seemed of doubtful advantage—unless the hostess' visiting list amounted to five hundred, there was a beautiful room, good servants and a score of interesting guests. All bores should be eliminated. "Weeding the social garden of thorns" was what Harris called it. Visiting hour was prey to all bores who would descend and fill the sofas and chairs. In vain would the hostess desire to discuss with a distinguished man his books, Mrs. Bore and her daughter would drive him away, and the hostess would be left distributing her teacups to the very dullest people. Back he is onto his theme of Brummagemism with suitability of dress: long trains and shadeless bonnets, which were only tolerable in open carriages where there was an idle hand to hold aloft a parasol, and paper-soled boots, fit only for velvet carpets, were incongruous in the underground and ridiculous when worn by housemaids, cooks and farmers' daughters. Why, the "present writer" had beheld little girls attending village boards in blue veils and fashionable bonnets and, in Wales, a buxom damsel scaling a six-foot wall in a dress with three flounces and a train.

The suburbs[5] came in for as close a scrutiny as the buxom lady with her flounces had received. Here people were still able to imitate a country life, but not without the inconvenience that comes from living in close proximity to other people. Neighbors[6] disturbed one another by jingling pianos, crowing cocks, barking dogs, invading cats, rabbits and pigeons that poached upon next door's fruit trees and vegetables. Often the roads were not paved, and Mr. and Mrs. Bore got badly splashed with mud and slush in winter and coated with dust in summer. Suburban life was one burdened with anxiety, bustle and responsibility. Everything—eating, sleeping, taking pleasure—was bound by the clock.[7] In eagerness to save time and make the most of the day there was little leisure left for idle occupation, which formed the real charm of life. "The great feature which life in the suburbs has developed among Englishmen is that they seem to live in a perpetual condition of catching trains. Doctors could perhaps inform us how many digestions are ruined by the hasty swallowing of an early breakfast, and the subsequent rush along the streets."

Everywhere there was an increase in building. Land, no matter

5 "Suburban Sorrows," April 22.
6 "Neighbours," February 29.
7 "Clock-worship," March 12.

what the fields had been, was exploited by market gardeners, roads were being marked out, houses erected, their foundations sunk into manure and mire. "Whether we are not considerably over-built in the matter of suburban residences is, we suppose, a question for speculative builders to settle among themselves; but the work goes on apace, and it requires the strong faith of a devotee of political economy to believe that the supply is . . . regulated by or proportional to the demand."

There was no quarter in London or any other English city for struggling artists and writers; yet Bohemia, like Harris, was essentially urban. Neither had an existence outside cities.[8] "Everywhere the magnificent restaurant is busily engaged in ousting the humble tavern or chop-house which contented a previous generation; and the Bohemian finds little in the glitter and glare of our modern palaces of refreshment to attract him. . . . Here and there a few of the old places remain, undemolished by the craze for improvements, and not 'exploited' by the speculative builder. The sanded floor, the wooden chairs, a plentiful supply of sawdust and spittoons, a comfortable fire—these are to be found in more than one alley and bye-street not many miles from the neighbourhood of St. Paul's."

On April 18, to stimulate the diet, there is a sensational account of a private whipping; the atmosphere is furnished with dialogue. The culprit was an undersized twelve-year-old who had tried to steal some cauliflowers from a barrow. He was sentenced to twelve strokes of the birch to be administered in the prisoners' waiting room, an apartment twelve foot square, lit only by a skylight. A good-looking jailer unlocked a cupboard and removed a bundle of birch twigs, which had to be soaked for half an hour. A leather-covered stool was brought, the boy told to get ready.

> Slowly, and with an occasional snivel, he takes off a coat that might have been borrowed from a scarecrow, a waistcoat recalling Johnson's definition of network, and a greasy velvet cap, till he stands in a pair of corduroy trousers and a ragged flannel shirt minus one sleeve, and revealing a bare lean arm, less in girth than a turkey's drumstick, with a dirty claw-like arm at the end of it. His sobs increase in vehemence as he proceeds to unloose his trousers, but he does this with a readiness eliciting the remark from the gaoler that he "knows all about it." The gaoler then grips

him by the arms between shoulder and elbow, and the policeman in charge takes him by the ankles. They lift him up and place him face downwards on the office stool.

The boy is weak and the blows shall be regulated accordingly. They tighten their grip, straightening their captive like a bar of iron laid across an anvil. The twelve strokes swish down in mercifully quick succession, each jerking out a cry from the victim; as the last three fall he tries to writhe round and look up into the face of the executioner. Amid howls he is replaced on his feet. "Lord bless you, there is a difference in the way boys take it," observed the inspector. "Some of 'em don't mind it one bit, but just shut their mouth hard and won't let a cry be knocked out of 'em, but this is a poor little devil." And the poor little devil slunk out with the prospect of another private beating, this time from his father, for having been discovered.

Soon Harris the man of letters had changed wholeheartedly into Harris the reporter, busy getting out and about. He hurried along to madhouses, prisons and parks, sitting on benches interviewing the other members, mainly on the subject of their incomes. Here he discovered a "super,"[9] who on being offered a cigar was pleased to reveal his weekly budget: four shillings went on lodgings; twopence a morning for a breakfast of cocoa and two chunks of bread and butter; dinner was bread and cheese, with meat once a week; sometimes a party "piles it up"—then it was a feast of sheep's head or bullock's heart. In "Knights of the Broom"[10] readers were introduced to two crossing-sweepers. One, noted for the shakiness of his legs, took up his position north of Bedford Row and had never been seen sweeping. Every morning his wife arrived at 8:45 with an armchair and a broom. He sat in the chair while she gave a quick sweep to the road. Then he spent the morning sitting there saying "Goo' morning" and getting tolerably well paid for his politeness.

Once, outside a pub, Harris met a tin-whistle player,[11] all woebegone and hopeless in the freezing wind, trying to whistle "God Bless the Prince of Wales." Soon he was inside drinking a glass of hot toddy in front of a roaring fire telling Harris that sometimes he got as much as a pound per week, sometimes he could not pocket seven shillings.

[9] "A Super's Story," June 23.
[10] May 21.
[11] "The Tin-Whistle Player," June 10.

He would play jigs and reels to poor girls, who, with shawls over their heads, liked to dance in the streets. Harris gave him three drinks and prepared to slip away. His guest did not notice. "He lifted his whistle to his lips and blew a weird, fantastic strain that bore a remote resemblance to 'Ye Banks and Braes.' . . . Turning on my heels, I took a last view of him as he crouched over the fire exposing the yawning seams and threadbare brilliance of his shabby coat, and playing softly to himself. Then I left the poor fellow alone with the dregs of his whisky."

One final example, and perhaps one of his best pieces, comes on June 25.[12] He had been strolling down Hogg Street in Southwark and had witnessed a dreadful fight. Tom Crondal was beating his wife. His face all torn down the right side, his coat in shreds, Mr. Crondal repaired to the pub, where the representative of the *Evening News* was quick to get beside him. "So yer one o' them noospaper chaps, are yer," Tom Crondal said, in the vernacular, glaring at Harris, who was pretending to drink "four arf" out of a battered pewter. Could Harris do him a good turn? "Let the publick know o' my gal's goin's on. . . . Say as Mrs. Marther Crondal is the biggest waggerbone in 'Ogg Street." Mrs. Marther Crondal, it turned out, had pawned her husband's boots and trousers and had hurried off to spend the money on drink, leaving him in Mrs. Wilkin's petticoat. Ted Green retrieved the goods, and off went Tom Crondal to hit his wife. "I cops her inside the Wiceroy, and drags her out. She'll be quiet for a week now, I'll lay! She ought to be biled, ought Marther, in salt and winegar." At this point three repulsive faces appeared at the partition all heartily cursing Mr. Crondal. "Persephone, Hecate and Alecto," Harris murmured wittily to himself. Nor was Medusa wanting, for the gin-inflamed visage of another hag rose slowly into view. In vain did Mr. Crondal threaten it with a pint pot. The furies howled like a tempest. "D'ye think Parlimint 'ud do her any good?" Mr. Crondal appealed to Harris. "She wastes a power o' money in drink. They might have her up afore Gladstone and Mr. Henderson, and say a word to her. Wot? Yer don't think they would? You're sure of it? Then, what's the good o' Parlimint? Wot's Parlimint for, but to take care o' the people?"

Between interviews Harris was pleased, he tells us, to accept dinner invitations and luncheons on Sundays—although at this stage he spent

---

[12] "A Wifebeater's Appeal to the Public."

most weekends with the Folkestones. Twenty years later their eldest son, then Lord Radnor, remembered in a letter to Harris many pleasant talks "in the old days," when he played listener, and he recalled the breadth and depth of Harris' information and knowledge. Lord Folkestone had taken Frank under his wing; he sent him to his tailor and saw that he was properly turned out, and then he introduced him into society. He also gave him some paternal advice about drinking. With his coffee Frank liked to drink five or six glasses of cognac, and this, no doubt, after liberal quantities of wine. Although he showed no signs of being drunk, this amount of alcohol, Lord Folkestone said, would certainly ruin his constitution. Harris was deeply hurt by this criticism and says that he gave up all drink for a year and began to take exercise, running and walking for several miles a day. It is unlikely that he abstained altogether, for he loved to drink wine, while talking about it for hours on end, but no doubt he moderated the amount. In any event Folkestone was a good friend—and one of the few not to be tarred in *My Life and Loves* with some sexual defect; another was Arthur Walter, the editor of the *Times,* with whom Frank would spend half his summers, near Finchampstead. Eight or so years later, in 1892, Frank was godfather to Walter's son. In 1885, no doubt soon after he had been made editor, he bought a house, 23 Kensington Gore, in order to entertain at home. "The fact remains that after my first month as Editor of the *Evening News* I did not dine in my own house half a dozen times in the year and had to reject more invitations than I could accept," he wrote in *My Life and Loves.*

Harris was intoxicated, if not by the numerous glasses of cognac, with his success and with London.

> If you have never been intoxicated you have never lived [he wrote in his memoirs]. London made me drunk for years and in memory still the magic of those first years ennobles life for me and the later pains and sufferings, wrongs and insults, disdains and disappointments all vanish and are forgotten. I wonder if I can give an idea of what London was to me with the first draught of its intoxicating vintage on my hot lips and the perfumes of it in my greedy nostrils.
>
> London in the early eighties; London after years of solitary study and grim relentless effort; London when you are twenty-eight and have already won a place in its life; London when your mantelpiece has ten times as many invitations as you can accept,

and there are two or three pretty girls that attract you; London when everyone you meet is courteous-kind and people of importance are beginning to speak about you; London with a foretaste of success in your mouth while your eyes are open wide to its myriad novelties and wonders; London with its round of receptions and Court life, its theatres and shows, its amusements for the body, mind and soul: enchanting hours at a burlesque prolonged by a boxing-match at the Sporting Club; or an evening in Parliament where world-famous men discuss important policies; or a quiet morning spent with a poet who will live in English literature with Keats or Shakespeare or an afternoon with pictures of a master already consecrated by fame; London, who could give even an idea of its varied delights?

In his third volume of memoirs he brings in a refrain: "London, to me, is like a woman with wet, draggled dirty skirts . . . and at first you turn from her in disgust, but soon you discover that she has glorious eyes lighting up her pale, wet face. The historic houses, such as Marlborough House, Lansdowne House, Devonshire House and Cadogan House, and a hundred others, are her eyes; and they are simply wonderful treasure-houses of past centuries, with records of each age in gorgeous pictures and books, in tapestries and table silver—all the accessories of good taste and comfortable living."

Off he would hurry to his parties, his art galleries and theaters, there to review exhibitions and performances; he would brave the icy blasts of Covent Garden to see Salvini as King Lear. Here we have the first glimpse of Harris the hypochondriac huddled in overcoats and wraps. It was, he said, a "night too rough for nature to endure," and he wanted to know if the management could do nothing to keep out the piercing drafts that whistled along the stalls. It was hardly an exaggeration when he said that to attend performances at Covent Garden in winter was to run the risk of severe illness.

During these years he met any number of people. He visited Karl Marx, he said, on Haverstock Hill, an encounter which seems to have been an exchange of delightful flatteries: Marx complimenting Frank on his fine German rhetoric and fluency, Frank rejoining by complimenting Marx on the importance of his book on the English factory system. He became friends with Alfred Tennyson, son of the poet's elder brother, who later gained a bad reputation and who taught

Harris all he knew about silver and furniture; and with the Duke of Marlborough, because according to Harris of the sheer similarity of their natures—they both liked good dinners, noble wine and women. It was, he says, at Mrs. Jeune's[13] "omnium gatherums" that he met most people—all celebrities, from Parliamentary leaders (Tom Crondal would have liked that) to figures of art and literature. One of his first meetings with Oscar Wilde is supposed to have been there. He met and knew Charles Dilke fairly well, and existing correspondence in the British Museum shows various professional dealings. He claims that he defended Dilke as best he could when he was cited for divorce by Mr. Crawford. While he spoke French excellently, apparently Dilke knew nothing of French literature or art, caring only for politics. As for Lady Dilke, Harris did not take to her at all. She was the only blue-stocking he ever met in England; he describes her as short and stout. This plain description[14] may have had something to do with her apparently caring more for her own opinions than for Harris'. He tells a story which happened when he had acquired a reputation as a Shakespearean scholar. She invited him to meet Jusserand, and the two were introduced in a small first-floor drawing room. She then proceeded to inform the two gentlemen that Shakespeare was not Bacon, from which point she launched into a long story about a Baconian whom she had met at Lincoln College. It is a nice tableau: Jusserand and Harris listening to Lady Dilke with polite inattention as she talked on for an hour. They were still listening when the dinner bell rang, neither of them having got in one word.

Some of his funniest passages occur in Volume II of *My Life and Loves* where he describes attending the Lord Mayor's banquet in his capacity as editor, first of the *Evening News,* then of the *Fortnightly Review* and the *Saturday.* His descriptions of the gluttonous festivities and anal evacuations of the Lord Mayor and his aldermen nearly caused him, on their publication in 1925, to be prosecuted for obscenity. One of his main themes was that while gluttony, bestiality at table and over-weight were accepted by society, self-indulgence in making love—which he believed to be a beautiful and noble act—was looked upon as

[13] Mrs. Jeune, according to Henry Hyndman, had a remarkable selection of people at her soirées: Robert Browning and Lecky, Fitzjames Stephen and Whistler, Oscar Wilde, Joseph Chamberlain, Randolph Churchill, Lady Dorothy Nevill.

[14] Roy Jenkins describes Lady Dilke, who had been the wife of Mark Pattison, Rector of Lincoln College, as remarkable both in talent and appearance.

immoral. "What I want to know is, why shouldn't one speak just as openly and freely of the pleasures and pains of sexual indulgence as of the pleasures and pains of eating and drinking?" he would demand. While, as in the case of making love, he took great care to inform himself about food and wine, escorting his dinner companions through their mysteries, he viewed overindulgence in either as "simply loathsome and disgusting to all higher natures."

He found apparently plenty to disgust higher natures at the guildhall. It is a lovely scene: the editor of various important journals gazing superciliously all round him while the red-faced aldermen guzzle like pigs at their troughs, letting down the human race from the heights to which Harris had ordained it. "Till that night," he says, "I had thought that as a matter of courtesy every man in public suppressed any signs of greed he might feel, but here greed was flaunted. The man next to me ate like an ogre; I took a spoonful or two of turtle soup and left the two or three floating morsels of green meat. When he had finished his first plateful which was emptied to the last drop in double-quick time, my neighbour while waiting for the second helping turned to me: 'That's why I like this table,' he began, openly licking his lips, 'you can have as many helpings as you want.' " Harris, in his best park-bench style, settled down to interview him. He discovered that his neighbour was the master of the Cordwainers' Company. At their table servants were instructed to be courteous and they all expected a tip.

"Why do you leave that?" the master of the Cordwainers' company exclaimed, pointing to the pieces of green meat on my plate. "That's the best part," and he turned his fat flushed face to his second plateful without awaiting my answer. The gluttonous haste of the animal and the noise he made in swallowing each spoonful amused me; in a trice he had cleared the soup-plate and beckoned to the waiter for a third supply. "I'll remember you, my man," he said in a loud whisper to the waiter, "but see that you get me some green fat, I want some Calipash. . . ." "Is that what you call Calipash?" I asked pointing with a smile to the green gobbets on my plate. "Of course," he said, "they used to give you Calipash and Calipee with every plateful. I'll bet you don't know the difference between them; well Calipash comes from the upper shell and Calipee from the lower shell of the turtle. Half these new men," and he swung his hand contemptuously round the table, "don't know the difference between real turtle and mock turtle; but I do."

And the editor of the *Evening News* was told that if he would eat up the green pieces on his plate they would go to his ribs and make a man of him. Why, the head of the Cordwainers—who was growing redder and redder, hotter and hotter, gobbling down three platefuls of mutton and consuming three bottles of champagne—had gained three pounds at his first banquet!

Another year Harris had the honor of sitting beside a little tub of a man. For a while he could not account for his wrigglings and apparent discomfort, until on investigation he observed that the tub had between his legs a huge bottle. "What's that?" Harris asked nosily. "A jeroboam of Haut-Brion '79," ejaculated the tub. When the banquet was over Harris had to help him to his brougham, and the tub's legs were not his only part to revolt that night; they had not reached the brougham before he was sick. Another time, he tells us, during an interval he happened to meet George Wyndham outside the door and was quick to draw his attention to the stench that hung about the guildhall. "Good God!" cried George Wyndham. "What a revelation!"

But it was the Lord Mayor himself, Sir Robert Fowler, who, according to Harris, was the master farter. He has a wonderful description of dinner at Sir William Marriott's, M.P. for Brighton. Sir Robert Fowler had the unusual distinction of being elected Lord Mayor twice, in the years 1883 and 1885. He was a rich man, an out-and-out Conservative, five foot ten in height, much more in girth, and a good scholar. Harris had gone to Marriott's dinner reluctantly, he says. Lady Marriott was a washed-out, prim little woman, kind but undistinguished. Marriott was just plain boring, with a small dining room to boot, which seemed even smaller by the time Fowler had waddled in. Harris had just taken a mouthful of clear soup when his nostrils were arrested by an unmistakable odor. By the time they had finished the roast beef and Yorkshire pudding, which Fowler had attacked like an ogre, and were enjoying the game, the atmosphere was appalling. The partridges were so high that they fell apart when touched. Harris, who had never, he said, been partial to rotten meat, trifled with his bread and watched Sir Robert Fowler smacking his lips and swallowing huge gobbets of meat, while his veins stood out like knotted cords and beads of sweat poured down his great red face. Lady Marriott's visage meanwhile was displaying a noticeable shrinking. Suddenly there was a redolent explosion. Sir Robert Fowler mopped his head serenely and returned to his plate. Little Lady Marriott was as pale as death. Harris, Knight of the Malodorous Table, escorted her out into the fresh air.

Not content with his dinner party scenes, Harris dishes us up a savory. The Honorable Finch-Hatton, he said, had been elected to Parliament. On one of his first nights on the House of Commons he sat next to Fowler, who got up and made a long speech. While he was speaking Finch-Hatton showed signs of restlessness, and toward the end of the speech moved some three yards away. The speech ended by Fowler saying he would not conclude with any proposal until he had heard what his opponents had to say. As soon as he had sat down, Finch-Hatton sprang up, holding his handkerchief to his nose. "Mr. Speaker," he began, and was at once acknowledged by the Speaker, since this was his maiden speech. "I know why the Right Honourable Member for the City did not conclude his speech with a proposal; the only way to conclude such a speech appropriately would be with a motion!"

Ironically, just at the time when he was preaching against hypocrisy Harris was guilty in his own columns of a gross sham. He had made his name with sensation; he had exposed scandals and poverty, the mimicry of the nouveaux riches. He had taken up the cause of women and he had inquired into the evils of prostitution; and here he had fallen down. It was tame stuff, made essentially of paper—not what one would expect from a sensation-monger. No doubt he found the articles difficult; no doubt to be frank, in that climate, about such matters on the front page of a Conservative newspaper was easier said than done. Nevertheless a lot of polite waffle emerges, reinforced with quotations from Voltaire, Lecky and Taine. "The Sisterhood of Sorrow" (April 8, 1884) refers to "those unhappy creatures who are doomed from girlhood to what is termed, as if in bitter irony, 'the gay life' of the streets." He did try to expose the miseries involved with the life—the drink, the poverty that came the moment the girl was no longer fresh and seductive—but the fiber is too limp to hit anyone.

> It is impossible to read the story of such hapless victims of brutal passion without feeling that in some sense society, or the existing order of things whose disorderliness we strive to mask under that

polite abstraction, is responsble for much of the suffering that has filled their young lives with sadness. . . . Have we done all that lay in our power to deliver these unfortunates from evil! Have we striven as we might have striven to open up to them some other path of life than that very broad one which at first seems invitingly strewn with roses, but which ere it has been long traversed is seen only too plainly reddened by those pilgrims of sorrow who have trodden its thorny way with bleeding feet.

He concluded a little more firmly. It was the greatest prudery, he said, to refrain from discussing these things, and he urged educated and earnest women to debate among themselves in the plainest terms how to stop these women from falling; so far every effort by good women had utterly failed to diminish what M. Taine called "the plague-spot" of London. It was not prostitution but destitution that filled the Haymarket, Strand and Regent Street with their "deplorable procession" that M. Taine pictured in his *Notes on England*. "Vice and its Victims" (June 3, 1884) discusses juvenile prostitution and its alarming increase. Harris quotes various laws and cases where children had been discovered brought up in one room that must serve both as nursery and brothel, and where young girls had been sold.

A year later, in July 1885, came W. T. Stead's famous exposé of vice and prostitution in the *Pall Mall Gazette*. Stead himself was a puritan, but there were no paths of roses or reddened, thorny ways in his piece; he called a virgin a virgin; moreover he ordered five to be procured for the purpose of seduction. This was not paper; it was real.

On Monday, July 6, 1885, on his mission for purity, backed by Cardinal Manning, he set out to show that there was a great and infernal traffic in vice. The crimes were classified:

i The sale and purchase and violation of children
ii The procuration of virgins
iii The entrapping and ruin of women
iv The international slave trade in girls
v Atrocities, brutalities and unnatural crimes

For a month, Stead said, he had oscillated between the noblest and meanest of mankind; he had wandered under the glare of the gas lamps with all the vices of Gomorrah surrounding him. And he had plenty of gory tales for evidence to support his list of classified crimes.

Tuesday, Wednesday and Thursday were taken up by these. He had talked to children who had no idea what "being seduced" meant; he had ordered five virgins to be specially procured for him and examined by the doctor—girls who would sign an agreement that for a present of £4 or £5 so-and-so could "have" them. One, Stead reported,

> was a nice simple, and affectionate girl of sixteen, utterly incapable of understanding the consequences of her act. Her father is "afflicted" . . . her mother is a charwoman. . . . She was to have £4; of which the firm were to have £2. The poor child was nervous and timid, and it was touching to see the way in which she bit her lip to restrain the tears. . . . She was very frank and I believe perfectly straightforward and sincere. The one thing she dreaded about being seduced was having to be undressed. Poor child, it was the only thing she could realize. Her lips quivered and her eyes filled with tears as she pleaded to be allowed to escape that ordeal. What being seduced meant beyond the formula that she would "lose her maid" she had not the remotest idea. When I asked her what she would do if she had a baby she started and then said, "But having a baby doesn't come of being seduced, does it? I had no idea of that." "Of course it does," I replied. "They ought to have told you so." "But they did not," she said; "indeed, they said, babies never came from a first seduction."
>
> Nevertheless to my astonishment, the child persisted that she was ready to be seduced. "We are very poor," she said. "Mother does not know anything of this: she will think a lady friend of Miss Z's has given me the money; but she does need it so much." "But," I said, "it is only £2." "Yes," she said, "but I would not like to disappoint Miss Z (the procuress) who was also to have £2. . . ." "Now," said I, "if you are seduced you will get £2 for yourself; but you will lose your maidenhood, you will do wrong, your character will be gone, and you may have a baby which it will cost you all your wages to keep. Now I will give you £1 if you will not be seduced; which will you have?" "Please Sir," she said, "I will be seduced." "And face the pain, and the wrongdoing and the shame, and the possible ruin and ending your days in the streets all for the difference of one pound?" "Yes Sir," and she burst into tears, "we are so poor."

Stead's report does not carry details of the seduction; nevertheless this is strong beer beside Harris' wishy-washy essence. Here Stead had, to all appearances, actually been party to seducing young virgins to prove his case. Harris, who had made his success with sensation, had been huffed at his own game. Moreover, the *Pall Mall Gazette* was a competitor of the *Evening News*; the exposé was an outstanding success, the editions were sold out—and eventually Stead was arrested and imprisoned. No paper was more virulent in its attack than the *Evening News*. "The article is simply hideous," it announced on July 8. "The writer revels in the description of the most atrocious and filthy forms of vice—vice so horrible that probably 99 men out of a 100 are unaware of its existence, even supposing that it *does* exist anywhere except in the writer's putrid imagination. The harm that has been done to public morality may be gauged by the fact: In every principal street in London City scores of boys—scarcely in their teens—may be seen reading this pernicious stuff and pointing out passages to their companions. The outrage upon public decency is still more glaring." It was the contents of a vile sewer, thundered Harris, it ensured general pollution, and further steps must be taken to stop further contamination and to punish the authors.

Clearly Harris was ashamed of his attack. He never mentions it and in his autobiography waves aside Stead's "crusade against the lust of what he called 'The Modern Babylon' " as a silly exaggeration that got him into prison for six or eight weeks. Stead (who went down in the *Titanic*) he describes as "an extraordinary specimen of the lower middle-class type of Englishman—without classical education, without any understanding of any other language or people, save his own. He had a great energy,[15] however, and a very complete realization of all the forces in England, particularly the forces of religious prudishness and nonconformity." He has one story that came from Mrs. Julia Frankau, who wrote under the name of Frank Danby. She told Harris how she had once made up to Stead and encouraged him until at last one day he fell on his knees and put his arms round her; he was going to pray, he told her, that she might always be faithful to her husband.

The end of Harris' *Evening News* editorship came in 1886. The story, according to Frank, is that, exhausted, he went off to Rome desiring complete change and recreation. There he had a lovely time, galloping all morning on the Campagna—how delightful it was to be

---

[15] An energy that, however, was reserved for himself. In the 1890s Horace Wyndham wrote to Stead asking for advice. He got back: "I don't see why I should be bothered to advise you or anybody else, and I decline to do so. Nor do I want to read *your* silly specimens which are returned forthwith."

hunting foxes over hills where Peter and Paul had walked, Caesar and Pompey had marched; out hunting, he soon encountered many Romans of excellent position, anxious to invite him into their palaces. Afternoons were hours for poets, scholars and studying antiquities. Soon the Dorias were asking for his interpretation of one of their Titians and a short discourse on Renaissance love. On his way to the Doria palace he fell upon a veiled soothsayer who peered closely at his hand and impressed him by detecting therein his passion for Byron Smith. She could see upward movements in his life, she said, but later the curve descended, and the end was misted in a great sea of blood; that evening he would return over the seas to England. This, scoffed Harris, was a shockingly bad guess; he intended to stay with his horses in Rome for a few months yet. Sure enough, no sooner had he presented his views on Renaissance love at the Doria palace and was just being congratulated by the British ambassador than he received into his hands a telegram. Lord Folkestone was summoning him back to England. Kennard, it seemed, was planning a row so that he could replace Harris with his assistant. Frank—in retrospect anyway—was astonished. He had worked hard, without breaks, to make the paper pay and he had plans to fill the pages with astonishing stories; he had his eye too on a morning paper with a circulation of a million. But Kennard, he claims, disliked having to pay him a share of the profits and therefore discharged Harris with a thousand pounds' solatium. Whatever the reason, there is no doubt that he left the *Evening News* and by July was editor of the *Fortnightly Review.* And there is no doubt that the *Evening News* went downhill. It tried to continue the sensational policies of the former editor but unsuccessfully. At the beginning of October 1887, through shoddy research, it made a major error. Colonel Hughes Hallett had seduced his stepdaughter. The *Evening News* took up his cause: Miss Selwyn was not Colonel Hughes Hallett's daughter at all, they said, and as for claims that Colonel Hughes Hallett should step down from Parliament, all they could say was that there were a good many members on both sides of the House who ought at once to apply for the Chiltern Hundreds. And then they found they were on the wrong track. The *Society Times,* which had been hounding them over the affair, gloated: "We have now finished the performance of a very unpleasant duty. We have demonstrated to conviction the hollowness and wickedness of the contentions of the *Evening News,* and we trust our words will be taken seriously to heart by that paper. Let it continue to publish the longest and most disgusting accounts of divorce cases that it possibly can secure; let it revel in virulent abuse of workers in the cause of public progress and purity; but let it not openly champion immorality in the stately homes of England lest a far worse thing than contempt befall it."

Something did; by the time Lord Harmsworth bought it in 1894 it was in very bad straits indeed.

CHAPTER 8

Women

IN Volume III of *My Life and Loves* Harris tells us that losing the editorship of the *Evening News* caused a crisis in his life. No doubt he was hurt and depressed, but it was not long before he had secured a superior job as editor of the *Fortnightly Review*. What is more likely is that he was unhappy and unstable over an affair he was having with an American girl. "Love didn't come into my life until I was nearly thirty," he told Ben Rebhuhn fifty years later. He believed he was in love with her, certainly he was obsessed; the affair began in 1883 and lasted in his memories all his life. In 1892 Princess Alice of Monaco, who was Frank's confidante at the time, refers to her in a letter as "the friend of America." Cheap ware she called her; there was *nothing* good, believe her, in the cause of his misery. As revealed by Harris in *My Life and Loves,* the affair exposes mostly his vanity and immaturity. "I used to take her to the theatre in Munich," he told Kingsmill when he was sitting up in bed one evening in Nice in 1912, "to be alone with her, away from her mother who hated me. And there in the darkness, at the back of the box she gave herself to me. Again and again. Ah, what hours! But she resented my dislike of her mother. We were always quarrelling about the wretched creature. And at last I had had enough, and more than enough. She came into my room while I was packing. 'Where are you going?' she cried. 'Away,' I answered, and lit a cigarette. But it drove me to the verge of madness.

At Basle I weakened. There was a train back in half an hour. But I held to my resolve, went on home. I used to see her in the mirror. In the corners of the room. But I wouldn't go back. I had suffered too much!" From then on, he told Kingsmill, he was permanently ill about the heart.

In his approach to women Frank was always romantic and idealistic.[1] Their bodies he treated objectively, like marble statues; with their lustrous eyes, their subtle, hesitating curves, they were like works of art to possess, rather like his Chippendale chairs and Adam silver; he would peer at them critically, finding fault with their parts. Their minds, however, were something different. Both education and the attitude toward education for women in the 1880s still left much to be desired. The general feeling was that while a new embroidery stitch, a new piece on the pianoforte should not be too taxing, excessive learning might lead to the straitjacket. As Harris related[2] when the mathematician Mary Somerville studied by night, her mother ordered that her candle be removed and her otherwise indulgent father exclaimed, "We must put a stop to this, or we shall have Mary in a straitjacket." But the benefits of higher education were improving. There was no necessity, as Harris put it, for distant journeys to hot springs of mental vigor; rivulets of knowledge now seemed to run down every street—a promising bit of irrigation—and soon people could expect to see the feminine mind blossoming like a rose. Alas, there would always be a bountiful supply of commonplace women who would prefer the idlest sentimental novel to the noblest essay, to whom petty gossip, the excitements of dressing and flirting would prove more interesting than philosophy. It was most important, in Harris view, that the education of women should proceed in both higher and middle classes, since what one wanted was not merely highly cultivated governesses and learned professors' wives but also a proportion of thoroughly trained intellectual women of the highest ranks. Hitherto it had been believed that for a lady to become a doctor would be to rob her of the "gentler qualities which have always been regarded a peculiar charm"[3]; the lecture room and operating table were generally

[1] He positively disliked anything unladylike. He tells us a story of how on his first meeting with Lady Colin Campbell she was toasting her legs in front of the fire with her skirt hitched up. This seemed to Harris to be gross, and it put him off both her and her articles—which seemed just as unsubtle.

[2] "Finished Young Ladies," *Evening News*, January 31, 1884.

[3] "Lady Doctors," *Evening News*, January 15, 1886.

looked upon as ordeals to which no pure-minded woman could be subjected without harm. As for the vote, objections roughly stated that the influence of the husband would be sure to color female political decision, so that the practice would simply duplicate voting power. In theory Harris firmly believed in equality of women and that they should have the vote. In matters of education, he argued, women had justified everyone's expectations and were in every way a fair match for their male companions; how, then, was it possible to deny to such women the right to a voice in the government of the country? In practice, for complicated reasons, he acted as a mixture between Casanova, an indulgent father and an institute for higher education.

Generally speaking, being deprived of a mother at an early age causes the child some difficulty in maturing. He is unable easily to nourish himself and grow. In all probability, for the first three years of his life Harris' mother was frail, distant and depressed. She was consumptive, almost certainly insecure and withdrawn. The only emotion he can recall at her death is shock at the disruption of the household; it was not so much loss as inconvenience. For the majority of his childhood we know that he was dependent on his father and elder brother; that it was an unhappy, insecure, frustrating dependence from which he escaped at the age of fifteen by running away, having learned as his major lesson that he wanted to win and be at the top in everything.

He emerged as two people: one a private, melancholy and uncertain person who idealized mankind, the emotions and the functions of the body; the other an overexcitable public performer who loved to talk about everything, including mankind, the emotions and the functions of the body, often in rough bawdy language—and amuse everyone by reciting what he called naughty stories and verses, not always only in male company. He believed, somewhat condescendingly, that women found it flattering to be taken out on equal footing with him and told smoking-room stories—man to man, as it were. One of his favorite terms of disapproval, which he used for certainly over twenty-five years, was that such and such a lady had a cunt the size of a horse collar.

All his life Harris moved from man to man, from father figure to father figure, changing them as his needs changed, from man of letters to man of action to poet, idealizing them progressively. One might make the mistake of supposing that in the same way he moved from woman to woman seeking a mother figure. This was not so. As he molded himself on the father figure he in turn needed to become paternal. He did not need children, he needed women whom he could feed with his knowledge and guide through the mysteries of literature[4] and luncheon tables and up the stairs to the velvet-hung private chambers of Kettner's, the Café Royal, the Star and Garter at Richmond and countless other establishments, there to introduce them to sex and— somewhat incompetently—to the processes of biology, procreation and his magic syringe. As with everything else, Harris believed himself to be an expert in gynecology.

He was, he wrote in his biography, a connoisseur of sex and food.[5] Shaw, in his preface to Frank's *Oscar Wilde*, says that although he never saw Harris drunk, he ate and drank heavily—in spite of his confessed fastidiousness about overeating and drinking. He believed, Shaw said, that his virility, of which he was inordinately proud, could be maintained only by lunching on at least two entrecôte steaks and a mix of highly flavored cheeses, with plenty of Burgundy to help them down and several liqueurs to finish up with. "I have heard him say to a lady after an exhibition of this kind 'we do this for your sakes.'"

Affairs provided adventures, the reassuring means to escape from the melancholy uncertainty that he dreaded. They were celluloid romances, apprehending Hollywood—nothing to do with reality. With their elaborate sets, their paraphernalia of swishing skirts and pretty new hats, they were opéra bouffe; sometimes in retrospect, with their heavy passion, they were epics, played by heroes and gods.

[4] There is a letter existing written in French on May 28, 1890, at the Hôtel du Pompadour, Fontainebleau, from the American novelist, playwright and poet Amélie Rives (Chanler), afterward Princess Troubetzkoy. Harris, it seems, is giving her a course in French literature and her letter is an exercise. She had read *Mademoiselle de Maupin*, she said, all afternoon, and she found it was absolutely marvelous. "Les pages me semblent étincelantes de pierres précieuses et illuminées de fleurs dorées des missels. J'entends le frôlement de soie, les murmures affublés de velours, le cliquetis des grosses bagues de différents émaux à tous les doigts des mains de la Beauté." She could not write all she would like on the subject, but she wanted to send Harris her first impressions at once—she was sure he would be indulgent. She was going to translate it into English to better her style. Could he tell her please the titles of several other books that he would like to see her study? Would he like her to read Flaubert after Gautier or more Gautier? "Vous ne vous figurez pas comme j'ai faim de commmencer mes études. Je voudrais être une Hydre et parler une langue différente avec chaqu'une de mes cent bouches."

[5] "I have a friend at Nice," he wrote to Mencken in 1926, "who has 30,000 vols. of naughty books in half a dozen different languages. Every one represents the woman as feeling just what the man feels: she gets excited, comes to an orgasm and therewith content. It is a lie: the woman goes on getting more and more excited sometimes for an hour or so and then hysteria! I'm the first to tell this truth: the first, too, to explain that passionate women feel thrilling and nerve shocks all through their lower belly and down the inside of the thighs to the very knees."

Before he penetrated a lady he liked to ensure that she cared for him; he needed to win her affection and trust, preferably her adoration. Then he would explore every nook and cranny of her body and mind —he did not like it if she were not a virgin, he wanted to be the initiator—he would interview her as though they were on a park bench enjoying a cigar: When exactly did she discover the facts of life? What exactly did she feel? He would observe her closely, cultivate her, feed her, demand her attention by every post, and when she had revealed all she had to show he became bored and passed on to the next. "Fresh cunt, fresh courage," as he observed coarsely in his autobiography, having penetrated a Lawrencian matron up to the hilt and saturated himself.

Harris was unable to rest companionably and peacefully with anyone. He must always be stimulated and stirred. He could not enjoy a flower, a touch on the leg, without tears flooding his eyes, blood rushing up his veins. He would not be refreshed, but excited. He could never like people spontaneously for themselves, but placed them on pedestals and admired them for their bodies, their minds, their ability to make him thrive. It was more the emotions, the electric ideas that others incited in him with which he was infatuated than with the men and women themselves. The moment he stopped reacting to a person, that person ceased to exist for him. In order to be stimulated he needed an audience, and for an audience he needed to entertain and be entertained. Friends, he said, meant more to him than any other influence—they proved to him that he was alive. To entertain he needed money. He had built up his intellect as a reservoir from which he hoped to draw money, position and power; a means to collect beautiful things and women; to conduct his adventures in the proper way. As he grew older he staged his affairs more and more carefully and expensively. Kingsmill believed that Harris was convinced that love was a manufactured article. Harris' heaven was made on earth: paintings, books, buildings, sculpture and love were man-made—by godlike men.

The clue to his continuing obsession with the American girl, Laura, was that she never revealed everything, she never quite trusted him. He believed she had had a lover before him, even been pregnant. She would *not* tell him. The more he probed and demanded the "truth" the less she said and the more he believed she was concealing, and he became frantically jealous and obsessed. With her carelessly coiled chestnut hair, her large round hips, her small breasts, wrists and ankles, she was, said he, made to his desire. Later on she would lie and pose for him in his bedroom, adopting the posture depicted in a copy of a Titian hanging over his bed. Her curves were finer than the model's. She was also a marvelous actress, someone with whom he could play out the noble role he had allotted to himself in life.

They met while he was living in Endsleigh Gardens, before working for the *Evening News*. He had been asked to call at a boarding-house and see someone who had written an article for the *Fortnightly*. An untidy maid had shown him into a ground-floor parlor. And then a girl was also shown in and asked to wait. She was rather tall—about five foot five inches—and was wearing a blue cloak. She moved singularly well, swimming rather than walking, in the Spanish way. Her eyes were long and hazel, her forehead broad, her face rather round, and there was the mass of his favorite chestnut hair, brightened a little with strands of gold. As a matter of fact, Harris recalled that the long cloak and the apparent self-possession gave her the air of a governess. At once they discovered something in common. She was, she admitted, half American and half English; he was able to tell her that this was his case, except that they must substitute Welsh for English. But then she revealed that, to be strictly accurate, she was half *Irish*. How delightful Harris found her command of languages, her good accent in German, French and Italian. Next day he had the honor of meeting her mother, a fat little woman from Memphis, Tennessee, with an air of dignity—or rather imperiousness tinged with temper—small gray-blue eyes and a pug nose. Her father was a handsome man of five foot eleven inches, fifty years old, stout and gray-haired, but with excellent features and splendid hazel eyes: a good-looking, happy-go-lucky fellow, Harris summed up, who had been unfaithful to his wife.

Now Harris tells a story that smacks plainly of editorial adaptation. Mr. C—or Mr. "Clapton," as he called him (suggesting something ominous, as Kingsmill said, in connection with love)—wanted to go to Brighton for Christmas, and off they all went to the Albion Hotel, Frank apparently furnished with his piece on Hendrik Conscience, which we know was published on October 20. It is more likely that they went for a late summer holiday. The *Brighton Times* visitors' list reports that from September 6–15 a Mr. and Mrs. and Miss Carter were staying at the same time as a Mr. Harris at Como House, 30 Montpellier Road. We do not know the Claptons' real name and we do not know whether this is Mr. Frank Harris, but the coincidence is worth noting. Apparently Frank spent some time reading out his piece on Hendrik Conscience, which, from the finished article, one can see was eminently suitable, full of "sweetness of nature," "inherent truth and beauty." Laura was suitably impressed. How wonderfully he read, how lovely the prose was, what a great writer he was going to be. Harris did not nod—a great speaker perhaps—and he passionately repeated, he says, the last words of the article, which are: "I am one whom God endowed at least with moral energy and with a *vast amount of affection.*" The next moment his arms were round her and his lips on hers. But immediately he was spoiling it all, thinking how often she must have given her lips. . . . But how beautiful she was. Flatterer, replied Laura automatically. No, this was not flattery. Harris was in earnest. He loved her figure, with its small breasts and large hips. He felt great pity too,[6] he said, for the girl because of the difficulties between her fat mother and unreliable father and the lack of money. He told her how much he loved her. Would she give him six months to a year and he would win a position in London with money?

It can clearly be seen that the "Clapton" family did not find him a prize. Laura may have been excited and fascinated by him, but she did not trust him. He wrote fine-sounding articles, but before Lord Folkestone had got to him he was likely to be down-at-heel and dubiously dressed. It seems there was some friction over money, since in retrospect Frank finds it necessary to maneuver himself into a superior position. It is he who pays the bill at the Albion—one of Brighton's most expensive hotels; and "Clapton" had drunk champagne in his room and tried to borrow money from him to boot. Harris compensates himself further on paper by conducting them back to their lodgings in Gower Street and discovering that their rooms were not prepared—unlike his own, which were of course all neatly swept and garnished.

Soon he had occasion for the first pangs of jealousy. He was, he said, going along the Strand to the Lyceum Theatre. He stood outside looking at the advertisements while people passed him on their way in. As he turned, a young man, unmistakably American, jumped out from a four-wheeler. He was broad and good-looking, and he proceeded to hand out Laura and her mother. He seemed, Harris noted disagreeably, to be showing a remarkable interest in Laura, talking to her all

[6] In a letter written to Kate Stephens on July 4, 1915, he told her how he had come to passion through pity and grew to devotion. "She had been loved, been badly treated, revenged on my passion her doubt of man, her disdain of men."

the time, even when helping down her fat mother. She, it appeared, returned the sympathy. Harris thought wildly of confronting them, but instead, furious, he stood aside while they passed into the theater. It was to Harris a grievous disappointment, as bitter as death, he said; she had not even waited three months.

When he became editor of the *Evening News* he did not find her to marry. He was working hard, he said, and tasting the first sweetness of society. Besides, once more he had seen Laura, the fat mother and the American at a theater, and this time he had seen the American holding Laura's bare arm and how she had turned and smiled her beautiful open smile.

And then, sometime in 1885, he saw the mother and Laura descending the stairs of the Lyceum—this time alone. And Laura smiled that radiant smile and Harris was once more captured. Would they dine with him at the Criterion? And in his memories his soul is overpowered with admiration, and Lady Watkin Williams Wynn's herbaceous borders rise before him, his senses are ravished, his eyes flooded with tears. . . . But in the cab the mother was as ghastly as ever. The window must be shut, the hour was late, the father was waiting. . . . However, there was Frank's foot touching Laura's and her right foot was on the other side, and if only he could put his knee forward he could touch her legs, and she—the goddess—smiled a kindly glance. That supper was delicious, seasoned by Laura's clever flattery and genuine interest in Frank's work. She had read his columns in the *Evening News*. Was May Fortescue really so pretty? It seemed that night as though everything was on velvet. The Perrier-Jouet was chilled just right, and there was a meeting promised for the next day at Kettner's in Soho—in a private room. Harris was drunk with excitement.

He had by now moved into his rooms in Gray's Inn, furnished, on the instruction of Alfred Tennyson, with Chippendale chairs and Adam silver—also, it seems, a bidet. Harris planned to bring Laura to see them. After the first lunch at Kettner's he locked the door, kissed and embraced her. And then he drew back to ventilate some singular biological observation. What was this? The red of her lips was not uniform, which, he believed, pointed to some unfortunate occurrence in her womb. Altogether, what with one thing and another, Laura was rather put out. How strangely Frank kissed, all on the inside of the ununiform lips. Soon, said he, she grew hot and her eyes long in sensuous abandonment. There he stopped, for, he said, he wanted a memorable gift, not a casual conquest. To Gray's Inn they would repair the following day.

The seduction scene, as related, was elaborate and one with which Harris himself was delighted. "I think my Laura chapter reaches in the poetry in the end an even more intense expression of passion than Shakespeare has reached in Othello. You see I am modest," he wrote to Hesketh Pearson on May 2, 1927. The stage was set so that the actors could act out their passion in all facility. At one o'clock the heroine entered dressed in silk, rustling with petticoats. The hero showed off the lunch—which had been sent round from the Café Royal—the Chippendale chairs and the table silver of the Adam brothers, expatiating importantly. To eat, there were hors d'oeuvres with special caviar, a tail piece of cold salmon trout, a cold grouse, fresh but not high, a glass of chablis with the fish, two of Haut-Brion '78 with the grouse, and a bottle of Perrier-Jouet 1875 to drink with the *surprise* masking fragrant wild strawberries. And then Harris made coffee, a performance of which he was extremely proud and one over which he made a great deal of fuss all his life. They talked and they talked. All the while Frank was jealously conscious that there was a change in her and determined to hunt down the mystery; Laura was reticent, which Frank concluded gloomily was a bad sign. At four o'clock he took her to the bedroom and asked her to undress. Did he really care for her, she wanted to know. Ah! he loved her as he'd never loved anyone in his life—he was hers, do with him what she would.

Ten minutes later, in his new pyjamas, he was conscious only of reverence:

> If only the dreadful doubt had not been there, it would have been adoration. As I pushed back the clothes I found she had kept her chemise on. I lifted it up and pushed it round her neck to enjoy the sight of the most beautiful body I have ever seen. But adoring plastic beauty as I do, I could only give a glance to her perfections; the next moment I had touched her sex and soon I was at work: in a minute or two I had come but went on with the slow movement till she could not but respond, and then in spite of her ever-growing excitement, as I continued she showed surprise. "Haven't you finished?" I shook my head and kissed her, tonguing her mouth and reveling in the superb body that gave itself to my every movement. Suddenly her whole frame was shaken by a sort of convulsion; as if against her will, she put her legs about me and hugged me to her.

"Stop please!" she gasped, and I stopped; but when I would begin
again, she repeated, "Please," and I withdrew, still holding her in
my arms.

In the next room were the bidet and the syringe, to which he led
her. He was now certain that "she had given herself in that d—d year
and a half to someone else." If she would trust him and tell him, he
would marry her, if not . . . When she returned from her ablutions it
was time for Harris to play the voyeur. Bit by bit he studied her figure,
which he now discovered was not perfect: her neck was a trifle too short,
but her breasts were as small as those of a girl of thirteen, her legs
were long, her hips were perfect, her belly almost flat. Afterward, in the
dining room, they were incredibly hungry and set once more upon the
food.

Laura had brains and a personality that Harris called queenly. She
was also astonishingly supple, due apparently to some Swedish exercises
that she would perform; she could stand with her back turned to the
wall with her head bent backward almost to the level of her hips, her
spine as flexible as a bow. Month in month out they would meet in
private rooms once or twice a week, and once a fortnight Harris would
take the mother and daughter to a theater and supper. Now and then
she would complain of pains in her lower body, giving Harris an opportunity to surmise that her womb had been inflamed by a willful mis-
carriage. He would bully her to confide in him, and always she was
reticent. She was influenced in this, he believed, by her mother, who
disliked him. "He can talk but so can others," she would say disagreeably, her eye on her husband. Laura also disliked very much Frank's
habit of interviewing her. When questioned about herself she became
vague and mysterious, which in turn drove Harris on more furiously;
he simply could not get out of her everything he wanted.

Occasionally there were dinner parties at 23 Kensington Gore;
afterward there would be music and singing. The mother, he tells us
crossly, was no bonus at these gatherings. She made herself a center of
rudeness. One evening Mrs. Lynn Linton, who, according to Sir H. H.
Johnston, could at the end of the eighteen-eighties talk about little
but Harris' talents[7] and how he was going to be the wonder-worker of
the world, was there. Laura, who had been apparently trained by
Lamperti, sang. Her voice, however, was small and of a drawing room

[7] Sir H. H. Johnston, *Story of My Life*.

variety; but afterward she acted a scene from *Phèdre*. Everyone praised her warmly, while the fat mother looked on, pinched and disapproving. Mrs. Lynn Linton, who was a kindly old lady, and wore gray-rimmed spectacles and a flowered cap, took Harris to one side. The girl was lovely—was he going to marry her? Laura was within hearing, so Frank said that he was. Well, Mrs. Lynn Linton advised, the mother must be got rid of first, she was no friend to him.

In 1886, Harris tells us, he made a lot of money through a certain broker; according to Bell, this was a Jew called Lowenstein, who ran a bucket shop and for whom Harris wrote brochures and pamphlets. Now he paid Laura ten pounds a week, often supplementing this with a check for fifty pounds. He gave her father money, he said; also he gave his sister Annetta and her husband, Henry Price-Williams, the funds to leave Tenby and join William and Vernon in Lawrence. Certainly Harris liked to be generous, a mixture between genuine desire to give and needing to purchase gratitude. All his life it was his habit to tip waiters hugely, buying good service and recognition; but often he would help artists, writers and others genuinely in need. Generosity not only purchased gratitude but attention.

> One day Laura asked me, "Have you helped father recently?"
> "What do you mean?" I asked.
> "Well, he was hard up a little while ago and bothered mother, and then he got money and got afloat; and yesterday he wanted to know why we never had you now to the house at dinner or for the evening, and I just guessed. Was it you who helped him?" I nodded. "And you never told me!" she exclaimed. "Sometimes I adore you. I've never known anyone so generous—and not to speak of it, even to me. You make me so proud of you and your love," and she put her hand on mine. "I'm glad," I said, "but why don't you now and then try to give me pleasure in the act?" "I do," she said blushing adorably, "but I don't know how to. I've tried to squeeze you, but you ravish me and I can only let myself go and throb in unison. . . ." "There," I said; "that pleases me as much as my gift pleases you."

These were moments remembered as Harris would have liked them to have been. But the affair seems to have rolled up and down on waves of jealous uncertainty. He was jealous of everything, Laura's ability to dance, for example—an ability that he himself did not possess. At every party she was picked by the best dancers, with whom she moved in easy rhythm—a poem, said Harris, in motion. He would watch furiously. Again and again his leg was between yours, he would insist, you must have felt a thrill. At one point Laura and her mother went off to America, whence Laura drove Frank crazy by sending him photographs of herself in bathing dress. On their return they stayed at the Charing Cross Hotel while looking for rooms. One evening, Harris said, he went to the hotel with news of a play that he knew would interest Laura. Miss "Clapton," he was told by the no doubt well tipped headwaiter, was in a small salon on the second floor. Obligingly he ran up the stairs and threw open the door. Two people were sitting on the sofa; they must, Harris knew, have been sitting with their arms round each other, so quickly did they spring apart. He was hardly able to speak. Possessiveness rushed through him like a cold drench; Laura, he noticed, was in evening dress, her small breasts outlined. He would never marry her now; no, she was a traitor. Again and again he imagined the arm being pulled away until he thought he would go mad. At Kensington Gore he tried to be reasonable. A life as a kept mistress was plainly not good for her; if he married her tomorrow she would be faithful. Or why could he not treat her purely as a mistress? Tell her that if there was one more suspicion he would never see her again; she would not like to go without all his nice presents. But behind his anger and his hurt vanity he felt guilt. He had failed to marry her. He could supply only the celluloid romance, not the security. It was an impossible situation: he was obsessed with the things that he imagined had taken place, he would not marry her until she had revealed them; but had she done so he would no longer have been in love, he would have become bored; besides, there was the very real drawback of her mother.

He consoled himself with his maid. "It has always been my custom," he explained ambiguously in his memoirs, "not only to tip liberally but to take a personal interest in dependents and so I often get extraordinary services." His maid had lovely Irish eyes and was "kindness itself." "As she stood by me after helping me to something, I put my arm around her, and nothing loath, our eyes and then our lips met. Soon I found she cared for me and this spontaneous affection did me good, took the unholy rage and bitterness out of me and brought me back to quiet thought and sanity. To cut a long story short, I consoled myself with Bridget's affection and fresh prettiness, and the fears of madness all left me."

129

Next day Laura had a perfect explanation. Harris smiled a mirthless smile and told her not to sit so close on the sofa next time or she would never see him again. Understandably, she was furious. What did he suspect? It was a public room. Harris makes the point that he records the incident in its "naked brutality" because he was really frightened of himself, frightened that he would never regain control. Soon after this Laura and her mother left for the Continent.

Harris returned to his maid, who proved to be a gratifying mistress and interviewee, supplying her master with frank stories of her early life—how she had been naughty as a girl. "Oh, oh," she cried, apparently the first time he kissed her, "I won't ask you again for more kisses: my heart's in my mouth, and flutters there—no, no more I'm near hysterics. . . . I hope there's nothing to fear." "Nothing," Harris replied, "you can trust me." But the poor girl, we are told, went round for quite a long time, heavy-lidded. Suddenly one morning she was cheerful again. "All's well that ends unwell," she is supposed to have said. As soon as Harris knew all there was to know about her and her past, he tells us, he lost interest.

It must have been the god's day off when Harris sat down in Nice to write Chapter 4 of Volume III, wherein he describes all this, for he excuses his behavior by saying that man is really a primitive beast. "What devil is it in a man to make him desire at all times the Unknown, the new?" he asks his readers. "It has never been explained, and never can be explained rationally. It is a primary urge, the keenest desire of the male; and the individual is not responsible for it in the smallest degree. He was fashioned in the far past of time, a creature of unregulated, impassioned desires."

Sometime in 1887 Harris had met Emily Mary Clayton.[8] We may be certain of one thing: primary urges and unregulated desires had no part in this encounter. He himself claims that they met in Scotland staying with the Mackenzies of Seaforth. Rebecca West believes that it was her uncle, Edward Fairfield, who introduced them: Mrs. Clayton had been pursuing Fairfield for some time, but he meanwhile was enjoying a happy affair with Miss Fortescue (presumably the erstwhile fiancée of Lord Garmoyle), and had managed to maneuver her along to Harris; Sir H. H. Johnston believes it to have been the flowery-capped, kindly Lynn Linton who brought them together. She was not well read,

---

[8] On the certificate recording her marriage to Harris she is marked as Edith Mary Clayton. This is a mistake, according to all other records.

said Harris, but she was sympathetic, she entertained delightfully and there were often charming lunches and dinners at her funny little squeezed-up house, 34 Park Lane.

In 1887 Emily Clayton was forty-eight and for seven years had been the widow of Thomas Greenwood Clayton, from whom she had inherited over ninety thousand pounds. After twenty-three years of marriage to a man thirty-eight years older than herself and seven years of widowhood, she was plainly ripe for some life. Originally, at seventeen, she had been engaged to Thomas' son, Henry Greenwood Clayton, a graduate of St. John's College, Oxford. He, however, disappeared in his early twenties and presumably died abroad. On July 1, 1857, under the offices of the Lord Bishop of Durham at Marylebone, she became, aged eighteen, the wife of the fifty-six-year-old widower. Born in Calcutta, she was the youngest daughter of a captain in the Bengal army, James Remington, and Louisa, the daughter of Lieutenant Archibald Watson. When Emily was three her father died at Kanpur. At eighteen she was the bride of a respectable Bradford man. Thomas Greenwood Clayton was one of those men who were the backbone of Victorian industrial society, who served their country in a quiet undistinguished sort of way and who vanished leaving few marks behind them. He was a man of iron, having made his money during the boom of railway building. Chairman of the Bierley Ironworks, he had lived from 1842 at Bierley Hall (now demolished), originally the home of the botanist Richard Richardson, whose gardens were shaded by one of the first cedars of Lebanon to grow in England and ornamented by Druid's circles, subterranean caves and cascades. Clayton would take the chair at the Bradford Anti-Corn-Law Association, stand as a Poor Law Guardian and donate to the Teetotal Association. In 1857 besides being a widower he was a magistrate of the West Riding and a chairman of the Bradford Banking Company. Perhaps it was his bride who preferred to move from the encroaching smoky, muddy environs of Bradford, with its depression, its starving paupers, its compound of villainous smells, to prettier parts. Perhaps, since the Bierley Ironworks had been bought by the neighboring Low Moor Company, Clayton desired to retire and lead the life of a country gentleman. At any rate he and his bride moved to Bessingby Hall—donating almost at once five pounds to the Philosophical Society—and soon purchased a large house on the banks of the river Ouse, in the small village of Clifton, a mile from York. Ousecliffe (now also demolished) marched on Clifton Holme, which belonged to the Munbys. The Claytons, however, do not appear in the diaries of A. J. Munby; either they were unneighborly neighbors or they spent most of their time in London. The census of 1871, however, discovers them at home enjoying a spring family party. There is Emily, aged thirty-two, her husband, aged seventy, her mother, Louisa Ramsden, aged fifty-eight—widowed for the second time and better suited to the host, one would have thought, than her daughter—Emily's two sisters, Louisa, wife of Major Jeffery, and Helen, wife of Colonel Turner, with her two children, Louisa and Constance. There is an army of servants: a butler, a cook, two footmen, a lady's maid, three housemaids and a kitchenmaid.

Clifton, as described by A. J. Munby, was a delightful riverside village of sunsets, umber washes, gray cloud curtains, rich bronzes and golden lights. Paths led along by the river. Munby describes the gray and tender days of July, the birds in the autumn shrubberies, the rooks cawing and wheeling over Red House, the osier beds and gray willow tops, the woods and Poppleton reflected in the polished waters of the Ouse, which would change from saffron to duck-egg blue, sliding between dark, shaded banks, with sweet curves in its channel, through fields and under trees. Blessed is the house that has a river near it, said Munby. Vermilion mists would curl up, it would be a dream of a world. Each year opened with the bells of York Minster ringing out across broad water meadows dotted with cattle; each dawn rose with a prospect of city walls and red roofs; each winter evening closed with barges passing, drawn by trotting horses, their cabin fires glowing red.

Ousecliffe was filled with all kinds of rich baubles. When, in 1881, the house and a good deal of the contents were auctioned, the widow obviously preferring a London life, the list[9] included billiard tables, rifles, pistols, globes on stands, gypsy and loo tables, wool mattresses, whatnots, Wedgwood calabashes, scent jars and commodes, Indian china fruit dishes, Canterburies, tabinet curtains, mahogany bedsteads, marble pastry stands, ottomans, jardinières, and "a great variety of Useful Articles," including a library of books in every department of literature.

Emily Clayton, according to Sir H. H. Johnston, was a kind woman. She had been used to a comfortable, hothouse life, preferred London to the country and had a large acquaintance of conventional people with whom she would attend race meetings and shooting parties and travel

[9] *York Herald*, Saturday, May 14, 1881.

abroad to fashionable resorts. Much of her life had been spent with an elderly, apoplectic husband;[10] clearly she was now looking round for a younger partner—ideally, one with a cause.

Harris was always perfectly honest about his reasons for marrying Emily. In the letter of July 4, 1915, in which he had told Kate Stephens of his passion for Laura, he tells her also about his marriage to a woman of "great position." Not only was she sympathetic but she was marvelously flattering. Unlike Laura, she believed he was capable of great things; why did he not go into Parliament? She gave dinners and introduced him to the leaders of the Conservative party, fired and fed his ambition. Here was the cause she had been looking for, matched to a young man. It seemed ideal. She became his friend and confidante. He confided to her his sad obsession with Laura, how she had taken her mother off to Marienbad without notice to him. "The English friend" told him that the girl did not love him. "I can't help it," wailed Harris. "She paints the sky for me." "The English friend" told him to put away childish things—in short, to marry her and she would make him into an English Bismarck.

So on November 2, 1887, they were married by Archbishop Plunkett of Dublin, at the Kensington Parish Church. They planned to spend the winter traveling abroad. They started off their honeymoon, according to Harris, in the Hôtel Meurice in Paris; that first night he went to bed well satisfied—at last his political ambitions were going to be fulfilled. However, by the end of a week he was laughing on the other side of his face. The rows, reproaches and tears, he said, began the next morning: the most perfect and sympathetic friend had been turned overnight into a madly jealous woman. He arrived at the breakfast table to find his bride crying into numerous letters, two of which had apparently come from heartbroken ladies—and she had opened and read them. She was furious. He was a brute, she had understood he had nobody, was unhappily in love with the American girl. She raged on. Clearly the new Mrs. Harris was as jealous and obsessed with her new husband as he was with Laura. It is ironic that he should have landed a fish of equal weight. She was, he said, so jealous that he called it a disease. Even if he looked at a woman in the street there was a scene. Often she would walk out of the theater rather than see him, she said,

---

[10] When, after five days of apoplexy, Thomas Greenwood Clayton died, in July 1880, at his house, 28 Grosvenor Street, Jane Burroughs of Bermondsey is marked as being present at his death; there is no sign of Emily.

stare at a pretty girl. All of this was the more annoying to Harris, since, he said, he was so shortsighted that he could not see anyone distinctly at half a dozen yards. He tried to school himself. In Italy he used to select a corner in the hotel restaurant that looked onto a bare wall: "anything for a quiet life was my motto, and as I had married for selfish reasons, I felt I ought to give full play to my wife's egotism, and peculiarities." If he lived properly and respectably with his wife, he told himself, he would get into Parliament.

Unfortunately, they were just passing through Bologna in the train when he pulled up the blind and there were Laura and her fat mother going past down the platform. "I thought I should choke; pulses woke in my throat and temples: in one moment I realised that I had bartered happiness for comfort and a pleasant life, that I had blundered badly and would have to pay for the blunder, and pay heavily."

In Rome a young Italian came daily at ten o'clock to read Dante with Frank until about half-past eleven, when Mrs. Harris would desire to take their morning walk. One day she entered while they were arguing over the meaning of a passage. Harris was an emotional talker. In a Latin way he would touch people as he spoke, throw an arm round their shoulders, clap them on the back; in this case it seems that he had hurt the boy and had a hand on his shoulder. On seeing this Mrs. Harris swept from the room to her bedroom, almost crazy with rage. "You caress your friends before my eyes," she cried, "you beast," and she beat his chest with her fist. From that moment, Harris said, the marriage ended. They lived and entertained together, but Harris went his own way, retaining 23 Kensington Gore, where he kept Laura and conducted other affairs. For the time being, however, they continued to travel and visited Sicily. Mrs. Harris was delighted by Taormina and its scenery, but she was not at all interested in the antiquities or the remains of the theater. They were, as Sir H. H. Johnston remarked, an ill-matched pair.

Plainly one of her troubles was that she was terrified of her age; she was wildly infatuated by her husband and jealous of anyone younger or more intelligent than herself. Harris tells a story of an Irish lady, both pretty and intelligent, well read in French and English literature, coming to lunch at 34 Park Lane. Naturally, said Harris, he was interested in her. His wife went on about it for days. How shamefully he had behaved, showing so plainly his admiration, her knowledge of French books was only a pretext to show off . . .

Frederic Carrel, who, it is likely, was a guest at 34 Park Lane during 1893 and 1894, presented a convincing physical description of Mrs. Harris. He describes her as a fair-haired woman—of a blondness that was assisted by all that science could offer—with regular features that had once been handsome, teeth so faultless that they smacked of artificiality, and extremely in love with her husband. There hung about her the faint aroma of wealth. Her ways were girlish, her waist little, her bust ample, her face wore the signs of rouge and a life of ease, opulence and satisfaction. Her clothes were made with a carefully studied simplicity and belonged to someone not quite reconciled to growing old. Everywhere she went she was followed by a procession of companions, hairdressers, masseurs and couturiers. She was a snobbish lady, with blanks in the subjects of art and literature, ashamed of her husband's origins and of her father-in-law, who Frederic Carrel described as a little old sea dog, all shabby and broguish, entering unexpectedly among a smart party of friends—which would have been quite possible, for Thomas, according to the Navy Pension List, had left Tenby and was living in London. Carrel also suggests that Mrs. Harris' relations were horrified by her marriage. This is certainly true. Her only relations that can be traced are the descendants of her niece Constance Lake, née Turner—Emily has vanished, like her first husband, leaving little mark—but they confirm that everyone at the time thought that she was extremely foolish to make the marriage.

Sometime around the spring of 1888 the unhappy couple returned to England. Harris now set his face toward politics. His life at 34 Park Lane was comfortable and social. There were luncheon and dinner parties and often he would dine out by himself. He could meet, he said, intelligent or more or less intelligent people every day, and if he wanted more stimulating guests than could be found among his wife's lists he would invite his own friends. He was not happy, but he could at least indulge in his favorite entertaining and discourse at length on cooking, wine, meat and game. Vincent O'Sullivan, in his book *Opinions*, says that he had the baronial hall conception of hospitality. The most incongruous people would meet around his table. His wife would have a set luncheon party; Harris, passing along the Haymarket or Pall Mall that day, might encounter two or three from his large acquaintanceship, and he would bring them to lunch. "Exclusive people boring themselves and each other, would say: 'The Harrises have asked us to luncheon. We may see something amusing.' And they went."

Nevertheless the snobbishness that surrounded them exasperated Harris, made him feel uneasy and inferior. He was on the defensive with his wife's friends, who were more interested in origins than intellect. He knew that among them he would always be an outsider. He discovered that everyone was nicer to him than they had been before. Here he was, editor of the *Fortnightly Review*, with a house in Park Lane, entertaining, moreover, royalty: altogether he was nicer to know. He resented it all. Grant Allen, who was a regular contributor to the *Fortnightly*, would often lunch at Harris' little house, Grant Richards said,[11] in Kensington Gore, opposite the park. His description is exaggerated, but its point is to show how *exotic* Harris was. Never, Grant Allen told his wife, Nellie, had he had such an experience; it seemed as if the Arabian Nights had come to life. The front door swung open and behind it stood a Nubian, well over six feet high, with a scimitar in his hand. He saluted and led Grant Allen to an Oriental salon in which the host was seated cross-legged on the floor surrounded by beautiful women and handsome, witty men. They ate, no ordinary food, but caviar. Grant Allen had met Harris at the Grand Hôtel du Cap at Antibes, where a regular bevy of people practicing or interested in literature congregated. Harris found recruits for the *Fortnightly* and an audience for his talk. Indeed, he could talk his listeners silly, but all men agreed it was magnificent, and when he was not talking he was telling stories. Some years later he was at a luncheon party and began to talk about the sufferings of the Boers during the Boer War in such a manner that the whole party, including a general from South Africa, was reduced to tears. Finally Harris burst into tears himself, jumped up and left the house. Mrs. Allen had been so amazed at her husband's description of the luncheon that she desired to resume the acquaintance. Harris was invited to lunch—to talk; Grant Richards made up a fourth. Never had any heard such talk, or had anyone captured Grant Richards' imagination so quickly. To hear Harris talk was to be enthralled, seduced, violated. He talked incessantly through lunch to coffee and then rose to go. Mrs. Allen pressed him to stay on. Harris was touched by her and Grant Richards' admiration. He could not stop then, he was already late for an engagement. Nevertheless he would return in the afternoon; and return he did, and continued to talk sincerely,

---

[11] *Frank Harris: His Life and Adventures*, with an introduction by Grant Richards (Richards Press, London, 1947).

learnedly, earnestly, but with hardly a touch of the truculence that in later years went so far to destroy his conversational charm.

Had the world been made of the admiring Grant Allens and Grant Richardses the truculence and the disappointment might have stayed at bay, but as it was, surrounded by his wife's friends and relations, the next eight years reinforced his uneasiness and awkwardness, and he failed ultimately in the career that he had set for himself. As with all things, so long as he had not won, the struggle obsessed him; now, as soon as he was on the home straight, with the winning post in view, he could see that he was on the wrong track among the wrong people.

One of his troubles, he suggested in his memoirs, was that he was a good talker. Englishmen, he said, distrusted good talkers and new ideas; certainly they distrusted his socialist leanings, which to his wife's friends were anathema. By now he knew how to dress and had charming table manners, yet he appeared with a slight brogue, self-assured, with ideas that ran counter to those of the English government; above all he was small, and Harris put down much of his unease and failure to his lack of height. The English, he liked to say, knew that the only beauty of man was height. All the men who had succeeded in England had height to help them: Kitchener and Buller were preferred to Roberts, who had more brains but fewer inches; Burton was more esteemed than Stanley; Parnell, Randolph Churchill, Dilke, Chamberlain and Hicks-Beach were all above middle height. Nevertheless, small, fast-talking and starting up the wrong track as he may have been, his success at this time was undeniable. He loomed majestically, Vincent O'Sullivan said, before many and various people. He knew everyone— artistic, political and financial—he exercised considerable influence, he had power and most of the world's goods at his disposal, his talk was amusing for the violence of its nature. But his looks, Vincent O'Sullivan had to admit, were not to his advantage. He had the air of an American bartender, or boxer-manager, with his big moustache and thick hair parted in the middle and plastered down over his forehead. He spoke and acted like an Englishman, and was recognized as such by all the well tipped continental hall porters and headwaiters; yet in England he passed as an American, and later, in America, he was believed to be an English Jew.

CHAPTER 9

Hypochondria, Hackney and the Fortnightly Review

DURING the first four years that
Harris edited the *Fortnightly* he concentrated on politics, in summer
radiating enthusiasm and energy. In winter he traveled abroad for his
health—for Harris was a hypochondriac and lived a slave to his chest.
Though his fears were endorsed by the death from consumption, in
January 1887, of his brother William, his correspondence with Coventry
Patmore the previous year reveals a valetudinarianism of no mean
proportion. Like all hypochondriacs, he understood that the state of
his health was of the greatest importance to everyone else and treated
everyone accordingly to a full bulletin.

> My dear Sir [he had written to Patmore out of the blue on
> October 8, 1886]. I read an all too short article of yours in *The St.
> James Gazette* the other day which induces me to think that an
> article from you on "Lord Randolph Churchill's Opportunity" as
> distinguished from his temptation, might not only be of general
> interest but also of real worth to the Conservative party and
> through them to the cause of good government in Great Britain.
> Will you write me such a paper? I had intended writing to you
> before now to ask you to contribute to *The Fortnightly*—prose or
> verse—as you might see fit. I should not think any list of contribu-

tors to the Review complete that did not include your name. But having only very recently assumed the Editorship of *The Fortnightly*, I have had such a lot of work that I put off writing to you until a more convenient season—a season that is when I should have already imparted to the Review its new bias. But you can help me in this: the question is will you, and, if so, how soon?

On October 11 "without losing a moment" he is writing off to say that he shall be very glad to get an article from Coventry Patmore—on William Barnes. "I can understand your wish to have more time to consider the proposal I, at first, made to you and I hope you will see your way ultimately to do the sketch of Lord R. Churchill. Men of letters should I think write more upon matters connected with politics than they do. Detached as they are from the passions inseparable from political life their judgement should be sober, their insight into the *permanently* valuable clear. I should much like to see you if that were possible as I have some matters I should like to talk over with you."

On October 15 a sharp attack of bronchitis "stayed my hand as well as my breath." Nevertheless hourly he was expecting the article on Barnes, and was hoping to spend the Saturday to Monday with Patmore on the thirtieth of the month and talk "at leisure over a pipe." He tells in *Contemporary Portraits* how he stayed with the Patmores at Hastings in their mansion, set out in three or four acres of ground converted into an Italian garden. He was delighted with Patmore, who was a mystic receiving much joy and inspiration from St. John of the Cross, believing that he enjoyed with his wife the sort of ecstatic love that the soul feels for Christ. Such a doctrine would have been eminently attractive to Harris. The desire of the soul for Christ was as erotic as the desire of men for women; heaven became very intelligible when it was discovered to be a woman. Unfortunately, in spite of such divine revelations and stimulating discussion, the rigors of Hastings proved too much for Harris and he contracted a dreadful cold which precipitated him "under the Doctor's hands." Unfortunately, too, Patmore's article on Barnes had not been reviewed in the penny papers as it deserved to be. "Had your name been known as it should be they would have exhausted their vocabulary of praise. I say this after reading your poems carefully, they have been with me for the last two days and I have scarcely been able to lay them down even to sleep. I cannot say more. They are all clear to me 'The Unknown Eros' especially, after our conversation on the same topic.[1] Apparently Harris, who loved to be at the center of intrigues and have his fingers in as many pies as possible, was scheming on behalf of Coventry Patmore's son. He concludes his letter: "As I told you I shall see Lord Charles Beresford this week and I shall discuss the matter we spoke of with him and let you know the result."

Alas! by November 10 the doctor had given place to the surgeon, and the patient was unable to leave his bed and see the Home Secretary. However, he told the Patmores comfortingly, no one was to be disappointed or impatient. Delays in such matters were inevitable. All he could say was that he would make a good opportunity of approaching him on the subject and utilize the occasion, when it came, to the uttermost of his poor powers; he did not by any means despair of getting a favorable answer. Meanwhile "a great lady whom I know well [who smacks of his future wife] is even now getting up a series of dinners to the party-leaders at one of which I shall get a good chance to find my petition ably supported." In the meantime, however, the invalid was behind with his work, he found it a strain to sit down and write, yet on matters relating to the private affairs of others was unable to employ his secretary. This brave letter was rewarded by an invitation from Patmore to dine on November 26 at the Grosvenor to meet Edmund Gosse[2]—an invitation that Harris was delighted to accept, concluding importantly, "I am still quietly arranging the sweep of the net."

It was the opinion of Vincent O'Sullivan that the *Fortnightly* under Harris remained a stodgy review. Brilliant and enthusiastic as its editor might have been, a regular contributor, Sir H. H. Johnston, remembered him as an untidy, messy worker who was often losing pieces sent to him. His carelessness was attacked on November 9, 1889, by "The Man of the World":

> Mr. F. Harris is one of the editors who are not writers, and he is evidently not sufficiently careful in reading what his contributors write for him. In an article on the Drama that appears in the current number of the *Fortnightly* the critic, who is no critic, talks of "waving" when "waiving" is obviously intended, "the moral" of a question, and speaks of the deportment of Turveytop—a piece of ignorance for which the writer who signs the article is, of course,

[1] Harris to Patmore, November 3, 1886.

[2] Plainly Edmund Gosse was not sympathetic either to Harris or to his opinions, since Frank describes him in *My Life and Loves* as a professor, knighted for mediocrity in England.

primarily responsible. Turveytop for Turveydrop is almost as good as the old lady's copperful for Copperfield. It is not so long that the same review fell into a ridiculous blunder over the *pari-mutuel,* which was rendered in the *Fortnightly* if you please, as the "Paris Mutual."

John Addington Symonds too was furious at Harris' slapdash ways. Harris dispatched frantic telegrams about an article called "A Page of My Life," and then ignored his proof corrections. Phyllis Grosskurth, in *John Addington Symonds,* tells us that Symonds was furious and sent an outraged protest to Harris as well as an open complaint to the *Pall Mall Gazette* on May 27, 1890, about his "villainously ill-edited essay." Harris replied that he had been unwell when the magazine went to press and his substitute had not been familiar with "the peculiarities of Mr. Symonds' handwriting." To this the editor of the *Pall Mall Gazette* rejoined: "The only peculiarity we have ever noticed about Mr. Symonds' writing is that it is peculiarly clear and scholarly."

Verschoyle apparently did more work than Harris; he was a hard worker and kept the fort while his editor wintered abroad. Every afternoon from four until seven the office would become a sort of debating club, but most of the time Harris worked from home; articles would be rushed round for him to read and correct energetically and untidily. In his contemporary portrait of Whistler he recalls having a disagreeable conversation with the artist. His appointment as editor of the *Fortnightly,* Whistler said, had set everyone guessing. Was he a man of genius, or just another editor, "don't ye know?" All the guests at the dinner party were by then goggling. Of course, Whistler continued, everyone knew how a man of genius would edit such a review. First would come an astonishing number, a reckless criticism of some great painter by a poet, then a poem by a painter, something novel, "don't ye know," the caricature of a bishop by Carlo Pellegrini—something unexpected, amazing. All the world would rush to buy the next month's number, but there would be none to be found, the editor would be resting, gone to Monte Carlo. The month after, another gorgeous surprise. . . . But no, Whistler said, you've not done it in the brilliant, erratic way of genius—every month the review appears regularly, just what one looks for, a work of high-class mediocrity—lamentable, you know.

Everyone laughed at this. One may imagine how much Harris disliked it all. He got his own back by saying he had only just been talking to Degas in Paris and Degas had never heard of Whistler. "Vistlaire? Connais pas: jamais entendu ce nom-là. Que fait-il?" In despair Harris had tried to describe Whistler's marvelous color schemes, his amazing arrangements, as well as his wit—the wittiest talker in England, he had assured Degas. "Dommage," Degas had rejoined—much to the delight of the dinner party—he should paint with his tongue, then he might be recognized as a genius.

It was the new editor's policy to collect within his net fish from every pool in the ocean, so that he had a band of experts on all subjects to call upon. He would read widely and write to authors suggesting certain subjects which, as treated by them, would surely excite widespread interest and warm discussion in all the leading papers of the United Kingdom. Vincent O'Sullivan believed that his literary appreciation depended on whether a book or a piece was of use to him or not. Edward A. Freeman, no doubt in happy ignorance as to the identity of his erstwhile reviewer, appears, writing on the prospects of home rule; Mrs. Lynn Linton, in her steel-rimmed spectacles, is a regular contributor, encompassing all aspects of women and adding a historical perspective including the Roman matron, the mistresses of kings and ladies of chivalry. Grant Allen writes on various topics including "Falling in Love," "Plain Words on the Woman Question" and "American Jottings"; and Lord Carnarvon states his views on Australia.[3]

Wolseley was Harris' man on military matters and during 1888 contributed several articles on military genius. Harris would write to him when he needed details of certain guns and gunpowders, and harass him, like all his other contributors, with telegrams. He was keen on the telegraph service; he would dash off cryptic messages referring to articles or proofs which would penetrate the most medieval fortresses, sweeping over the moats and up the croquet lawns of England. "I have not yet even read more than a small portion of Maurice's article on war. So I could not deal with it here, as I have not got it with me," Wolseley replied to one such communication. "I shall be very glad to let you have it for the 1st January, remember." He had been so pressed with official work, he explained—three and a half hours, for instance, under examination yesterday by Lord Hartington's committee—that he had no

[3] In return, in 1889, Lord Carnarvon asks Harris his view on the publication of the Chesterfield letters. Would Harris run down on Thursday, October 16, to Highclere Castle in time for dinner and talk over at leisure the benefits of shortening the publication?

time for any pleasant occupation. Then, when it was done, he wished it were done better; he could not by word of command dive into his sea of reminiscences; had Harris given him more time he was sure he would have done better.

In fact, Wolseley was impressed by Harris and by his ability to absorb military information. "I had no idea you were so well read in the history of wars until I read in your letter your able outline of the Waterloo Campaign," he told him in the summer of 1888. "I was astonished at your intimate acquaintance with points about it which I had thought were only known to military students."

The navy exercised Harris equally. He believed that a large sum of money should be invested to modernize the force and sustain naval supremacy. To support his views, in November 1880 the Admiral of the Fleet, Sir Thomas Symonds, Lord Alcester and Admiral Sir G. Phipps Hornby each wrote an article asserting that the navy should be almost three times as strong. According to Harris, Lord Randolph Churchill resigned because he objected to the naval estimates in general, and in particular he objected to spending the money necessary to put the ports and coaling stations in a proper state of defense. Harris tells us that he had convinced Lord Randolph of the necessity of constructing a Channel tunnel—a measure that would permit trains to run through to the Continent and re-establish the Port of London as the first port in the world. "And there was big money in the gamble," Harris tells us. Lord Randolph, he said, had promised to speak and vote for the project, but "to cut a long story short," when the debate came up a new thought entered Churchill's head. Humorously he pictured the Secretary of State for Home Affairs hearing that 5,000 French troops had seized the tunnel and were advancing on Dover—should he or should he not blow them up? The whole picture was idiotic, roared Harris, "no French troops would take such a desperate risk; both ends of the tunnel could be raised above water level, so that they could be easily blown to pieces by a mere gunboat. No general would send troops through such a defile, and if he did, ten to one they'd all have to surrender the next day. . . . At the moment I was wretchedly disappointed, for I had been fool enough to say that Randolph Churchill would defend the scheme, whereas it was he who damned it altogether. He had made a fool of me and merely grinned when I told him how I had come to grief through believing in his word: from that time on my faith in him was shaken."

And from that time on Harris was busy hatching up malevolent exposés of his erstwhile political patron, not only to get his revenge on him but also on his son, Winston, who, he believed, let him down much later on. In an unpublished sketch—presumably a preliminary to the one that appeared in *My Life and Loves*—he explains how he was introduced to Lord Randolph by Lord Folkestone, in a private room in the Carlton Club. Lord Randolph's creed, he says, was one of Tory democracy, and he promised to help Harris as much as he could. Next they dined—invited by Harris—at the short-lived Amphitryon, where Randolph talked brilliantly, flashing "snapshots" of his life at Oxford, in Paris and in the House of Commons. After dinner, Harris says, he drove him to a political meeting at Paddington where Churchill was to speak, and insisted that Harris sit on the platform. The speech was eloquent, but "Randy," as Harris calls him in the article, with his bulging eyes, thrust-out chin and upturned black moustache, was no speaker; he had no grace of gesture or accent, no wide choice of words or fluency of speech. Often he would practice, said Harris, to a thin house or during the dinner hour. Harris himself was given the job of making popular whatever was good in English conservatism. In five years Churchill had become a popular and unconventional politician, Chancellor of the Exchequer and Leader of the House of Commons. Then he resigned— thereby, it seemed to Harris, letting him down.

So in his sketch he reaches for his pen and blacks in a good deal of "human interest," in the form of rumors that were supposed to have emanated from Louis Jennings.[4] How Lord Randolph was supposed to have been given a stirrup cup at the Bullingdon, and passed out, to wake up, with a nasty hangover, in bed with a dirty pillowcase and an old hag with one long yellow tooth, which waggled when she spoke. Twenty-one days later he was in high spirits at dinner with the master of Balliol, Jowett, when he was suddenly stimulated by a small itch, and there was a fiery red spot, a perfect example of a syphilitic sore. Harris concludes his revenge by telling a paranoiac story. Years later he sat opposite Lord Randolph at a dinner given by Sir Henry Thompson, the famous doctor. As they sat down, Lord Randolph, his face drawn, his skin leaden gray, his eyes gleaming with hate, anger and fear, bowed coldly to Harris. With the soup Frank leaned across to his neighbor

---

[4] Louis Jennings died of cancer soon after Lord Randolph died of syphilis, which he contracted not from the old hag with her wobbly tooth but, according to Anita Leslie, from a French mistress he kept in the 1880s.

Lord Morris and said something about Ireland. To his astonishment Lord Randolph interrupted angrily: "You know a great deal about Europe, Mr. Harris, and of course all there's to be known about America . . . but what do you know about Ireland?" Harris replied that he was born in Galway and brought up in the Royal School in Armagh. All through the next course Lord Randolph did not speak a word. As the game was being taken round, the footman noticed that it had not been properly cut, so he passed Lord Randolph quickly to carve it at the sideboard. "At once Lord Randolph pointed, squealing out as if in pain: 'Eeeeeee!' His host was solicitous, inquiring the matter anxiously. 'Eeeeeee!' repeated Lord Randolph, pointing his finger after the footman. 'I want that—eeeeee! Some of that—eeee!' 'It shall be brought back,' said Sir Henry. 'I'm very glad you like it.' Lord Randolph helped himself greedily. Suddenly he stopped, put down his knife and fork and glared at each face round the table, apparently suspecting that his strange behaviour had been remarked. He was insane that was clear. From that moment on I could drink but not eat. Lord Randolph Churchill mad! Like Maupassant!"

Needless to say, when this account was published in 1925 the Churchill family did not find it in the least amusing. According to Anita Leslie,[5] Lady Randolph Churchill had thought Harris ghastly; he had arrived once at her house in Connaught Place, uninvited, and had been asked to leave. Harris says that he met Leonie Jerome, Anita Leslie's grandmother, at dinner years after Lord Randolph had died, and regaled her with his experiences at Sir Henry Thompson's table. Anita Leslie says that he spoke once to her grandmother and after that talked and wrote as if he knew her well.

In 1889 Harris started out on two major ventures; both began brilliantly, both petered out dismally and helped to lead to his growing sense of isolation and feeling of being out of step with the society he had invaded. He became secretary of the Father Damien Fund for research into leprosy, and after several years of hoping and looking for a suitable constituency he was adopted as Conservative candidate for South Hackney. The year before he had been encouraged by Wolseley: "I hope you are going into Parliament," he had written. "Why not try to succeed poor Colonel Duncan who died yesterday? I believe it is a very safe Conservative seat and being in London would just suit you.

[5] Letter to the author, May 28, 1972.

This govt. will be in for the next three years, so now is your chance. I hope you will think of this." Now, on Saturday, May 25, 1889, the Hackney *Mercury* reported: "On Friday evening a thoroughly representative and influential deputation of South Hackney Conservatives interviewed Mr. Frank Harris (of the *Fortnightly Review*) at the Manchester Hotel, with a view to his succeeding Mr. Pearson-Hill as the Conservative and Unionist candidate for that division. Mr. Harris gave a brief and eloquent outline of his political convictions which, at intervals, was interrupted by warm applause. It was decided to invite Mr. Frank Harris to address an aggregate meeting at an early date."

So far so good. Now Frank was obliged to put in an appearance at the functions of the South Hackney Conservative Club. At the beginning of June a presentation was made to the resigning secretary, a most animated appearance, recorded the interested *Mercury*, causing the concert room to be tastefully embellished with a select and brilliant audience. There was a musical program and then the presentation of an illuminated address, a timepiece and an engraved silver shield. The function was attended, during the course of the evening, by Mr. Frank Harris himself, who made "a few succinct and inspiring remarks."

On Saturday, June 22, the *Mercury*, under the headline "Enthusiastic Proceedings," reported his official adoption. From a platform nicely decorated with flowers and foliage plants, as well as Sir W. T. Marriott (whose wife was nearly asphyxiated by the evacuations of Sir Robert Fowler), Harris delivered a speech that, according to the *Mercury*, thrilled everyone present, and one could have heard the conventional pin drop during portions of it. The *Mercury* reported that "Mr. Harris is a thorough going earnest politician and a deep thinker as well as a brilliant debater. He is the nearest approach to a *bona-fide* liberal-conservative of any man. . . . He was mentioned some time ago for N.E. Bethnal Green . . . but lengthened absence abroad, in a journalistic capacity . . . obliged him to forgo the honour." The *Mercury* went on:

> Mr. Harris has undoubtedly qualities which should commend him to any constituency. He has all the fire and spirit of pure patriotism in him, leavened by a strong humanitarian feeling. He has displayed this in many ways, and the latest instance of it is perhaps the zeal he is evincing in connection with the Damien Memorial Fund, of which he is the hon. sec.—the Prince of Wales being

president. He is an Englishman by actual birth and he is proud of it, but he is also a cosmopolitan, a citizen of the world, and his political creed, in its broad sense may be summed up in a determination to leave that world better than he found it. In the distinctive and possibly narrower meaning of the term, he is a Conservative . . . He has travelled much, and because he has travelled he believes in unity. "Look abroad," he will say to any interrogator, "and you will find every nation binding themselves together, America, Germany, France, Russia, Italy; and we, the British race, alone think of separating, of cutting ourselves asunder, and drifting until we become finally wrecked against the first rock we strike against." Added to his other qualities Mr. Harris has the inestimable gift of youth on his side. That he will reach the goal of his ambition—the House of Commons—there can be no doubt. It is only a question of time. But we will go further and say that if he but follow up and accentuate the excellent impression he has unquestionably made, that goal will be found in South Hackney.

The audience, said the *Mercury*, was enraptured after their new candidate's able, scholarly, masterly speech. It was proposed that Frank Harris, Esq., with his political views, was a fit and proper person to represent the constituency in the House of Commons. It was a magnificent speech, said one Mr. Whittaker, a speech that was sinking deeply into their hearts by reason of the speaker's clearly expressed sentences. They would never forget it. Mr. Whittaker had heard of speeches being written in gold; never yet had he heard one that was more deserving of such a description. A more thoughtful, a more original speech and one more free from claptrap would be impossible to listen to, agreed Sir W. Marriott, who added that he had known Mr. Harris for years; he was patriotic to the core and would carry them all through the next election to the House of Commons. The retiring candidate, Mr. Pearson-Hill, said that Mr. Harris brought with him, in addition to great knowledge, the fiery heart of youth, instead of the more sober sense of serious old age.

Harris, who was clearly enjoying himself, let no opportunity pass for further talk.

I don't quite understand what Mr. Pearson-Hill has said about the fiery heart and sober sense [he replied, causing laughter]. I think it is very hard to make fire without a fire and equally difficult to rouse enthusiasm in anyone unless one feels it oneself; and I know of no better method of convincing others than by speaking from heart to heart [at which point there were loud cheers]. At any rate as I can speak I have spoken with entire frankness. You have yet to see me work and fight. I only hope that in the working and the fighting, I may not be less enthusiastic than I am at the present time in speaking. Your duties are my duties, neither more or less, and how can I ask you to do your duty unless I first carry out my own? But if I do mine I want you to do yours also, and quite as well, and with it the sobriety of extra years and better sense.

With loud laughter and cheers ringing in his ears Harris stepped gloriously down from the platform, all set, as he told Kingsmill, to become the British Bismarck—"whatever he imagined that to mean," H. G. Wells added in his autobiography. "He may have been thinking of his moustache."

Moustache or no, Harris had been in his element that June night. This was the stuff of life, when he could enrapture audiences and have papers reporting that his words were made of gold; it was fine, too, to hurry down to the House of Commons, listen to a debate, discuss it afterward noisily over a pipe and the Perrier-Jouet 1875. He felt potent and appreciated; that his ward was really sympathetic toward him. But he was an actor; he could play only his part, descending from a fine carriage, sweeping onto the decorated platform, and talking the evenings away in a series of repetitive lectures under the benevolent eye of his chairman, Mr. Hogsflesh. It was not the working and the fighting but the performance—that was the thing; the extended references to enthusiasm, political warfare and Thomas Carlyle, the graceful gestures, the tears, the words trembling here, roaring there, pouring out like cream, may have been fine, but they buttered no parsnips. The constituents required a humbler, more practical approach. A letter published in the *Mercury* on October 19, 1889, signed "Anxious," said that while it was pleasing to know that there were a number of enthusiastic workers in the unionist cause in South Hackney, it would be still more gratifying to see the result of their labors. Why did they not prevail on Mr. Frank Harris to "come amongst us to make himself known to, and popular with those from whom he looks for support when the time of election comes? At present he is practically a stranger to the general body of electors."

His colleagues in the other wards of Hackney were more diligent: Mr. H. H. Marks and Mr. Sebag-Montefiore were to be seen at billiard matches and smoking concerts listening to "Queen of the Earth," enjoying anniversary suppers, children's parties, flag devices, Chinese lanterns and Punch and Judy. Stimulated perhaps by "Anxious," Harris cantered down to Hackney and bombarded them with more words. "There is little doubt as to his popularity throughout the division," noted the admiring *Mercury,* as he stood without notes, wishing "to chat in a quiet way" about music halls, colonies, India and Ireland. He concluded by saying that his audience's courtesy and kindness encouraged him very much, and he believed that it arose from a certain sympathy with what he said. That winter he put in two dinners; besides some "capital songs" the toast of "Our Candidate" lifted through the commodious premises of the Conservative Club. "Our Candidate" was pleased to reply that it was essential that the good work continue, and departed, loudly cheered by the whole company.

All this time Harris had been apparently keeping or anyway meeting Laura at 23 Kensington Gore. Soon after his return to England they had met. She, we are told, had been most distressed at his marriage, believing that he loved his wife. Then one day she had seen Emily in the street, a sight that provoked laughter and an immediate letter to Frank. Their relationship of quarreling and jealousy was resumed. This, together with the excitement of the dinners, seems to have purchased a decline in "Our Candidate's" health, for during 1890 there is a remarked absence of his presence in South Hackney. The children's party, the house supper, the smoking concert and "Sally in our Alley" were all enjoyed while he was "unfortunately prevented from attending by illness."

Then he returned in October and began on a series of lectures that were indirectly to end his political career.

On November 17, 1890, Captain O'Shea won his divorce suit, in which he cited Charles Stewart Parnell. The scandal filled the newspapers and the drawing rooms. Parnell was attacked on all sides, one of the most virulent attackers being Stead. It was demanded that unless Parnell stood down from Parliament, there could be no possible confidence in Mr. Gladstone and his party. It was one of those cases that arise periodically, anyway in British history, and awake in the public generous measures of hypocrisy and stupidity. Harris was far too egocentric not to identify closely with Parnell.[6] Certainly he was outraged by the display of public dishonesty and hypocrisy—what Lord Macaulay called the most ridiculous of all imaginable sights, the British public having a periodic fit of morality—but was he not skating near the same piece of ice? Here he was, unhappily married, a vigorous adulterer and just returned from a trip abroad with his mistress; to speak openly for Parnell meant speaking openly for adultery; this is exactly what Harris did. He hurried off to Hackney, and on November 29, under the heading "The British Empire," he criticized at length before Mr. Hogsflesh, Mr. Whittaker and company the public view of the scandal.[7] His own opinion was that if adultery was to be punished as a crime, the best thing they could do was to set to work and get the law altered; since, however, this offense was not punishable, how dare they get up and pretend—for it was only pretense that Mr. Parnell should be hounded from society. Harris tells us that he was applauded; next day eighty members of the committee resigned.

All seemed patched up by January, however. On the tenth the *Mercury* reported that at the Annual Ward Dinner Mr. Frank Harris remarked that many present had taken him to task because he was so delighted with the Parnell episode. He felt that the Irish question had been settled for all time by Kitty O'Shea; she was to a certain extent a second Joan of Arc—she had positively saved England.[8]

> Honestly he meant it, for the fight was so undecided, so many thousands of voters had followed Gladstone, blindly even in the wrong, that he more or less felt that the battle would be lost in the next election. But when he found that they had won so completely, he could not avoid speaking about the means—bad as they might be—by which the victory had been brought about. Having further

[6] He had met both Kitty O'Shea and Parnell, he tells us. Parnell, he says, had greatness of character, but he was curiously ill read and ill informed, added to which Harris felt there was an insane streak in him. His superstition, Harris was sure, showed mental weakness. He remembered walking with him once to his house for dinner. At the door he stopped and would not enter. Did Harris mind walking a little before going in? After a turn he was still dissatisfied and took yet another stroll, this time successfully. "I hate four and eight," he is supposed to have said, "but when my last step brings me to a count of nine, I'm happy. Seven, even, will do, but nine's symbol of real good luck and I can go in rejoicing!" And with a smiling face, in he went.

[7] *Mercury*, November 29, 1890.

[8] The resignation of Parnell meant that the prime mover for home rule in Ireland had been deposed. Harris, with his policies of binding England, Ireland and the colonies together into a federation of states, was against the whole question.

> animadverted upon this topic, Mr. Harris in conclusion said it was the duty of everyone who thought and felt upon questions of politics to make his influence felt as widely as possible.

Publicly he may have wriggled out of his unpalatable views on adultery, and turned them to his own and party advantage, but privately he was still exercised by the attitude toward divorce and adultery —and particularly a politician's divorce and adultery. In the February number of the *Fortnightly Review*, under the title "Public Life and Private Morals," Harris, supported by Dante, Carlyle and Goethe, under the signature of "M," launched an attack on the national voice of righteousness, the system in general and his old rival Stead in particular. Mr. Stead, he said, could be righteousness caricatured—a professional righteous man: murder excited in him calm, impartial disapproval; adultery had unmanned him in hysterical horror and indignation. If the *Inferno* had been written not by Dante but by Mr. Stead, it might have been difficult to say precisely what sort of hell we should have had, but of one thing we could be perfectly certain: Judas Iscariot would have been taken out of the mouth of the devil and Francesca da Rimini put there in his place. Adultery and the divorce courts meant the grave for the politician. A politician guilty in the divorce courts was inconclusively shown to be unreliable in his public character: unholy, unsafe. But, argued "M," Carlyle, Dante and Goethe, the state's attitude was totally illogical. Adultery's essential wrong was seen by Mr. Stead and his like to be a sin against God: marriage was a sacrament, indissoluble therefore; if the divorcing party married again, he or she committed adultery; it was not so much an injury to human society as a desecration of some divine mystery, blasphemy in action. But this meant that the nation took a sacramental view of marriage. This it did not do—it demonstrated that it regarded matrimony simply as a civil contract; its law sanctioned divorce; its church married divorced people. There was no logical right to condemn adultery. The vulgar idea of an adulterer, "M" said, was a man whom no mother would admit into her house for fear of attempting her daughter's virtue; but there had been many adulterers who had been consecrated by their passion. If such atheists as Mr. Bradlaugh and Mr. Morley were tolerated, such felons as Mr. Gladstone, how could a nation be otherwise than hypocritical in pretending to be unable to tolerate Mr. Parnell on account of a love affair? "We must say," concluded "M,"

Carlyle, Dante and Goethe, "it has been probably one of the most demoralising outbursts ever witnessed in this country; for, whilst proposing to aim at exhibiting vice as hateful, it has only succeeded in exhibiting what calls itself virtue as ridiculous."

Thereafter in South Hackney during 1891 there was silence. The work of the club had not been of an exciting nature, the *Mercury* reported in May; it had consequently suffered in membership from the usual amount of apathy and the unfortunate illness of Mr. Frank Harris, which had necessitated his absence that winter. As faithful as ever, the *Mercury* continued: "Mr. Harris is popular wherever he goes, and it is certain that when the time for more active work arrives he will find the strongest support."

But on December 12, 1891, three months after Parnell died, the *Mercury* was obliged to make its final insertion: Mr. Frank Harris had definitely decided to retire owing to the pressure of literary and other work. The British Bismarck had failed with both his parsnips and his bread; unlike the prince, he had not found the side with the butter.

Progress with the philanthropic work proved no less disillusioning. In May 1889 the Belgian Father Damien had died in Hawaii from leprosy, which he had contracted through working among the South Sea Island leper colonies. With its horror and flavor of self-sacrifice it was a death that took hold of the British public's imagination. It took hold of Harris' also; there was nothing he liked more than a good martyr, and the whole tragedy smacked to him of the early Christian ones. Mrs. Vyner was present at one of his Park Lane lunches when he was discoursing at length about the whole business. She was a close friend of both Mrs. Harris and the Prince of Wales, and, Harris recalls, wonderfully sympathetic; one felt after talking to her the same sort of intimate sympathy that is present in a love affair. This was endorsed by her daughter, who said her mother was so sympathetic that she entirely gave her attention to her companion, and it was as though she was for that moment in love. In any event, at that luncheon Mrs. Vyner's attention was given to Harris, who was declaring that modern science should turn the sacrifice of Father Damien into a triumph; he believed that modern doctors could discover the microbe of leprosy in six months; therefore a fund should be raised, with the Prince of Wales as president and himself as secretary. So it was arranged, although apparently there was a slight hitch when the Prince of Wales failed to recognize Harris in his new role. "I could hardly believe it was you,

Harris," he is supposed to have burst out at their first business meeting. "Your naughty stories are wonderful, but what have you to do with leprosy and a fund to cure it?" Once this was settled, the meetings were held at Marlborough House, and the first one especially was a great success. All the "first men of England came," said Harris with satisfaction, claiming that £20,000 were subscribed in the first half hour. Donations were boosted with society concerts and private efforts from Harris, who wrote round to his friends and contacts. "The cause you are working for is a noble one," Wolseley told him. "The priest was a real hero in these days of golden idols, pinchbeck statesmen and sham heroes." Nevertheless, sorry as he was to turn down any proposal coming from Harris, he had little to give away annually and that little he reserved for old soldiers and their families. However noble the cause and substantial the donation, the executive power fell into the hands of the doctors, all of whom, Harris said, had formed their opinions from one hour's reading—"Why you could tell the text book each had used." Clearly all of them thought little of their secretary with his new ideas. "Each had his own fad to air and his own personality to advertise," he explained. The team of investigation was appointed by the College of Surgeons, one of whom was Sir Jonathan Hutchinson. He was a gentleman of whom the fund's secretary thought nothing. He believed that leprosy came from eating stale fish; it had been his belief when he was a student and he was sticking to it—in spite of the fact that the theory had been disproved in Norway. Sir Jonathan knew nothing of modern research and insisted on appointing someone who believed in the stale-fish theory. Consequently the commissioners went off to India and discovered nothing; Harris' idea had been to send two men to Norway, two to the leper colonies at the Cape of Good Hope and two more to Calcutta. In the meantime he was attacked in the *World*, accused of social climbing, of jumping from Father Damien's shoulders through the windows of Marlborough House. Next, strange rumors seeped in from Hawaii: Father Damien, it was whispered, had contracted leprosy through carnal knowledge with some lady lepers. There was some commotion. "Here's a pretty kettle of fish!" Harris, in *My Life and Loves*, tells us the Prince of Wales cried. " 'Of course it's not your fault, but this Father Damien must have been a nice person. Fancy choosing lepers—eh? It gives one a shiver. . . . We must change the name of our fund, though—what shall we call it?' 'Why change, Sir?' I asked. 'That would be to condemn Damien without a trial. I don't believe a word of the vile story.' 'Whether you believe it or not,' cried the Prince impatiently, 'everyone else believes it, and that's a thing I have to consider. Such stories are always believed, and I can't afford to be laughed at like they laugh at Damien. I don't want to be taken for a fool; surely you see that. We may believe what we please, but I have to consider public opinion.'

" 'As you please, Sir,' I said, realising for the first **time** that in these democratic days Princes, even, are under the hoof of the ignorant despot called opinion. 'The name can be changed. "The Leprosy Fund" is as distinctive a title as "The Father Damien Fund," but I regret your decision.'

" ' "The Leprosy Fund" is excellent . . . we must be worldmen, men of the world I mean, and accept opinion and not be peculiar; you get laughed at,' and so he ran on expounding his cheap philosophy, the philosophy of the average man of the street. Fancy a prince afraid to be peculiar." After this Harris tells us that he washed his secretarial hands of the matter; it had lost its essence of self-abnegation.

It was in the south of France that Harris chiefly saw the Prince of Wales. During the years 1888 to 1895 most winters would be spent in the Mediterranean, mainly on the French Riviera, which during the season of January and February sparkled. As recounted by Harris, his relationship with the Prince of Wales is one of court jester and wit to a sort of prep-school boy. He presents the two of them pacing round various salons and gaming rooms, the prince's arm thrown lightly round Harris' shoulders, Harris' low, deep voice lifting and falling, punctuated by the prince's laughter, while waiting discreetly in the wings for the performance to close are various eminent people, Randolph Churchill and Lord Hartington for two. One evening, says Harris, at Monte Carlo, Sir Algernon Borthwick touched his shoulder and said, in a low voice, that the prince wished Frank to be presented to him. The prince, speaking with the accent of a German Jew, told Harris that he had heard a great deal about him from the Duke of Cambridge, who called him the best storyteller he had ever heard. The prince hoped that he was going to hear some of the stories. Meanwhile, since he had noticed him playing at the tables with such luck, perhaps he would be good enough to place some notes for him. Afterward, when they were both stuffing money into their pockets, Harris was visited with a notion that perhaps no one had ever told the prince a dirty story.

> There was a young lady at sea
> Who said—"God how it hurts me to pee."
> "I see," said the Mate,
> "That accounts for the state
> Of the Captain, the Purser and me,"

recited Harris. "Tell me another, tell me another," cried the prince, only failing, in the narrative, to clap his hands. So Harris gave a recital of more verses. One evening, he tells us, he arranged an entertainment with Jeanne Granier, the actress, who regaled the company with stories of this director kissing her, that manager pinching her bottom. The prince was rejuvenated.

Just as Harris was giving up his position on Father Damien's committee the prince is supposed to have said to him, "I find you too serious, Harris. What I really want are some more of your naughty stories." So Harris went along to dinner, and this is apparently one of the stories with which he amused His Royal Highness:

> There is a story told in New York of the friendship between an Englishman and an American who were out together one day on Long Island. They came upon a pretty girl fishing in a very, very shallow little brook.
> "What are you fishing for there?" exclaimed the Englishman. "There are no fish in that shallow brook; what can you hope to catch?"
> She swung round on the rock she was sitting on and said cheekily: "Perhaps a man."
> "In that case," laughed the American, "you shouldn't sit on the bait."
> The girl tossed her head. . . . Half an hour later the Englishman burst out laughing.
> "I didn't see the joke at first," he said.
> "Joke," said the American, "it was pretty plain."
> "I didn't think so," said the Englishman. "How could you know she had worms?"

Harris remembered telling the prince about the malodorous Lord Mayor's banquet. "He laughed, but said it was a pity to tell anything against one's own country; he would rather forget it." And the story of Fowler making it impossible for Lady Marriott to enjoy her dinner seemed to him appalling. "He hoped I would never mention it." "We should forget what is unpleasant in life" was his guiding rule—a rule that encouraged Harris all the more to repeat the tale. His account of the end of the affair with the prince reveals how, overexcited by people and, no doubt, wine, he was capable of extraordinary tactlessness and rudeness.

At a reception by the Vyners one night, the Prince walked up and down the room with his arm on my shoulder while I told him one or two new stories. Suddenly I said to him, "You know Sir, I mustn't accept any more of your kind invitations as commands because I must get to work; I must withdraw from all this London life and try to make myself a writer. . . ." He seemed huffed, greatly put out. "You are the first," he said, "who ever spoke to me like that."

"It is my necessity, Sir," I said, "that drives me to work. I shall always be proud of your kindness to me."

"A strange way of showing it," he said, and turned away.

Once later at Monte Carlo I was talking to Madame Tosti, the wife of the well-known London musician, when the Prince came directly across the room to speak to us. I don't know why, but I felt sure he meant to be rude to me so I took the bull by the horns and copied Beau Brummel's famous words to King George. "Now I leave you," I said to the lady, "to your stout friend." And I turned away, but I could see the Prince was furious.

CHAPTER 10

A True *Friend*

Sometime, probably in 1890, Harris met Princess Alice of Monaco, who became a close friend and confidante and who really loved and admired him. Frank may have had a ferocious public manner; he may have been thickset, with his hair plastered against his skull, have had the air of a lion tamer, as A. J. A. Symons said, and a pugilist, he may have dressed like a parvenu millionaire; but with his powers of conversation, his knowledge of literature and the world, he was to some women unbelievably fascinating. Alice was one—and one, incidentally, who hardly appears at all in his autobiography, suggesting that, with the exception of Laura, the women in his memoirs are mostly make-believe. It was a perfect alliance; she was flattering, fascinated and deeply romantic. It seemed to her that Frank was a magic carpet that could whirl her away into a glorious wonderland where men were gods and everything was beautifully artistic. She was the perfect audience, content to sit and listen to him by the hour. The affair contains all the ingredients of Harris' carefully arranged romances: dinners given at Claridge's, reading and recitation in Monte Carlo and pairs of gloves purchased for the Prince of Monaco.

> I am longing to see you [wrote Alice from 25 Faubourg Saint-Honoré in Paris on June 29, 1892], but I feel that fate is dead

157

against me and my énamouré. . . . What are you doing? What are you working at? Your poor heart tossed and beaten by the waters has it found some sort of haven where it can rest? Is there no chance of your coming over, I would *so love* to see you—you don't know how fond I am of you and our friendship has been such a solace to me, that, when my thoughts wander back to the happy— oh very happy hours of soft sweet sympathy passed together I feel tears come up to my eyes—you are such a *TRUE* friend and how I love and admire your qualities. Yes, I am intensely grateful to Providence to have met you and I feel we can rely without any doubt on each other.

Alice was in all probability a spoiled, discontented, pampered woman, certainly idealistic and romantic. She was an heiress, the stereotype of a Henry James heroine, and by her marriage to Prince Albert of Monaco she preceded Grace Kelly by seventy years. She was born Miss Heine in New Orleans in 1858. Her father, Michael Heine, was described in the New Orleans directory as a "commission merchant," and later established a branch of his bank in Paris, where Sarah Bernhardt was one of his clients and called him affectionately her *"cochon d' or."* Alice was chaperoned by her mother to Europe and successfully married to the Duc de Richelieu. When he died five years later, his widow, an excitable, emotional girl of delicate health, ravaged by her loss, was hurried to Madeira to convalesce, reported the gossipy *A la Plage*,[1] and there fell in love with her Jewish doctor. Her father, who, *A la Plage* tells us, was delighted with his daughter's marriage and enjoyed addressing her as the Duchesse de Richelieu, bundled her off to Biarritz, where she fell in love with a second Jewish doctor. Soon, however, she returned, out of love, to her château in Sarthe, Haut-Buisson, which stood on the summit of a hill surrounded by a splendid park crossed invitingly by undulating paths. Isidore de Lara, who dedicated to her *Many Tales of Many Cities* and who was one of her greatest friends and one of the reasons for the collapse of her marriage, describes her at a party at the Château de Monchy, a party that was very much to poor de Lara's taste, sparkling as it was with titles. It was a "delightful time" he remembers that he had with his new friends,

---

[1] *A la Plage*, November 29, 1966.

"surrounded by all the luxury and magnificence which recalled the splendid receptions of the Third Empire." And there sat the Duchesse de Richelieu, her delicate face crowned by a halo of pure gold and illuminated by a wonderful smile. Known to her friends as Mona, she was generous, warm and pessimistic, with great enthusiasm and a magnetic presence, and, said de Lara, a genius for friendship; her belief in those she cared for was more like a religion, her faith was a cult, her loyalty heroic. She saw her friends idealized by reflection "on the mirror of her generous and noble heart." And she loved flowers. At Haut-Buisson there were long hedges covered with sweet peas. She was a marvelous and extravagant hostess; her cooks were superb. Englishmen, it was said, would cross the Channel simply to dine with her. Her teas were renowned for their brilliant guests.

In Paris she lived in the Faubourg Saint-Honoré, holding celebrated salons for writers, politicians and artists. Albert of Monaco was a neighbor. He was divorced from Mary Victoria Douglas-Hamilton, daughter of the Duke of Hamilton. Their marriage had been arranged by Napoleon III, and over it, like vapors, curled strange rumors. The bride had returned to her mother five months after the wedding, pregnant; Albert, it was whispered, had beaten her when she accused him of chasing other ladies. *A la Plage* reported that the prince was possessed with a "timidité presque maladive," that he was chiefly interested in scientific matters, and that the scandalous liaisons were an effort to compensate for this. Albert desired to marry Alice, but his father did not approve the match. Soon after their meeting the duchesse became his mistress. In 1889, when Prince Charles of Monaco died, they were married. They were a great contrast, the Earl of Lytton wrote to his daughter: "she [Alice] full of quick silver, he [Albert] very staid and subdued, never laughing, rarely smiling—but then with great sweetness —the dominant note of the whole man, a sad gentleness. But they adore each other!" Yet the marriage was not a success, and her letters to Frank show that she was in almost as distressed and low a condition as he.

A la Plage reports that she was horrified the first time she saw the gambling at Monte Carlo. Deeply concerned about the suicides and vanished fortunes, she implored her husband to close the tables. However, her attitude changed rapidly, and she began to take a closer interest in the management of the Casino, which was in the hands of the Le

Blanc brothers, and to complain about it.[2] "Tout le monde reconnut que c'était la Princesse Alice qui aboutit à une nouvelle concession de cinquante ans, et qu'elle se montra en l'occurrence une affaire épineuse," reported *A la Plage*. She arranged also that an opera house be constructed—which was finished in 1892. It emerges that she was, with Frank, planning to take over the management of the Casino and, backed by her father, turn it into a sporting club. On September 28, 1891, she was writing to her "dearest friend" from her yacht *Princesse Alice* that the "Governor," as she called her father, would be in Paris on October 5 so that Harris could see him and ascertain what could be done in that direction. Harris tells us that he had the idea of a sporting club. When he first knew the prince he was always complaining about the gambling house—which paid all the expenses of Monaco—and the Le Blanc brothers.

> I knew the "gambling house" at Monte Carlo extremely well [Harris says]. I had spent a good many winters at the Principality, and it was apparent to me that the way to give tone and importance to the whole place was by founding a special Sporting Club which would have all the best visitors as members, especially the best English and French and American. One day I outlined this scheme to the Prince of Monaco, saying that if he decided that he had to leave the "gambling house" as it was, the way to improve it would be by establishing a high class Sporting Club in close connection with it. He asked me to make out the whole scheme. I told him it would cost some time and labour and he wanted to know how he should reward me. "Very simple," I said. "You can make me a permanent secretary at a decent salary."

extrait *des Quarante Bergères*

Un grand banquier, un grand cardinal,—or et rouge
Tels sont les éléments au destin de *Mona*,
Le financier comptait, le prêtre sermone,
Et le croupier ratisse. Un grand premier ministre,
Un grand thésauriseur et le trois plus sinistre,
Qui voit le suicide échoir à ses tripots.
Et cependant Mona goûte de doux repos.
Elle songe parfois, lorsque la rouge règne,
Que, de l'homme d'État, la robe encore saigne
Et veut bien empourprer l'espoir du tapis vert.
Et, pour la consoler, lorsque la noire perd,
Le vieil économiste augure que sa fille
Rattrapera son dû d'un prochain tour de bille.

[2] There is in the Bibliothèque Nationale in Paris a satirical portrait of "Mona," alias the Princess of Monaco, by Robert de Montesquiou.

A little later it was rumoured that the Prince of Monaco had concluded a treaty with Monsieur Camille Blanc, the chief share-holder in the "gambling house" and had given him a fresh extension of his lease, on condition of receiving some millions of francs. One night in London I mentioned the matter to one of the kings of finance; he laughed outright. "So you're the culprit," he cried. "That's a jolly one on you . . . that wily fox, the Prince of Monaco, got you for nothing to frighten M. Blanc so that he has concluded a new contract for fifty years to come on most favourable terms." . . . The Prince of Monaco sold the whole idea of the Sporting Club as constituted by me, to Camille Blanc and got another large sum for it, taking care not to encumber the deal with a permanent secretary, and so cheated me.[3]

From 1891 to 1893 Harris was mostly in a state of depression, anxiety and uncertainty. He would spend some time with Laura, it would end with the usual jealous row, he would return to his wife, ill and down-hearted, and she would nurse him jealously. At last, toward the end of 1892, he ended his liaison with Laura. It was a painful time and through it he was supported by the warm, sympathetic, scarcely legible letters from Alice, who was also disillusioned and unhappy. She was so deeply attached to him, she scrawled, that she suffered here "like a pang at the spot of the heart which is yours" when she received his letter.[4] She was "oh so glad," so happy, so rejoiced, she was so fond of him—not in a selfish way, no! For such a long time his letters had been miserable and disheartened; that creature was unworthy of him and, thank God, he was nearly cured. She had always told him his wife was an angel to him, she was a trump and her devotion to him was very touching. Alice was very fond of her, she told him, and she had always said she had a nice nature. He ought to drink O and then he would see how well he would feel.

Oh, how she raged, she wrote from the Palace of Monaco, when she thought of the many hours she could have spent with him, dear, instead of seeing him among all the fools and snobs who came to see her and probably loathed her. There was no one she was so devoted to as him. She felt his friendship was made of cast iron, her devotion was a

[3] The negotiations, it seems, lasted for nine years, for the lease was not renewed until 1899–1900.

[4] Harris' letters to Alice, together with all her papers, were by her wish burned on her death by her executor, Isidore de Lara.

sweet, soothing comfort, how she admired him, his talent and his intellect, beyond all, his heart! He didn't know how miserable she had been, she told him from her yacht, anchored at Dartmouth, he *did* alter so, how keenly he must have suffered, it was a pain to have seen him in London so miserable and wretched and she cursed the cause of his depression. Might it *never* return—it would leave him a wreck, he was far too good for such cheap ware. She missed him so much, his "dear low voice" clung to her ear. Cruising in Sicily, she wondered had he forgotten her. What had she done? Was he happier? Had the friend of America returned? She only could make him forget her, she thought. And his wife—what had he done, returned to Park Lane? Her cruise she found monotonous, each day she drifted in the commonplace, further and further away from her illusions. She supposed she was an impossible creature who couldn't make up her mind to everyday routine, who was hurt and wounded by most things in life. Visiting the Greek and Roman ruins had made her think of Frank and wish she could see them with him—she thought of him when any art impressed her strongly, she longed to be carried away from her petty, small life.

In 1893, while sailing round Sardinia, she declared once more that their friendship was sacred to her, and she had felt that he was ailing physically and morally. So he had been ill and *she* had tried to go back and he did *not* see her. Poor heart of his, what harm *she* had done him, oh, how he had loved her and loved her still, what a heart he had got, of the purest gold, how she wished he could be happy, how she wished they could both be happy, but life was a fraud! Would rest come at last? Peace of heart and mind and a place where one can't think?

In this low state, his political career teetering, his secretarial post come to nothing, his marriage and his love affair causing him much anxiety and distress, Frank, encouraged by Alice, turned in 1891 to writing—and a worse pursuit for someone like Harris, with his fear of isolation, his uncertainty, his horror of being alone, cannot be imagined. Into his first stories, as Stead detected, he poured all his bitterness against Laura and his unhappiness over women in general. His uncertainty started at once. Would he be able to write better than Balzac? Could he compete with Shakespeare? The admiring Grant Allens were staying at the same place on the Riviera and assured him that he could. Were his stories equal to Maupassant at his best? Harris would tell the Grant Allens a story one night and write it down the next day; in fact,

Grant Allen said,[5] he told the stories one winter and returned with them in proof the next. All his friends were pulled in for advice. Would a comma improve that semicolon here? Should a phrase or an adjective be eliminated there? The Grant Allens apparently sent off "A Modern Idyll" and "Montes the Matador" to Meredith. Two weeks later a letter came back: he did not care for "A Modern Idyll," but he was delighted with "Montes"—better than Prosper Mérimee, he said. "If there is any hand in England can do better than *Montes* I don't know it."

Alice was there with her scribbled enthusiasm. He was so wonderfully clever and saw all faults and defects so quickly, never had she known such a sure judgment as his, and would go blindly by anything he would say; she loved his letters, they read exactly as he talked. He was not to be depressed. Believe her, he was well rid of the past; he would feel far more content as time went on and he saw what a name he was going to have. He was not to give up, and he would love his work as he lived in closer intimacy with it. He would find it so companionable. Indeed, with his writing technique Harris made it as companionable as he possible could—he was never really alone. When not reading his work to his friends he would be dictating it to his secretaries or showing round and dispatching proofs and complimentary copies to anyone he could think of who might give him praise and reassurance.

The first short story to appear in the *Fortnightly* was "A Modern Idyll," published in June 1891, the story of a love affair between a Baptist minister and one of his deacon's wives.[6] It caused a furore. "Your 'Modern Idyll' in the *Fortnightly* is a disgrace to have published," wrote an anonymous correspondent. "It is a licentious and I may say blasphemous production, evil and punishable. Your first article is by an acknowledged adulterer ["The British Army in 1891," by Sir Charles Dilke] and your final product a wicked justification of sensuous iniquity and mark this if the author (yourself) dies in the condition that gave it inspiration damnation will be your reward." "Permit me to express my surprise and regret that the article 'A Modern Idyll' should have appeared in such a review as the *Fortnightly*," wrote Newman Hall. "To me its spirit seems not only immoral but anti-religion.

---

[5] Grant Richards' introduction to *Frank Harris: His Life and Adventures.*

[6] Arthur Symons found something turbulent and disturbing in the story. It occurred to him to turn "this rather revolting material" into a one-act play, on which he and George Moore collaborated—*The Minister's Call.* It was performed on March 4, 1892.

Linking high profession and devout prayer with deliberate sentimentality and hypocrisy. I should remonstrate with any of my congregation having such a publication within the reach of young people who would not read it without injury."

The reception, however, was by no means all bad. Elmer Gertz's collection of papers in Washington contains the correspondence received by Harris on his debut in short-story writing. Much of it is praise. Indeed, this first batch of stories, set in America, is drawn fresh, firsthand, and does not come, like much of his later writing, as jaded, talked-out stuff. Professor Tyndall had read both "Montes the Matador" and "A Modern Idyll" and had recognized in both of them the literary gift of a writer. Froude had read his story with interest; he always thought Harris had something considerable in him, he wrote, now perhaps it would come out. John Addington Symonds, recovered from his ill humor over the proof corrections, said that "A Modern Idyll" was neither bad nor indifferent but decidedly good, a fine study of mixed motives, and one must felicitate Harris on his Americanisms and accompanying dryness of humor. He wondered what the philistines could find to object to in it, to him it seemed so natural and ordinary— but then he never could understand the philistines. Frederic Harrison told him that the "Idyll" was a most vigorous and effective piece of work and would attract most unusual attention. There was a "trenchant realization" about it and a subtle analysis of character, and the briskness and vraisemblance of the local color and speech were wonderfully vivid: good people would be sorely tried. He concluded that he did not think Bret Harte did anything new to beat Harris' sketches. Beerbohm Tree thought it was a most powerful piece of writing—terribly modern in its unblinkingness of "the great fact"; Harris must have committed a most successful rape of poetic justice. Fletcher Moulton said that he had read his tale with interest and made him his compliments upon it. Harris had done his work surely and well; it must give him the rarest pleasure, that of being quite satisfied with what he had done. But how about Stead, Fletcher Moulton wanted to know; he was going off to buy the *Review of Reviews* to see what Stead had to say about it. "I half fear he will be wise enough to hold his tongue."

Stead, however, did not hold his tongue. "If Mr. Harris has nothing better in his wallet than the narrative of the growth of an adulterous passion of a Baptist Minister for the wife of one of his deacons, the world has not lost much by the fact that the editor of the *Fortnightly* has hitherto refrained from any attempt to make a name among contemporary writers" was his opinion. After all the commotion, Stead's opinion was apparently endorsed by the publishers, Chapman and Hall. They asked their editor not to submit any more stories for publication, and their editor, much offended, resigned. The day was saved only by Meredith and his support.

With all this worry and private uncertainty, Harris' public manner became more ferocious. H. G. Wells has a marvelously funny illustration of this, his first interview with the Great Editor. In July 1891, the month after the furore had raged over "A Modern Idyll," Harris, in the same number that contained "Montes the Matador,"[7] had published a paper by Wells, "The Rediscovery of the Unique,"[8] which was described by Wells himself as ingenious but very ill-written. The publication was a success and Wells sent along a further article, "Universe Rigid," which Harris at once dispatched unread to the printers. In proof he and his staff found it incomprehensible.

> This was not surprising [explained Wells in his autobiography], since it was a laboured ill-written description of a four-dimensional space-time universe, and that sort of thing was still far away from the monthly reviews in 1891. "Great *Gahd!*" cried Harris. "What's the fellow up to?" and summoned me to the office.
>
> I found his summons disconcerting. My below-stairs training reinforced the spirit of the times on me, and insisted that I should visit him in proper formal costume. I imagined that I must wear a morning coat and a silk hat and carry an umbrella. It was impossible I should enter the presence of A Great Editor in any other guise. My aunt Mary and I inspected these vitally important articles. The umbrella tightly rolled with a new elastic band, was

---

[7] Stead had reviewed "Montes the Matador"; a great improvement upon "A Modern Idyll," he had said, "which but for its unpleasant motif would never have attracted any notice. The story of 'Montes' although culminating in jealous and deadly revenge in the last two pages is, for the most part, a vivid picture of the life of a matador. It may be noticed that here, as in 'A Modern Idyll,' Mr. Harris makes his woman absolutely detestable, false, selfish and immoral. Perhaps in his next attempt he will give us a female less worthy of perdition, otherwise the uncharitable will say that he knows no other woman, which would be unjust."

[8] Harris' account of the story is that when he took over the *Fortnightly Review*, Mr. Morley—the retiring editor—pointed to two large boxes in the corner and said that they were full of manuscripts. Harris went through them and discovered "The Rediscovery of the Unique," which, he said, was charmingly written in a simple style. He called H. G. Wells to see him. Wells had a timid manner, spoke very little, in a cockney accent, and was so self-effacing, colorless and withdrawn that he wiped out the good effect of his paper, and Harris forgot all about him until he got the *Saturday Review*.

not so bad, provided it had not to be opened; but the silk hat was extremely discouraging. It was very fluffy and defaced and, as I now perceived for the first time, a little brownish in places. The Summons was urgent and there was no time to get it ironed. We brushed it with a hard brush and then with a soft one and wiped it round again and again with a silk handkerchief. The nap remained unsubdued. Then against the remonstrances of my aunt Mary, I wetted it with a sponge and then brushed. That seemed to do the trick. My aunt's attempt to restrain me had ruffled and delayed me a little, but I hurried out, damply glossy, to the great encounter, my début in the world of letters.

Harris kept me waiting in the packing office downstairs for nearly half an hour before he would see me. This ruffled me still more. At last I was shown up to a room that seemed to me enormous, in the midst of which was a long table at which the great man was sitting. At the ends were a young man, whom I was afterwards to know as Blanchamp,[9] and a very refined-looking old gentleman named Silk who was Harris' private secretary. Harris silently motioned me to a chair opposite himself.

He was a square-headed individual with very black hair parted in the middle and brushed fiercely back. His eyes as he met my shabby and shrinking form became intimidatory. He had a blunt nose over a vast black upturned moustache, from beneath which came a deep voice of exceptional power. He seemed to me to be of extraordinary size, though that was a mere illusion; but he was certainly formidable.

"And it was you who sent me this Universe Rigid!" he roared.

I got across to the table somehow, sat down and disposed myself for a conversation. I was depleted and breathless. I placed my umbrella and hat upon the table before me and realized then for the first time that my aunt Mary had been right about that wetting. It had become a disgraceful hat, an insult. The damp gloss had gone. The nap was drying irregularly and standing up in little tufts all over. It was not simply a shabby top hat; it was an improper top hat. I stared at it. Harris stared at it. Blanchamp and Silk had evidently never seen such a hat. With an effort we came to the business in hand.

"You sent me this Universe Gur-R-R-Rigid," said Harris, picking up his cue after the pause.

[9] Shaw, in a letter to Harris dated December 16, 1900, refers to Harris' assistant Beauchamp. It is likely that the young man Wells met is he and that "Blanchamp" is a misreading.

He caught up a proof beside him and tossed it across the table. "Dear Gahd! I can't understand six words of it. What do you *mean* by it? For Gahd's sake tell me what it is all *about*? What's the sense of it? What are you trying to *say*?"

I couldn't stand up to him—and my hat. I couldn't for a moment adopt the tone and style of a bright young man of science. There was my hat tacitly revealing the sort of chap I was. I couldn't find words. Blanchamp and Silk with their chins resting on their hands, turned back from the hat to me, in gloomy silent accusation.

"Tell me what you *think* it's about?" roared Harris, growing more merciless with my embarrassment, and rapping the proof with the back of his considerable hand. He was enjoying himself.

"Well, you see . . ." I said.

"I don't see," said Harris. "That's just what I don't do."

"The idea," I said, "the idea . . ."

Harris became menacingly silent, patiently attentive.

"If you consider time is space like, then . . . I mean if you treat it like a fourth dimension like, well then you see . . ."

"*Gahd*, the way I've been let in!" injected Harris in an aside to Gahd.

"I can't use it," said Harris at the culmination of the interview.

"We'll have to disperse the type again"—and the vision I had had of a series of profound but brilliant articles about fundamental ideas, that would make a reputation for me, vanished. My departure from the room had been mercifully obliterated from my memory. But as soon as I got alone with it in my bedroom in Fitzroy Road, I smashed up that hat finally. To the great distress of my aunt Mary. And the effect of that encounter was to prevent my writing anything ambitious again, for a year or more.

But even such tonic as unnerving young writers with wet top hats did not make Harris more confident of his own abilities. He was uncertain what to do—whether to abandon politics and write, or keep matters unsatisfactorily as they were. He hurried off to Cap Brun, Toulon, at the end of October and dispatched his stories to Coventry Patmore, who so far had remained silent.

I only ask your impression of my stories. I am afraid you will condemn at least one of them, "A Modern Idyll," and I should like to know how far it is condemnable. Besides I lost my head a little, and stand hesitating at a point whence roads innumerable stretch to every part of the horizon.

Your judgment will I think help me much, although I feel ashamed to ask you for it on such a slight pretence.

I think you understand me well enough to know I would rather hear the truth stated in the harshest manner than have it mitigated out of any earthly consideration—and you are the only person I know whose judgment would weigh really with me on many points.

Coventry Patmore's reaction was favorable, for when the collected edition of stories[10] was published in 1895, under the title of *Elder Conklin*, he reviewed them, praising their severity; Kipling, he said, never did anything better than "Eatin' Crow" and "Best Man in Garotte."[11] As we know, Harris abandoned politics—and the Prince of Wales—for writing. He tells us he had turned some of his stories into his best French, and they were published in the *Revue des Deux Mondes*.

"My dearest friend," scrolled the admiring Alice from the seas of Sardinia, longing for some story to be dedicated to her and dropping an unfortunate brick, "how could you allow your beautiful Conklin to be disfigured in translation—I can't read it—the first three pages make me boil." And then, from the Faubourg Saint-Honoré: "But now tell me *who* translated your 'Modern Idyll' because it is not good. Your dialogues were extraordinarily brilliant in English and I don't like them in translation. They fall flat."

[10] *A Triptych*, published September 1891, was also reviewed by Stead under the title "Mr. Frank Harris's Third Effort":

> Mr. Frank Harris who has abandoned politics for art—the literary art of writing short stories—gives us a third sample of his peculiar genius in three sketches of life in a Western mining camp, entitled "A Triptych." The third is better than either of those which preceded it for one reason, because it is not disfigured by the presence of a woman, and hitherto Mr. Harris has only given us women whose room is very much better than their company. There is life, character and colour in this Triptych. Mr. Harris's range is wide, and we look forward with pleasure to his further efforts in this new line. It is somewhat odd Mr. Harris should only seem to feel at home in society which reeks either with murder or adultery.

There Stead was plainly hitting back at "M," in the February *Fortnightly*, who had claimed murder excited in Stead calm disapproval, whereas adultery unmanned him.

The other stories' publication dates were: "Elder Conklin," June 1892; "A Straight Flush," August 1892; "Profit and Loss," September 1892.

[11] Not only did Coventry Patmore compare Harris to Kipling but Professor Dowden said that his work betrayed unmistakable evidence of Bret Harte. The *Daily Chronicle* declared that Mr. Frank Harris' *Elder Conklin* was perhaps the best piece of work of that year, and the *Athenaeum* commented that no doubt Balzac could have drawn such a figure as Elder Conklin, so stoutly pathetic, so hopelessly repellent.

CHAPTER 11

The Slipping Grip

IN 1894 Harris lost the *Fortnightly*; at about the same time he decided once and for all to leave his wife, thereby forfeiting her financial support—although officially he was still listed at 34 Park Lane until 1895. After the affair with Laura had finished he had, it seemed, found balm in being promiscuous, which in turn had made his sexual vanity overpowering. "He not only became a discursive amorist," Wells said, "but he talked about it, and there ensued an estrangement and separation from his wife and her income and Park Lane. His dominating way in conversation startled, amused and then irritated people, and he felt his grip slipping. The directors of the *Fortnightly* became restive and interfering. He began to drink heavily and to shout still louder as the penalties of loud shouting closed in on him."

Harris' own version of losing the *Fortnightly* was that the publisher, Chapman, being a conservative man of old-fashioned type, became more and more difficult to work with. On September 1, 1894, an article appeared, "Some Anarchist Portraits," by Charles Mulato, in praise of Henry and Ravachol, two anarchists who had thrown bombs at the houses of those magistrates who had passed sentence on people involved in the Parisian riots in 1891. Henry's bomb had killed eight people and he was sent to the guillotine, but not without the *Fortnightly* calling him the sweetest and noblest of men. Chapman was scandalized, and finally gave his editor two months' notice. Harris says that, overwhelmed and hurt, he fled to Maidenhead, where his nights were sleepless, his days curdled with misery and regret. A friend, Willie Grenfell, instructed him in punting, which helped a little—but only a very little. As Wells said, "As soon as he ceased to work vehemently he became unable to work. He could not attend to things without excitement." He needed momentum, bustle and fuss. When he had time to think he was in danger of being overcome by his private melancholic, uncertain self. He was happiest when he was rushing importantly about interviewing this person, dispatching that telegram, correcting the other proof, talking and eating magnificently, playing chess. When the pace stopped, the wind was taken away, and he wallowed, uneasy, vulnerable to every wave of thought. Being constantly on the move and reacting to everything and everyone was extremely tiring, and since Harris had no means of restoring himself he had begun to burn himself out. In 1894, where the waters of Maidenhead ran silent, green and cool, he was all at a loose end, "and suffering for the first time in my life with nerves. I often sat in the corner and cried. I was unable to control myself, and could not get any better, and was very near to an absolute breakdown. And the fatal day when I should be out of work was coming nearer and nearer. Sometimes I began to feel I should go out of my mind. Neither the exercise in the open air with Willie Grenfell nor the regular quiet life did me any good. At last, almost in despair I left Maidenhead and returned to London."

Around October 1894 he purchased the *Saturday Review,* telling us that he offered the owner, Lewis Edmund, Q.C., a pound for every reader. It seems that the magazine changed hands at £560. With his new organ Harris felt better, potent once more. His aim was to furnish the *Saturday* with as efficient and talented a staff as possible, with a view to constructive rather than destructive criticism. Hesketh Pearson, in "Rebel Artist,"[1] says that Harris gave a drinking party to launch the *Saturday,* an account of which went the rounds, shocking the reputable critics who had been shown the door. Hilarity broke loose, and the office wastepaper basket was used as a football by the happy drinkers, with much horseplay ensuing, the editor leading the revels. His new crew was certainly muscular. Shaw accepted the offer on December 4 to become drama critic at six pounds a week; John Runciman secured the post of music critic and personal assistant; and D. S. MacColl

[1] *Extraordinary People.*

reviewed art. Max Beerbohm, Chalmers Mitchell and Arthur Symons were all to contribute, and H. G. Wells was summoned to review novels. His cockney accent had disappeared, Harris observed, and he had an air about him of quiet self-confidence. In his autobiography Wells once again gives a delightful account.

> The office was in Southampton Street, off the Strand, and it occupied the first and second floors. I found people ascending and descending and the roar of a remembered voice told me that Harris was on a higher level. I found Blanchamp in a large room on the drawing-room floor amidst a great confusion of books and papers and greatly amused. Harris was having a glorious time of it above. He had summoned most of the former staff to his presence in order to read out scraps from their contributions to them and to demand, in the presence of his "Dear Gahd" and his faithful henchman Silk, why the hell they wrote like that? It was a Revolution—the twilight of the Academic. But Professor Saintsbury, chief of that anonymous staff, had been warned in time by Edmund Gosse and so escaped the crowning humiliation. Clergymen, Oxford dons, respectable but strictly anonymous men of learning and standing, came hustling downstairs in various phases of indignation and protest, while odd newcomers in strange garments as redolent of individuality as their signatures, waited their turn to ascend. I came late on the list and by that time Harris was ready for lunch and took Blanchamp, Low and myself as his guests and audience to the Café Royal, where I made the acquaintance of Camembert of the ripest and a sort of Burgundy. . . . I don't think we talked much about my prospective contributions. But I gathered that our fortunes were made, that Oxford and the Stuffy and the Genteel and Mr. Gladstone were to be destroyed and that under Harris the *Saturday Review* was to become "a weekly unprecedented in literary history."

Wells describes Harris at this time as a star that was still high in the London sky. He had lost his wife, her financial support and Park Lane, and therefore the goodwill of her circle of friends, but "he was still a star of the magnitude of Henley or Whistler or Oscar Wilde and we, his younger contributors, were little chaps below him." To date, anyone who has written about Harris has presented only the brash, noisy extrovert, booming all over the place; the private view, revealed by his letters, shows a melancholy introvert living much of his life in depression and fear of illness. He was not a good letter writer; his letters hardly ever contain funny or interesting observations or a zest for life—they are too occupied with himself. Nearly always written when he was depressed and alone, they are efforts to share his isolation, and emerge chiefly as complaints over his physical and mental state and wild plans to ensure that health, wealth and happiness would be his any day. He wanted, as Francis Hackett said, two things—the joy of full self-expression and the prestige and power that could be earned by it. Also he wanted money. Gradually, as it became evident that his writing was not winning for him the glory he craved, he became disillusioned and obsessed with making money as a means to authority. Arthur Symons said that during the seven years he knew Harris intimately—while he edited the *Fortnightly* and the *Saturday*—he seemed to him a man of prodigious talent, which all too often he misused; he had immense vitality, vivacity and violence—his voice reminded Symons of a beaten Eastern gong; he was the best and least exacting editor Symons had ever come across.

He may have boomed at and upset certain members of polite society, but he still had his admirers. Mrs. Devereux told Arnold Bennett[2] that she had met Harris in 1895, when he was forty-three, and that he was convinced he was going to die at forty-four (the age of his mother at her death). The reality—that in 1895 he was thirty-nine—does not alter the fact, as he was pleased to tell his many correspondents, that during the last four years he had been decidedly sickly, living in fear of consumption. No party was complete without him, Mrs. Devereux said; and obviously Harris had selected her to confide in and impress, for not only does she talk admiringly about his anticipated death but also about his great bass voice—the greatest bass there ever had been—and how Lamperti had offered him five years of free tuition if only he would study. She was not totally taken in, however, for she said that he was easily influenced and intoxicated by his own eloquence, and although he was generous, he was the sort of man who would stab another in the back, rob him of all he possessed, then give the entire proceeds to another.

It is useful at this stage to draw together the descriptions of his contemporaries so that we may make a picture of Harris as he appeared to them. A. A. Baumann[3] suggests that it was his unpunctuality that

---

[2] *The Journals of Arnold Bennett*, 1896–1910, edited by Newman Flower (Cassell and Co., London, 1932).

[3] Grant Richards' introduction to *Frank Harris: His Life and Adventures*.

finished him off with the *Evening News*. (Presumably Baumann meant the *Fortnightly*, to which he contributed.) In any case, either from insolence or genuine inability to mark time, he was seldom less than two hours late for an appointment. Once Baumann asked him to lunch at the Café Royal at one-thirty and waited until three o'clock, when he appeared, without any apology. Grant Richards, on the other hand, remembers that he was extremely civil and took endless care to acknowledge civilities. Violet Hunt, in her book *The Flurried Years*, shows that he was capable of extraordinary behavior. She has an account of a dinner at Gwen Otter's where she sat between H. G. Wells and Frank, who sent away "all Gwen's beautiful viands preferring to munch dry biscuits out of a paper bag, which he crumbled all over the cloth, and offered to me and H.G. . . . in his interesting fingers."

Kingsmill has a story in his *Frank Harris* which he tells with relish and which is by now well known but is worth repeating not only for amusement but because it shows how disorganized Harris was. It had come to Kingsmill from Hesketh Pearson, who had had it from Robert Ross, that sometime, probably toward the end of 1895, Harris gave a large luncheon party at the Café Royal. Ross received an invitation one morning: "Will you lunch with me at the Café Royal 1 o'clock today? Only a few friends to meet the Duc de Richelieu [Alice's son]." Ross arrived and found that Harris had forgotten to reserve a table. He and the other guests, about fifty of them, waited while a large table was placed in the middle of the main dining room, and all the other lunchers at their small tables were squashed against the walls. The lunch began and Harris and the duke were soon in conversation. Suddenly Harris' huge voice rose above the general conversation: "No, my dear Duke, I know nothing of the joys of homosexuality. You must speak to my friend Oscar about that." Silence fell in the dining room. "And yet," Harris mused, in more subdued but still reverbatory tones, "if Shakespeare had asked me I would have had to submit." Max Beerbohm, who was there, illustrated this with his delightful cartoon of Harris standing naked by the sea twirling his moustaches looking over his shoulder at Shakespeare, "who with starting eyes, trembling hands, and loosened knees gazes in anguish upon his awful mate."

Sisley Huddleston, in *Bohemian, Literary and Social Life in Paris*, remembers Harris claiming to be an Irish-American. Many of Huddleston's friends later said unkind things about Harris, but Huddleston did not care to know these aspects—he preferred to think of the Harris that he knew, a passionate and earnest man, intensely human, whose eyes would fill with tears when he spoke of beauty, who was moved sincerely by misery or oppression, who recited for hours significant passages from Browning. Raymond Blathwayt, in *The Tapestry of Life*, remembers him as one of the most interesting persons he ever met. A small, wiry, eager personage with a fiercely upturned moustache, a voice harsh and penetrating, a keen wit and a pungent outlook; if ever a man possessed the primary qualities of greatness, surely Frank Harris was that man. Alas, said Blathwayt, he was always his own worst enemy, far more generous, kind-hearted and noble-minded than many of his petty adversaries, but he could not hold his tongue or hide his scorn. A little more complacency, less tendency to pugnacity, and there was no pinnacle of honor to which he could not have climbed.

Harris himself tells a story, with which he was extremely pleased, of meeting Alfred Austin, the poet laureate—who he said had no more poetry in his composition than a housefly—with Wolseley, when the latter was the ranger at Woolwich. Harris did not care for Austin at all; he considered him to be a mere journalist and place hunter, without talent or personality. That evening, apparently, his tone toward Harris was condescending, high and mighty.

"I hear now that you write poetry as well as prose," Harris remembered that he said to him. "Which do you intend to use in the future?"

"Oh, now," Austin replied, "I must write a certain amount of poetry."

"Why?" asked Harris, pretending ignorance.

"Oh, to keep the wolf from the door," Austin replied, with a smile.

"I see," Harris retorted, "I see, very good: you read your poetry to the wolf, eh?" Harris was mightily pleased with his *mot*—perhaps, he says with rare humility, because he was seldom witty.

His rare instances of wit and his more frequent occasions of frankness were more than many good people could stomach. Shaw tells a story of how Harris dined one night at a London club that preserved a traditional large communal table. His host noticed that he was peering gloomily into his claret glass. Was his wine all right, he inquired solicitously. "Oh, yes," said Harris, looking round the room. "I suppose it is good enough for this collection of seedy prigs."

Shaw was a good friend to Harris—in later years he often rose to his defense—and to a certain extent he recognized his split personality. All the best people had been quite ready to lionize him, he said, at his first impact on them as a Tory democrat with a powerful pen. But contrary to opinion, Shaw explained, he was a martyr to the truth.[4] He was ostracized in London because he was so truthful. He would get overexcited, out of control, and then there was no knowing what ruthless candor would emerge, carried by a voice that filled the largest theater and dominated the noisiest dinner party. He never learned how much dissimulation was needed to make good society work smoothly, and he was incapable of the hypocrisy and polite mendacity necessary to consolidate a position in the London governing class. In perfect faith he assumed that every young woman over fifteen knew the tales of Maupassant by heart, was as open to the discussion of sex as Mr. Havelock Ellis himself and had a portfolio of Félicien Rops on the bedroom shelf. In the much quoted letter Shaw wrote to Harris on his final departure to America in 1915 he imagines a scene during which Harris, the buccaneer, takes in a bishop's wife to dinner. (This was a scene of which Shaw was very fond and one on which he elaborated to Hesketh Pearson and in his introduction to Frank's *Oscar Wilde*.) In a deep voice Frank pours out his scorn for the snobbishness and hypocrisy of the church, finishing with a reference to Mary Magdalene and Jesus, at which the poor lady withdraws and Harris finds himself between her husband, the bishop, and Edmund Gosse; whereupon he turns the conversation to Rops, pulling out a picture of a nude woman seated at an organ, every pipe of which, as Shaw wrote elaborating on his theme to Hesketh Pearson, represents a penis, and broadens the language into that of the forecastle of a pirate sloop. At the least sign of restiveness he redoubles his energy of expression and angry scorn. Upstairs the bishop and Edmund Gosse console themselves. "My God," says Gosse, "what a man"; the bishop says, "Impossible, quite impossible." Shaw had seen all this, and he was forced to admit that Harris was a monster—a phrase that has often been taken up by Harris' debunkers and used out of context. What they do not add is that Shaw's tone is teasing, amused and affectionate. Clever as Harris was, he continued, it was impossible

---

[4] Shaws preface to *Oscar Wilde*. More accurately, Harris was a martyr to his *frankness*—and his own tactlessness. He never told a deliberate untruth. Facts and accuracy were not, however, his strength; he was too impatient to check his work and too untidy. On paper he blurted out what he felt emotionally, and as he grew older his mind grew more muddled, and what he felt emotionally and remembered became embedded in fantasy, anecdote and gossip.

to ask anyone to meet him unless the person could stand up to the utter-most freemasonry of the very freest thought and expression.

This might have been disagreeable to snobs and conventional people, but it was not in the least disagreeable to Shaw; to him it was as natural as Beethoven walking through the Court with his hat pulled down on his eyebrows and writing "Brain Owner" on his visiting card, in the same way as his brother wrote "Land Owner." On Beethoven's part it was an assertion of special values, but it was also ruffianism; and the same went for Harris. One could ask Harris to meet Julia Frankau and Lady Jessica Sykes, but not Mrs. Humphry Ward; and unless one could be trusted to take Mrs. Humphry Ward in to dinner and leave her with the impression of either being very respectable or very charm-ing, one could not have a career as a journalist or a politician in Lon-don. Mrs. Julia Frankau had, said Shaw, seen how really sensitive Frank was, and had reprimanded Shaw for dealing with him as a buccaneer and not realizing what a daisy he was. When they first met, Harris was editing the *Fortnightly*, and would expostulate earnestly at being called a pirate from the Spanish Main. Shaw had first discovered him engaged with a visitor to whom he was speaking resounding and fluent German; it was all very impressive. After this Harris gave Shaw a nice dose of his hypochondria, telling him how he had upset himself by some ath-letic feat on the river. Shaw asked him whether he drank much, at which Harris poured out a long measure of his symptoms, diet and so forth. After this they were on unreserved and intimate terms.

Whatever his drawbacks might have been—untidiness, unpunctual-ity, vociferousness, munching biscuits from paper bags—he was always ready with generous appreciation, T. H. Bell said, quick to size up a man and to bring him out; ready with help and suggestions; willing to let a man work a thing out in his own way if he thought him responsi-ble. He had a great capacity for work, was a just and honest critic of literature and a wonderful conversationalist. If, as William Rothenstein said, his rather truculent manner drew repartee, he had a geniality and a boisterous vigor that won the loyalty of the *Saturday* circle, and he had a love for literature and an audacious critical insight. The *Saturday* under the new regime had become a lively and remarkable publication, causing much attention and some controversy. In the office, Shaw said, whisky flowed *ad libitum*, and though it had no more apparent effect on Harris than a can of beer on a sweating haymaker in hot July, it changed John Finlay Runciman from a sober young enthusiast to a fatal case of dipsomania within a year or two.[5]

Although Wells was remunerated quickly and efficiently, certain contributors found that the *Saturday* was slow to pay. Alice Herbert told Elmer Gertz that she was owed £20 accumulated fees. She dispatched the following verse:

> Dear Mr. Harris, when I heard you were in Paris,
> I thought it might embarrass you to dun you then
> But now that you are back again to gather up the slack again
> Do pay a faithful hack again—or just say when!
> So up-to-date and latterday and brilliant is the *Saturday*
> It can't want lean contributors to hang about its neck.
> I value every writing of my Editor's inditing
> And it shall not meet with slighting if I find it on a cheque!

She was paid within three days.

Harris was once more in his element. He entertained lavishly, recalls William Rothenstein in *Men and Memories*, usually at the Café Royal. "I remember especially a dinner he gave there at which Oscar Wilde, Max Beerbohm, Aubrey Beardsley, Robbie Ross and myself were present. Harris monopolised the conversation telling an endless story inspired by 'Étui de Nacre,' Oscar growing more and more restive. Max said, 'Now, Frank, Anatole France would have spoilt that story.' Harris then proceeded to tell of all the great houses he had frequented. 'Yes, dear Frank,' said Oscar, 'we believe you, you have dined in every house in London *once*'—the only time I heard him say an unkind thing." Another time Rothenstein was lunching at the Café Royal and Harris was sitting near with a lady friend. As they passed his table on the way out he called out, twisting his moustaches: "You're getting older, Will, I'm getting younger."

In spite of all that food and drink, with his nervous energy, and later the use of his stomach pump, it is unlikely that Harris was ever fat. He retained always his dislike for grossness. When he first met Oscar Wilde, he says, he was shocked by his appearance—although Hesketh Pearson suggests that the shock may have been invented,

[5] According to Sir Steven Runciman (in a letter to the author, January 1974), the family disapproved of John's connection with Harris, whom they considered to be John's evil genius.

because Wilde at first disliked Harris and his noise. Lord Alfred Douglas said that Wilde always avoided Harris; then they met at a dinner party and Harris told a story about an Australian fighter being attacked by the crowd and fighting the whole lot with his back to the wall. Wilde was fascinated at how Harris told the story and complimented him. They immediately became friends.

Fleshly indulgence and laziness were written all over Wilde's face, Frank wrote. When they shook hands, Wilde's hand, flashing with a great scarab ring, felt flabby and greasy in just the limp way that Harris disliked; he was overdressed, and his lips had the heaviness of a Roman emperor. To crown the appearance was a black front tooth that affronted the world when he laughed. "But then," said Harris, relenting, "it was a tribute to the man, who with his vivacious beautifully expressive eyes, his fascinating talk, could overcome his unpromising appearance." He first met him, he said, when Wilde was living with Frank Miles—and a charming, aristocratic home it was too, where tea was served by a pretty girl called Sally Higgs, who soon became famous and was painted by Lord Leighton as "Daydreams." Frank makes out that almost immediately they became friends, but this is almost certainly untrue, since at this point his anecdotes are taken from other people. But Wilde was exactly the right contrived image for Harris to idealize—to represent for him estheticism and beauty and art nourished by classical Greece, smacking of golden figures, purple shadows, white landscapes, naked youths moving against deep blue, tables heaped with red wine and roses. There is no doubt that he was deeply affected by Wilde's prosecution. Shaw said that he quite lost his head over the whole affair and raged impotently at the cruelty of law and the savagery of the sexually excited mob. To him, certainly in retrospect, the trial was symbolic, and he identified himself with the victim. For had not Harris abandoned politics and put all his energy into becoming a writer and a prophet? The whole of English opinion, he felt, was set not only to persecute Wilde but himself; all men of letters, poets and art itself were, he saw, attacked by a deep-rooted prejudice; the two prevailing British passions, puritanism and philistinism, were united to crucify a gentle person personifying civilization and wit and art. The state was malevolent, prison was a hell from Dante's inferno, and Wilde was a martyr. And he was quite powerless to do anything about it. Everyone shunned the name of Oscar Wilde and would publish nothing in his cause. At one point he approached his friend Arthur Walter, editor of the *Times*, but Walter would do nothing. During a lunch with Mrs. Jeune it was generally agreed that Wilde's punishment had been too slight; while one guest said two years' imprisonment with hard labor usually resulted in idiocy or death. Harris seethed and declared to the company that he was a friend and admirer of Wilde's; a glacial silence spread round the table. It was Lady Dorothy Nevill who helped. "Are you talking of Oscar Wilde?" she exclaimed. "I'm so glad to hear you say you are a friend. I am too, and shall always be proud of having known him, a most brilliant and charming man."

Since the publication of Harris' *Oscar Wilde* in 1919 there has been a barrage of assaults dismissing the book and its author in general, and Harris' claims to have helped Wilde financially and otherwise in particular. Where there is evidence to support him it is explained that any help he might have given was for reasons toward his own profit. Certainly there is much in the book that is mere romancing and too much injection of the author himself, recalling astonishing conversations that do not sound right. Too much "Do you remember Verlaine, Frank?" and "You are not offended, Frank, are you, for making you meet two caryatides of the Parisian temple of pleasure?," too many " 'No, no,' I cried's." But what is clear is that Harris genuinely believed that Wilde had been destroyed by Lord Alfred Douglas, whom he makes the villain of his piece. During his research he was given to read by Robbie Ross the letter known as "De Profundis," a sad, desperate, bitter letter written by Wilde, while he was in prison, to Douglas in which he told Douglas that he had worn him out; that he was a spoiled, demanding boy wanting presents, attention and visits to every sort of amusement and expensive restaurant; that between the autumn of 1892 and the date of his imprisonment he had spent on and with Douglas £5,000 in actual cash irrespective of the bills that he had incurred on hansoms, turtle soups, luscious ortolans wrapped in crinkled vine leaves, amber-colored champagnes and jewel-encrusted sleeve links. Harris says that each time he saw him during these years it seemed to him that Oscar had grown grosser, more purple-lipped and Roman-emperorish than ever. He noticed the growing discomfort of people; less and less did they wish to be seen in Oscar's company or to meet him, less and less did restaurants desire the patronage of Wilde and Lord Alfred Douglas. Shaw was present one spring evening in 1894 at the Café Royal just before Wilde's arrest, when Harris not only begged Wilde to leave the country before it was too late but also accurately forecast the outcome of the trial.[6]

> I myself was present at a curious meeting between the two when Harris on the eve of the Queensberry trial prophesied to Wilde with miraculous precision exactly what immediately afterwards happened to him and warned him to leave the country. It was the first time to my knowledge that such a forecast proved true. Wilde, though under no illusion as to the folly of the quite unselfish suit-at-law he had been persuaded to begin, nevertheless so miscalculated the force of social vengeance he was unloosing on himself that he fancied it could be stayed by putting up the editor of the *Saturday Review* to declare that he considered *Dorian Gray* a highly moral book, which it certainly is.
>
> When Harris foretold the truth, Wilde denounced him as a faint-hearted friend who was failing him in his hour of need and left the room in anger. Harris's idiosyncratic power of pity saved him from feeling or showing the smallest resentment; and events presently proved to Wilde how insanely he had been advised in taking the action, and how accurately Harris had gauged the situation.

The first trial resulted in the jury disagreeing, and Oscar was refused bail and sent to Holloway. Through the kindness and cooperation of the Home Office it has been confirmed that Harris visited Wilde there on May 4, 1895. Among their papers there is a letter from Silk to the governor. Through his solicitor Wilde had expressed a wish to see Mr. Frank Harris (still officially addressed at 34 Park Lane) to obtain advice on matters connected with his literary work. Mr. Frank Harris had not been well enough that day to make his application in person, and Silk, as his private secretary, had done so for him. Harris' own story is muddled and he has probably mixed two visits into one. It was a miserable visit, he says, in the presence of a warder. Wilde had an unshaven face, a sad and frightened air and a toneless voice. Harris was sickened by the regulations that denied Wilde his watch or cigarettes; as a result he could not sleep and the nights seemed interminable. On leaving, Frank turned round to look at the medieval castellated front of Holloway; how fitting, he thought, that face was— the whole institution belonged to the middle ages and not to the

---

[6] Introduction to *The Dark Lady of the Sonnets*.

present. Soon after this Wilde was granted bail on, according to Harris, "his own recognizance of £2,500," with two other sureties of £1,250 each. Harris tells us that he made preparations for Wilde's escape—preparations that were pooh-poohed by Sherard years later.[7] He claims that he had arranged for a steam yacht to be waiting at Erith—complete with a small library furnished with French and English books and supper in the cabin, with lobster à l' américaine and a bottle of Pommery—and a closed carriage at Hyde Park Corner to convey them thither. Wilde, however, refused to leave. The second trial opened on May 21, before Mr. Justice Wills, and Wilde was sentenced to two years' hard labor. On October 1, on *Saturday Review* writing paper, Harris applied again to the prison officials for permission to see Wilde about his bankruptcy. To the letter was appended a note that Mr. Harris must state fully the reasons why he thought it necessary to have an interview with the prisoner Wilde and whether a letter and reply from the prisoner would not answer his purpose. In December, More Adey and Adela Schuster wrote to Harris with ideas for Oscar's release. On January 4, 1896, via Silk, Harris dictated a mysterious reply to More Adey: "I have been working hard in the way I thought best calculated, but I have been baffled;—and now I find I must leave for South Africa on the 11th; and shall not return for some months. The petition if finally determined upon should to have a chance of being of avail be signed very widely by literary men." The petition was, in fact, shelved for a year, and Harris vanished to South Africa.

His visit was to change his outlook radically. The reason for his hurried departure was the Jameson Raid. On January 1, Dr. Jameson, apparently in response to an appeal for help from the British women and children in Johannesburg, advanced. Harris set out to unearth the facts and discovered that the mastermind behind the affair was Cecil Rhodes. Harris had known him since 1887; correspondence shows that their views of the colonies were similar and they had enjoyed long,

[7] Robert Harborough Sherard was obsessed with Wilde and spent a substantial amount of time writing books about him and abusive pamphlets attacking his other biographers. Shaw, largely to help Nellie, who was in great financial difficulties after Frank's death, wrote a preface to Harris' *Oscar Wilde* to help promote its publication. Sherard, helped by Kingsmill, who offered to dash off and see Shaw on "his ill-advised recommendation of Harris's book," rushed into the attack and published *Oscar Wilde—Drunkard and Swindler?* and *A Reply to George Bernard Shaw* (Vindex Publishing Co., 1933), which were published in the U.S.A. in 1934 as *Oscar Wilde Twice Defended from André Gide's Wicked Lies and Frank Harris's Cruel Libels* (Argus Book Shop, Chicago). Sherard's tone is as poor, as crazy, as paranoid, his assumptions as inaccurate, as ever Harris was at his worst.

imperialistic talks together. Harris had admired Rhodes's abilities and liked him—unlike Arthur Walter, who did not, considering him a lout. Mrs. Jeune did not think much of him either; he had kept the gentlemen at her dinner table so long after the ladies had withdrawn that she had to send down several times, and it was between eleven and twelve o'clock when eventually they appeared—and then Rhodes was extremely argumentative.

Rhodes had been deeply influenced at Oxford by Ruskin, that brilliant and melancholy solitary who wandered in a dream world of passionately unconsummated love with fantasy women—the last of whom was Rose la Touche, aged nine years old. His Slade inaugural lecture in 1870 had filled Rhodes's head. It was the duty of the young men of England to go forth, Ruskin pronounced, take natives' lands, exploit them in the name of the Empire, found colonies as fast as they were able, seize every piece of fruitful waste ground.

This was precisely what Rhodes was proposing to do. South Africa's mineral wealth was enormous, while her internal situation was complicated. There was a Cape Colony, which was recognized as British and administered by the imperial government and Cecil Rhodes, and which had few minerals apart from diamonds; and there was the Boer Republic—the Transvaal—whose territory was richer both in minerals and agricultural land than any other portion of South Africa, but whose internal conditions were muddled by the large number of aliens, mainly English, who were there only to mine the mineral wealth. Rhodes had been casting his eyes toward the Transvaal and Johannesburg for some time.

Rhodes's life had hitherto been fairly tough, and it is not altogether surprising that Arthur Walter and Mrs. Jeune found his manners uncouth. At the age of seventeen his health had broken down and he had been packed off to Natal, where his brother was trying to grow cotton on land cut out from the bush. They disposed of the farm and went off to Kimberley with two spades in search of diamonds. During the long, slow journey by ox wagon, the oxen walking as if in sleep, chewing with sideways, rhythmic jaws, during the long nights when wild flesh was roasted, he dreamed of gold and diamonds, fertility and cattle. At the age of twenty-four he had a heart attack, and this helped him to form "the cause" for which he was to live. He had come across the *Pall Mall Gazette* while in Kimberley and found much about the imperialistic Stead to admire. In 1877 he had dispatched to him a document. It was his wish, he said, to make himself useful to his country: "I contend that we are the first race in the world, and that the more of the world we inhabit, the better it is for the human race." He would work for the furtherance of the British Empire, for the recovery of the United States, for the making of the Anglo-Saxon race into one empire, he would develop a secret society whose aim should be to extend the British rule throughout the world. He would be the general, over a junta of three—Stead, George Brett and Lord Milner.

Toward the end of 1895 Rhodes, it seemed, had decided that the Transvaal and Johannesburg were ready to be added to the British Empire. With this he was helped by President Kruger, who, instead of trying to turn all those Uitlanders, who had arrived in the mid-eighties during the gold rush, into contented citizens, denied them all political and municipal rights. It was clear that there could be a rising and Rhodes was determined to stimulate one. Alfred Beit, the director of the Chartered Company, would share all expenses, and the hoped-for result would be extended territory not only for the British Empire but for Rhodes himself and his companies—the Chartered Company, de Beers and the Consolidated Goldfields of South Africa.

First, Harris discovered, Rhodes had acquired a farm at Pitsani Springs—the only farm near the Transvaal border where there was water for a large number of horses and men. There he assembled a force of six hundred men, ostensibly British South African police being sorted for eventual distribution. Then on January 1, in response apparently to the desperate appeal from the Uitlander women, Dr. Leander Starr Jameson advanced. The whole maneuver, as Harris discovered, was grossly incompetent. At Pitsani the day had been one of vocal and alcoholic celebration. One trooper was sent off to Pretoria to cut the telegraph wires, but he was so drunk that he cut and buried long strands from a farmer's fence instead, so that Kruger was kept fully informed of the troop movement. The fight began on Wednesday at midday and ended in surrender on Saturday morning. A white flag—an apron borrowed from an old Hottentot nanny—was hoisted. Dr. Jameson and his officers were imprisoned, and Rhodes had a heart attack and resigned.

Much to Harris' indignation, the roles were now reversed. Where once he had supported Rhodes against the opinion of many who disliked him, most national papers, including the *Times*, fought passionately to save him and gave a good deal of space to maintaining that he was in no way implicated. It made Harris all the more indignant that his friend Walter had refused to give any space to helping Oscar Wilde—a man who had written a great play did not rank in his esteem with a man who had stolen, or had tried to steal, a piece of land from some barbarians and annex it to the Empire. From South Africa telegrams exposing Rhodes flashed almost hourly on a hot line to the office in Southampton Row. Harris' facts, accounts and interviews have all been confirmed by Chief Justice Kotze. When Elmer Gertz and A. I. Tobin were preparing their biography they wrote to Kotze, they told Vincent Brome, and received a long reply in which he substantiated virtually everything that Harris had said in the *Saturday* on the subject of South Africa. Almost at once Gertz received a second letter from Kotze, this one frantic in tone. Since writing to Gertz he had heard for the first time about *My Life and Loves* and did not wish to have his name mentioned in connection with Harris.

It was with Kotze that Harris went to interview President Kruger, who had extended an invitation for the visit to take place at six o'clock in the morning—an hour not at all to Harris' liking (he explained to the President he got up only when the day was well aired). Even with the day well aired, Kruger's parlor could raise little enthusiasm. There was a round table of the sort that one saw in British cottages and western American farmhouses, carrying the usual devotional books; there was a cluster of wax fruits under an oval glass dome, and upon the walls sugared confections of Samuel and Ruth; stiff-backed chairs stood like soldiers at mathematical distances. Kruger had been a famous athlete and was made of stern stuff. Forty years before, he had amputated his own thumb, and when visited with toothache he had prized out the sore tooth with a knife. He was a large man clad in a frock coat with what appeared to be soup stains all down the front; his clothes were of the same cut and material as those of a western Methodist minister, but dirtier and more crumpled. His complexion was unhealthy, gummy bags lay under his eyes, and before the interview could begin, he kicked open a great spittoon and spat.

All this factual reporting seems to have unnerved Harris' imagination, for thirty years later he bolted off in *My Life and Loves* on an expedition to the Victoria Falls, where we are treated to some astonishing tales of mystery and imagination, culminating in a recovery from death comparable only to the belladonna incident. His tent flap was interfered with by a lion; he fell ill from malaria and blackwater fever; was deserted by his bearers—with one of whom a baboon had fallen in love—after they had smashed the medicines and stolen everything except for one tin of soup and six of sardines. He wandered about for a month with a raging temperature, shot a hippopotamus and ate its tongue, together with berries, leaves, the sardines, a small boiled snake and a disgusting caterpillar. He traveled in a canoe to a Portuguese settlement, through which he walked carrying a kettle, so terrifying the inhabitants that they ran away. After spasm upon spasm of indigestion he returned to London.

After all these adventures, Harris claims, he was told by a well known specialist that he had only a short time to live; his heart was virtually inaudible to the specialist's practiced ear. It was at this stage, his digestion ruined by the ravages of ingesting snakes, caterpillars and sardines, that Harris says he was introduced to his famous stomach pump—the perfect toy for a hypochondriac and the perfect toy for Harris. He seems to have played happily with it for hours, peering at this and that good matter returned from the mysterious interior of his stomach. Now everything could be remedied by a good "wash-out." It was like cleaning his teeth. If he drank too much, ate too much starch or oil, he would "wash out" twice and go to bed with his stomach as clean as his teeth. Bread and butter were dangerous. Two hours or so after swallowing them he would be interested to detect a slight pain in his forehead. Ah, yes, he had indulged too freely. The pain would pass away, he would take his usual light dinner. "Four hours or so later I would wash my stomach out and suddenly the butter, eaten at lunch twelve hours before, would appear. The stomach had allowed all the rest of the lunch and dinner to pass on into the intestines, but had retained the butter to be washed out in due course."

Because of his hypochondria, Harris developed all sorts of theories and notions. His main fetish was exercise. His view was that indigestion in adults came from the fact that they did not move the middle part of their bodies enough. Accordingly he devised all sorts of exercises involving that portion. And then, as if poor digestion and lungs were not enough, he discovered that he was going bald, or, at least, he discovered a bald spot on the top of his head. It was wearing a hat, he surmised, which prevented the hairs blowing about and thus being exercised. Cleverly he thought of a substitute. He began to scratch his head, so as to excite the hairs surrounding the bald spot. Yes, that did the trick: the hairs gradually came back after six months and the baldness disappeared. But next his eyes grew dim. Soon he had contrived contortions which had his eyeballs circumnavigating the room and which proved so wonderful that in *My Life and Loves* he was able to tell us that he would at the age of seventy read for ten to twelve hours a day without experiencing any fatigue at all. Harris never recovered from South Africa. Two years later Meredith was to remark how fatal the trip had been; besides a wrecked digestion, he returned with an outlook set firmly against the Empire and an obsession with money. Money occupied his mind for the rest of his life; every now and then he would pause, take up his pen and dabble in art, but profit came first. Out there, he says, he had come to know the world of modern finance.

Soon after his return he had met Ernest Hooley, the *fin-de-siècle* millionaire. He was in the heyday of his prosperity, and all the world went, hoping to make their fortunes, to the Midland Grand Hotel, where Hooley had taken a whole floor for his offices—in all, about fifty rooms. He had started out with prospects in a Long Eaton lace factory, but had preferred to deal in millions. He claimed that he was the man who established cycling all over the world, because it was he who put Dunlop tires on the market. The year of Harris' return from South Africa Hooley had bought Papworth, a grand place sixteen miles in circumference and furnished regardless of expense by his friend Sir John Blundell Maple, containing a cellar holding £2,500 worth of cigars and £12,000 of drink; wine came from the cellar of the German Emperor, port from the King of Portugal and sherry from Buckingham Palace. The lunches he gave at the Grand Midland Hotel were world famous. Anybody who felt hungry had no need to go without a meal provided that he was decently dressed. Bedrooms and sitting rooms had been converted into small private luncheon rooms. Sometimes as many as six lunches would be going on simultaneously. Hooley would dash from room to room, having hors d'oeuvres in one, soup in another, fish in another. Once he bought the royal yacht *Britannia*, but his life was mostly spent with little recreation, buying and selling anything. From ten in the morning till six in the evening, Harris said, the Midland Grand Hotel was filled with people, while Hooley, all black beard and moustache, whisked from room to room. There would be Li Hung-chang desiring a loan of sixteen million for his imperial government; Arthur du Cros waiting to discuss the Dunlop promotion; and a singular Spaniard who had arrived with the news that sugar could be made with sea water and hoped to make a million out of his discovery. Hooley was generous and would often ask people to Monte

Carlo, causing his wife unending astonishment by constantly paying the bills of at least a dozen other people.

More and more the columns of the *Saturday* became occupied with promotions and matters of finance. Harris explains that various publishers had taken exception to the lively, constructive reviews that were being published under the new regime. The Oxford University Press had been insulted by a review published anonymously, but written by Churton Collins, pointing out that there were three hundred grave errors of fact in one of their books. Grant Richards says that often a minor contributor would want to lay out more money than usual on lunch. He would drop in and see what highly priced books had come in for review, and take a selection forthwith to a secondhand dealer. As a result important books were not reviewed, and when publishers complained they would be told in good faith that the books had not reached the editorial desk. To fill the gaps Harris hurried off not only to the Midland Grand Hotel but also to the salon of Alfred Beit, which, with its palm trees, brown rockeries and green ferns, was more like a woodland grotto than a drawing room. Alfred Beit himself seemed to have run all to head—the huge round ball appearing far too large for his little body; he had a nervous hesitating manner and a curious trick of twirling his tiny dark moustache with his right hand without actually touching it. Very soon the *Saturday*'s advertising columns were filled with advertisements for pneumatic tires, South African mining companies, horseless carriages, warehousing and railway companies. There was a funny column, something like a lonely-hearts' corner, giving advice to would-be investors. "Diogenes: The name is not quite correctly given in your letter, but sufficiently so for identification. The venture is still highly speculative, and this must be borne in mind by the purchasers." And to "Disgusted, Birmingham": "You are right. They are worthless and should be sold even at the present price." Sometimes it would explore incompetent or swindling promotions, and found fault particularly with the New Sociable Bicycle Company with their silly "Grilli" apparatus, which could transform an ordinary bicycle into a two-seater, the seats being placed side by side. "The attractions held out in connection with this invention apart from 'the pleasure of being able to talk with your companion side by side on one bicycle' are the advantages of being in a position 'To hold your umbrella, or read your book, which make it much more sociable than the tandem.' We should think so! But would it not also be possible to play cards or have a game of chess? Seriously, we cannot discuss this company from its purely financial aspect, because it is absurd to suppose that anyone would be so wildly foolish as to invest in it."

Harris claims that he was behind Hooley with the Bovril promotion, which figures a great deal in the pages of the *Saturday*. Before Hooley took over the concern the *Saturday* had complained that in their opinion the Bovril Company was not at all a well managed undertaking. Rumors circulated that Bovril was concocted from the carcasses of broken-down horses. "They very foolishly advertised their indignant denials together with a declaration that the company had only one horse in its possession—a statement which served to make their conduct more ridiculous. The same Directors hold office today, but we cannot say if the horse is still in existence."

As soon as Hooley had purchased the shares for two million pounds, Bovril miraculously changed into an excellent beverage. Doctors were unanimous in recommending it, and rapidly it was becoming a refreshing drink instead of tea, coffee and alcohol. The *Saturday*'s advice to its readers was to "apply for at least double the shares you really want." On November 21, 1896, the most splendid prospectus appeared, coming apparently directly from the pen of Harris himself for the sum of £5,000. With the help of the famous eighteenth-century cook Mrs. Hannah Glasse it set out fully the appetizing values of this delicious beef tea from the moment of catching the oxen fresh from their herbage to serving them embrothed, steaming and fragrantly nutritious. This was the first of several promotions in conjunction with Hooley, the liaison collapsing with the bankruptcy of Hooley in 1898. "Terah-rah Hool-ey-ay" was sung at the Palace Theatre,[8] and the *Daily Mail*

[8] "Terah-rah Hool-ey-ay"
I will sing the crowning care
of a certain millionaire,
To a most familiar air
(But that is neither here nor there)
He's a man of mighty fame,
For he conquered, saw and came,
He played a most gigantic game
And everyone knows his name.
Terah-rah Hool-ey-ay!
Terah-rah Hool-ey-ay!

Tear not your wool-i-ay!
Don't fret and mope-i-ay!
But live and hope-i-ay!
You may yet rule-i-ay!
Terah-rah Hooley-ay!

hinted darkly that Harris, along with some other journalists, was trying to obtain money from the Public Receiver under false pretenses.

It was partly through his dealings in speculative matters and partly through his own boasting that Harris acquired his reputation for blackmailing. There is, however, no evidence that he ever defrauded anyone. Eric Linklater, in the *House of Gair*, depicts him as a clever and calculating swindler, in league with a writer who would write a couple or so chapters describing the indiscretions of an eminent man, who in turn would pay handsomely to suppress them. Eric Linklater[9] says that he never met Harris and formed an opinion of his character from various friends' accounts. They all endorsed the fact that Harris himself took great pleasure in his own assertions of rascality; they found the impossibility of deciding whether or not they were true most exasperating. H. H. Johnston too features Harris—Bax-Strangways in the *Gay Dombeys*—as an ugly and disreputable trickster with a tremendous reputation as a lover. George Sitwell, Osbert Sitwell's father, was chairman of the board of directors of the *Saturday;* he claimed[10] that he resigned on observing that the policy of the paper was calculated solely in order to blackmail a celebrated public man—he never knew who it was.[11] Years later, after Harris' death, Lord Alfred Douglas, who by

> First his mighty Dunlop deal
> Made the world financial reel,
> But now he's got a punctured wheel,
> Which will take some time to heal.
> What a shame he doesn't stop
> After his three million "cop,"
> Schweppe's soda "proved a useful prop"
> Now, like the corks, he's gone off pop.
>
> At Bovril then he had a dash,
> But oh! Hydraulic's Joints went smash;
> And now alas! he's pushed for cash
> He really ought to make it known
> That he now wants one of his own,
> For Li Hung-chang might grant a loan
> If rung up on the telephone.

[9] Letter to the author, November 1973.

[10] Osbert Sitwell, *The Scarlet Tree.*

[11] This story still persists. In an article in 1974, in the *Sunday Times*, Frederick Raphael remembers Somerset Maugham declaring that Harris used the *Saturday* to blackmail people, which is why he was sacked.

then hated Harris, wrote to Elmer Gertz that Harris, while he was editing *Vanity Fair*, had tried to blackmail him. Douglas was editing the *Academy*, and Harris apparently sent Edgar Jepson, who was on his staff, to see him. Jepson said that he had come to tell Douglas that Harris had written an awful article about him in the next week's *Vanity Fair*; it was about the Wilde scandal and would do Douglas a great deal of harm. What was the idea of coming to tell him? Douglas wanted to know. Well, said Jepson, he thought the matter could be arranged. Douglas asked how. Jepson said that Harris was very pushed for money and he thought that a few hundred pounds might make it right. Douglas declares that he told Jepson to go back to Harris and tell him that if he published one libelous word about him he would go straight to Bow Street Station and get a warrant for his arrest. He heard no more, and no article appeared in *Vanity Fair*, and from then on Douglas attacked him in the *Academy*, poking fun at him. Harris again and again tried to make it up. Douglas claims he refused. He says that Harris got his revenge by making him the villain in *Oscar Wilde*.

Shaw, however, wrote in 1932 to defend Harris against Douglas' accusations. Harris' business morality, he said, was so American that he supposed it was possible that he regarded blackmail as a legitimate way of making money out of journalism. But Harris behaved exactly as if he knew nothing of the attempt. He took no notice of Douglas' attacks in the *Academy*, Shaw said, and was genuinely astonished and hurt by Douglas' treatment of him when he attacked him in the Café Royal. If there had been an attempt to blackmail Douglas, was Douglas quite sure, Shaw asked, that Harris knew anything about it?

Wells tells us in his autobiography that Harris' reputation for blackmailing was pure romance. " 'I'm a blackmailer,' he announced, time and again, and represented himself as a terrible wolf among financiers. Possibly he did something to justify his boasts; in later life he seems to have told Hugh Kingsmill some remarkable stories of cheques extorted and bundles of notes passing from hand to hand but manifestly in the long run it came to very little." Further on, Wells continues with his theme: "He achieved neither the wealth nor the jail that are the alternatives facing the serious blackmailer. He was far too loud and vain, far too eager to create an immediate impression to be a proper scoundrel. I have been hearing about him all my life and I have never heard convincing particulars of any actual monetary frauds." Hesketh Pearson's theory was that it was a consequence of his frankness that too much attention has been paid to dredging up possible trickeries and not enough to his liberality. During the years following Harris' death people were delighted to see him as black as he sometimes painted himself, and certain writers took advantage of this, says Pearson, implying that he was capable of extortion in its least attractive form.

It is far more likely that Harris hoped to make money not out of blackmail but out of various libel cases. Years later, in 1925, when Aleister Crowley was thinking of taking out a libel action against Lord Beaverbrook, Harris' advice was that he should find some powerful solicitor who would go halves with him and make Beaverbrook pay; in this particular case he thought there should be twenty thousand dollars to be made out of the action. This is typically one of Harris' wild financial fantasies; the libel actions that were brought while he was editing the *Saturday* made no one's fortune. The first was in 1896, when Sir Alexander Mackenzie, the principal of the Royal Academy of Music, sued the *Saturday* because of an unsigned article by John Runciman, written on January 4, 1896, which charged Mackenzie with permitting the manipulation of a scholarship "at the cesspool of academical musical life." "The *Saturday Review* seems to have changed from its old form," reported the *Musical News*. "Its once smart writing has now descended into a condition of scurrilous and very malignant criticism." Harris, in defending Runciman, blustered out excuses: he himself had been ill, he had been ordered by the doctor on a sea voyage, the *Saturday* had been in the middle of changing printers, there had been confusion because of the Jameson Raid, Runciman was "a very, very hot partisan of English music"—an opinion that the *Musical News* found "quite delicious." Damages, though Mackenzie expected £2,000, were assessed by the court at £400.

Next, in April 1897, was the case of Pennell vs. Harris and Walter Richard Sickert. Pennell claimed damages against Harris and Sickert for an article Sickert had written stating that Pennell was incorrect in his description of a particular artistic technique, thereby causing people to think that his product was commercially more valuable than it really was. William Rothenstein says that Harris had promised to support Sickert and "stood most of the racket." During the case Harris for the first time came to blows with the well known solicitors Lewis and Lewis, who acted for Pennell, publishing their letters in the *Saturday*, questioning their grammar and punctuating them liberally with *sic*'s.

"We presume that it is useless to suggest to Messrs. Lewis and Lewis that their letters should for the future be revised in the interests of good English by some competent person," he wrote on January 9, 1897. "In their letter to us of last week there was a mistake in grammar which we took to be a careless slip, and therefore passed it without comment but in the above letter it really looks as if they were unduly excited, for they outrage not only grammar but intelligibility." In spite of the corrections to Messrs. Lewis and Lewis' syntax, judgment was given for the plaintiff, Pennell, for the sum of £50.

The third case was more complicated. In 1874 John Pym Yeatman, a paranoiac lawyer, had published *A History of Common Law of Great Britain and Gaul.* The pre-Harris critic had reviewed the book on February 28, 1874: "We must honestly confess that on reading it we had not the faintest notion what it all meant, and now that we have gone more fully through the book we have, if possible, even less notion what Mr. Yeatman is trying to prove than we had before we began." Apparently Yeatman, under the impression that this article was written by a barrister, swallowed his pride and, in 1896, published *The Gentle Shakspeare: A Vindication.* Churton Collins reviewed it in an unsigned article, calling it a singular publication. Yeatman informed his readers that his book was written "but with very little preparation and with only a previous very little knowledge of the works of Shakspeare—in just three weeks." Shakespeare, he claimed, was an aristocrat, a Roman Catholic, and died mad. He quoted John of Gaunt's speech in *Richard II:* "This land of such dear souls, this dear, dear land" as "This land of such dear souls, our mother's dowry." "Our mother's dowry" appeared in huge capitals at the bottom of the page with the note: "The words printed in capitals are printed in substitution of those usually printed which Shakspeare could not have written, not only because these words are nonsense, but they are obscure and destroy the meaning of the passage." The book, said Churton Collins, was "miserable twaddle" and "an insult to literature." "It is really lamentable that it could find a publisher; a more nauseous and despicable compound of unctuous sectarian cant, bemuddlement, ignorance, dogmatism, and fatuity it has never been our unhappy lot to inspect. We implore Mr. Yeatman to . . . be dumb."

Mr. Yeatman was convinced that this article was written by a clique of barristers, that there was a barristers' campaign to persecute him through the pages of the *Saturday.* He had written to the *Saturday,* he told the court, to protest about the article, but his letter had not been published. He had quoted extracts from other articles appearing in the *Sportsman* (laughter), *News Agent* and *Vanity Fair* to demonstrate that the writer in the *Saturday* was unfit to criticize Shakespeare. He could prove that those who conducted the *Saturday* were filled personally with ill feeling toward him, since on May 8, 1897, they had published a commentary on a matter that he had attempted to bring before the whole profession of barristers at the annual meeting of the Bar Committee. "We notice without much surprise," the *Saturday* had commented, "that these gatherings at Lincoln's Inn are becoming more and more a kind of debating society for the cranks of the profession." Yeatman had decided to instruct solicitors to sue for damages. The last straw came in October 1898, when the *Saturday* referred to one of their letters: "After our first feeling of amusement on receiving the letter had subsided, we felt disposed for very pity's sake to send Mr. Yeatman a five-pound note." The jury was absent from court for ten minutes, and found that the articles in question did not exceed the bounds of fair criticism; judgment was given for the defendants. Mr. Yeatman had discovered two years after a review had appeared that it was unfair and libelous and stopped the sale of his book. What a pity he had not reversed the process and devoted the two years to writing the book and the three weeks to considering whether the review was fair! Had he done that, the review might have been more to his liking.

It was unlikely, then, that Harris made vast sums of money through either blackmail or libel cases, but there is no doubt that his time with the *Saturday* had anyway the aspect of prosperity. He was living now at Kingston, William Rothenstein recalls; every day he drove a fine, spirited horse to the office and back. Apparently so much did he admire Rothenstein's studio at Glebe Place that he invited him to Kingston with a view to rearranging the interior there. Being tired and nervous after a hard day's working—to say nothing of a hard day's talking, eating and drinking—Harris was glad, Rothenstein tells us, to hand over the reins and drive out to the green peace of Kingston Vale. He was generous with his prosperity; happily and loudly he would order on the spur of the moment beautiful things and offer money to unfortunate poets and friends. Frank Vizetelly wrote to Elmer Gertz that when he was with the *Fortnightly Review* Harris went forward and offered to bear all the expenses of Vizetelly's divorce trial—Queen's Proctor vs. Vizetelly. Unfortunately, especially later, when the beautiful things were ready, the poets and friends eagerly awaiting their presents, Harris would find that a certain speculation had come to grief, that his financial position was not so strong as he thought, and he was very sorry, but after all . . . William Rothenstein has a story that illustrates his spontaneous generosity perfectly. Arnold Dolmetsch had made an exquisite clavichord, with a keyboard painted by Helen Combe. Runciman brought Frank to see it and he seemed really moved by its beauty. He boomed and bellowed enthusiasm, wanting at once to possess it, and hearing that it had been specially commissioned, he insisted that Dolmetsch make a similar instrument for him. Some months afterward, when the clavichord was ready, Harris' enthusiasm had cooled. For a moment he wanted to get out of his bargain; then, in his impulsive way, he gave the instrument to Runciman.

Harris has not really been given credit for the number of times he was generous to Wilde[12] during the last years of his life—although the occasion when he withdrew an offer of financial help has often been broadcast. In June 1896, when Harris had returned from South Africa and was struggling with his own health, news came through that Wilde's condition was deteriorating. "I saw him [F.H.] yesterday," Adela Schuster wrote to More Adey on June 7, "and he promised he would do all I asked in a fortnight or 3 weeks time—till then he had not a moment." The idea was to approach some doctors and secure their opinion that it was dangerous for Wilde to stay in prison. If necessary, More Adey believed that they should "buy" the option, a measure Adela Schuster felt might be a false step. She put her faith in Harris, believing that the eloquently expressed opinion of a clever man might move even the doctors. Two days later she wrote again to give a progress report. The Home Secretary was to be approached by two different persons; "other steps are being taken also by Mr. Harris, who however is quite broken down by illness, and not able to do much. Would you send me *at once* the names of any very respectable and well known people, *who would not mind* their names being mentioned to the Home Secretary, as being anxious for O's release."

Harris now went off to see Sir Evelyn Ruggles-Brise, the head of the Prison Commission, described by Harris as a compassionate and intelligent man, who, according to him, was asked to draw up a special report on Wilde. Certainly he succeeded in rousing Ruggles-Brise's

---

12 Rupert Hart-Davis, in his edition of Wilde's *Letters*, does mention his generosity.

anxiety, for on June 13, 1896, it is revealed by the Home Office files that an order was granted for Mr. Frank Harris to have an interview with Wilde—in sight, but not within hearing, of an officer. To the order is fixed a note from Ruggles-Brise: Would the governor of Reading Prison be good enough to report confidentially and as soon as possible the mental condition of Oscar Wilde? To which the medical officer replied that the prisoner's condition was perfectly satisfactory and had been for all the time that he was in prison. Harris' account was not so satisfactory. Wilde appeared older and thinner, his hair streaked with gray. His description of life in prison was distressing. The bad ventilation, the foul-smelling dark cells, the diet of bread, water and coarse Indian meal, the lack of books and occupation, the isolation and harshness caused even the most hardened man to have diarrhea and delusions; for Oscar it was very nearly unbearable. Eventually he became so weak, with abscesses of the ear, that he was admitted to the prison hospital.

On July 2 a petition from Wilde himself was forwarded to the Home Office by the governor of Reading Prison. A visiting committee of five men—Cobham, Thursby, Palmer, Hunter and Hay—went off to Reading and on July 10 reported in much the same terms as the medical doctor: Wilde had put on weight in prison and showed no signs of insanity. Ruggles-Brise, however, was plainly not satisfied, and this could only have been the result of his talk with Harris. On July 15 he suggested that an independent medical inquiry should be made. Shortly after this the Home Office ordered the governor to allow Wilde light, writing materials and books in his cell. Although there is no evidence to support Harris' claim that he visited both Wilde and Sir Evelyn Ruggles-Brise again on November 21, there is no doubt that he was at this time working on a petition. Ruggles-Brise, Harris said, believed that if a petition were got up, signed by men of letters, asking the Home Office to release Wilde for his health's sake, it could diminish Wilde's sentence by three or four months. Harris was confident of getting Meredith's signature at once; after that the rest would follow. But a telegram dispatched from Harris in Torquay to Adela Schuster informed her that Meredith would not sign.

Although Frank applied for permission to visit Wilde again in the middle of January, taking with him Charles Ricketts the artist, Wilde —much to Harris' pain—preferred to see More Adey on legal business, and he did not see him again until April 7, just before Wilde was due to be released. Then he went to him with an invitation to go on a driving tour to the Pyrenees. "When I saw him he was most cordial and friendly," Wilde wrote to More Adey on May 12, 1897, "told me he had made a very large sum of money—some £23,000 in South Africa—and that he had come to put his cheque-book at my disposal. I was greatly touched, I admit, at his spontaneous and unsolicited kindness, and told him that if I were set free from money anxieties I thought I could produce some good art. He said he had come for the purpose of doing so, and would send me a cheque for £500 before my release. . . . I now learn he has sent a verbal message through you to say he is very sorry but cannot do it." Here had been one of Harris' grand gestures, and then when the time came near to paying, affairs were none too steady. He had the anxiety of standing "the racket" over the Pennell libel case, he had just invested heavily in Schweppes—an investment that was to end disastrously with Hooley's bankruptcy—and there was, perhaps, the Dolmetsch clavichord ready for delivery. Very understandably, Wilde was devastated. His bankruptcy and his terrible time in prison had, not surprisingly, made him neurotic about money and paranoid. Locked up in his isolation, it seemed to him that not only had Harris failed him, but so had everyone else. After he came out of prison he would play one friend off against another, telling one that the other had not paid a penny to help him, and vice versa, when his pockets held substantial sums from both. That last month in prison he was worried and bitter, convinced that all were out to swindle him. He quivered, he said, in every nerve with pain. He was wracked with recurring tides of hysteria. He could neither eat nor sleep. He accused Harris of blowing lying trumpets, and as for an excursion to the Pyrenees, nothing would induce him to go.

> I hardly suppose he expects it [he continued to More Adey]. Would you kindly write to him that you gave me his message and that I was a good deal distressed, as I had unfortunately received similar messages from everyone else who had been kind enough to promise me money, and that I find myself in such a painful and parlous state as regards my finances that I could not think of any pleasant pleasure excursion such as he has proposed till I had in some way settled my affairs and seen a possible future. This will end the driving-tour, and there is nothing in the message that could hurt his feelings. It is the secret of his success, just as the fact that he thinks that other people have none either is the secret of his

failure that lies in wait for him somewhere on the way of Life. . . .
I loathe the promise makers. . . . I have nothing but contempt for
them. The Frank Harrises of life are a dreadful type. I hope to see
no more of them.

This passage has often been quoted to illustrate what a cad Harris
was. But previous writers on Harris have failed to point out how bitter
and egocentric Wilde was, and how everyone else came in for equally
vituperative attacks. It is also not indicated that Harris' financial affairs
improved toward the end of May and that Wilde wrote to him from the
Hôtel Sandwich in Dieppe: "Just a line to thank you for your great
kindness to me, for the lovely clothes, and for the generous cheque.
You have been a real good friend to me, and I shall never forget your
kindness: to remember such a debt as mine to you—a debt of kind
fellowship—it is a pleasure."[13]

In fact, Harris' feelings had been extremely hurt when Wilde had
chosen not to go on the driving tour with him, and it also came to
Wilde's ears that he had made a great scene over the letter from the
Hôtel Sandwich, saying that it was not "sufficiently elaborate in
expression."

"This I can hardly credit," Wilde wrote off to him on June 13 from
Berneval.

> It seems so unworthy of a big strong nature like yours, that
> knows the realities of life. I told you I was grateful to you for your
> kindness to me. Words, *now*, to me signify *things*, actualities, real
> emotions, realised thoughts. I learnt in prison to be grateful. . . .
> But I cannot say more than I am grateful. I cannot make phrases
> about it. For *me* to use such a word shows an enormous develop-
> ment in my nature. . . . But I must say again that I no longer make
> roulades of phrases about the deep things I feel. When I write to
> you I speak directly. Violin-variations don't interest me. I am grate-
> ful to you. If that does not content you, then you do not under-
> stand, what you of all men should understand, how sincerity of

---

[13] Sherard claims that this letter is a forgery; he would have nothing else and refused
to listen to Reginald Turner, who had seen the original. "In this letter supposed to have
been written from the Sandwich Hotel in Dieppe . . . he [Wilde] is represented as
thanking Harris for 'his great kindness' to him 'for the lovely clothes and for the
generous cheque.' Anyone inclined to doubt that this letter is sheer forgery is invited to
compare it to a letter as to the authenticity of which there is no possible doubt which
was written just at this time by Wilde to More Adey"—and he quotes the letter written
to More Adey on May 12.

feeling expresses itself. But I dare say the story told of you is untrue. It comes from so many quarters that it probably is. I am told also that you are hurt because I did not go on the driving-tour with you. You should understand that in telling you that it was impossible for me to do so, I was thinking as much of *you* as of myself. . . . If I had gone with you, you would not have been happy, nor enjoyed yourself. Nor would I. You must try to realise what two years' cellular confinement is, and what two years of absolute silence means to a man of my intellectual power. . . . I have now no *storage* of nervous force. . . . Had I gone with you on the driving-tour, where we would have of necessity been in immediate contact with each other from dawn to sunset, I would have certainly broken off the tour the third day, probably broken down the second. You would have found yourself in a painful position: your tour would have been arrested at its outset; your companion would have been ill without doubt; perhaps might have needed care and attendance in some little remote French village. You would have given it to me, I know. But I felt it would have been wrong, stupid, and thoughtless of me to have started an expedition doomed to swift failure. . . . You are a man of dominant personality; your intellect is exigent, more so than that of any man I ever knew; your demands on life are enormous; you require response, or you annihilate. The pleasure of being with you is the clash of personality, the intellectual brain, the war of ideas. To survive you one must have a strong brain, an assertive ego, a dynamic character. In your luncheon parties, in the old days, the remains of the guests were taken away with the *debris* of the feast. I have often lunched with you in Park Lane and found myself the only survivor. I might have driven on the white roads, or through the leafy lanes of France with a fool, or with the wisest of all things, a child; with you it would have been impossible.

Harris, however, continued to sulk into the autumn and winter of 1897 and "be so offensive to me and about me that I don't think negotiations possible with him," Oscar told Leonard Smithers on October 19, when they were trying to get *The Ballad of Reading Gaol* published. By March of the following year, however, Wilde, from Paris, was negotiating for a little more money: "You have been so good and generous to me that I hate to have to ask you to be generous again. But I am entirely without money, and if you could let me have £5 you would be doing me a great kindness. . . . I long to see you here, and to have the dinner you asked me to at *Reading*." The money was evidently dispatched with all briskness, for on March 7 Wilde was writing a well buttered letter: "Just a line to thank you for your generosity, and the sweet way in which you make your generosity dear to one. Many can do acts of kindness, but to be able to do them without wounding those who are helped in their trouble is given only to a few, to a few big, sane, large natures like yours. I long to see you and catch presence and power from your personality."

CHAPTER 12

Between France and Putney

THE dinners—and plenty of them —came later that year. Meanwhile literature was once more exercising Harris' mind. In March he had published the first of his articles on Shakespeare, "The True Shakespeare: An Essay in Realistic Criticism," which continued in ten parts through the spring and summer and on which he was to work intermittently for the next ten years. It was a series that he used again and again, both in print and in lectures, and which eventually became *The Man Shakespeare*. No doubt, although he hardly mentions it, he was stimulated by the publication, on February 26, of Dr. Brandes' book.[1] The attitude toward Shakespeare at this time was adoration of an unknown god. There was a spate of books coming out on this enigmatic deity, including John Pym Yeatman's "miserable twaddle." But Harris' (and Brandes') idea was that Shakespeare the man could be found in Hamlet and Macbeth and in a thousand different ways. Harris tells us that he started with the assumption that the deepest psychological study of any writer was one in which he necessarily revealed most of his own nature. He took Hamlet, in Shakespeare's case, and began by proving that Romeo and Jaques were preliminary sketches of Hamlet. Next he proceeded to prove that when Shakespeare wrote *Macbeth* he unconsciously pictured

[1] *William Shakespeare: A Critical Study*, translated by William Archer and Mary Morison with the assistance of Diana White (London, Heinemann, 1898).

Hamlet again in the character of Macbeth, though everyone until his time had taken Macbeth for a rude, barbarous, Scottish thane. Harris discovered that he was merely the gentle, humane poet masquerading in galligaskins. He went on to show a dozen other characters in which Shakespeare fell into the Hamlet vein and so revealed his own nature.

From the theory that Shakespeare was to be found in Hamlet, Macbeth, and a dozen other characters Harris eventually progressed to the discovery that he himself was to be seen there also, that Shakespeare was exactly like himself. For the poet, in Harris' play *Shakespeare and His Love*, published in 1910, is conceived as a broken-hearted melancholic, enormously sentimental, and is presented with pathetic tenderness—tragic, bitter, pitiable, wretched and broken among a robust crew of Jonsons and Elizabeths.

That June 1898 Meredith wrote to Harris—just a gentle chiding. His start in fiction had been excellent, but he came to "the stop abrupt." Why? The course had been clearly marked for him to take the lead. Meredith had not seen the Shakespeare papers, he said, but he doubted if they would satisfy him in comparison with his expectation of Harris' work to come; South Africa seemed to have been a fatal gap. Perhaps Meredith played a small part in Harris giving up the *Saturday*. Various reasons have been suggested, one of Harris' own being that he wanted to devote more time to writing. Ill health of the editor was the general one. "The *Saturday Review* has had many brilliant pens at its disposal but seldom one so brilliant as that of our retiring editor," announced the *Saturday Review* on November 26. "We hope that a better climate will restore him to health." Kingsmill's view was that trouble arose over Harris' attitude to Sir Alfred Milner. On April 24, 1897, Harris, the great expert on South African affairs, had published in the *Saturday* an open letter to Milner on his appointment as governor in South Africa. It was arrogant in tone. "I am merely going to talk to you about yourself, your new position and prospects, and if I happen incidentally to give you some advice, I ask your pardon. . . . Did I know you better, I might be seduced into telling you of the various faults and shortcomings which intimacy had discovered in you; but as it is you will be spared that amiable privilege of an old friendship. I am concerned rather with your personality and if I touch upon your talents or your training it will be because of the great colony you are called upon to govern." Harris went on to exhort Milner to do his best; he had to win Mr. Chamberlain to politeness, President Kruger to trust, and keep the

peace between the Boers and the British. "Look to it, Sir," he concluded, "you have a great, a unique opportunity. Everyone in England
is wondering whether in you Oxford has at length produced a great
man or only another commoner who wins a pension by obsequiousness
and a peerage by time-serving." A year later, in June, Harris found
himself dissatisfied with Milner's conduct and wrote that he would soon
have to come home, "and we doubt if he will speedily find another
Egypt to restore his lost credit." This attitude in an important Conservative weekly toward the government's difficulties in South Africa,
explained Kingsmill, was extremely embarrassing to Chamberlain.
Harris was approached by Lord Hardwicke and asked if he would sell
his shares in the *Saturday Review*. He agreed, but after the transaction was completed, Rhodes and Beit, who were supplying the purchase money, learned that Harris still possessed 500 deferred shares,
which gave him the control of the editorship and staff of the paper.
They had little choice except to ask Harris what he required for the
deferred shares. Under their supervision it was announced on November 26, the same issue in which Harris' departure was reported, that
"the wiseacres and panic-mongers will have it that Sir Alfred Milner
has been summoned home by Mr. Chamberlain to confer on a crisis. . . .
There is really no crisis in South Africa at this moment."

Frank himself claims that, among other reasons, he gave up the
Saturday for money. "Excuse this pencil-scrawl," he wrote to Shaw on
November 30, 1898, "but my nerves won't stand the slooping that
pen-and-ink demand. . . . You ask me why I gave up the pulpit. First
because they (The True Blue Conservatives) offered me more for that
antique object d'art than it was worth. Secondly because I *needed* the
money, thirdly because I wanted nerve-rest, fourthly because following
your example I want to try my hand at books and plays and stuff more
enduring than articles." According to A. A. Baumann,[2] when the purchasers of the *Saturday Review* came to look into their assets they
found that all was not well. The chief advertisers in the paper were
the Café Royal, a carriage builder in Bond Street and a firm of gun-
makers in South Audley Street. All these owed considerable amounts
for advertising. On inquiring, the directors were told that Mr. Harris
had a large unpaid bill for luncheons and dinners at the Café Royal
and they had agreed to pay themselves by advertisements; the coach-

[2] Grant Richards' introduction to *Frank Harris: His Life and Adventures.*

maker explained that Mr. Harris had bought a brougham and victoria for which he had not paid, that the advertisements were being set off against the bill; the gunmaker had just sold Mr. Harris a pair of guns . . . Baumann himself was a director, so he knew.

Harris' domestic arrangements during 1898 are puzzling. It seems that he was running two ménages—one in Saint-Cloud with an actress called May Congden, with whom, according to her granddaughter, he lived about a year,[3] the other in Roehampton in a house called Lime-hurst with Nellie O'Hara, who, according to information she gave to various authorities in later life, was eleven years old, and with whom Harris lived for the rest of his life. Sometime during the year he added to his establishments by purchasing the Palace Hotel in Monaco, for which he had grand schemes, proposing to make his fortune. Judging from the amount of time that he spent in Paris entertaining Wilde, it was the Saint-Cloud ménage that seems to have claimed most of his attention.

In April, at Foyot's restaurant, Wilde had introduced him to Henri Davray, who was to remain a lifelong friend and who was to translate Kipling's works and Harris' *My Life and Loves*. "Frank Harris was most hospitable and nice to me here," Wilde wrote to Robert Ross in July 1898. "I dined with him every night, except one. . . . One night I made Frank Harris invite Bosie to dinner. We dined at Maire's, the bill was terrific. . . . Runciman and Mrs. Harris (No. 2) were of course present. Frank was wonderful on the subject of the Greek passions of Christ and Shakespeare—especially Christ. He insisted that the betrayal by Judas was the revenge of a great lover discarded for 'that sentimental beast John.' "

Wilde's words "Mrs. Harris (No. 2)" afford some interest, since there is no evidence as to which Mrs. Harris he means—May Congden, who would at the time have been seven months' pregnant, or Nellie O'Hara, according to her 1920's passport, aged eleven. Wilde the following year mentions "your charming wife," but again there is no evidence of which one he knew. Lord Alfred Douglas claims that Harris had lived with Nellie as early as 1894, but this is highly unlikely: there are no letters covering this time—and she would apparently have been seven.

On September 3 Frances Mary was born to May Congden and

<hr>

[3] Verbal evidence from Dr. Teresa Hankey.

Frank Harris. Her father seems to have selected the sophisticated pleasures of Paris and Wilde rather than the domesticity of her nursery; and then, closing his affairs at the *Saturday Review*, he vanished to the fogs of Roehampton, whence he wrote to Shaw in November: "The longing for sunshine I feel in me gives me a sort of unspoken promise of renewed health." In December he returned to wine and dine with Wilde, making it a point, according to Douglas, of taking Wilde to Durand's, which was a haunt of British Embassy people. "We have dined and lunched together every day at Durand's," Wilde wrote to Robert Ross on December 14. "At least I lunch at one o'clock, and dine at eight o'clock. Frank arrives at 2.30 and 9.15. It is rather a bore, and no one should make unpunctuality a formal rule, and degrade it to a virtue, but I have admirable, though lonely, meals. Frank insists on my being always at high intellectual pressure; it is most exhausting; but when we arrive at Napoule I am going to break the news to him—now an open secret—that I have softening of the brain and cannot always be a genius." There in Napoule Wilde saw himself among the petals and perfumes of southern flowers, the gold dust of the sun, by the sapphire wall of the sea. There Harris intended to spend the beginning of 1899 writing his book on Shakespeare and supervising the renovations at the Palace Hotel in Monte Carlo. Wilde, it was thought, in the peace and charming climate, his financial worries erased, would himself be able to produce a chef d'oeuvre. But instead of escorting Wilde to Napoule in December, Harris was seen rushing "express rate into the unknown." "I myself thought that you might have been summoned to London on business," Wilde wrote to him, "or that you were flying from Runciman. I am charmed to know that it was love and affection that made you take wings"—although after which bird he was flying we do not know.

What had happened was that May Congden wanted to leave Harris, Saint-Cloud and Frances Mary, who was, according to her daughter, a sickly baby with rickets. Her grounds for departing were that Harris' smart, well known friends were not taking her seriously and she wished to advance her acting career. Harris apparently did not want her to leave, but nothing would change her mind. In England, with the cooperation of May Congden's mother, Frank set up his daughter in a farmhouse in the care of a friend, who herself had had an illegitimate son. Here Frances lived for three years, endowed with £8,000 by Harris to be invested in order to support her.

Wilde meanwhile had advanced to Napoule. Everyone there was anxiously awaiting the arrival of Harris, who was expected to be something of a regenerator of the place. Wilde, mildly bored, wandered among aromatic pinewoods and over porphyry rocks and wrote off fretful letters to his friends. "Your coming is anxiously waited for by the hotel proprietor, and by the worthy Ribot, who wants to place his son, a nice youth of seventeen, in the Palace Hotel to learn his *métier*," he told Frank. "Ribot is anxious to place on the porphyry rocks by the sea small glass-walled pavilions for eating oysters in! I told him you would not allow it."

By February 2 the public anxiety was somewhat assuaged. Harris had arrived, having apparently been to Corsica, and was safely "upstairs thinking about Shakespeare at the top of his voice." It was a pleasant life, the days supposed to be spent writing, the evenings talking and drinking quantities of wine, Wilde was able to grumble away contentedly to his friends. "Frank Harris is of course exhausting," he wrote to Reginald Turner on February 3. "After our literary talk in the evening I stagger to my room, bathed in perspiration. I believe he talks the Rugby game." Harris was always restless, never able to stay in one place for long. He lasted only until February 15, and dashed off again, sending Wilde, penniless, to the Hôtel Terminus in Nice with instructions to find him a villa. This soon led to financial disaster for Wilde. "You were kind enough to promise me three months on the Riviera," he wrote off, "and I have had two of them, and since I arrived you have given me £30. Do let me have £20 now, and I shall go off to Switzerland on the 1st: full of pleasant memories of your great kindness, and of our charming evenings together. But, for goodness sake, send at once."

And Harris, who was in London struggling with the John Pym Yeatman libel case, did send at once, for on February 18 Wilde was writing: "Many many thanks for your enclosure and letter. . . . I hope you don't really think that I had forgotten about the money you so kindly gave me in Paris, but that I spent before coming down in paying my hotel and other bills. I was only alluding to what you had given me since our arrival, nine weeks ago. And I trust you don't think I have rushed you too much, or been recklessly extravagant." Four days later Wilde was again in financial distress and obliged to travel to Monte Carlo to see Frank, having raised ten francs on his ring for the journey. He had been unable to leave the Nice hotel, since he could not pay the bill; he had been forced to have his meals *table d'hôte;* and the "middle-class English" who were in the hotel had objected to his presence.

"You have not forgotten that you invited me to spend three months on the Riviera as your guest," he wrote to Harris around February 22. "My bill at Napoule for eight weeks amounted to £35, of which you gave me £30, and I cannot think that it was very extravagant of me. The choice of Napoule was yours, and £4 a week is not very extravagant. Of course at Nice it is different. My bill is forty francs a day at the hotel. You asked me to go there and to look out for a villa for you. My one anxiety has been to leave the place, but I have not been able. Now I am turned out, and everyone at the hotel knows it. My dear Frank . . . you cannot, and you will not abandon me . . ."

By March 1, however, he was safely away to Switzerland, staying with Harold Mellor, and on March 19 was writing to know if Harris would allow him to dedicate *An Ideal Husband* to him. Harris would; the dedication reads: "To Frank Harris / a slight tribute to / his power and distinction / as an artist / his chivalry and nobility / as a friend."

But Harris' complications at this time seem, anyway in retrospect, to have been too much for him. He tells us that he took a house in San Remo, where, he boasts, astonishing orgies took place. He conjures up a picture of himself earnestly reading Dante in the garden and writing his Shakespeare on Monday, Tuesday, Thursday, Friday and Saturday, with Wednesdays and Sundays set aside for pleasure. With the cooperation of the Italian gardener, this recreation was a sort of beauty contest, with prizes offered by Harris and the gardener for the prettiest of the young local virgins, who were obliged to strip naked and flutter prettily about the room and the bed before submitting to a champagne luncheon. So delightful and successful, Harris said, were these orgies that he had peers and younger sons traveling from Monte Carlo especially for their delights. The number of girls grew weekly until a certain lord and the gardener were enjoying a bevy of twenty of them. There were all kinds of novelties too for those who liked variation: naked bathing, whipping, dildoes. Douglas claims that this all went on at the Palace Hotel in Monte Carlo and the Cesari Réserve at Eze; that Harris boasted about seducing young girls—children of thirteen and twelve—at Eze and any place that he could get hold of them. Douglas had heard him say, while he was with him in Monte Carlo, that he cared for only very young girls. Thomas Bell, his secretary over these years, dismisses this. He did think that he recognized in the Italian gardener a character something like the Italian gardener of the Cesari Réserve at Eze, a jolly fellow with whom Harris would pass a few rough jokes. But, says Bell, during the years he knew him Harris seemed a totally ordinary person, in his middle age, given to hard work and new schemes for making fortunes, more concerned about his health and his dinner than love affairs. The picture of the gay dog full to the brim with physical vigor, roving round recklessly after women, plunging from one voluptuous adventure to another, magnificently virile, was ridiculously different from the Harris that he knew: Harris the hypochondriac, always looking at his tongue, trying his weight, swallowing a soda, groaning about his bronchitis, raising a scene because his shirt had been aired before the fire only ten minutes. Douglas' account, he believed, arose because of Harris' boasting and because of what he called Harris' "rough talk." Besides, if he had been seducing and purchasing young girls, it would have come to the "ears of someone else," a person of "great importance" (presumably Alice). All through his correspondence to Elmer Gertz he hints about this person—in fact, there were, he said, two people: "I dare not tell you about them."

In "Oscar Wilde Without Whitewash" Thomas Bell supplied a full description of Harris' business matters at Eze and Monte Carlo.

In London, sometime about the end of 1898, I replied to an advertizment calling for an accountant who spoke French fluently, to fill a temporary job in the South of France. In accordance with an appointment I presented myself at a stockbroker's office in Queen Victoria Street. The advertizer, name unknown to me, was a middle-aged man, rather under the average height, well and strongly built and well set-up, a handsome man, with an intelligent face, his broad nose just the least little bit up-tilted, over a mustache. Dressed in the style of a city business man, but richly, with a fur-lined overcoat, he wore a great deal of jewelry and carried a gold-headed cane. A distinguished-looking man, one evidently quite sure of himself, walking with a little swagger. His voice when he spoke to me I noted as one of the most musical and resonant I had ever heard, carefully cultivated, no doubt. His accent was perhaps a little less than usual of the drawl. His manner was courteous and pleasant.

He spoke to me in French. Excellent French. His pronunciation of the è and of the au clear and distinct, not the English diphthongs. Fortunately, my own French was then still very good. Did I know Paris? Which of the Boulevards did I remember? Had I been sometimes to the Louvre? Did I know the Beaux-Arts? When had I acquired my French? I told him that I had spent a year in Paris when I was a young fellow and that I had spoken French well before I went there. Had I ever listened to lectures at the Sorbonne? They were fine , eh? Yes I had thought so. Had I ever been to the Côte d'Azur? No.

I had handed him some testimonials from former employers, and he noticed that they spoke of my German and my Spanish as well as my French, so he changed over to German. His German seemed to me perfect. My own was only just passable and I was not much of a judge but his German at any rate was very good indeed. He told me that he had lived in Germany when he was young, in Berlin, and Munich and also in Vienna. . . . When he shifted over to Spanish, however, it was evident to me at once that he had only a very little of it. He spoke in the Castilian way. He told me that he had only as much as was needed to take him on a trip through Spain.

By this time I was beginning to feel more at my ease. I had been very nervous when I came in. . . . But he was talking to me now in such a very pleasant, friendly and democratic way—and in such an intelligent way—that I took courage and told him honestly where I had perfected my Spanish—on the Texas border and all over Mexico. Indeed! He himself had been on the other side for some years—New York, Chicago, Colorado, Kansas. He complimented me on both my French and Spanish: that was the way to learn a language—to go where it was spoken. As he was now plainly interested I warmed up still more and told him of having no difficulty with Portuguese in East Africa and even of being able to follow the Taal at the Cape. He was still more interested; he too had been in South Africa. . . . He was talking freely now and he was evidently very well informed both as to the languages he spoke of and as regards the countries in which they were used. "The Taal, but that is not proper Dutch as it is spoken in Holland; it is just a kind of jargon?" Yes, I told him, it was a simplified Dutch with some English and a few native words; but I confessed, I read the European Dutch too. "Well, why don't you tell of these things; your letter speaks only of French; is it modesty?" No, I repudiated the modesty; it was because of my conviction that most employers did not care to take on a man who knew much more than they happened to require. Yes he supposed I was right, but for his part he never would be grumbling at that. He talked for a while still of Dutch and its close relationship to English, and of Frisian even closer. Somehow or other we got round to Chaucer. Did I know Skeat? Why, yes. Grimm's Law? Yes, I knew it. Had I ever heard this language? I listened, and then told him that I had read Dante in the original, though I would not undertake to converse in Italian. How about this one? He gave me a piece of great rolling syllables, splendidly delivered, which I took to be Homer, but which I had to tell him sorrowfully was all Greek to me.

With both of us laughing at this talk which had so little to do with the job I was after, languages were at last dismissed. What he wanted me for, he explained, was to go to Monte Carlo to investigate the finances of a hotel he had there and still more to investigate a new venture he had made at a place called Eze, halfway between Nice and Monte Carlo. The man in charge of them, Mr. Cesari, was an able man all right; but it seemed strange that he had to press so constantly for money and his letters did not seem to explain. I was to go into the situation and report. He gave me the money for my fares and expenses—I was to stay at the hotel —complimented me once more on my accents and linguistic ability, shook hands with me heartily and told me his name was Harris.

I went away very pleased. I liked him very much indeed. He seemed to me more like the best type of American employer than the usual British one; British employers are more reserved, fuss more about their dignity; this Harris talked man to man. I was flattered by the way he had accepted me; he had not asked about my accounting at all; he had not put me off to see anybody else but had taken me at once; he had handed me the money without troubling about inquiries. He was evidently a fine linguist and undoubtedly a very intelligent man; I could never be comfortable with a stupid employer; this time I seemed to be in luck.

During the six years that Bell was Harris' secretary he liked, respected and admired him, and worked for him with great pleasure; each of them, he believes, developed quite an affection for the other. Often they quarreled, had violent rows and angry breaks, but when things quietened down, Harris would show up at Bell's house with a jovial grin on his face and an outstretched hand and they would start again. Later Bell was to depose Harris as an arrant liar. But there was no lying during these six years, he said. He did not recall Harris on any occasion lying to him. He describes what was happening in the south of France after his interview that winter of 1898.

Well, I went off then to Monte Carlo. There I presented myself to Mr. Cesari and next day drove out with him to the new venture at Eze.

At one time the only road between Nice and Monte Carlo was by the famous "Corniche"—the cornice running along the mountain tops on a magnificently picturesque route high above the sea. It was originally a military road built by Napoleon to give him ready access to Italy, and he had built it away up there instead of down along by the sea shore partly to keep his troops out of gunshot of British ships and partly because the shore route was blocked by rocky promontories over which there would be too much climbing up and down. But in the course of time the railroad pierced these promontories by tunnels, and a while after that a carriage road paralleling it was finally pushed through.

Harris, with his American experience of how values go up when the road goes through, was early on the spot. He found on the east side of a little bay called the *Petite Afrique* (because of being so well sheltered by the mountain behind it tropical fruits like bananas ripen there) a little cape which took his fancy. It was being used most of it as a place on which to keep pigs. But it was in a lovely situation, with glorious views on both sides, just the place, he saw, for some sort of resort, some half-way house in which the rich tourists driving along the coast by the new road between Nice and Monte Carlo would stop for *déjeuner*.

It is generally quite difficult to acquire a piece of land there. A death means always that the land belonging to the deceased is divided up into still smaller pieces, and these smaller pieces at that have generally mortgages attached to them and often the claims of minor children making things so complicated that the would-be buyer drops the matter in despair. Here at this place there were two different pieces to be acquired. Harris, however had overcome these difficulties. He had acquired the ground, cleared off the pigs, planted the slope and built on the point a "Réserve," that is to say a high class restaurant with several apartments attached; and with a tank at the side cut out of the rock, where with the sea washing in, a supply, a "reserve," of live fish was retained.

The slope down from the road was laid out in the most beautiful fashion; the guests descending passed through groves of flowers and fruit trees, picking their own oranges on the way, passed on to the tank and selected the fish to be served to them at *déjeuner*. The idea was excellent. The design was good—except for one point, the architect, a southern Frenchman, had made no provision whatever for warming up the restaurant. True, that, as a rule, did not matter in sunshine of the Riviera, but when it did matter it mattered a lot. The guests complained bitterly that however good the food they could not enjoy it with cold fingers. With that one exception, however, the job seemed to me a strikingly successful one.

When Cesari told me that it had cost only £7,000 I congratulated him warmly. But my job consisted, of course, in an examination of the accounts; and at the end of a week's delving, alas, I had to tell Cesari that the place had cost not £7,000 but £14,000! Cesari had evidently kept track of the cost mainly by figuring the checks he had actually paid out; almost oblivious to the accounts not yet rendered. He was a perfectly honest man, a splendid *maître d'hôtel*, a man of excellent taste and judgement in all that related to the trade, but he was certainly no business man.

The situation at the Cesari Palace Hotel, Monte Carlo, was worse—much worse. The hotel was indeed quite close to the Casino—but in a back street with nothing but a street view from the front windows and an alley view from the side. People come to Monte Carlo not merely for the gambling but because it is one of the loveliest places in Europe. And people to whom money is no particular object—the class to whom the hotel was to cater—did not care for the idea of coming to Monte Carlo to look out on nothing but a street or an alley. Cesari in taking over the building had spent many thousands of pounds on altering the interior. He had practically reconstructed the interior and it was indeed palatial, quite magnificent. But it did not require any great knowledge of business principles to see that in doing that he had blundered—in spending thousands of pounds on the alteration of a building held only *on lease*. I found him still full of confidence that he could make it go: but my own impression was that only in very good seasons when the other hotels were full could he hope to make it pay. A good deal of Harris's money was evidently already lost.

. . . Harris, in receiving my report was thoroughly awakened. He hastened out to the Riviera himself, checked things over with me, at first much alarmed and very angry, but in the long run recognizing that the fault had been his own. At the Réserve the money had not been thrown away. Cesari had made a few mistakes, of course. It was hardly worthwhile putting in such a splendid parquetry floor if it was going to be hidden by equally expensive rugs. It had been foolish to spend so much in blasting out a place for a stable up the hillside when the carriages might just as well have parked in the yard below while the drivers were kept in good humour by a good lunch and a bottle of good wine. The money put in levelling and building up the little cape in front had been already washed into the sea by the first big storm.

But on the whole, at Eze, Cesari had obtained good value; and his taste was very fine; the prospects were as good as ever; the only trouble was that now more capital was required, because even with the £14,000 the job was not finished. (Ultimately £21,000 was put into the place.) So Harris promised to put in more money, when he got it. He was just a little short at that moment. I had the job wished upon me of dealing with the creditors. I had gone off from London on a job which was to last only three weeks—it lasted six years.

But in the month we spent in Monte Carlo, Harris and I got better acquainted. We had taken to each other from the first, though I did not know yet really who he was. The man in the fur-lined coat, with rings on his fingers, gold-headed cane in hand, gold chains on his waistcoat, whom I had met in a stockbroker's office, had looked to me at first a typical successful business man. But I had noted from the first that the business man could talk literature in a fashion quite beyond any business man I had ever met before.

He began talking with me about literature one afternoon while we stood waiting for something at the Réserve: "You told me that you read Dutch; did you find anything worth reading in it?" I had in reality read one author only, Dekker. "Dekker, Dekker, Dekker? ah, that's Multatuli; is it not?" Yes, Dekker wrote under the name of Multatuli; but I was very much surprised, it seemed to me extraordinary that he a London business man should know of Multatuli—who was then and still is almost unknown to the English reader. Harris, I suppose had read him in French; the French place him very high. . . . But, good heavens, a London city business man reading Multatuli: a strange business man surely!

Talking with him one night however, some turn in his phrases started up a vague recollection in my mind; I remembered that he had been in Colorado and Kansas and I suddenly burst out with, "Why, it must have been you who wrote 'The Best Man in Garotte.' " Yes, it was he, no doubt he was flattered by my recollection. I had noticed two or three of these stories of his appearing in magazines and I had been struck by them, not only because they were brilliant but because they dealt with that western life from which I myself only a few years before had returned.

Harris spent 1899 between Eze, Monte Carlo, Roehampton and Paris thinking up and setting in motion various schemes to make money, constantly promising Bell substantial sums next week, next month, next year. He was confident that his schemes would work, that his fortunes would be renewed, but meanwhile the state of his finances was precarious. His extravagant entertaining, his presents to Wilde, his ménages, dowry to his daughter, legal expenses, and above all the heavy expenses that he had incurred at Eze and Monte Carlo, had drained his reserves. Matters were not improved by the fact that one of Harris' most important patrons—Alice—was forbidden by her husband to visit either his hotel or restaurant. The marriage was breaking up, and in spite of all the good advice Harris had offered him ten years or so before on subjects involving naval architects, in spite of the special pairs of gloves purchased and Alice's assurances that "he *does* like you immensely," Prince Albert took exception to his wife's friendship not only with Isidore de Lara but with Harris also.

That year Lord Queensberry died, and Harris went to dine with Lord Alfred Douglas at Chantilly at the Hotel Condé, where he was living. Douglas tells us in his autobiography how they sat up till two in the morning discussing Oscar's complaints of Douglas' meanness. Oscar, he said, was hoping for £2,000 now that Lord Queensberry was dead, and Douglas had no intention of handing it to him. Harris suggested that, instead, Douglas should pass it over to him and he would put it into a scheme he was floating that would bring him £2,000 for life. Douglas should come and stay as his guest at Monte Carlo. Soon his hotel would be paying 50 percent on the capital, and if Douglas so wanted, he would let him into the company. But down the road he had a much bigger thing—a real gold mine; at that point he preferred to say nothing. Douglas went. He said that the Cesari Palace Hotel was small, consisting of beautifully furnished ultra-expensive suites—bedroom, bathroom and sitting room. Harris' idea was to attract the same American, South African and other millionaires he had hoped to catch with his sporting club, who enjoyed spending large sums of money on luxury. The cook was excellent. Harris entertained Douglas magnificently and drove him to Eze for a delicious lunch, eaten sitting on the terrace overlooking the sea while a Hungarian band played. The restaurant[4] was full of clients and appeared to be doing a roaring trade. "You see the sort of business we are doing," said Harris over liqueurs and cigars. "This is my gold mine." He had, he said, a concession from the French government allowing roulette and trente-et-quarante. Douglas was impressed, paid his £2,000 and received 2,000 shares for the Cesari Réserve Syndicate. Bell, too, says that Harris brought Douglas along to question him about the Réserve, and he could assure him that the enterprise was thoroughly sound if new capital could be put into it. The Réserve was a company; Cesari had brought in two or three of his friends who, like Harris, knew him as an able *maître d'hôtel*—indeed, Madame Melba was one of them. Bell says:

> I liked Douglas and it was evident that he liked me too, and two Scotsmen abroad can generally trust each other. I think, though he has forgotten it, that it was my assurance which confirmed him in his idea of investing £2,000.
>
> Well, I was happy indeed to have the financial difficulties of the Réserve shifted off my shoulders, as it appeared they were going to be, £2,000 would relieve our worst troubles. Harris went off to England. I had to stay in the south of France: the creditors were grumbling badly. Soon it came to the point where we must open up again. The money I did not have yet. Douglas had come through in Paris; he had given Harris a check for £2,000, I understood. Harris in return gave him a certificate of stock in the Cesari Réserve Company. I stayed on in the Riviera, expecting to receive the money soon, when the affair was completely settled and the check had been cashed. But the thing dragged until I grew desperate —and finally, alarmed, I rushed off to London, faced Harris, and demanded the money. He owned up; the money had been already spent. He had used it for some purpose of his own.
>
> It looked to me that Harris had not only stolen the £2,000 but had used me as bait to obtain it, getting me to assure Douglas that everything was right, and I was furiously indignant. I threatened

---

4 There are two descriptions of the Réserve at Eze that are of interest. Someone who signed himself Lucifer wrote in the *English Review* of how he was motoring with Harris along the Corniche when they approached a lonely, strange romantic building on a rock overhanging the sea, shut off apparently from all approach. "My hotel," explained Harris. Grant Richards says that Harris had planned to have a coach-and-four running there every day from the Casino at Monte Carlo. He and Edward Clodd went to the restaurant, which was at the time managed by Bell; the claret—a rare one—was brought in an ice bucket.

that if the £2,000 was not paid into the reserve funds at once, I would charge him with its theft. No, Harris kept his temper, kept his head, kept his attitude of apology and regret, begging me to listen to his explanation; he had not stolen the money from the Réserve, he had not stolen it from Douglas, nor had he any intention of robbing either of them. He had acted, in fact, in the best interests of both; if I would only listen and be reasonable. He had used the money because he had received it at the most critical moment in his fortunes; if I raised a row now, he would be ruined for life. Nay, not only he would be ruined, but everybody connected with the affair would be ruined. The Réserve would be ruined, and Douglas's money would be lost with it. If I would only listen, he was on the point, as he explained to me, of a great coup which would put him back on Easy Street in a very short time, within a few days, in all probability. He would pay in then, not only the £2,000 of Douglas's but a greater fund to finish up the Réserve in good shape and start it off full sail—to success. . . .

Douglas, in one of his books, speaks of Harris having swindled him in the affair of the Réserve. He tells of the ideas Harris said he had in his mind as if they were matters of imagination to get the money out of him. No, these schemes of which he says Harris told him were quite genuine and quite practical at the time. Harris did have brains all right. Harris did not swindle him in that way but in another way which evidently he never understood until I explained it to him. . . . The dodge played by Harris was this: when Douglas paid in his £2,000 Harris handed him a certificate for 2,000 shares of stock. That was all right; the certificate was quite genuine; but it was not 2,000 shares of stock from the still unsold capital stock of the company . . . it was a transfer of 2,000 shares of the stock of the company *already belonging to Harris*. The check, therefore, made out to Frank Harris, quite legitimately could be cashed by Frank Harris as paid to him, not to the company.

Harris had received that stock, with some other stock, in consideration of his transfer to the company of the land on which the Réserve was built. It was good stock, all right, at that time; the swindle came in the fact that Douglas when he paid the money in, thought it was going into the funds of the company, where it was so desperately needed, whereas it was really a case of Harris drawing out an investment already in, getting out from under and letting Douglas take his place. . . . I think still that Harris was quite serious at that time in his promises. He did feel sure of making that fortune, and if he had made it I am quite certain that he would have paid in not only Douglas's money but whatever more was required to make things right.

The spring had been an expensive one, entertaining Bell, Douglas and Davray at the Palace Hotel and Wilde at the Terminus in Nice. Harris had returned to London via Paris, crossing the mountains in a motor, and now his schemes for renewing his fortunes were diverse. Besides finishing his book on Shakespeare he intended to start a new review, with the hope of selling patents and promoting parts of motors, and an art gallery. Henri Davray was his right-hand man in all these ventures. He was to translate the Shakespeare into French, and act as agent negotiating with French automobile companies[5] and with Rodin. Already Harris had purchased two Baryes; now he was ordering Rodin's bronzes. "I hope you've ordered the bronzes and got the big one. I'm going to have the *best* shop in London soon—soon," he wrote to Davray on June 11. On June 22 he had no time that day to write about motors: "But t'will be hard to sell patents in England for some time . . . for God's sake get the Apollo from Rodin if you *possibly* can, and the others *soon soon,* or the season will be over. The notice in the *Plume* says I paid 1,500 francs instead of 15,000, this 0 is *nothing*! But it makes a d—d great difference."

On July 3 he was complaining about Rodin's prices. "Rodin really seems to me extortionate. 100,000 francs for his bronze Apollo that will be exhibited in London and Monte Carlo and that will certainly make him better known to the Anglo-Saxon public both here and in the United States. I think half the money or say £250 or 6 thousand francs plenty. A word in *La Plume* saying that I had paid 15,000 francs for 2 Baryes would help me, don't forget . . . for goodness sake let me know when I can get those bronzes. I want them now, now, now . . . every hour saved will be of advantage to me." By September it was clear that the *Automobile Review* was not going to grow past the smart writing paper that was already printed. Harris was negotiating, he told Davray, for some unnamed paper, for which he would have to pay £24,000. "Please get me the 'Baiser' of Rodin. . . . My Shakespeare is growing."

[5] In the beginning it was the French who manufactured and exported motor cars to England.

At last the "Baiser," "Apollo," the "Nymph" and the "Faun" had all arrived with others and were all duly exhibited to large crowds in January 1900 in the Carlton Hotel. But the newspapers did not carry a single notice, Davray told Rodin: "Toute l'attention étant absorbé de l'autre côté du détroit, par cette stupide guerre de Transvaal." Harris' luck was out. His disintegration, which came through a combination of bad luck, bad timing, bad judgment and bad management, had begun.

Bell claims that Nellie O'Hara was one of the main reasons for the decline of Harris; she encouraged in him irresponsibility and extravagance. Bell could not under any circumstances bear her and referred to her as "that O'Hara woman" (not, it is interesting to note, "that O'Hara little girl," which suggests that in later life Nellie faked her age—which would have been quite in character, as she was terrified of growing old). He believed her to be a thoroughly evil woman, a most wretched parasite, dragging Harris down and encouraging him to be unscrupulous. He was convinced that she was a woman without any thought of truth and honesty and was faithful only so far as he, Harris, was her meal ticket. She never opposed the most foolish waste, he told Elmer Gertz, and was ready with her approval of any possible way of getting money. With a decent woman Harris would not have been so bad. H. D. Turner also wrote to Elmer Gertz and told him that he believed that Harris would not have descended to such bad ways had Nellie not encouraged him in every rascality. He insisted that her affection was merely a matter of hanging on to a man who had been rich once and might be rich again. He described a sister living in Central Africa who was in very much the same situation and who wrote to Nellie cynically and cold-bloodedly offering her advice. It is not known where or how Harris met Nellie. It has been said that he extracted her from a convent; Nellie herself told Rebecca West that she had given up a fine career on the mandolin to be with Frank. Whether she was eleven years old or not, she was exactly the type to attract Harris, with that long red-gold hair he loved and hips that he described as vase-shaped. Almost thirty years later Leo Rosten described her as a Dresden doll with big blue eyes and red hair, very *creamy*; her creaminess against Frank's swarthiness was fascinating. She was the source of much amusement to Shaw many years later—somewhat insipid, he thought, and he giggled like a schoolboy over her. There is no record of her birth among the Irish registers; on the certificate of her marriage to Frank in 1927 it is recorded that her mother was Mary Mackay, her father Patrick O'Hara, suggesting that she was illegitimate. Certainly this would be an easy explanation for her insecurity—for she was as frightened, as vain, as unwilling to be alone as Harris himself. Coming from that uncertain Irish background—with a father who, it is rumored, drank—she longed for a glamorous life, exciting but secure, with money, pretty clothes and a nice house surrounded by beautiful flowers. Harris, with his riches from South Africa, his luxurious hotel in Monte Carlo, his restaurant on the Riviera, his victoria and brougham, watch chains and jewels, his seeming self-assurance, his carefully arranged dinners, his flattery, his romantically quoted poetry, must have seemed the mercurial father figure she needed. He was married, it was true, but separated, and he had every intention of marrying Nellie at the first opportunity.

For someone of Nellie's temperament, the waiting while he rushed off to his meals, meetings, Monte Carlo, Paris and heaven knows where else cannot have been pleasant. At the beginning he was running his other household simultaneously, and no doubt the affair was conducted with some discretion, with Nellie being kept behind the scenes. Often he would be held up with some business or other and would not make the arranged rendezvous. "Oh, darling I'm so disappointed," he scribbled hastily after such a fiasco. "I thought you would know that when I didn't come yesterday I'd come today. I couldn't wire you yesterday—I was so sick—a big party came in after you left and I didn't get home until almost 7 a.m. Oh, darling I feel miserable! You don't know how hard it was to get away today and now it was all for nothing. You are out! and I had so much to tell you. Darling I'm so unhappy."

It was probably in order to make the arrangement more settled that Harris moved Nellie into Limehurst. Possibly she, like May Congden, was pregnant, for Gwladys Price Williams told Elmer Gertz that Nellie had given birth to a daughter, who died aged two or three years old as the result of a vaccination. In May 1899 it appears that Frank wished to settle her further, for he was inquiring from Wilde about the address of Arnold Point the jewelry designer, wanting to have a ring designed for his emerald—a ring that he very likely gave to Nellie and that later spent much of its time sitting in the pawnshop. Ever after Limehurst, the memory of Nellie and their bed there would return to Harris with the fragrance of new-mown hay—the scent of Nellie herself and their bedroom. Twenty years later, lonely and miserable in New York, Harris gave himself up to rare nostalgia.

I did not look at you undressing, but when I got into bed and put back the clothes, your nighty draped you and you showed your left breast and the great vase hips and your eyes looked at me half inviting, half shy, you were adorable. I slipped in beside you and covered you up and then kissed you and you slid your arms round my neck and your right leg came against me and I felt you were ripe with desire. I put my hand up your clothes (always to think of it gives me shivers of delight) and touched your sex and in a moment it opened and I got over on you and you moved to take me in and your eyes were divine with love and tenderness—one red-gold plait was by your half-flushed face—you lovely Titian darling. At the first thrust you closed your eyes as if in pain and then when I cursed myself for not being gentler, the eyes opened smiling and you moved your body to take me in further and opened your legs to receive me and bring me nearer and draw my sex further into you and as I began to move, your legs closed again and suddenly you open wide and push down on me and then your legs twine about mine and you moan and sigh a little and all inundated with tenderness you put your hands down drawing me into you for your desire is at its height and you want, will *have all* of me.

And there we lie with pleasure making music in our twin bodies that are one and your dear mouth kisses and your dearer eyes caress me and your hands touch me like flowers, and your deep breast sighs, and you are adorable, my love, my delight who can combine as *no one else can* tenderness, in a flood with passion sharp set as hunger.

Nellie may have been passionate and tender, but she felt inferior. Things may have been more settled and regular now that they lived in Roehampton, but there was no avoiding the fact that she was a kept woman, and she disliked very much being alone and having to stay behind when Frank went off to Monte Carlo or to various grand friends and acquaintances on money-raising trips. Harris meanwhile lived in constant fear of scandal. He urged and warned that there must be none—this would spell ruin to his career and to his future, to *their* future. But Nellie was weak and she needed to be surrounded by as constant a cloud of admiration as Harris himself. No sooner had he set off to Monte Carlo for a week or so's rest and writing than Nellie was unwisely accepting invitations from tongue-wagging ladies—and worse, was inviting strange gentlemen to luncheon with her at Limehurst. The whole thing threw Harris into a frenzy:

> Oh Nellie how could you? How could you? I've warned you against Mrs. Vandam and her friends and you give a man lunch at Limehurst. No gentleman lunches with a lady he doesn't know save at her express request, personally made . . . you do this in my absence I'm hurt to the soul. I'm here and getting the news from London that stocks are going down, down, down and then you do this! Nellie you have ruined my holiday. I can scarcely write. I shall do no good now here. . . . I trusted you so. I trusted you and again you wound me. You are too weak. God, how I suffer! I don't know what to do: it was right of you to tell me; but my God why do it when I warned you? I feel like a wounded dog I cannot even howl; the pain's too great. One thing is certain. Mrs. Vandam shall pay for it! Remember from now on I don't want you to know or meet her! Tell her if you please it is my wish. I don't wish you to know her or *any* of her friends. So one acts *after* the event *after*; yet I warned you before Nellie. You tell me you love me and you can't do what you promised for one short week. Now I take a new tone. If you care at all for me or our future together, be more than Careful. If you ever see or speak to Mr. Gardiner again and I know it, I shall understand that you care no more for me. Be careful, be careful! But what's the good of warning you. If love does not make you careful nothing will—nothing.

There is no doubt that Harris believed himself to be deeply in love with Nellie; certainly he was deeply obsessed by her. As with Laura, there were jealous scenes, and as he grew older he became bad-tempered. It seems that after the first few years they were not often happy together, but when Harris was away he was not happy either. "I miss you every moment: day and night," he wrote in a letter of which only a torn fragment remains. "I check myself from calling Nellie. You are throned in my heart and brain you alone you only! Don't doubt that darling ever: I have never loved and reverenced anyone as I do you: be sure of that. Sometimes I think you don't care for me as much since that unseemly scene but really I was not to blame really, but I was frightened a scandal would rot us of all the fruits of my hard work."

One of these fruits was, presumably, *Mr. and Mrs. Daventry*. Through 1899 and the first half of 1900 Harris was in touch with Wilde, sending him money and keeping him informed as to his progress with the *Automobile Review*, the gallery and Shakespeare. "He was a mist and you have made him marble," Wilde told him. "If you are rolling in gold and have achieved your victory over Beit and the other lost tribes of Israel do send me a tenner." Silk dispatched twenty pounds—"a bank note of extraordinary beauty," Wilde told Harris. "I long to learn about your book, your Baryes and your automobiles."

In May and June 1900 Harris was in Paris once more, not only to entertain Wilde sumptuously but to run round to his laundry and pay the bill.[6] "Frank Harris is very wonderful and really very good and *sympatique*. He always comes two hours late for meals, but in spite of that is delightful," Wilde told Robert Ross. Pleasantly, over various expensive lunches and dinners, Harris proposed that they should collaborate over the play that was to be *Mr. and Mrs. Daventry*. Originally it was to have been called *Love Is Law*, and its plot had come to Wilde when he was working on *The Importance of Being Earnest*, but he had been unable to do any work on it before he was sent to prison. Harris departed, and August and the first half of September passed agreeably, with a further sum of money sent off on the eighteenth. On September 19 Harris and Wilde had a row. Harris had proposed collaboration; he had disappeared, to return with the play finished.[7] Oscar had not seen a line of it, he told Frank in a letter written the following day, and he suggested that Harris should buy the plot and

[6] See footnote, p. 223.

[7] Harris did not alter the original plot much, and *Mr. and Mrs. Daventry* is chiefly of interest in that he uses it as a vehicle to discuss idealistically what he calls the "new woman" and his preoccupation with marriage and adultery. "The decay of Christianity and the belief in a future life has had for chief consequences 1st the demand on the part of people for a better life on this earth—socialism—and 2nd the demand by the other oppressed class, woman, for a larger satisfaction of her instincts in this world," Harris told Shaw (November 27, 1900), who had written criticizing his "sardonic bitterness" against Wilde's "beautiful kindly humour." "This new woman wants nothing but love, whatever form she may individually effect, affection or passion. I have taken her to demand affection in this case."

"The world is more charitable than it used to be, I think," he makes Mrs. Daventry say. "People are beginning to see that no single mistake—not even marriage should be allowed to ruin a whole life. We have a sort of second chance now and most of us need it." While Mrs. Daventry is optimistic, the romantic hero, Mr. Ashurst, is remarkably like Harris himself, always going off to buy motor cars in which to drive over the mountains to Paris, and bearing gifts of red roses—"roses for my Queen!"—at which Mrs. Daventry looks up with passionate affection in her eyes and buries her face again and again in her flowers.

the scenario for £200 in cash, £500 of shares in the Cesari Réserve, and a quarter profit of the play.

What happened then has been described by H. Montgomery Hyde in his introduction to *Mr. and Mrs. Daventry*. The play opened on October 25 at the Royalty, with Mrs. Patrick Campbell and Fred Kerr in the title roles, and ran until the death of Queen Victoria, on January 22, 1901; the theater reopened for the play's hundredth performance on February 5 and was withdrawn on February 23. As soon as the production had been announced, a crowd of people applied to Harris, each one claiming that Wilde had sold the play to him. Harris was compelled to pay money to Mrs. Brown Potter, Horace Sedger, Ada Rehan, Louis Nethersole and Leonard Smithers, and accordingly he withheld £150 of the money due to Wilde. Unfortunately, Wilde was not well and about to undergo a serious operation, necessitating a check for £60 and the attentions of a hospital nurse all day. The situation threw Wilde—and, later on, Sherard—into his most nervous state. Harris was to send £125 at once, he raged on November 12. No one had any right to the options; Harris was breaking his agreement, and he had no right to do that either. For himself, he was tortured with apprehension, in a state of fever, rarely sleeping, stuffed with morphine, covered with unhealed wounds—and it was all due to Frank.

On December 14 Robert Ross wrote to More Adey. He had been to see Oscar, recovering from his operation, who was saying how much he had suffered but was shouting with laughter and telling stories about the doctors and himself and his grievances against Harris. "Oscar, of course, had deceived Harris about the whole matter. . . . Harris wrote the play under the impression that only Sedger had to be bought off at £100 . . . whereas Kyrle Bellew, Louis Nethersole, Ada Rehan and even Smithers, had all given Oscar £100 on different occasions and all threatened Harris with proceedings.[8] Harris therefore, only gave Oscar £50 on account, as he was obliged to square these people first—hence Oscar's grievance." Oscar was at his most paranoid, telling

---

[8] That Oscar had sold the play to anyone else was angrily dismissed by Sherard. Harris had seen a "phantom crowd." Imagine the Oscar Wilde of *The Importance of Being Earnest* selling a play to anyone for £100! he asked us. And as for Robert Ross's letter to More Adey—which Harris had originally quoted in his *Oscar Wilde*—this was another forgery. Reginald Turner, who had seen the letter, was mistaken. "Knowing Reggie's absolute good faith I cannot but think he must be mistaken in saying that he actually saw this letter. . . . I would rather believe that the message in Ross's letter—with all deference to dear Reggie Turner—is an interpolated forgery by Harris."

Ross apparently: "Frank has deprived me of my only source of income by taking a play on which I could always have raised £100."

Oscar never recovered. Furious with Harris, he lay drugged, in pain, his head in ice, refusing to have mustard plasters on his legs. Desperate for money for Wilde, Reginald Turner sent a telegram to Harris, who with Alfred Douglas had made himself responsible for Wilde's debts and who, being laid up with his usual bronchitis, sent Bell along with money and instructions not to part with it if Wilde were drinking.[9] He believed that Reginald Turner's remark that Wilde was really in a very poor state, both in health and finances, was made only to get the *Mr. and Mrs. Daventry* money.

Bell arrived and obtained Wilde's room number from a chambermaid who was carrying a bundle of washing and seemed momentarily startled. Bell mounted the stairs to find the bedroom door open; he thought that Harris must have been right, that Wilde had gone out, quite well, on his customary round of cafés. Then in the room he saw a white-coifed nun sitting by the side of the bed and waxed tapers burning. Wilde had died a few hours previously; the nun was keeping watch over his body.

---

[9] Bell's visit to the Hôtel d'Alsace—which he had described in the New York *Bookman*, May 1930—was "entirely imaginary," according to Sherard. It was entirely imaginary that Harris, on hearing that Wilde was in distress, sent Bell with money; Bell took no money, he never went to the Hôtel d'Alsace, he had no idea what the place looked like. Sherard demonstrated his theorem by a long argument based on Bell's description of the hotel's side entrance, which, Sherard said, did not exist—which threw Bell into a fury. It would have been interesting to know what Sherard would have made of the following note addressed to Wilde from his laundry, who he would have imagined had concocted it. It conjures up a ridiculous picture of Harris, Ross and Reginald Turner sitting in Durand's scratching their heads over fictional "mouchoirs" and "chaussettes noires."

Monsieur Osc Wilde

Lorsque Mr. Harris est venu pour solder votre note qui se montait à 110 fr. 80 cm il n'avait que 100 fr. et me les a remis. Il devait revenir le mardi chercher le reste de mouchoirs qui n'était pas revenu de chez la blanchisseuse. J'en ai 11 et une paire de chaussettes noires comme il n'est pas revenu je ne savais pas quoi faire.

Vous pourriez faire prendre quand vous voudrez en fuissant de régler la note. Quant au reçu que je lui ai fait signer c'est un reçu certifiant qu'il enlevait *vos* affaires et les *siennes*. Depuis j'ai retrouvé un petit étui en cuir pour mettre des crayons je le tiens aussi à votre disposition.

CHAPTER 13

Quarrels and The Candid Friend

HARRIS was never content for long without a paper. Not only did he physically need the power and excitement of the world of journalism but, since South Africa and his City exercises, he needed an instrument with which to play the stock market and promote shares. "Qui dit noble, dit riche" logically would continue "qui dit riche dit noble"; alternatively, "qui dit pauvre dit bourgeois." Harris' goal—to reach the top, be noble—could not be pursued without the necessary funds—or rather, Harris' particular brand of "nobility" could not, requiring as it did grand and generous entertaining in the capitals of Europe and equally grand and generous appurtenances to accompany the noble sentiments. Heroes and heroines should not be subjected to petty economies, as he told Arnold Bennett several years later. Heroines, particularly, should be beautiful, sincere, adoring, free from drudgery, to develop their minds to the utmost under the skilled guidance of their masters. Petty economies were bourgeois. So, to avoid this unpalatable condition, in May 1900 he had written to Joseph Pulitzer hoping to become the London correspondent of the *World*; according to Bell, he was going to be allocated large proportions of the column to write. However, this came to nothing and instead he started *The Candid Friend*, sending for Bell to come to London and lend a hand. Shaw detected that this would be a waste of time and the start of Harris' decline. On December 16, 1900, he wrote to Harris on receiving *Montes the Matador*,[1] his second published volume of short stories. "Sonia," he said, was a very fine shot at a star, and a bull's-eye at that. "In Sonia and Mrs. Daventry you are shewing the top end of your range. Why you want to plunge back into the journalistic mud bath again Lord knows! You are the most extraordinary chap with your genius and your shiny hats and Café Royal and Hooleyisms and all sorts of incongruities! And now you want to give your struggling soul a final good chance of damnation by coming into a paper with sixteen pages by Beauchamp, one by me, no advertisements and a note by you every two months or so. All pure waste of time: even parliament would be better. We are too old for it: journalism is not for men over forty."

Plans for *The Candid Friend*, however, continued. On March 26, 1901, a circular was sent round to prospective readers and contributors:

The bare name of *The Candid Friend* is, we think, in itself an introduction. We shall try to live up to it, and to add to the amusement of our readers by drawing attention to the virtues and failings of public men and public institutions. But we shall not find fault in any self-righteous spirit; nor put on airs of superiority nor try to make our own virtues shine by dint of shady comparison—we shall always try to remain friendly to those we criticise. . . . We don't even pretend that *The Candid Friend* will supply an urgent want to the public, or fill an aching void in the general heart; we are persuaded however that there is room for us, and we mean to elbow our way in and take up as much place as we can in the public favour.

[1] Stead waited until April 1901 to review *Montes the Matador*—favorably. "It is some years since Mr. Harris published his *Elder Conklin and Other Stories*, which stand out among the most vivid and masterly pieces of workmanship in that kind of writing that English literature possesses. It was understood that Mr. Frank Harris had abandoned short story writing and was devoting his attention to a great work on Shakespeare, endeavouring to reconstruct the man from his works. Hence the pleasant surprise which I felt on receiving this new volume.

"In all Mr. Frank Harris's stories, but especially in the first and the last, there is manifest power and capacity for vividly picturing strongly-marked characters in very dramatic situations. There is also a subtle analysis of human emotion. His women are by no means divine. Sonia, to a certain extent redeems the short comings of the others, but Mr. Harris has not yet given us his ideal heroine, for Sophie Peroffsky, or Sonia, as he calls her, although full of the vague longings and the vast aspirations of the Russian Nihilist, is a creature of disordered nerves, who charms us as much by her weakness as by her strength. . . ."

This was followed up on May 20 by a further circular, distributed by Harris to "most of the contributors who wrote so excellently for the *Fortnightly* and the *Saturday* under my editorship. . . . Might I, in all courtesy, ask whether I may count upon your help as one of the staff of *The Candid Friend?*" Bell was somewhat surprised when he saw the title. Surely, he felt, this was an error of judgment for a man who had edited the *Fortnightly* and the *Saturday Review*. Here was a "society" paper, and it did not look to Bell in the least like a paper edited by Frank Harris. John Davidson—who had in 1898 written, "If these telepathic miracle-mongers would only hurry up, so that I could sit here and convey through the air . . . and musically how much I like Frank Harris, and his talents and genius: a slow-developing genius that will advance instructions from great things to greater"—told Bell that he could not bring himself to write for Harris' society paper, he did not like it at all. Soon it became obvious to Bell that the paper was not being published for any literary ambitions but was a handle to make money by influencing the stock market.

It was on May 1, 1901, that the first number appeared: a sort of eccentric *Tatler*, with photographs of the Duchess of Cleveland in a donkey cart, covered with dogs, the Marchioness of Headfort veiled with hair, and the Duke of Connaught smothered in tartan; the Empress Frederika lay in repose and H.M. Queen Alexandra in a basket chair. A. G. Hales had been requested by the editor of "this literary spice box" to tell his readers all he knew about himself; and Le Gourmet, alias Harris, who had an attack of incipient gout and had been ordered to drink Moselle by the doctor, advised where to dine in London. First he recommended the Café Royal with its French cuisine and its cellar—the best in London. Then, in fear and trembling, Le Gourmet passed to the Midland Central and ordered his meal. The soup was good, the fish surprising, the entrée eatable, the roast excellent, the sweet omelette made with really fresh eggs. But coffee and brandy? No, the Gourmet thought he would not tempt Providence. The coffee might be immemorable, the spirit raw. Unconsciously Le Gourmet had spoken aloud. The waiter assured him the coffee was "vary gut." "But the brandy?" queried Le Gourmet—not for him any three-star fire, and if he drank coffee he must correct it with a *chasse*. At that moment the smiling headwaiter stopped. "We can give you as good a glass of liqueur brandy as you can get in England," he assured Le Gourmet. "Stuff that will make me see stars," sneered he ungraciously, somewhat provoked. "Oh no," rejoined the headwaiter pleasantly, "the best brandy to be found in Paris." Le Gourmet counterrejoined that it was jolly hard to get good brandy in Paris, what with the phylloxera spoiling all the grapes. Back came the headwaiter, still smiling, with a bottle of Bignon's 1800. "Yes, Bignon of the Avenue de l'Opéra! How well I knew the label!" The bottle was opened, the golden essence gurgled like oil into the glass and the aroma brought back to Le Gourmet forgotten days and friends long silent.

What fashions had the first days of warm weather brought out, what fascinating stuffs, swirling and swishing, pale spotted voiles, satin surfaces, new clinging poplins, nets and cream taffetas glacés. And what sunshades—pink silks with clematis sprays, turquoise silks with flounces of lace, frills of chiffon, ruches of gauze. What hats and toques, with everywhere flowers—roses, pale heliotropes and primroses, colored apple blossoms; picture hats of cream, scarves with cream lace, wreaths of pale pink rosebuds. What evening gowns, what pretty curving figures, what Turkish embroideries, crystal buttons and pearls, in ropes and collars and rows.

Advertisements were included for "Vicar's Lustrine," a Turkish bath at home, and *Montes the Matador*[2]—"that brilliant collection of stories by Frank Harris." There was *The Candid Friend* postcard competition—"All you have to do is to write on a postcard, in column form, a list of the twelve ablest Englishmen," for which you would receive £100 in cash. Another ploy was to buy a copy of the current number of *The Candid Friend*, show it to your friends or any other person with whom you might come in contact, and ask each of them to sign his or her real name, address and date in the list that should be made for the purpose, "ruled foolscap being the most suitable." The worker who succeeded in sending the largest list of genuine names and addresses— a hundred must be in each list—would receive a magnificent piano valued at fifty guineas.

As 1901 continued, there were features on actresses, from Sarah

[2] On August 10, 1901, there was a rapturous piece by Edgar Jepson on Harris "as a writer of short stories." Jepson believed that such fine, sincere work was wasted in the English tongue and would have had more of a chance in French or Italian. There was Mr. Harris' look, honest, unblinking, utterly opposed to the Englishman's sentimental conception. Mr. Harris was a great artist—was it the sense of beauty and form that was strongest in him or was it the sense of life? The writing was never a note above or below the subject, the English of clarity and vigor: perhaps "nervousness" would be a better word. Here was a musician with an amazing grasp of life, and a grasp of emotion that was no less amazing; his men and women were fuller of will than Balzac's.

Bernhardt—photographed traveling with a retinue of servants, dogs, secretaries and companions—to May Congden, "who has not been quite three years on the stage and who is now performing at Oxford by permission of Mr. Wyndham in whose new play she is shortly to take part. . . . During her short career she has proved herself a mistress alike of piquant daintiness and deep pathos. For though Miss Congden is a born *comédienne* and is usually cast in comedy characters she is equally at home in pathetic parts and the charm of her musical voice is great." Shaw contributed "All About Myself"; the editor wrote a piece on Lord Randolph Churchill, pointing out that he was a very bad speaker, losing the thread of an argument, his knees knocking together like castanets from nervousness; Lord Methuen was described as a flanneled fool and a muscular Christian; and Lady Warwick was evoked in her famous Garden of Friendship, "containing delightful blossoming contributions from the fair gardener's friends," and at work in her charming lingerie shop in Bond Street—all part of her scheme for the advancement of women.

The death of Rhodes inspired from Harris on April 5, 1902, streams of abuse. It enraged him that all the newspapers dished out praise; "warp and woof and fantastic lies" was what they were writing in Harris' opinion. It made him furious that people still did not recognize that the Jameson Raid and Rhodes's other sorties into Matabeleland and Mashonaland (now Rhodesia) were for motives of greed and financial profit only. The *Daily Mail* waxed so lyrical over his death scene that it reminded Harris of the death of Tennyson. Rhodes died at six o'clock in the evening. The moon, said the *Daily Mail*, which was slowly waning, streamed through the windows, throwing a silvern glow everywhere while the personal friends of the dead man reverently performed the last rites. The main message to emerge from all papers was the contempt that Cecil Rhodes was supposed to have held for money—a parrot cry repeated on all sides, snorted Harris. The *Daily News* said he was not a mere money grabber, he valued riches for the power they conferred. The *Times* said that diamonds and gold occupied but the surface of his mind. "These writers wish us to believe that a man can rake together 4 or 5 millions in 15 or 20 years without caring particularly for money." "No one," observed Harris bitterly, "gets millions who is not extraordinarily greedy. It's no use to have big ideas if one has not the money to carry them out—and the only big ideas that he had depended on money for their fulfilment." In conclusion he remembered a witty quip he had delivered, before the first sitting of the South African Committee, to Rhodes and another gentleman: " 'We admit the raid,' said the gentleman, 'we admit everything, but at any rate, give us credit for good motives—eh? We wanted to help the Uitlanders.' 'I suppose,' I replied, 'if I found you and Rhodes in the vaults of a bank, it would be plain that you had gone there to make love to the cook.' Rhodes laughed grimly."

As Harris' fortunes dwindled he grew more insecure and obsessed with money, always ready to accuse others of greed and obsession. With Rhodes his accusations were stimulated by a sense of injustice: he was furious that the newspapers should offer praise and support to someone who appeared to him an avaricious, profit-mongering imperialist, guilty of theft, while they had ignored Oscar, a noble, gentle poet, guilty of nothing, victim of a barbaric law. Prince Albert of Monaco, however, he charged more subjectively. At first Albert clearly had liked and admired him; they had shot together and Harris had bought him pairs of special gloves and introduced him to bicycling. At the end of Alice's letters she would send love and "all kinds of souvenirs and amities" from her husband. They had fallen out mainly over the sporting club. To Harris it seemed that the prince had cheated him twice: Albert had renewed the lease of the Casino in a way that had made his own fortunes greater while ignoring Harris, and he had helped to spoil Frank's own chances as grand hotelier and restaurateur by withdrawing Alice's patronage. In June 1902 Harris raised his pen on the occasion of the "judicial separation" of the Prince and Princess of Monaco. "Most people are not likely to understand the true inwardness of this proceeding, though they know by rumour at least . . . that Prince Albert of Monaco has never been a model husband," he gossiped. "The scandal of his first marriage shocked Europe: he had married a daughter of the Duke and Duchess of Hamilton and one day this lady ran away from her gilded prison . . . I do not need to reproduce the stories she told of Prince Albert's petty tyrannies and intolerable nature. . . . Prince Albert took time enough over his second marriage: for nine or ten years he was known as the devoted admirer of the Duchess of Richelieu before he could persuade her to risk marriage with him. In an evil hour for herself she at length consented."

The piece continued in praise of Mlle. Alice Heine—her inherited love of literature, music and every form of art; how she won universal admiration and affection as the head of every good movement in the principality. Through her hands Monaco became one of the art centers of the world; she founded picture galleries, brought success to the opera. But both her charities and her patronage of art lost money, and her generosity was offensive to the prince, whose avariciousness "has made his name a by-word. Prince Albert's love of money is a monomania. For years he pretended to hate the gambling house from which his main income is derived, he told everyone he intended to shut it up in 1910 when the lease expired, he used to beg his guests not to set their feet in that 'foul den' as he called it. . . . A couple of years ago he renewed the lease for fifty years on huge terms: a gratuity of some millions and 80,000 a year besides for himself. And meantime his son by his first wife is staved off with a beggarly allowance and he gets a judicial separation from his wife in order to punish the woman whose will he cannot break, while keeping a tight hold on her fortune." This piece Harris initialed, and concluded it ominously in parenthesis "to be continued." And continued it was. The princess, it was revealed, had refused to live with the prince in his house in Paris, or on his yacht, where she was seasick, or at Marchais, in northeast France, where the prince, surrounded by vast marshes and flocks of geese, was in his element, being an enthusiastic sportsman. He had telephones erected linking the keepers' huts with the bedrooms so that he would know when the wildfowl alighted on the ponds. This the princess did not like at all. She was unable to sleep at night with the telephone bells ringing at all hours.

Later, in 1915, Shaw claimed that *The Candid Friend* was run by a titled lady, Lady Jessica Sykes, by then dead, who was never known to be sober and who kept it afloat with reminiscences and photographs of aristocratic friends. To this Harris indignantly replied that he was glad Shaw had buried the poor lady before making fun of her: "I never heard of her before." With or without a titled lady, there were plenty of photographs and social pieces, with descriptions of Mr. and Mrs. S. R. G. Graham's garden party at their "pretty house St. Albans at Hampton" to watch the Molesey Regatta, and their guests, Mrs. Mullino, "a very pretty fair woman," and her friend Mrs. Spencer Day, "handsome, dark and tall." There were descriptions of trips to Esher, "an old-fashioned rural English village" complete with village green and red-brick houses, to visit Mr. Kitcat, "one of the most delightful writers of our time."

On January 4, 1902, *The Candid Friend* announced an expedition round the world, to be undertaken by Dr. Lehwess, who loved all things mechanical and automobiles particularly. He intended to travel across Russia and China, and was at pains to explain that he was not trying to compete with Phileas Fogg. Before setting out, Dr. Lehwess was invited to write "About Myself." This he found very difficult; his egotism seemed to have oozed out through the top of his penholder, he told his readers—however, what trickles through is that this scheme had more to it than meets the eye. Dr. Lehwess was, he explained, an ardent student of political economy, and he had devoted much time to considering the benefits to Western Europe of opening up Siberia. Lehwess held that nothing was known of the great mineral riches or of the possibilities of the terrain as a fruit- and corn-producing country; he had set his eyes also on a great gold belt running from the Behring Straits to Southern Patagonia. Plainly Dr. Lehwess was to go forth, sponsored by *The Candid Friend,* and return bearing tidings of gold, corn and fruit, which Harris, and perhaps he, would reap.

In the interim "The Old Woman" promised advice to ladies: how to do their hair, buy frocks, retrieve money they had been foolish enough to lose on the stock exchange, answer a letter with discretion, a telegram with significance, get rid of the attentions of one man and serve the good fellowship of another. She told Maisie to "revive the jet gown with transparent yoke and sleeve of lace" (Dickins and Jones was the best establishment for lace); Millie was to wear a little sac lace coat over her blouse with bell-shaped sleeves, permitting a view of the blouse sleeves beneath. (The coat, which she could buy only at Allenby's in Conduit Street, would cost three guineas and would take all suggestion of stoutness from the waist.) Millie was suffering from a very common complaint, but since she had not asked "The Old Woman" for a cure, merely for a cloak, she was to have the lace coat and let "The Old Woman" know how she liked it.

The Candid Friend was not altogether a success, and Bell says that eventually Harris took in with him a partner, a Scot, Campbell-Everden, a sedate businessman with a serene charm of manner who was interested in company promotion. Things went from bad to worse; both men seemed on the verge of bankruptcy. Then Campbell-Everden came up with a new scheme for getting all the Scottish collieries into a trust.

> Harris took the documents [says Bell] and went with them to
> Morgan's offices. . . . He has told me how that when he put the affair

finally over for many millions—and he certainly had a splendid tongue for promoting any deal of that sort—he was at his wit's end, and had only a few shillings in his pocket. Nevertheless, he told me, he was inflexible in his demands. He fought it out with the Morgan people all afternoon stubbornly until they gave way to the percentage he required. Yes, that was Harris, I am sure that tale of his was true, his nerve was always all right.

The Candid Friend, however, was far from all right, and, disillusioned by the whole publication, Bell returned to the Mediterranean, where matters were worsening. Suddenly he had an urgent call from Harris to return to London on a mission that he thought only Bell could fill. For many years Harris had been connected with a man called Catton, a company promoter in whose office Bell had first met Harris (they had been partners in various schemes).

Harris insisted to me how that the partnership was rated as a permanent one and that the understanding was distinct that if either of them brought off a success the other should have his share in it in accordance with the assistance given him. Catton's schemes up to that time had not been successful, but just lately, at last, he had made quite a great kill. Harris thereupon had seen him and demanded his share. They had disagreed, Catton maintaining that the affair was his own entirely in which Harris had no part; and they quarreled very bitterly. . . . Catton had taken to me especially after one occasion in which I had frankly told him that his way of spending life was silly and the fortune he was striving for not worth the effort. He had the reputation as a company promoter of not being any more overburdened with scruples than other promoters; but as a man and a friend he always seemed to me a pretty good fellow. . . . Catton received me in very friendly fashion. He told me of his success in the promotion of a tea company which in its branches all over the United Kingdom gave with each pound of tea sold life insurance for a certain limited time. He laughed at the affair himself and compared the result with his first promotion, an entirely honest, straight and intelligent one: he had attempted to organize a company for the manufacture of modern baking machinery . . . in which the flour went in one end and without touch of human hand came out loaves at the other. In that he had failed completely; the public would have none of it. This time—with the tea insurance—he had done extremely well.

He was quite willing to discuss with me the thing I had in

hand. But he remained inflexible. I think he would have been willing to do what he considered the square thing but Harris in the last
row had struck him. Harris was a strong man, much heavier and
stronger than the light-weight Catton who was, moreover, slightly
lame. I could not get him to forgive the blow.

Harris reinforced his blow by rushing into print. Catton was a
wretched little thief, a Jew, he told Bell, and on December 14, 1901,
published an exposé under the title "The Nelson Teapot, a New Financial Concoction," brewed by Mr. J. "Morris" Catton and Mr. D. H.
Evans (the famous draper). Some time before, Harris said, he had
been amused by reading a prospectus of the Nelson Tea Company. It
was trying to get customers for its teas by a new plan of so-called insurance. Every married woman who bought a pound of tea per week
from the Nelson Tea Company and whose husband died while she was
a customer was entitled to ten shillings weekly for the remainder of
her life. It was, however, said Harris, evident to an insurance expert
that the scheme was not financially sound. The Nelson Tea Company
had been bought for £40,000 and turned into a new company called the
Nelson Share Syndicate, with Mr. Catton proposing to manufacture
and peddle the shares. "I imagine very few people will care to drink
any of his watery concoctions." And he concluded by adding that the
unfortunate Marquess of Queensberry was a major investor with 10,000
shares. In return Catton informed Bell that the Marquess of Queensberry had bought 2,000 shares of stock in the Cesari Palace Hotel
shortly before it became bankrupt. Harris, Catton explained, had gone
down to see Queensberry, who was drinking heavily, and talked him
into investing £2,000, as his brother had already done.

During the two years that *The Candid Friend* was published, Harris won himself at least as many new enemies, and renewed ill will
from an old one. On May 24, 1902, Countess Cowley sued *The Candid
Friend*, which had announced that Lady Cowley showed "contempti-
ble snobbery" in keeping her title after she had divorced Lord Cowley and remarried. Harris rushed in aggressively. Mr. Eldon Banks,
Q.C., prosecuting counsel, was a man of fine presence, he told his readers, tall and well made, of fine face, chiseled features and quick eyes;
he had the face of a scholar and thinker and gentleman, yet Mr.
Banks chose to treat the "small crime" of *The Candid Friend* as an
accusation of unutterable villainy. "No language of mine can fairly

stigmatize the atrocity of the accusation," he had said. "Poor gentleman!" wondered Harris, describing his statement as gaudy rhetoric. As for the judge, Mr. Justice Kennedy, he held the reputation for footling his summing up. The jury knew better, Harris said, but because the plaintiff was a lady they gave her £100. And then there was the solicitor. "This is the third libel action I have had in twenty years' journalism," concluded Harris inaccurately. "All three actions were brought by Sir George Lewis or Levi, or whatever his race may be. If I could afford to waste the time, I would give my readers a pen-and-ink sketch of this little Jew and his petty social ambitions but on the same page there is a sketch of his face which will tell more than words to those who care to study the Saurian type."

Many people must have sighed with relief when the last number of *The Candid Friend* appeared on August 9, 1902. Harris' affairs were no better abroad than they were at home. Frank and Nellie had moved from Roehampton to Melbury Lodge, Kingston. Frank, who was "really unwell," was sent into a fever by news from Bell in Monte Carlo. The cellars of the Palace Hotel were stocked with the finest wines, and it seemed that the best thing to do was to ship some of that treasure, together with some other wines, and sell them—'92 champagne, he assured Bell, was the same as gold in London. "Send *that* wine . . . all you conveniently can. As soon as I sell it I'll let you have some money and in case the company doesn't go the wine will be the only source from which I'll be able to help you. . . . Tell Cesari to cut expenses everywhere: we *must show* a profit this year however small. . . . I should think our king will go to the Riviera in March. What do you think of his title: Edward the Caresser: King of the Jews: In truth I'm so down in the mouth sometimes that it is only laughter can help me: laughter at the strange tragi-comedy of life."

Soon the situation in the Mediterranean became so desperate that Cesari abandoned Harris' hotels and became the head of the Elysée Palace Hotel in Paris. Bell duly reported:

> I begged Harris again and again to let me dispose of the hopeless affair there for just whatever I could get—enough to pay the creditors and leave a little something for himself. But Harris, rightly or wrongly, always considered himself on the brink of another great success. He wanted me to play a delaying policy, assuring me constantly that in a month or two, just a few days, he

would be out of his troubles and sending me all the funds required for victory. I had postponed matters to an extent which seems to me even now almost incredible; but in the long run the blow fell. The creditors made the Palace Hotel bankrupt; and the owner of the building, Sir William Ingram, of the *Illustrated London News*, took possession of his property so greatly—and so expensively—improved. The Réserve at Eze dragged along a while longer, but it too was finally seized by the creditors.

Now, both of these enterprises were supposed to be companies. On my first investigation I had found, nevertheless, that neither of them had been properly registered as such, as required by the laws of Monaco and of France. The indignant creditors of the Réserve seized the opportunity to make directly responsible both Harris and Cesari from whom, indeed, they had received their orders. This was a very serious thing for both of them. Cesari indignantly denied that he was the proprietor of the place and responsible, but he had a fine position in Paris and the creditors saw an opportunity, they thought, to hold him liable and squeeze something out of him. Harris, in England, they could not get at; but they had him in another way. The piece of land bought by Harris included a part not necessary for the Réserve; that part, about a quarter of the piece, Harris had not transferred to the Réserve Company but had retained with the intention of building thereon a place for himself. Now the creditors naturally seized that bit too.

When Cesari denied liability and refused to present himself in Nice, the creditors, playing a bold stroke, had him arrested in Paris, brought to Nice and clapped in jail. The affair was beginning to look very serious indeed. It certainly looked like ruin for Jules Cesari. Everything connected with the Réserve affairs had been done in the most careless way. I had found for myself for instance in my first investigation that the land had not then been properly conveyed to the Company, though the restaurant had been built on it. Letters and instructions were signed not in the name of the Company but merely by Frank Harris or Jules Cesari. Cesari . . . was a thoroughly honest man, but no doubt he had yielded to the temptation of lording it a little as Jules Cesari and now here was a dreadful mess for him.

Cesari, in prison, was a nervous wreck because of the threatening attentions of the receiver, an unscrupulous fellow called Feraud. Bell found a fine lawyer, Maître Achiardi, and very soon they got Cesari released. Achiardi then started a long fight, which was to last for several years, to free Cesari and Harris from responsibility. Feraud tried all sorts of clever tricks, endeavoring to make himself rich at the expense of everyone else. He tried to sell the Réserve to an accomplice in the heat of summer when there were no outside buyers present. Another scheme was to try to sell the stock of magnificent wines to another accomplice for a song. All property had now been made over to Nellie O'Hara. Bell, with the aid of a new lawyer, managed to sabotage Feraud; they hunted up a number of victims who had been similarly exploited and hounded. After many threats and extortions Feraud's nerve finally gave way and he suddenly bolted for Constantinople.

A new receiver was appointed. Bell knew that the property at Eze was valuable and should be sold at the proper time to someone who saw its possibilities; a price should be obtained that would pay back the creditors in full—including Harris, who came in as a creditor because he had supplied its wine cellar from that of the Palace Hotel and because on several occasions he had advanced sums to keep the Réserve going. Always Harris would assure Bell that success was just within his grasp, and then he would buy the place for himself, nobody would lose a penny—not the shareholders, not the creditors. At last Achiardi won his case; it was wound up, and the court granted Harris his claim to his bit of land and to a reasonably substantial sum of money.

Throughout the affair, even when Harris had dispatched his last £8 to Bell—"which exhausts my bank balance"—he was assuring him that "the outlook begins to look clear." Though he was a pauper, he told him, he had this huge thing in his head, that great play. With the success of *Mr. and Mrs. Daventry* ringing in his ears Harris had written *Black China*. He was feeling very seedy, he told Bell, on February 13, 1901, had fainted twice with indigestion, but Alexander[3] had practically accepted *Black China*. "He jumped at it . . . he says it's the most charming play he has read for years." "I believe the second great deal is launched," he wrote again, with renewed vigor, from the Star and Garter Hotel in Richmond on November 13, 1902. "If I'm right I can live at my house, Daisyfield is already called 'The House Beautiful.' The third great deal is on the tapes, I don't want to be poor again."

No doubt, much of the previous two years had been spent dodging creditors. Harris and Nellie had moved from Limehurst to Melbury Lodge to 22 Gilston Road, Fulham, and now Harris had bought Daisy-

---

[3] (Sir) George Alexander (1858–1918), actor-manager and manager of St. James's Theatre, London.

field and he was also thinking of buying his friend Alfred Tennyson's villa at Eze. But it had to be cheap, Nellie told Bell, no fancy price for him. The sale was completed on February 21, 1903, for the sum of £800 of fully paid ordinary shares in United Collieries Ltd., Lanarkshire, Scotland. This soon became something of an embarrassment. By August £600 were required to finish the decorations. Harris did not have it, yet both he and Nellie wanted the house finished during the next two months, he told Bell; trees were to be planted—mimosa, lilacs and eucalyptus. He had a couple of good things in his brain, it was sure to be all right, so Bell must borrow 16,000 francs on the property and every franc must be spent in finishing it—18,000, if he could, because the steps up to the drawing room were lacking any ornamentation. Meanwhile he was trying to get some few thousand on a coal deal and he had dropped the Shakespeare book for the time being and was working hard at finance. "I'm trying to make this year memorable." Soon Harris became so pressed with affairs that he wanted Bell to stay with him at his house so that they could get through the work better. Harris did have a marvelous capacity for work, Bell said; even when everything was threatening to fall into ruin he could shove his troubles aside and do competently what had to be done. Bell remembered that in the midst of ruin Harris found time to dictate to him what Bell called some really good pieces of literature. Living at such close quarters gave Bell an opportunity to know Nellie and Frank better. He did not like what he saw. Harris, he said, could be unbelievably thoughtless and rude, and he believed it was Nellie who made him worse.

Harris told me when he came home one evening that a man had been introduced to him in the City, an old man, who had been foreman of some steel mill and had some invention which he declared would revolutionize manufacture. But the old fellow knew nothing of business, it appeared, and was terribly afraid that what he had would be stolen from him. It is not easy in steel affairs, nor in anything else, to sell a thing without showing it; the old fellow had failed so far, and was absolutely broke. Harris had then . . . a charming manner when he cared about being charming; he was not at all a snob and was more apt to be pleasant with a humble person than with an important one. The old man had talked to him and told him his story. He wanted Harris to take the matter up. Harris had not had the time or opportunity to discuss the matter with the old fellow, but he suggested that the old chap should come next day to his house at Putney, when they would go into it thoroughly. If Harris did not take it up he would give the old man a pound to repay him for the trouble and help him along.

Harris had been speaking about this next day at lunch, saying however, as he thought the matter over, that he did not see any chance of his being able to do anything with the affair. Just as he was telling us this the maid came in to say that an old man was at the door and wanted to see Mr. Harris. Harris put on a bored air, "I suppose I shall have to see him and give him that pound I promised." Mrs. Harris said something quickly to him. He hesitated a moment then, to my surprise, told the girl to say that he was out. The girl went out with the message but in two or three minutes she was back . . . the old man had walked down from London to Putney and . . . if he did not see Mr. Harris he would have to walk all that distance back. Harris did look doubtful for a moment, but he confirmed his outness. Mrs. Harris scolded the girl afterwards for daring to question it.

Yet that evening just as they began to think of dinner, the dinner cooked, an excellent one, by their own servants, Mrs. Harris took it in her head that "poor Frank would best be cheered up by a little dinner in town." Off to town they went, all the way up in a cab. They ate at the Savoy and came back to Putney, all the way down in a cab; spending in that fashion six or ten times the pound he had welshed on the old man.

He had had grouse instead of chicken. And the next morning Bell told him that he was leaving for America; the case of the old man had upset him.

Clearly both Nellie and Frank were deteriorating. For Nellie's part she was learning not to believe Frank when, again and again, he assured her that this time it really would be all right, this time they would win, never again would they be poor. Her mercurial father fig-ure, with his glamorous hotels and restaurants on the Riviera, had turned into a sickly middle-aged egocentric, jealous and ill-tempered, with no capital apart from his energy—which in turn he blew trying to get capital—in whose protection she shuttled from address to address, hotel to house and vice versa. Matters cannot have been improved by the begging letters that she received—and these raise an interesting point. On Harris' death one must suppose that someone, probably Nel-lie, destroyed a number of Harris' papers; for example, none of Nellie's letters to Frank exists. Harris kept all his correspondence with a view to selling the so-called important letters. Yet apart from Alice's and some crazed love letters written to him on the publication of *My Life and Loves,* few letters from women exist. Bell tells how he delivered notes to Harris in Monte Carlo from a famous French actress—once Nellie caught him and there was a frightful scene—how every Christmas Emily Harris would send him what Bell called "a letter of real feeling" and quite often some money. None of these exists. One must assume that someone had edited his papers for posterity, with "important" letters retained and, more curiously, the crazed love letters and begging letters from illegitimate children. One, a desperate plea for help and money from some destitute woman, had "blackmailer" written beside it, probably by Nellie, and to most of the begging letters she had added explanatory notes, usually unsympathetic. Bulking considerably in the pile are those from Norah Stack, an Irish cook, who is possibly the Bridget of Kensington Gore who used to say, "All's well that ends unwell." If this is the case, all was neither well nor unwell; she had given birth to Harris' daughter—who was also called Norah—fifteen or so years before. At the turn of the century, when she was writing her letters to Nellie, poor Norah Stack was having a bad time in Battersea. She was in debt, her strength was giving out and she was nearly blind; her daughter had a bad situation, for which post she had been fitted out with new underlinen by Nellie.

> I must write to you as I have no one in this world to tell my trouble only you [she wrote off to Nellie]. Norah is leaving Bognor, on Friday. Mrs. Wolfe the lady that took her from London has treated her most shamefully. I get a letter every week from Norah telling me that Mrs. Wolfe's mother calls her out at 5 o'clock every morning and has to go without a bit of breakfast until 9:30, so that when she gets it she is too ill and broken hearted to touch food. . . . She has a very bad swollen throat and face and not a kind word day or night from them. She tells me the change has done her a lot of harm. She has got very thin. I wish I could run down today to fetch her back as there is a cheap train running but I am not worth one shilling. I am now nearly four weeks out and looking all over London for a job. I do not know why God is unkind to me so and I am good and kind to man and beast. I have not had a dinner of any sort for the last eleven days. I shall soon be out of this world. I wish I could take my child out . . . and away from bad people. I would be happy to see [her] dead now so that she should never

know any more unkindness. Dear Madam I hope this will not make you unhappy but you are the one Friend we have on Earth.

Norah, the daughter, had aspirations higher than being a nursery governess. She had, in the opinion of a certain signor with an illegible name that looks like "trampoline," a great gift. So impressed was Signor Trampoline with Norah's singing that he begged her to go to him for free lessons. But how could she pay her rent unless she earned some money? "It seems a terrible thing," she wrote to Nellie in equally terrible sloping-backward handwriting, "that my whole life should be blighted for want of a start, a nursery governess position is always the same, the wage would never enable me to support my mother." Meanwhile Ian Robertson, the brother of Forbes Robertson, had also heard her sing and had offered her a part, but that was no good either, since she was away with Mrs. Wolfe when the letter came, and the part was gone when she returned. "God is most unkind to me and I don't deserve it. I am willing to do anything you may suggest. In the last place after I had payed my rent I had 2/– left for myself and consequently I have no suitable clothes to go after anything, Dear Madame I am relying on your gracious kindness. I am your grateful Norah Stack." To this Nellie had noted: "Wired on receipt and met this girl and she lies worse than her mother if that's possible. It all turns out she now wants to go as chorus girl at Gaiety this is the third start I've given her. Have promised to keep her till she gets some engagements. I have already sent her new dress etc."

"I cannot go to bed tonight until I thank you for your great kindness," wrote Norah. "I have often imagined what you were like and now I have seen you. . . . I will pray for your happiness and perhaps God will hear me." This was followed by another letter: "I have a feeling that you are angry with me I cannot shake it off. I know this must worry you so much and I am so sorry, I am just sending these few lines to tell you I am thinking of you and that I love you, although I have only seen you once. I know now, that such a being as a beautiful, and at the same time kind and sweet, woman does exist."

While Nellie was growing disillusioned Frank was growing frightened. He felt out of control and depressed; he tried to throw off his anxiety by the bustle and rush that had once been so therapeutic. He dashed from one deal to another, Shakespeare to *Mr. and Mrs. Daventry*, England to France, telegraphing sudden changes of plan and changing houses and countries as easily as he changed clothes. But the old magic had gone; he dissipated his energy and achieved very little. As he realized that he was losing way he required more flattery, more attention and more sexual reassurance. And as he flagged and his confidence went he talked more and more, louder and louder. Wells said that his talk was most effective at its first hearing, but after some experience of it, it began to bore Wells so excessively that he avoided the *Saturday* office when he knew Harris was there; he remembered it all as a "rich muddy noise." T. E. Epstein listened to Harris talking and remarked: "That man has stopped thinking." Kingsmill relates how once when Frank was staying in a country house he ran into the bedroom of his neighbor, who told the story to a friend of Kingsmill: "Harris in his billowy night-shirt was trembling: he had heard weird noises in his room, he said. What was he to do? The man appealed to was of a saturnine temperament, and seems to have reassured him rather curtly." Harris himself tells a story of how he had been working hard and late and one night had to go home by train. He drove to Waterloo and got into the usual carriage, the porter holding open the door for him. Harris had not asked the porter whether it was the right train; this he wanted to do when suddenly he found that he could not remember his station. A terrible fear came over him and then he found he could not even remember his own name. Thinking sleep would help, he settled down. Just as the train started, a man jumped in. "Is this the Richmond train?" he asked. "Ask the porter," snapped Harris, "and leave me alone," and he fell asleep. Waking at Richmond, he left the train, found a cab and told the driver to drive him back to Putney. He fell asleep once more, and when he reached home he was in his right senses, with his memory back. But after that, fear was always with him, he said. He was terrified of going mad.

From France, Monte Carlo and various parts of England would come his miserable melodramatic letters to Nellie, written, many of them, in the cold dark hours before dawn, showing that he felt he was losing sympathy with even such real friends as Ernest Beckett, whom he was approaching on some fund-raising scheme.

> Dear my sweet. I shall have to wire you in the morning that I can't get away till Tuesday: I've done my best but Beckett insisted I must stay for it seems *Royalty*—the Duke and Duchess of Connaught—are coming tomorrow—what good I'm to get out of

that God alone knows but I can't go. I'm out of spirits. I've not had a moment to make my request: I must wait till he returns to London: one thing I have done is—convinced him about Everden —I long to see you; I'm tired of this rot—this society rot! all false and insincere—rotten and I want you whom I love to console and help me to do my work for the fashion of this world is passing away for me and I would fain finish what I have in mind before the curtains ring down. Dear love, love me, I need you so. I'm not fit to be here—I hate the people. I love you and kiss your sweet face and bathe in the golden-chestnut hair and thank God for your sweet affection.

Harris concludes Volume II of *My Life and Loves* with a chapter called "A Foretaste of Death from 1920 Onwards." He had often heard, he said, that sixty-three was "the grand climacteric" of a man's life. He had no idea what this meant until he was well past that age. Here he is relating "the grand climacteric" to virility and his own impotence. But to use the term in its more general sense, meaning a change of life, a critical stage in a human life specially liable to change in health and fortunes, there is no doubt that Harris reached it in 1898, aged forty-two. In his chapter he does attribute other symptoms besides impotence to the condition: a deterioration of general health and digestion—which we know from Bell and from Harris himself that he was suffering—and a softening of judgment, with which there is no doubt he was afflicted. The mixture of bad digestion and poor judgment, coupled with his "frankness," was fatal and led to performances that were offensive and insensitive. Kingsmill gives an example, when ten years later, he and Dan Rider were sitting in the Café Royal with Harris. Two prostitutes, stout and simple, were sitting nearby. Harris growled, "When I came to London as a young man, stuff like that wouldn't have been allowed on the streets." The women tried at first to take it as a joke, then became gradually red and confused. Rider and Kingsmill, who were both at the time under Harris' spell, excused the episode by telling themselves that an overwrought prophet must not be judged like other men.

Harris himself, in Chapter 1, Volume III, of *My Life and Loves*, explains his insensitivity as impatience:

> My worst fault, I think, has always been my impatience: it often
> gave the impression of bad temper, or cynicism, or worse, for it was

backed by an excellent tongue that translated most feelings into words of some piquancy. Consequently this man spoke of me as truculent and the other as callous and the third as domineering, when in reality I wished to be kind, but was unable to suffer fools gladly. This impatience has grown on me with the years and as soon as I gave up conducting journals, I limited my intercourse to friends who were always men of brains, and so managed to avoid a myriad occasions of giving offence unnecessarily.

This sharp-tongued impatience was allied to a genuine reverence for greatness of mind or character; but again this reverence brought with it an illimitable disdain for the second rate or merely popular. I was more than amiable to Huxley or Wallace, to Davidson or Dowson, and correspondingly contemptuous of the numerous mediocrities who are the heroes of the popular press. So I got a reputation for extraordinary conceit and abrupt bad manners.

CHAPTER 14

"The Waiter's Terror"

By July 1904 Harris' finances were once more precarious. He sold "the house beautiful," Daisyfield, to Herbert Beerbohm Tree, who lived opposite, and once more he and Nellie were on the move, avoiding creditors. "I remember you have not got my address," he wrote to Max Beerbohm, "and so I will give you one herewith that will always reach me, but I beg you to keep it private." He wanted Max to read his play—originally called *Shakespeare and His Wife*—on which Tree had bought an option for £500. Harris had written two love scenes for him, "but I don't like them coming together. . . . If you write this week I hope, you might direct to me here, 28 New Steine, Brighton, but don't please give either address to strangers." Harris' negotiations with Tree were not successful; in the end Tree found that the play was not quite suitable for him, just as he had found *Black China* was not right. In "Oscar Wilde Without Whitewash" Bell says that *Black China* was a good play but that the hero was represented as a thief; Tree decided he could not play a crook, and Harris was dreadfully disappointed.

Bell was very sorry to part from Harris—he felt that he was leaving him in the lurch at a bad time; both men, he said, had tears in their eyes. Voluntarily, on his own initiative, Harris had offered Bell a quarter of all that he could save from the wreck in France, and he told him he would send it along as soon as the money came through. With it Bell had intended to pay all the debts that he had incurred while Harris had been unable to give him any salary and put the rest into a little piece of land in California. "I'll send Mrs. Bell a fiver as soon as I can get hold of one," Harris, who was by now working on another paper, told him in December 1904. "Things are a little tight here till I get the paper registered. . . . I suppose by this time you have started for California. I think you ought to send me an account of some pretty place in Southern California as soon as you can, say Santa Barbara, or any other place that strikes you. You can imagine the motor-car and I can fill in the details of the drive if you give me the photos of the prettiest scenery you pass through. . . . I should be able to pay you something for them. . . . You might also find me a correspondent in San Francisco who would keep me informed of the chief events of that noble city." Bell waited a while in New York for the money Harris was to send. None arrived. So at last he wrote to find out what had gone wrong. The reply came promptly. Yes, Harris had received the money, but he denied that Bell had any claim to it. The blow, said Bell, was a hard one. He needed the money, yet he believed that if Harris had written to him acknowledging that he had gambled away Bell's share as well as his own, he would have forgiven him. As it was, he could have sued him, since he had the original letter offering the share and some notes signed by Nellie, in whose name the properties lay. But to present a case in an English or French court would have taken money that Bell did not have, and even more important, when he did win the case, the money would have been spent and impossible to retrieve. "I did what I have always thought since was the wisest thing. I got over it as well as I could, dismissed Harris completely from my mind, and set to work in New York to pay my debts." Only, understandably, Bell did not dismiss Harris, ironically adopting Frank's own tactics by raising his pen in revenge on several occasions over the coming years, both in print and in correspondence.

No doubt much of Bell's share of the money had been spent in Harris' new motoring ventures. With the help of Captain Dalrymple he had been trying again to get the *Automobile Review* off the ground. "I am glad you liked the 'dummy' of the *Automobile Review*," he wrote to Davray on January 9, 1905, "but I don't think you will do much with the Darracq as the Darracq is practically now an English company."

Harris had been quick to be interested in motoring and all things mechanized.[1] "I want a French automobile," he had told Davray in July 1903. "I want to know what a 9 Horse Power Renault will cost me in Paris." The *Automobile Review* was intended purely as a money-making organ, promoting, through its pages, shares and the actual sport of motoring—of which Harris was to become extremely fond,[2] as it suited him marvelously, giving him the feeling of superiority as he bowled along the roads pointing out to his companions the fine scenery and architecture en route. He was on the money warpath, he told Davray, he had no time for stories and plays—they were for the hours of leisure, "which by the bye, seem to get scarcer with me as I grow older, instead of more frequent." The *Automobile Review* office was all set up in Henrietta Street, the writing paper grandly headed—but, according to the journalistic directory, no issue ever saw the light of day. What emerged, however, was the *Motorist and Traveller*, on January 7, 1905. Sometime during 1904 Harris' pecuniary condition had been so serious that a friend had introduced him to Arthur du Cros, son of Harvey du Cros of the Dunlop Tyre Company, with the view to receiving some financial assistance. He did. He was appointed editor of the *Motorist and Traveller*, for which he received £500 salary and 7,500 shares in the magazine, which was to be edited in the interest of the Dunlop Tyre Company. "The Dunlop Tyre Company put in the money and I put in the brains," said Harris.

> We intend to concern ourselves chiefly, if not exclusively, with every development of the automobile industry [the magazine told its readers]. We shall write of automobiles, new and old, tell of their achievements, their utility, the pleasures they afford, and keep a record of their progress as motor-cars, motor boats and motor

---

[1] H. G. Wells, in *The War in the Air*, published 1908, depicted Harris as Alfred Butteridge, a very progressive gentleman who flew from the Crystal Palace and back again astride an apparatus with transparent wings, who came, it was variously said, from America, Australia and the south of France, and who had a loud voice and a swagger. "I lurve England but Puritanism, Sorr, I abhor," he said. "It fills me with loathing. It raises my gorge." He talked with tears of tenderness about his mother: "I owe everything to me mother. All we have we owe to women. They are the species, Sorr."

[2] In one of his novels, *Love in Youth*, the hero—called Bancroft—a young romantic fellow, drives the heroine through France in a motor car, opening her eyes to beauty and telling her stories about the history and architecture of places through which they pass. He is particularly anxious that women should be encouraged to become lawyers and doctors; women must be encouraged to grow and give. Take me, teach me, the heroine cries.

balloons; we shall even discuss other automobile papers and journals, whenever their work seems of sufficient importance . . . we
not only believe that the automobile has "come to stay" as the man
in the street phrases it, but also that it is destined to change the
face of the country and the conditions of life, and in many un-
thought of ways to exercise an incalculable influence on national
character. As the nineteenth century has been called the century of
railways and steam boats so the twentieth century may come to be
known as the century of automobiles.

The intention might have been to promote Dunlop Tyres, but the
product was a sort of motorists' *Tatler*, covering motorists' weddings,
motorists' parties and all the beautiful scenery and houses that there
were to be visited, particularly those belonging to motorists, with all
the wonders therein—waterfalls, canyons, rope bridges and Japanese
gardens. It was an erratic production, which lasted until March 1906.
Sometimes the photographs of statuary and billiard rooms appeared
in purple print, sometimes in orange and green. "One of the great
advantages of a motorist's tour round the shops," it assured its readers,
"is that it enables you to buy such a lot in the morning." Yet not many
people had motors, although Lord Radnor, the son of Harris' friend
Lord Folkestone, told Harris in a letter that he possessed two—not that
he cared for motoring as a sport—he preferred horses; but he was a
busy man and they enabled him to make speedy journeys across Wiltshire: "For business the motor car is almost a necessity now."

The *Motorist and Traveller*, or rather Harris' editing of it, was not
a success. Members of the Dunlop Tyre Company were not impressed
either by this motorists' *Tatler* or by the various scatterbrained schemes
in which their editor, on his warpath, tried to involve them. He
wanted Arthur du Cros to buy the *Observer* and appoint him manager;
he hoped to sell several of his own paintings and bronzes to Harvey du
Cros; and he advised the company "to identify with various bus companies." Once he and Arthur du Cros went off to Paris on business in
connection with a Chartreuse company in which they were to have
shares. After ten or twelve months the Dunlop Tyre Company was so
dissatisfied with its editor's services "in every particular" that it was
advised by a solicitor to dispense with him at any cost. The result of
the paper was a loss of between £8,000 and £10,000. Harris retired
offended, contributing for several months regular articles to *John Bull*.

However, a more satisfactory transaction, involving another son of an erstwhile colleague, had cropped up in the late autumn of 1905. Harris had met Winston Churchill through his friend Ernest Beckett, who was Lord Randolph Churchill's literary executor. Harris had liked him, and in 1901 a complimentary sketch had appeared in *The Candid Friend*. Churchill had been working on the biography of his father, and by the late summer the typescript was finished; but there was tightening to be done, Churchill felt, and the book had still to be sold satisfactorily. At the beginning of October Churchill arranged with Harris that he should look over the proofs, suggest any improvements and then sell the book: "I authorize you as my friend to talk in confidence and privacy to publishers about my book. I reserve to myself the right to decide freely on every offer—whether as regards whole world rights, or English, foreign or Colonial rights—even to the extent of taking a lower one if I choose. But if as a result of your negotiation I make a bargain, then I shall pay you 10 per cent on the excess net profit accruing to me from that bargain above £4,000 as such profit may be realized."[3]

By October 30 Harris had sold the biography to Macmillan for £4,000 and had been paid his £400. "I am much obliged to you for the skill and zeal with which you have prosecuted my interests; and for the advice and assistance you have given me. It is pleasant to me to think that you have been associated with me in this business, for I remember that the best appreciation of Lord Randolph's life yet published was from your pen." This dispatch Churchill followed up the next day: "You have certainly managed extremely well the difficult

[3] Harris' literary executor, Mr. Arthur Leonard Ross, is most anxious that nothing should be missed in this matter, or indeed in any matter concerning Harris and Churchill. He wishes to draw attention to the fact that Churchill's life of his father won the Nobel Prize for literature, 1953, and to the part that Harris had played. "I had given you all the data concerning the private and hidden [in the University of Texas] letters that Churchill had written to Harris when he was editing the life of his father which he received a Nobel Prize for . . . ," he wrote to the author in October 1973. "It is true that the reviews of the biography were almost unanimous in their opinion that it was the greatest biography in the English language, with one exception. The critic's review of the *Daily Telegraph* of London dissented, but it was prophetic in that he said, 'Some other hand or hands must have been at work on this manuscript, hands which seem to have been trained in the worst school of American journalism.' In your biography of Frank you should give him credit for his part in the revisions and editing as evidenced by Churchill's letters."

Mr. Ross was also anxious that it should be pointed out that there was a fairly substantial correspondence between Harris and Churchill: there exist, in all, fifteen letters and a telegram inviting Harris (but not Nellie) to Churchill's wedding in 1908. One letter thanked Harris for his wedding gift, some "really beautiful" saltcellars.

and delicate negotiations with the publishers. No one I venture to think would have been able to make so good a bargain for me as you have. It is remarkable and unusual that a shrewd business instinct and grasp of technical detail should be allied in you to distinguished literary gifts." Churchill, however, was still not quite satisfied. He had been considering the punctuation, he told Macmillan, and was seriously disquieted by a growing feeling that it was permeated throughout by a total lack of system; above all things he was anxious that the grammar and punctuation should be strictly correct. He wished that the book should be solely read for punctuation once again before going to press. "I should have most confidence in my friend Mr. Frank Harris, of whose scholarship and precision in such matters I entertain the highest opinion."

According to Kingsmill, Harris had hoped that when Winston came to office he, unlike his father, would support and advance him politically. He once informed Kingsmill that he had told Churchill that income-tax collectors had no idea at all of what some millionaires were worth. They were well equipped to deal with professional business concerns, but they knew nothing of finance. Now, Harris knew the City intimately—he would go down there whenever he was hard up and make a thousand or two. He assured Churchill that he could add millions to the income-tax returns, and Churchill promised to use him as soon as he came to office. Harris' mortification was real when eventually Churchill came to power and ignored him. His disappointment is evident in his contemporary portrait of Churchill: he was not more than thirty-two, he said, when he first met him, yet his hair was thinning and his figure showed signs of a threatening landslide. During the course of time that he worked through the proofs of the biography of Lord Randolph—which, he observed sourly, he had said in a weak moment that he would do—he discovered a thousand new reasons for believing that no son can possibly write a life of his father. Churchill, said Harris, was no man of genius; he was a climber, thinking not of his work but of his reward, of his £4,000. And what blunders he had made during the 1914–18 war when he was First Lord of the Admiralty! Harris added. Furthermore, Churchill knew no foreign language, read scarcely at all and loved stilted pompous writers like Gibbon and Macaulay.

However, in 1905 Harris was still a firm and optimistic friend, and the book being successfully lodged with Macmillan for publication that spring, Harris, who was ill with his usual winter malaises, departed to spend the New Year, without Nellie, at Haut-Buisson with Alice. He saw the New Year in writing a letter to Nellie. It was 11:36 and only Harris was still up. It had not been a particularly good evening; he had been bored out of his wits by the hand of bridge that de Lara, John Saville and the Duc de Richelieu had preferred to, perhaps, an evening of Harris ventilating his opinions and prejudices. And now he sat down, totally occupied with himself, to talk, as it were, to an extension of himself. He had turned Nellie in his mind into a gentle and adoring woman for whom he would create great things, who would always be behind him, soft and praising, reassuring, supporting and loving, with whom he need never again be alone, who was as interested as he was in himself, in his health, his symptoms, his diet and his comfort. She was his private audience for whom he created passion, melodrama and tragedy. And because in reality she was not like the image he had created, he spent the rest of his life having rows with the real Nellie, trying to turn her into his creation, for he could not, would not believe that she was different, that she was not thinking of him every minute and writing to him by every post. To lose her would be to lose part of himself; no letter meant silence, silence met death.

And now all was silent, the moon a small ivory sickle giving scarcely any light over the still fields as he sat down self-consciously, melo-dramatically to write:

> Dear Heart Mine, I shot this afternoon for a couple of hours and the air and exercise have nearly cured me. . . . I shall see the New Year in while writing this letter to you and I don't know how it could be better or more fittingly welcomed for you are the light in my sky, the assured hope of this coming, as of so many bygone years. But you don't write much: if I don't get a good letter from you tomorrow I shall feel dreadfully disappointed. And I feel in my bones that I'm not going to get one. Naughty child. . . . What are you doing, I wonder. Are you in London or New Brompton? thinking of me? Ah well—I'm thinking of you dear.
>
> The cider here is of many sorts: some strong, some weak, some sweet—some sour but none that I've fallen in love with or much prefer to our own. I've asked about the peas and strawberry jam: it appears both are made and the Princess says she will send some direct to 54 Acacia Road.

I've sat here long: there's no fire: the servants are all out; and I'm a little cold. I'll break off here—undress and then finish this later just as the clock strikes midnight. . . . It is 12 all but three minutes: Now one minute. And Now! the hour is striking—I kiss you sweet and send you all my best wishes for the New Year—all my hopes and all my love and most passionate affection. I love you better every year.

Alice, however, did not love Nellie at all. She was not invited to stay and was referred to coldly as "your pretty wife"—nothing more. There was no mention of her having a sweet disposition, as with the case of Emily, no devotion, she was not called "a real trump"; politely, strawberry jam and specially prepared peas were bundled off to her and that was that. Nellie was not accepted.

In January 1907 Harris' next venture wobbled into publication with the assistance of Richard Middleton and T. W. H. Crosland. After his motoring reviews Harris had tried to buy various newspapers, including the *Times*; all attempts had failed. "I put as much brains into the purchase of *Vanity Fair*," he told Kingsmill, "as Napoleon put into any of his campaign." To which Kingsmill added waspishly: "The brains he put into purchasing the paper were not so evident in its editing."

The first issue appeared on January 2, 1907. Churchill seemed more impressed than was Kingsmill. "*Vanity Fair*—excellent," he wrote from the "tents of Kedar" at Camp Thame. "What a power you have of breathing new life into a journalistic Lazarus." Certainly a great deal of energy went into raising the funds, for by June 1907 affairs seemed very black and *Vanity Fair* about to topple into the jaws of bankruptcy. Harris hurriedly dispatched letters to his friends. Churchill on his behalf interviewed one gentleman but had to report, on June 12, no success. Indeed, the "person" was quite indisposed to assist, not on account of any financial risk but because he disliked society newspapers and did not wish to be connected with them in any way. Ernest Beckett, now Lord Grimthorpe, although in foreign parts, was as staunch as ever. He forwarded the request to the proper quarter and hoped that it would be attended to: "You know that now, as ever, so far as it depended upon me, I should be only too pleased to do you a turn. I buy and have persuaded others to take *Vanity Fair*. Life with you has always been a pretty hard fight, but I have always felt confident that you would win through if your health stood." From Blenheim the Duke of Marlborough wrote: "I will do all in my power to help you in the difficulties in which you find yourself placed, for the sake of the friendship you had with my father and other members of the family. I am sending my solicitors £500 which they will give your solicitor when he calls on them tomorrow. This will keep the matter out of the courts for the coming weeks." Of the required £2,000 Marlborough was going to invest £1,000. Matters seemed saved for the moment and Harris set his face toward new financial horizons. "I am going to that awful America on 7th September," he told Ouida, the romantic novelist whose real name was Marie Louise de la Ramée.

He set off from Liverpool on the R.M.S. *Luciana*. The first thing he did was to lose a bundle of rugs—whether they were to keep him warm or to sell is not disclosed—and then the food on the boat was inconceivably badly cooked, the wine list incredibly stupid. However, Harris had a new role, he was a martyr, a martyr going on a crusade to make money for Nellie:

> This quivering rolling round putting me to dire sickness as I write lends a touch of resolute self sacrifice on my part to this poor testimony of your great heartedness. Often I blame myself that I don't *tell* you all this *oftener* but the passionate feeling of love and reverence is there in me all the time. For your goodness to me and solicitous love I bless you with every good thing in me and my resolve is ever to be and love with you and try to make you happier till the night comes which will still my inevitable being in eternal sleep. If I ever do anything big it will be yours as much as mine for without you I should be a poor lonely rudderless wreck. . . . I am better and as I grow stronger I want to kiss your dear hands and lips and limbs. Oh if you were here! I long for you night and day —never again with my will shall we be parted, never! It is like sundering body from soul. . . . The motion is dreadful here in the bows. I kiss you darling mine with all my heart and beg you to love me a little and not to forget me who love you so. My lips kiss your name Nellie dearest . . .

His trip to America suited him. He worked, according to him, like a dog, traveling from New York to Chicago, Salt Lake City, Buffalo, and Toronto in a train with a private drawing room, into which at every station officials would drop to see if Harris and his retinue had everything they wanted. From the Cobalt Mining Camp he wrote to Nellie: "I've met many people and they are all so kind and complimentary as soon as they know I am a writer. I've been treated like a prince." But then he falls to a less cheerful note: "You are all I have on earth to care for and love. It saddens me to think of my bad tempers, but you must take the good with the bad." By September 24 he was again cheerful and optimistic: "I believe this journey is the turning point. I hope to make money out of it as I made out of the South African trip at any rate we'll make enough to get out of fear for our future." The trip was certainly profitable, for besides financial benefit, he gathered substantial amounts of literary material. Knowing Harris, as he traveled in his glass observation car across the great plains, which thirty years before had been grazed by countless herds of buffalo, one may assume that he talked to numerous people. It was a long journey, and stories of Indians, gunrunning and cowboys must have abounded. From this trip grew his series "The Odyssey of the Great Trail," which began in *Vanity Fair* on January 1, 1908, and which followed a perfectly straightforward lot of articles, "Impressions of America." "The Odyssey of the Great Trail" was changed very slightly and repeated in *My Life and Loves* to document Harris' apparent life as a cowboy and was published as Harris' novel *On the Trail.*[4] The journey also supplied material for another work of fiction, *The Bomb*, which was published in 1908 and dedicated to H.S.H. the Princess of Monaco. This was a novel set in Chicago dealing with the case of the anarchists' bomb-throwing in 1886. Harris supplemented his material with stuff that had been told to him by Bell, which was supplied from Bell's own anarchist experiences. One of the most interesting points is that *The Bomb* was written in the first person from the hero Rudolph Schaubelt's point of view. What could be easier—besides pulling the series together—than for Harris, used as he was to the first person singular, to slip himself into the odyssey in the role of hero and give zest to his anthology of cowboy tales by supposed eyewitness accounts?

One thing really spoiled his successful trip: the food. In spite of his being treated like a prince, the regal fare was foul. The meat was tough and tasteless, the bacon as salt as fire, peas tinned rather than fresh, tomatoes with skins like leather, chickens with legs so long it seemed they had been walking up and down Mount Ararat, half-cooked trout that tasted like a blanket, peaches uneatable, bread as

---

[4] This was later adapted into a film called *Cowboy*, much praised for its authenticity.

fresh as dough, nothing palatable except for green corn. American cooking was ruined, said Harris, by the German cooks, who poured a greasy pomade over everything. Your fillet swam in yellow, your potatoes slid, your beans slipped. But he did have one remarkably good meal. In New York he was taken for the day in the yacht of Mr. D.; Mr. D. was thirty-eight, he had been everywhere and had seen everything. The yacht steamed out of the New York Yacht Club, past the little islands whose green lawns ran down to the water's edge, with here and there knots of ladies in colored dresses enjoying the parapet walks and scattered seats. Long Island Sound was busy with pleasure steamers, delicious in misty sunshine, the wooded slopes burning with russets and golds, the bays and promontories framed in autumn trees. Soon they arrived at their destination—the Huntington, a hotel perched above a white sandy beach. There a fine lunch was served, outside on the veranda, of kingfish, steak and golden plovers and a wonderful ice—grapefruit in maraschino. Later there was an excellent dinner; little bluepoint oysters—eaten with a marvelous sauce of chili and tomatoes—cutlets and snipe.

Harris got back from America in the middle of November, having traveled nearly 15,000 miles in forty days: "forty days in the wilderness," he told Ouida. From the proceeds he and Nellie were able to move house once more—to The Cedars, West Hill, Putney. He returned to the front at *Vanity Fair* refurbished, so to speak, financially and mentally. William Sorley Brown in his book on T. W. H. Crosland revealed that Crosland had a lot to say about the regime at *Vanity Fair*. Mr. Campbell-Everden—Harris used to say that something he would love to see would be Everden drunk and Crosland sober—had a similar story to that of Mr. A. A. Baumann. When he rendered accounts to such establishments and hotels as the Savoy for advertisements that had appeared in *Vanity Fair* he discovered that the advertisements had either been "taken out" by Harris in furs for Nellie or eaten by Frank and Crosland in lunches and dinners at the Savoy and other places. Certainly there are plenty of letters thanking Harris for his hospitality around this time. "Thanks for our famous time at the Savoy," Herbert Trench wrote on September 27, 1908. "It loosens the heart strings to meet one who cares more than oneself about the only things that matter."

"The waiter's terror" was what Crosland called Harris. One of his last articles was about Harris and his first meal with him, which took place, or rather did not take place, at a restaurant in Regent Street. Harris had ordered "pretty well everything a loving heart could wish," but on the appearance of the hors d'oeuvre he had roared at the waiter, "What do you call this?" It had been abjectly removed. Then the bisque had appeared. "Take it away," the author of *Elder Conklin* had roared. It was the same with the fish, red mullet or something of that sort—the author of *Mr. and Mrs. Daventry* had declared it was sodden with a scandalous sauce; equally the entrecôte, which the author of *The Man Shakespeare* proclaimed at the top of his voice to be horse flesh, and probably donkey flesh as well, and no fit viand for a Christian gentleman. Even when the proprietor appeared and inquired if anything was wrong, Harris refused to be placated, whether with cold chicken, York ham, grouse pie or anything with salad. The result was that Crosland had no dinner, and the next time he was invited to dine he arrived with a ten-ounce chop wrapped in greaseproof paper. On arrival at this new meal Harris started going through the menu with a blue pencil and Crosland put his parcel on a convenient plate in front of him. "My dear man," cried Harris, "what in the name of Chatterton, the sleepless boy, have you got there?" "Our dinner," Crosland replied—apparently using the royal plural rather than having any intention of providing for Harris. Harris laughed until the tears rolled down his face.

In fact, while Crosland was writing for *Vanity Fair* he was attacking Harris in the *Academy*. His language, Harris told Kingsmill, was too strong even for his stomach. He was about the vilest man he had ever met, he announced, after Crosland had died in 1925: "I employed him for some time as an assistant on *Vanity Fair* until I found out that he had borrowed money from everyone in my employ—from the typists and even from the office boys. When at length I remonstrated with him, he told me that his private matters had nothing whatever to do with me or my office." He was the only man he had ever seen who deserved a term of imprisonment, he told Robbie Ross in 1914, when Crosland was up before the courts: "you've got him on the hop—perjury too and blackmailing—'tis all excellent: he's been staggering from one to the other of these amusements for the last 12 years and on the way to getting drunk and assaulting his wife."

Vanity Fair is important in Harris' life, not for any merit of quality but because it marks a milestone. On the surface the paper appears similar to *The Candid Friend*. Both carry the same gossip of duchesses, kings and cabbages, at home and abroad. It reviews more books and theaters, but most of the old friends reappear; "The Eccentricities of Dining" are described by Le Gourmet, but now, rather touchingly, he has added "old" to his title. Through the pages of *Vanity Fair* it becomes evident that Harris has abandoned the future, new ideas and new material and has turned round and is retracing his steps. He begins to use up and embellish his past experiences. He is still guide, philosopher and friend, but he is escorting his readers to the exit by the way he has come. The sights are there, but they are *déjà vu*. His Shakespeare work is repotted and his portraits of acquaintances and friends begin in earnest, with many pieces, such as the one on George Meredith, occasioned by death. There are portraits of Thomas Huxley, Herbert Trench and Matthew Arnold. In April 1907 the first interview with Carlyle is written up, giving here merely his views on Darwin and Heine—who, apparently Carlyle held, was a dirty Jew pig. The summer of 1907, while the magazine was on the fringe of bankruptcy, seems to have inspired some astonishing nonsense from the pens of the contributors: Harris himself signs pieces entitled "The Cunning Ant" which are all about primroses, pear trees and daffodils. As the gale of financial disaster reached its height, Harris' fingers seemed to become greener and greener, his pen positively sprouted verdure. The May numbers blow with honeysuckle, lilac, chestnut, oak and ivy; there are Aesop-like fables featuring magpies, rabbits, foxes and sparrows, and burlesques on the seasons. One moment spring is calling lustily in his hot voice, forcing the little snowdrop to drop her white petticoats, and the "sun-lord of summer" is kissing the rose, making her shudder and tremble and wither, and the poppy is naked, shapeless and wanton in the cornfields; the next the retired editor of the *Fortnightly* and the *Saturday*, the waiter's terror, is penning: " 'Two of my sisters,' said Miss Spring to herself, 'are beautiful. Summer and Autumn, they are praised on all sides and therefore I suppose must be pretty; but after all, Summer is too lazy-hot and Autumn is too fat and coarse to be compared with me for a moment. . . . And my flower robes are too lovely for words, primroses, violet, cowslip and daffodil. . . . I must try to be kind to others.' " It is possible that the florals did not come from the nib of Mr. Frank Harris but from that of Miss Nellie O'Hara; she loved flowers, and a few years later she wrote several lush articles for *Pearson's* magazine.

Thatched cabins in the Claddagh, illustrating Bohermore as it was at Harris' birth [From *A Pictorial Record of Galway*]

Fishwives from the Claddagh [From *A Pictorial Record of Galway*]

Ruabon grammar school [Permission of Mr. Eifon Ellis]

Lawrence, Kansas, in 1879 [Kansas State Historical Society]

Byron Caldwell Smith

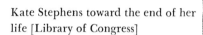

Kate Stephens toward the end of her life [Library of Congress]

William Arnold Horace Harris, Frank's second brother [Permission of Mrs. T. K. Harris]

Thomas Vernon Harris, Frank's father
[Permission of Mrs. T. K. Harris]

W. T. Stead, about 1885 [Radio Times Hulton Picture Library]

Cecil Rhodes, about 1890 [Radio Times Hulton Picture Library]

Oscar Wilde in 1885 [Radio Times Hulton Picture Library]

Lord Alfred Douglas [Radio Times Hulton Picture Library]

Princess Alice of Monaco [Permission of Mr. Arthur Leonard Ross]

Lady Dorothy Nevill in 1895
[Permission of Mr. Guy Nevill]

Harris horsed in Putney, aged about forty [Permission of Mr. Arthur Leonard Ross]

Romantic portrait of Harris [Reproduced in Stead's *Review of Reviews*]

"The Editor of the *Saturday Review*"—a cartoon by Max Beerbohm [Permission of Mrs. Eva Reichmann]

"My poverty, but not my will, consents" (*Romeo and Juliet* V, i)—a cartoon by Max Beerbohm depicting himself as apothecary and Harris as Romeo [Permission of Mrs. Eva Reichmann]

May Congdon in theatrical dress
[Reproduced in *The Candid Friend*]

A pastel portrait of Nellie Harris
and Cappie [Permission of Mr.
Arthur Leonard Ross]

"HAVE YOU SIGNED YOUR NAME YET?"

NO MORE UNEMPLOYED!

100,000 WORKERS WANTED AT ONCE.

There is Plenty of Money Waiting for You.—No Skill Required.
A Child can do it and Earn a Big Income.

READ THIS CAREFULLY.

Buy a copy of the current number of **THE CANDID FRIEND**, show it to your friends or any other person with whom you may come in contact, and ask each of them to sign his or her real name, address, and date in the list which should be made for the purpose, ruled foolscap paper being the most suitable.

Head the list as follows :—

" *We, the undersigned, hereby declare that a copy of the current number of* **THE CANDID FRIEND** *has been shown to us, that we have glanced through its pages, and have taken notice of its contents.*"

(Here follow the signatures)

As soon as you have compiled a list of 100 names, forward the same, together with a stamped and addressed envelope, to the Editor of **THE CANDID FRIEND**, 13, Henrietta Street, Strand, W.C., when a remittance of 5s. will be sent to you in return for your trouble.

TWELVE GOLDEN RULES.

1. A copy of the CURRENT number of **THE CANDID FRIEND** must be shown, and not a back number.
2. No person should enter his or her name and address unless he or she has been shown every page (including the advertisement pages) in the copy submitted.
3. The signature of each person must be in his or her own handwriting (either in ink or pencil), and no one is permitted to sign for another person.
4. Persons must not sign their names in more than one list. Therefore, every fresh list sent in should only contain names that have not appeared in other lists.
5. You can send in as many lists as you like, but each list must contain 100 genuine names and addresses.
6. For every additional 100 names and addresses a fresh list must be made.
7. Lists containing less than 100 names and addresses are disqualified, and will not be paid for.
8. A stamped and addressed envelope must be enclosed with each list.
9. Lists may be sent in at any time. *The name and address of the sender must be plainly written.*
10. Lists are forwarded at the senders' own risk, and will not be paid for until actually received by us at this office.
11. A remittance of 5s. will be forwarded by post for each complete list as soon as such tests have been made which the Editor thinks necessary for verifying the genuineness of the names and addresses.
12. Lists which are not made up in accordance with the above conditions will be declared null and void, and payment for such will be refused.

A GRAND PRIZE.

The worker who has succeeded in sending in the largest number of lists of genuine names and addresses (always 100 on each list) by the end of this year, will receive as a SPECIAL PRIZE A MAGNIFICENT PIANO, valued 50 guineas.

A USEFUL HINT.

In order to gain this Grand Prize, friends should combine by sending in their lists through one person, instead of each one forwarding his or her own list separately.

100 Additional Prizes,

Value some Hundreds of Pounds—a detailed list of which will be published shortly—will be distributed, *in order of merit*, among the next 100 Workers who have succeeded in sending in more than one list.

P.S.—Newsagents, Bookstall Clerks, and Newsboys, Time-keepers, Secretaries of Clubs &c &c, who have special facilities for obtaining signatures, should not delay in joining our large army of willing workers. It will pay them and add considerably to their income.

REMEMBER, this is not a speculation, but a CERTAINTY that everyone will receive payment for his labour, apart from the fact that he may win a Valuable Prize.

ANOTHER ASTOUNDING OFFER.

A FREE GIFT OF £1,000.

In engaging thousands of workers at an enormous cost for the purpose of making **THE CANDID FRIEND** known in every town and hamlet throughout the United Kingdom and the Colonies, the Proprietors, basing their calculations on the law of averages—which rules all human affairs—expect that a considerable number of persons to whom the journal has been submitted will become regular subscribers.

"Once a Reader, Always a Reader,"

is the motto which the Editor is determined to make especially applicable to **THE CANDID FRIEND**. He will spare no labour or expense to supply the British home with a most unique and always interesting periodical.

Now, in order to further stimulate the untiring efforts of our workers at home and abroad, we have great pleasure in making the following offer :—

If at any time between now and the end of this year (Dec. 31st, 1901) the monthly average circulation of **THE CANDID FRIEND** should reach a total of

25,000 copies per week, we shall give an extra bonus of	**£250**
50,000	,,	,,	,,	**£500**
100,000	,,	,,	,,	**£1,000**

to be divided amongst our workers in proportion to the number of lists they have sent in. A careful record of these should, therefore, be kept.

THIS IS NOT MERE FICTION. We can see no valid reason why our circulation should not go up to 100,000 copies within a comparatively short time. But as this depends largely upon the energy displayed by our workers, it is our sincere wish that they should derive some extra benefit from their successful labour.

In summarising the above, please bear in mind :—

1. That a fee of 5s. will be paid to you for every list of 100 genuine names and addresses, as a certainty.
2. That in addition, it is within your reach to win one of the hundred Prizes, its value being solely dependent upon your energy and the number of lists you send in.
3. That, provided our conditions are fulfilled, you will participate in the distribution of our cash bonus of either £250, £500, or £1,000.

MORAL—Set to work at once: "It is not work, but worry that kills."

One of Harris' money-making schemes for *The Candid Friend*

Ernest Hooley, "the fin-de-siècle millionaire," in action—a cartoon from *Hooley's Confessions*, by E. T. Hooley [Permission of Trustees of British Museum]

Arthur du Cros—a cartoon from *The Hooley Book*, by E. T. Hooley [Permission of Trustees of British Museum]

Sir George Lewis [Reproduced in
The Candid Friend]

Frank Harris at home with Saint Joan and Shakespeare—a cartoon by
Gabriel Atkin [Library of Congress]

Mr. and Mrs. Frank Harris and Cappie with friends [Permission of Mr. Arthur Leonard Ross]

Photograph of Harris taken in Berlin in 1927 [Permission of Mr. I. A. Tobin]

29 Waverly Place, New York City
[Permission of Mr. I. A. Tobin]

Left to right: I. A. Tobin, Nellie, Frank and Arthur Leonard Ross, during Harris' last visit to America in 1928 [Permission of Mr. I. A. Tobin]

Harris with cakes [Permission of Mr. Arthur Leonard Ross]

Harris hunting in Nice in 1926 [Permission of Mr. I. A. Tobin]

Drawing room at No. 9, Rue de la Buffa, Nice [Permission of Mr. Arthur Leonard Ross]

Harris shortly before his death [Permission of Mr. Arthur Leonard Ross]

It was perhaps a mercy that the flora, fauna and transsexual seasons did not occupy the pages for long. Soon the editor's teeth were into meatier matters. He saw himself as a crusader fighting the savage penal laws. He saw England in general, the Jewish race and Sir George Lewis in particular, lined up to persecute him personally. One of his main abhorrences was the injustice of the prison system and of judges and juries who convicted people unfairly and committed them to dreadful sentences. For a short time he ran a column called "Man's Inhumanity to Man," wherein he attacked the Home Secretary, Herbert Gladstone, for not repealing the sentence on Dorothy Downing, aged thirteen, sentenced for five years to a reformatory for petty thieving. He attacked Mr. Justice Phillimore for sentencing Von Veltheim to twenty years' imprisonment for writing a threatening letter, taking pains to expose the fact that Mr. Justice Phillimore was religious and against divorce. Here, said Harris, was apparently a fervent believer in the religion of love—the very man to inflict a barbarous and inhuman punishment. He attacked the vicar of St. Austell for ordering the arrest of a poor man who called at his vicarage asking for a pair of boots. "We say no more about the matter because we hope the vicar will take the opportunity of explaining his conduct."

Besides being persecuted by Sir George Lewis he was convinced that people were stealing his work, and he attacked them too. He found that Professor A. C. Bradley had annexed as much as he could from his theories on Shakespeare—while saying that he did not share many of Harris' views and that in any case he had arrived at almost all the ideas expressed in the lecture "Shakespeare the Man" before reading the papers. "Then," spluttered Harris, "he took almost my very words on the subject of Shakespeare's personality and Hamlet." Babyish was what he called Professor Bradley; he had not learned his lesson properly. Then he discovered that the American novelist Jack London had taken almost half a satirical speech that Harris had imagined in 1901 for the Bishop of London, entitled "For the Promotion of Public Morality," and had inserted it bodily into *The Iron Heel*, wherein, seemingly created for the purpose, it emanated from the mouth of a bishop. At this Harris wrote an offensive article: "Mr. Jack London: knave or fool . . . or knave and fool." He was infuriated when Jack London replied that he had never heard of Frank Harris, but he was either a guileless and precipitate young man or else desirous of getting free publicity. Finally Harris was forced to back down, which he did with very bad grace, grumbling that Jack London was not paying him a fee for reproducing his article.

It was not surprising that many people disliked his aggression and tone. The Duke of Marlborough wrote on July 30, 1908:

> I am glad to hear that all goes well with you and that you have been able to put your heel upon those who wished to devour you. I fear that you seem to be surrounded by a lot of enemies, this must be troublesome to you, I only hope you will be able to deal satisfactorily with them. I have been pestered by several people who have written to me about *Vanity Fair* and all that I have done is to acknowledge their letters. I feel though from these letters you have several enemies abroad. Take care that they do not do you damage. Declared enemies are easy to deal with but those who work against you in silence are the formidable ones of this world. No doubt you are well forwarned. I only hope that you will come out triumphant. I fear you must have had a lot of worry but this factor seems to be part of the general scheme of existence.

Solicitors' letters flew back and forth. In 1907 Messrs. Ehrmann were accused of marketing phony Château Lafite wine, and the Peninsular and Oriental Steam Navigation Company was informed that its management was idiotic and its passengers subjected to a Sunday School treatment. Not all lawsuits were on Harris' own behalf. He helped, encouraged and acted in one for Ouida, the romantic novelist whose heroes were always richly endowed with fabulous qualities. He had published her articles and received her letters, crossed and crisscrossed with her sprawling, difficult writing, since he had edited the *Fortnightly*. "Montes is admirable," she had told him. "The man *lives* and the bulls too." Ouida in 1907 was in a bad way; she had no money, a great deal of worry and a cough. De Lara remembered her some years before as something of a pest, always wanting to meet prime ministers to give them the benefit of her advice. Once, she, de Lara and Lord Lytton were traveling in a train to stay at Knebworth when suddenly a stout, awkward man dressed in ill-fitting clothes flung himself into the compartment. Lord Lytton introduced him, or rather passed him off, as a city wine merchant, and much to Ouida's horror they conversed all the way in a low tone until they reached Hatfield, whereupon the man got out. Very queer behavior, Ouida whispered to de Lara—fancy Lord Lytton associating with a wine merchant. That was no wine merchant, de Lara told her, that was Lord Salisbury. Ouida was furious—she wanted particularly to speak to Lord Salisbury and give him some very important advice. Besides calling her a pest, de Lara called Ouida a clever eccentric, who appeared at Knebworth in a white plush tea gown. At dinner she and Percy ffrench would "commence discussing," de Lara said, and when Lady Lytton rose with her candle at a quarter to eleven and all the ladies, each taking a candle, followed her, Ouida remained, quite unconcerned and indifferent to the discomfort of the men.

In July 1907 Harris, aggressive as he was, out for a good fight, had sent Ouida a telegram asking whether she approved of Madame Corelli's "impudent attempt" to get up a subscription for her, thinking she would like to "snub the half-educated creature." Ouida, however, had unfortunately replied to the editress of *Vanity Fair* and had addressed Harris as "madam." That little upset smoothed over, Harris, restored to his masculinity, was soon helping her against the *Daily Mirror* and the *Daily Mail*, which, Ouida said, had slandered, insulted and injured her by publishing articles that spoke of her poverty, particularly the *Daily Mirror*, which had paid an old peasant to be draped and to pose for a picture that appeared as Ouida.

> As you will see from the enclosed *Vanity Fair* [he wrote to her on August 16], I have used your letters as weapons against the *Daily Mail* and *Daily Mirror* and I think from what I hear that they will be disposed to come to terms with you if you bring an action against them. Please, please hold out for heavy damages. To make these brutes pay is the only way to teach them manners or morals. . . . It is really difficult here in England to avoid growing pessimistic about literature and art. The few who care for things of spirit in England are so few: formerly one could hear their voices from time to time; but now in the hullabaloo of the halfpenny papers and their vile and sordid and silly sensations the better voices are overpowered at last . . . the laws are harsh, and cruelly pedantically administered and the prisons of course . . . are the most soul-destroying places in Christendom.

On August 26, just before leaving for America, he wrote that he was quite willing to pay the costs of the action, if she cared to take it.

There was silence until his return, and then, invigorated from his success in America, he wrote on November 29: "I know if you brought an action they would pay you a thousand pounds cheerfully to keep out of court. That is the only way to punish these people." As ever he was too optimistic, but it is true to say that the *Daily Mirror* did offer to apologize and to pay a hundred pounds. Ouida, however, sent a sad telegram to Harris in the middle of January 1908, to which he replied at once: "Chère Bonne Confrère. Your wire, saying you were so ill, made me feel as if my heart were being squeezed in a vice: I do hope you are not really ill; but at any rate, I have determined to put all work aside and come down and see you and try to cheer you up. . . . Now cheer up please, we live by being determined to live, and all of us friends and admirers of yours look forward to seeing much work from you yet."

Ouida probably never got the letter—just as she never got the £100 or the apology; she was dead. Harris was outraged by the *Daily Mirror*, which, instead of apologizing and paying the £100, proposed to raise a subscription for a monument to Ouida and begged its readers to send their contributions to the editor. "The editor of the *Daily Mirror* in order to be sure that he shall do the thing which would have most keenly wounded Ouida, had the impudence to write that 'it proposes to institute a fund to raise sufficient money to pay for this monument, and to liquidate certain other expenses incurred during her life time,' " he told his readers. "The *Daily Mirror* had better pay the hundred pounds it promised to pay, and leave the memory of Ouida to those who honored her."

In the spring of 1908 came two cases, neither of which was to do Harris any good. In February he had a disagreeable altercation with Cecil Parr and Parr's bank, from which he endeavored unsuccessfully to dissociate himself, trying to get Parr's bank to draw up its own apology, which he agreed to sign. In vain, however. The dreaded Sir George Lewis—reminding Harris of one of those people scorned by Dante, despised by God and detested by the devil—was called in, and Harris was ordered to pay £5,000. From then on, whenever he could, Harris drew his pen to make some swipe, however small, at the members of Parr's bank. When Mr. Cecil Parr made a statement a month or so later against the nationalization of railways, his grammar came in for a slating and he was told that his sense of English style was worse than shaky.

In March the case came up that Harris had instituted against Mr.

Arthur du Cros, M.P., which in retrospect was to do him much harm, adding substantially to his reputation for blackmailing. Harris saw himself as the artist and man of letters persecuted by the businessman— and such a businessman, said Harris, whom a writer would have as much chance against him as a poodle or a pug-dog would have fighting a bull terrier; he identified with Whistler on the occasion when the latter was awarded a farthing damages. Harris, who was smartly dressed for the occasion in a white waistcoat and fur coat, stated that he had been Arthur du Cros's ghostwriter, and he was claiming £315 for literary and political services rendered in 1905 and 1906, comprising articles he had written for the *Bow and Bromley Unionist*, a biography of du Cros—with which he had had a great deal of trouble since du Cros wanted it altered to include his pedigree—and three speeches. He added that at the time, being hard up, he had wished to sell du Cros a Holbein, belonging to him, for £350; du Cros had taken it and kept it for a month and then offered to give Harris £200 against it, which would be redeemable in six months. After the election of 1906 du Cros had written asking Harris how much he was charging for his work; Harris had said £315; du Cros had refused to pay.

Harris supported his claims by producing a secretary who said she had typed the work and some letters written in 1905 and 1906. One was from du Cros, which read, "My dear Harris, your writing is exactly the thing"; another was from Harris stating that he had written a couple of little leaders but he had to send to the agent general in order to know the differences between the tariffs of two adjacent colonies: "you will remember the point I talked to you about the other day—one of the colonies under Free Trade and the other a high Protective one; I must verify my statement." He produced also two witnesses to plead that he was a creative artist, who could get £50 for a short story and £500, after dinner, for a play. Herbert Beerbohm Tree[5]

[5] Nellie, in her fragmented memoirs, tells us that Tree was very nervous about motoring. Once they were all going down Leith Hill and he covered his face with his hands and sat down on the bottom of the car trembling. There was another quite different incident in Boulogne. Tree turned up with Mrs. Reed, "an extraordinary beautiful woman," and they all went for a drive in a hired car to Le Touquet and the Grand Hotel. The maître d'hôtel recognized Frank at once and insisted on showing him all the rooms in the hope that he would stay there. They had "to traipse all round," said Nellie disagreeably. "Who would come here?" Frank asked playfully. "Why," said the maître d'hôtel, "we had Mrs. Tree and Mr. Louis Waller." "Can you imagine the scene?" Nellie asks us. Mrs. Tree was supposed to be in a little village in Hampshire with her daughters. All the way back Tree fumed, while Mrs. Reed looked delighted. The Harrises had to dine with Tree and his solicitor, "and we all had to repeat the waiter's story." Nellie felt

gave evidence of his high class as a playwright, and Mr. Massingham, editor of the *Nation*, of his distinction. It was ridiculous that such a man would sit up all night writing things for nothing. There is no doubt that at the end of the first day at least two papers supported Harris against du Cros. The *Star*'s headline was: "How Politics Are Made to Order for Wealthy Unionists."

Du Cros in his defense denied that Harris had written speeches for him; he said that Harris' total output was 5,000 words. And as for a biography, all he had done was to give Mr. Harris a biography written by the *Hendon and Finchley Times* and ask him to dress it up so that it should not read the same way. He said that since Harris had not hinted that he wanted payment until December 1905, he had understood that any work Harris had done for him was free, or at least in return and gratitude for the loan that du Cros had advanced him against the Holbein. And when he did ask Harris to submit an account, Harris had refused, because, du Cros surmised, he was expecting to do business with the Dunlop Tyre Company with reference to a coach company in which he was interested. He felt that Harris was keeping the claim in the background as a lever, which he hoped du Cros would use with his company to persuade them to accede to certain proposals. Du Cros then set about bringing in a number of side issues. He sought to make Harris seem a boaster and braggart. Why, he told the court, he had even claimed that he had edited Winston Churchill's *Life of Lord Randolph Churchill* from cover to cover. He added to this what Harris called a number of irrelevancies: the companies "the artist and man of letters" had proposed, the works of art he had offered for sale, his worthlessness as an editor, his stupidities as a man of letters. The gutter of the defendant's memory was dragged for any lump of mud to be thrown at his enemy, said Harris. Furthermore, an attempt at settlement was made by the plaintiff's solicitor, or was alleged to have been made, and forthwith a cry of blackmail was raised, though there was not one scintilla of evidence of any such thing. "It is a striking feature of this case that all the irrelevancies of it,

---

very sorry for Mrs. Tree. "Why shouldn't she have a lover?" she wanted to know. When they came out of the restaurant there was a victoria waiting, with the driver inside asleep. Harris and Tree got into the seat and drove off, leaving Nellie and Mrs. Reed behind laughing, said Nellie. The driver, thinking someone was stealing his cab, yelled. He got a "much bigger tip." Another trip was to an inn apparently called "The Good Little Bugger." Nellie thought that Tree would never stop laughing when he saw it written up in big letters.

and all the malice of it, were on the side of the business man," Harris commented afterward.

The attempt at settlement was as follows. In September 1907 the Dunlop Tyre Company had failed to renew their advertisements in *Vanity Fair*. In November Harris brought his action. It was suggested, therefore, that the one was the cause of the other—that Mr. Clinton, manager and proprietor of *Vanity Fair*, had been to see Mr. Wilson, director of Dunlop's advertising policies, and had suggested that if Dunlop resumed their advertising the action would be dropped—all of which Harris and Clinton hotly denied, Harris saying repeatedly that his claim had nothing whatever to do with Dunlop's withdrawal of advertisements.

In conclusion the Official Referee found that the £20 paid in to court by du Cros was sufficient as compensation for Harris—a conclusion that, needless to say, inspired a flow of comments from Harris in the *Vanity Fair* of March 25, and that reinforced, anyway on paper, his passion and his sense of self-sacrifice. "The most obvious lesson to be drawn from this trial, it seems to me, is that the man of letters or artist is always at a disadvantage in any legal contest with the business man." Whatever else may be drawn from the trial by his comments in *Vanity Fair*, a fine sketch emerges of Harris at bay. Whenever he felt that his position was weak his tactics were to lodge complaints and attack his opponents, and as he grew older his attacks became more frequent.

CHAPTER 15

"Frank's Glory"

Six months later, in October, Harris was busy packing off copies of *The Bomb* to anyone who he thought might be able to offer him praise, preferably published praise.

> I do not think that I need any introduction to you [he wrote to Jacob Tonson, alias Arnold Bennett], for you have written about my work and I have been grateful for what you have said. I think I wrote you once to this effect, but in my usual casual way I may have forgotten to post the letter. But now I send you my first long novel, *The Bomb*, a sort of confession of faith—the first reasoned defence of anarchy which has been seen in print. I should be obliged if you would review it. . . . I have never asked any favour of this sort before, but if I do it now it is because I want a little popularity and the hope of a little profit in order to get out the ten or twelve books which I have in me still. I have received nothing as yet for what I have written. Not even enough to pay the cost of printing and paper, which seems to me too little.

Jacob Tonson, alias Arnold Bennett, did review it, favorably, in the *New Age*, but this was the only really good review that appeared, according to Harris, although the *Observer* and the *Daily Telegraph* also praised the book. However, most of his friends, complained Harris, had massacred it. Shaw was too busy to write or say anything; H. G.

Wells thought that the first part was good, the second tawdry and bad, offending Harris by asking which part of it was his; Massingham had told him it was delightful and then had written the dullest review, in the *Nation*; Dilke had said to him that it was excellent and then wrote in the *Athenaeum* a notice that was grit in Harris' eyes and ashes in his mouth. Beerbohm had written that he had enjoyed the book and thought highly of it—however, ten such words published in the *Saturday* would have done more good, Harris told him, "and led a whole lot of weak-minded sheep. The fate of books, as you know, is decided in London now in a fortnight or three weeks, and if you delay much longer you will come in the rear of the elephantine main body, and your qualities as sharpshooter in the vanguard will all be lost, which is a roundabout way of asking you to deliver your soul at once in this matter. . . . I cannot be humorous about this, for I am too anxious, I want the book to be a success if possible."

Edwin Pugh, who contributed a little to *Vanity Fair*, wrote that Harris was a literary genius and that some day the world would wake up and do him justice. Alfred Deakin, the Prime Minister of Australia, who Harris hoped would review it there, wrote that in spite of his having been offended in 1907 by the incivility of Harris (who himself had been displeased that the Prime Minister, extremely pressed on an official visit, had not gone to see him), the book had taken him by storm with its force and fascination; he had not been so moved for years—the story was stunning. Perhaps, like Meredith, Harris would come into his own when the reading public were forced to recognize the value of original work.

Although *The Bomb* took only eight weeks to finish, Harris found writing difficult; it exhausted and depressed him. Generally he would do the initial work fast and then work over the material again and again. Years later he commented that reading things in typescript, though better than handwriting, was like seeing a statue in putty; never could he be sure of the writing until it was in print—the marble of writing. "We authors, like mothers, are apt to judge our offspring by the pain they cause us, and we cherish them to make up for the coldness shown them by the outside world," he declared to an unknown Mr. Browne in 1909. He wanted to do so much, he tried so hard, and yet his writing seemed to him often to fall flat. "You give a pictorial effect whenever you want to," he told Arnold Bennett, "and I cannot. I want to do the passion of the soul, the joy, the endeavour."

Having discovered that Jacob Tonson was none other than Bennett himself, Harris wrote on November 27 criticizing *The Old Wives' Tale*. The workmanship was astounding, he found; halfway through the book he was crying out to his wife, "An amazing book, I must finish it." But he was disappointed that the heroine, Sophia, was so ordinary. Why could she not have been seduced and abandoned? Then he wanted her to take her life into her hands and go on, making her body the servant of the spirit, determined to grow, to realize all that was in her, to get the knowledge she craved for and to reach the heights. Alas, Bennett preferred to bring her down to dullness, to make her a lodging-house drudge, her spirit quenched by petty economies. Harris wanted his heroes to have money, to be big enough to appreciate his noble heroines. Stay-at-home sisters were by comparison mangy tabby cats. Bennett, he said, had given his heroine a muck-rake instead of a soul. The book seemed to Harris but the pedestal of a statue, and Harris wanted the statue. "Or is this merely a proof of my thirst for ideal things, for figures greater than life, carved out of some enormous cliffside by a greater than Aeschylus? I should like to trace gigantic ebony figures out of the night itself with a flaming torch. I want the realism; but I want also to see the soul conquering its surroundings, putting the obstructions under its feet; heaping up the funeral pyre, if you will, from which the spirit may take flight."

"Now that we have met in this whirligig of a world let us keep in touch with one another," he added in December. "I think we can be helpful to each other."

Two months later he had finished his *Shakespeare*. "It had hung on me just over twelve years," he told Arnold Bennett, "and at last I have got done with it. I never want to hear the fellow's name mentioned again. I expect it will be difficult even to find a publisher for him!!" However, eight months later, on October 1, Harris was sending out corrected copies. "I hope you will review it in the *New Age*," he told Arnold Bennett. "Excuse tear in paper: it's better than the big blot I made." A week later he was shivering "with the obscene fever of influenza" at The Cedars, his nose streaming, his limbs aching, his throat a furnace and his eyes feeling as if grit had been rubbed into them, when a telegram from Bennett arrived that surpassed his most sanguine expectations. "Here's one," Frank shouted at Nellie, "who doesn't lie, whose impartial soul is moved to truth whom neither love nor friendship can seduce."

As Henry Savage remarked, the portrait in *The Man Shakespeare* was less that of the master dramatist than of Frank himself; nevertheless to many, particularly to young men, the book came as a blast of fresh and clear air. Desmond MacCarthy on finishing the book wrote that he could not resist the impulse to tell Harris personally how convincing he found it. The greatest of all poets was now a live man, insight and truth were on every page, he found himself enlightened. Yet, he concluded, such statements from strangers could not have been very interesting to Harris. How wrong he was! In spite of all the interest and praise, a year later he was telling Arnold Bennett that *The Man Shakespeare* had cost him £250. "I made out of *The Man Shakespeare* in England £25 and spent £250 in publishing." As a potboiler he was writing *The Women of Shakespeare* in the *English Review*,[1] which, in the opinion of George Moore, was losing Harris all the reputation he had gained.

Toward the end of 1909 Harris sold his shares in *Vanity Fair*, and against the advice of Lord Grimthorpe, Nellie and various other friends, he planned to write the life of Oscar Wilde. "My heart faints within me when I think of a new book," he told Arnold Bennett dramatically, "and I am as water spilt out on the ground without strength or cohesion." In this state he set off to Italy to begin writing.

It is curious that Nellie chooses 1910 as the year in which to begin what was to have been a life of her late husband. It was a desultory effort and she covered only two years. Scribbled in a flat, condescending, uninspired, uninspiring prose, it was obviously meant as a corrective, since it covers with some detail certain events over which, after Harris' death, there were controversial accounts, and she deals, or rather tries to deal, with Harris' lack of humor and his affairs with other women. Sometime in late November or early December 1909 Nellie, Frank and Miss Cot, a large-toothed, nervous secretary, with a high color and pale hair, set off to accept Lord Grimthorpe's invitation to winter in his villa, Cimbroni, at Ravello. They spent a few days in Paris, where Princess Alice, Nellie said, insisted that they use her "apartment . . . for we intended being there some days etc." She follows this up with boring details about a motor car that, Augustus John suggested later, Harris only pretended to own. "We also had a motor car. A Brazier that needed looking after and putting into repair. So

[1] Published in six installments, May–October 1910.

we took that along, left it in the repair works, said goodbye to our chauffeur—who begged us to employ him on our return. He was a very good fellow—so we said 'surely.' "[2] They had, said Nellie, ten thousand pounds, invested in her name. What with that and the articles that Frank would write, "we figured we could get along famously— go for Frank's glory." . . . Soon the three of them took the train for Rome. Somewhere, in the early morning, the train stopped and a waiter from the railway hotel appeared with hot coffee. At once Harris engaged him in conversation. When the train departed the waiter was still on board, and remained so until the train stopped about three-quarters of an hour later and, well lubricated by a handsome tip, he could alight, smiling. The whole thing was, in the view of Nellie, maliciously staged by the waiter on purpose to extract money from Frank.

In Rome they paused to visit the graves of Shelley and Keats, spectacles that, said Nellie, seemed terribly impressive, more impressive than anything else in Rome, mainly because there were *lovely fresh* violets placed daily on Shelley's grave. From Naples they traveled to Amalfi in two victorias. Never, said Nellie, would she forget that journey. She describes the country as though she had been through a course of landscape appreciation—which is very likely—at the school of Harris. The rounded hills and mountains blazing with sunlight, the fishing villages with macaroni spread out, like carpets, to dry—it all seemed like fairyland. At Cimbroni the journey had to be continued on foot, for the cobblestoned passages were too narrow to allow a carriage to pass. What an endless walk, said Nellie; she was tired out and it seemed too much like hard work, but what Romance. She sat on a wall and watched Frank, who was *engrossed* with the head gardener, a scholarly man who had been head professor at the Italian school of horticulture. Frank's eyes blazed (a favorite word), the gardener waved his hands so excitedly that you would have thought they were having a fight, and then they would smile and start off again, reciting

[2] An undated letter exists from an A. Liantard: "Well Sir, I love you so much, that I must assure you, I'll be at your disposal as soon as I can. I like your wife as much, she has been a so good Lady to me." Harris, it seems, was proposing at some time to travel from Paris to Biarritz and tour the Pyrenees—the journey he had never made with Oscar. A. Liantard considered the route such "a sad and dull one" that Harris had better travel by train and Liantard could meet him at Biarritz for the crossing of the Pyrenees. "I could also take my wife with me, she would be delighted to act as a maid to the Lady. She is a very good person and very useful. Her temper is as good as a child's. I tell you the very truth."

Dante to each other. Dinner was eaten that night in a room that was more like a cathedral than anything else.

So in spite of Lord Grimthorpe and Nellie begging him not to, Harris planned to spend the winter writing his life of Oscar Wilde. It took him three months. He worked regularly, the day revolving round the creator and his work. "I was only there to help and encourage," wrote Nellie, "which I did with all my heart." In the mornings he dictated to Miss Cot; in the afternoons she typed erratically, hitting the keys without decision, producing letters and typescripts in mauve, wildly spaced words, while Frank and Nellie walked, sometimes along narrow paths among herds of goats. For treats there were occasional day excursions to villages where there was reported to be "an image or a column of great beauty." Here they would sit on a bench and the whole village would assemble and stare at them as though they were something out of the zoo. Nellie was upset by the dogs: "poor things they were always so hungry and they got most of our lunch." Some days Frank, without Nellie, would go off with Mancy the steward, both mounted on donkeys, to far-off villages, and would return with a column or a statue. "I made excursions all through Calabria," he wrote to Arnold Bennett on April 7, 1910, "and made some wonderful 'finds' in the art way. Old columns and wells, funeral urns and medallions half life size, things to me of infinite value."

But generally the day was regular, and after the walk along the goat path, tea would be drunk and manuscripts read. Dinner in the baronial hall was gay—always galas, said Nellie. Afterward they would mount to the huge salon, with its domed ceiling and its stone floor "strewn with great chairs." Frank would settle into one of these and cover Miss Cot's purple typescripts with blobs of ink while Nellie and Cot stayed at the other end of the room. Cot would play the piano and Nellie would dance "Hungary dances," but always the two were subdued and nervous, for Frank was "rather intolerant of noise and I was afraid he would not approve of the dancing." On Frank's birthday the great hall was arranged with flowers ("ah such flowers!") and the steward Mancy brought up the best champagne and wines: "it was awfully sweet and touching." Perhaps for her purpose she found it politic to remember the time as a happy one. "How happy we were there," she remembered. "There was a great terrace that seemed to look over the whole world—Frank worked and we danced and life was a wonderful thing." Life was also a dull thing, as she revealed in another paragraph. The only distraction was the *Bombicade*, which started in the morning—sometimes at five o'clock—and continued for hours blasting trails of dynamite in celebration of the Virgin, or any other saint whose day it happened to be.

The view was wonderful—from every window Vesuvius was visible. The terrace, built by Lord Grimthorpe, was several hundreds of feet high and contained many statues and columns from Paestum—all the world came to see it—although unfortunately for Nellie, not when she was there. There was an Italian and a French garden and thirty gardeners. By the door of the "great domaine" was a small house that Lord Grimthorpe had never been able to buy. Nellie was fascinated by its occupants, who would swagger about—two or three women sitting on the doorstep in the sun, letting down their hair and searching for lice, a hunt which in Nellie's view added only to the picturesqueness of the place. Not that the sun put in much of an appearance, according to Harris. "The climate of this place is absolutely atrocious," he wrote to Augustus John on February 17. "It is worse than England. It rains persistently and is windswept to boot." But he had finished *Oscar Wilde* and for the moment was feeling in an optimistic mood and invited Augustus John to join them. John could not get there.

> This "Oscar Wilde" book is really gorgeous in places and will I think make a stir [Harris told him]. I had to write it; it was in me, and now I have done it I feel better. I am at last loosed and free to try my hand at a great novel or two, from the standpoint of my brains now, Shakespeare was in me twenty years ago, I had to get rid of him, and my enormous German reading; Oscar had been in me ten or fifteen years and I had to get rid of him. I should like to get rid of Rhodes and Randolph Churchill, but they don't count so much. At last I am free, as I say, to write two or three novels, bigger than anything in English, if it is in me to do it. And if it is not, the mere effort will do one some good. But at any rate I am now pregnant with four or five books—suggestions gradually taking shape in me, gradually clothing themselves with incidents and emotions, and if I can wait until they are ripe to be born, they ought to be worth seeing. For surely I can look over the heads and under the feet of the Fieldings, Thackerays and Scotts, who keep thrusting their little pictures between me and the great vision of life. I have done.

His hand meanwhile was being greatly exercised by the tipping. The tips were awful, Nellie said. Everyone had to be tipped, even "our wonderful gardener, who knew Dante by the yards." It was decided it would be more economical at Nice, so they answered an advertisement and rented a "small chalet on the hill."

There was no part of the world, except for that piece of London containing Wimbledon Common, Richmond Park and Kingston Hill, that Harris loved so much as Nice and all that coast from Saint-Raphaël to Menton, with its air like new milk, its red soil, its pinewooded hills, fragrant valleys with thyme and rosemary and sweet paths carpeted with pine needles. "I would rather have a peasant's cottage in the sun and eat bread and onions than a palace in the dull and gloomy north," he had written in *Vanity Fair* in his "Cunning Ant" period. "I love to see outlines cut sharp in translucent air and clouds that seem like masses of snow-white marble and shadows that are purple-black. . . . I love the twisted patient olive trees and the black green leaves of the oranges with the red-gold fruit. I love the old grey sunburnt walls where the little lizards play and the white-hot dust of the roads." To Augustus John he wrote: "The older one gets the more one turns to nature and her soothing beauty for rest from the foul ineptitudes of Philistinism." In fact, Harris' and John's idea of nature were very different. To Harris nature meant those nice tame pine-needled paths leading down between the rosemary and thyme to the facilities of the Promenade des Anglais and the comforts of hotels. To John this was not nature, this was suburbia.

They arrived in March at their chalet, Villa Tourterelle, Boulevard Boron. "Here I am again in God's country," he wrote to Arnold Bennett in his letter of April 7, 1910. "After a delightful winter spent in Ravello perched on a promontory 1,200 feet above Amalfi . . . I could not stick it out. Italy always makes me bilious. I suffered perpetually, but in spite of my wretched body I had a good time." "The house we had taken trusting the advertisements was very simple," wrote Nellie, "so simple it had no bathroom and the toilet was outside." It was surrounded by pinewoods and had flowers all round; "we each had a room and a room to spare for a guest," and how happy Nellie was once more putting carnations all over the house and washing herself "in pieces." All three of them used to go to a hotel nearby for a bath. "We found that very expensive."

She follows these careful trivia with an account of Augustus John's visit designed to contradict John's own unflattering statement, which had originally been published in *Horizon* in 1942, wherein Nellie, who was described in attire that was faded and secondhand, was supposed to have been offered to John by Harris as his prize concubine. According to John, originally he and Frank had met at a party in Wellington Square with Max Beerbohm, Charles Conder and Will Rothenstein. With his booming voice, baleful eye and hardy wit, Harris had impressed himself upon the company by sheer force of bad character, or so it had seemed to John. While he was booming on, John had suggested to Constance Collier that she should sit for him, adding that he would have to find a bigger studio. "Why not take the Crystal Palace then?" roared Harris, and everyone had laughed. He was very much the *pièce de résistance* of the party, John had observed sourly, and gave an impression of Mephistopheles with his basilisk eyes and hair of suspicious blackness rising low from the brow. Frank, on the other hand, was impressed by John's looks and more than once exaggerated his height, which was in reality five foot eleven; in his contemporary portrait he says he was over six foot in height, square-shouldered, and a good walker. Of all the men whom he had met John had the most striking personality, but he added that his pictures failed to satisfy him in spite of the really magnificent quality in them. "If John does not realize himself to the uttermost, doesn't mint all the gold in him, it will be, I am sure, because he has been too heavily handicapped by his extraordinary physical advantages. His fine presence and handsome face brought him to notoriety very speedily and that's not good for a man. Women and girls by the dozen have made up to him and he has spent himself in living instead of doing his work."

In April 1910 Harris was feeling restless and in need of a little living; he was anxious also to add John to his gallery of contemporary portraits. As soon as they arrived in Nice he invited him, once he had got his car from Paris, where it had been inundated by floods while being repaired; he would give him a great time, he promised.

> John was staying at a place near Marseilles with some gypsies [Nellie wrote]. Frank had some months of work accomplished so he was ready for some fun. He invited John to come and stay in our tiny cottage in the hills. . . . I am sure John thought he was coming into high excitement perhaps he had been having a dull time too. He arrived for Isadore de Lara's opera Messaline. . . . Frank got almost half a dozen people for a big box. John arrived about

eight. Frank insisted on bringing the unfortunate man to the
opera, after the opera we all went to the restaurant and had supper
and then home to our place on the hill. Of course Frank was full
of his work on Wilde and poor John who had come to Nice expecting a great time found this simple little cottage and Frank ladling
out his manuscript begging John to read it which he did—after two
or three days this must have got on John's nerves for one day we
went into the town and on our return we found John had flown,
leaving no word—nothing. Frank's face was a study—poor John. I
used to love to walk along the Promenade des Anglais with John at
that time he wore just a painter's smock and wooden sabots in
defiance—it was great fun to see the people and watch their faces.
Augustus John looking *defiant* and I was enjoying it all.

"Poor John" himself plainly had disliked every minute of his stay:
"pretty queer days" he called his time with Harris. The mixture of
suburbia and Harris' egotism had clearly been frightful to him and not
helped in any way by the presence of Nellie and poor Miss Cot. "I
went to Neece to stay with some people but I found they were so horrible I ran away one morning early before they were up. Neece is a lovely
place full of horrible people," he wrote to his eight-year-old son David.
In *Chiaroscuro* he says he could not understand Harris' longing for
his company. For his own part, he was able to resist the pressure to
travel to Ravello; however, when Harris returned "to his own villa at
Nice" he decided to travel thither from Martigues. The words "to his
own villa" reveal that John's story is not accurate; he remembered
that they were staying at Villa Édouard VII, yet this did not become
the Harrises' address until 1928.

I arrived at Nice with little baggage but my paints and panels.
Harris awaited me on the platform in evening clothes. He viewed
my corduroys with evident distaste before carrying me off to the
Opera House where he occupied a box lent him, he said, by the
Princess de Monaco. His wife, Nelly, awaited us, attired for the
occasion in somewhat faded and second-hand splendour. An opera
was being performed and presently the composer joined us, one
Isidor de Lara. This personage, I could see, regarded me with more
than suspicion. Frank and he were on the best of terms, vying with
each other in expressions of intense mutual admiration. I gathered
that I was assisting at a meeting between "the modern Wagner"
and "the greatest intellect in Europe." I was glad when the "up-

roar" ended. Then, Nelly having been sent home, Harris took me to some hotel where we sat up late, drinking champagne and, as far as my host's conversational flow would permit, listening to the nightingales. The "Villa Edward VII" was situated in a suburb of Nice, and was typically suburban in character. I was shown my room which, as Frank was careful to point out, adjoined Nelly's, his own being at a certain distance round the corner.

Next morning Frank and I went down to Nice. His method of transport was ingenious. There were always a few private cars waiting on the high-road, and he found no difficulty in persuading one of the chauffeurs to run us down to the Promenade des Anglais where we alighted in style. This manoeuvre not only saved us a walk but tended to reassure Frank's tradesmen. Frank was always reminding them that his Rolls Royce was still *en panne* and under repair somewhere in the centre of France. I guessed that this vehicle, like Elijah's chariot, was purely mythical. Frank had a talent for buffoonery and delighted me by his clowning. It was our only spiritual link. His longwinded discourses on the subject of Oscar Wilde, whose life he was writing, bored me stiff. When he showed me his manuscript, I found the text interlarded with pious sentiments and references to our Saviour. I asked him what the devil he meant by dragging in Jesus Christ on every other page. He looked black at this but did in the end largely purge the book of such allusions. Before many hours passed in the Villa, I decided I was either mad or living in a mad-house. What I found most sinister was the behaviour of Nelly and the female secretary. These two, possessed as it seemed by a mixture of fright and merriment, clung together at my approach while giggling hysterically as if some desperate mischief was afoot. On the evening of the third day, my relations with Frank Harris, always precarious, broke down altogether. He was looking his ugliest: neither of us now attempted to conceal our mutual antipathy. At dawn next morning I arose, gathered my belongings and silently departed: this time I descended to the harbour on foot and, entering a seaman's bar, breathed, with what relief, a purer air.

What actually did happen lies somewhere between these two accounts. John several times skeptically slants his story so that the reader will accuse Harris of boasting: the Princess of Monaco's box at the opera is one case in point, Harris's car another, while the Villa Édouard VII is a definite piece of inaccurate reporting. Hesketh Pearson says in "Rebel Artist" that John was secure in the knowledge that everyone would believe anything about Harris[3] and felt certain that a little picturesque embroidery of the tale would not be questioned. "Recalling the phrase 'Give a dog a bad name and hang him,' John did not hesitate to string up his former host."

Sometime after John's escape the Harrises moved to 2 Square Gambetta, and having supplemented the furniture from a secondhand store, they departed, leaving a maid in charge, and rented new British furnished suburban accommodations, The Corrie, Roehampton. Here, said Nellie, Richard Middleton[4] would come and stay, sleeping "on a couch in the sitting room." He and Frank would go off on long walks over Wimbledon Common, Richard Middleton shambling along like some great Newfoundland dog, grumbling about the *Academy*, for which he wrote and which had the audacity to change some of his words. The summer, spent between long walks, motor cars, literature, lavish tipping, luncheons and dinners and fine wines, reduced the Harrisian household to its usual financial difficulties. "I have run rather heavily into debt," he wrote to Austin Harrison, editor of the *English Review*, on August 21. In the words of Emerson, literature was a good stick but a bad crutch; he must make money another way. "At any rate literature will not pay for my motor car, much less for the primitive statues and the pictures which my soul desires."

However, literature coupled with morals exercised him into the summer of 1911. In February his "Talks with Carlyle" had appeared in the *English Review*.[5]

From the Villa Turtledove among the Niçois pinewoods he and

---

[3] Lew Head, for example, wrote to Elmer Gertz that Harris was separated from his fellowmen largely because of his "slant," which was quite pronounced. "Frank taught me the first lessons I learnt about homosexuality. I have not held it against him."

[4] Harris was an ardent believer in Middleton—he supported him constantly with praise, advice and, according to Henry Savage in *Richard Middleton: The Man and His Work*, financial help. "Your article The Magic Pool . . . is simply divine. Why don't you do a book of these things, man?" roared Harris. "I call for a book and as soon as the brute public read it they will call for more too." Unfortunately, "the brute public" did not; Middleton had nothing published before he committed suicide in Brussels, where he died penniless. Harris abhorred a system that allowed a poet such as Middleton to live penniless while rewarding millionaires and "mediocrities" and spending thousands on the South African war. He was deeply depressed by Middleton's suicide. He had offered him his flat in Nice and £20 for the journey, but Middleton had preferred to travel to Brussels, and in December 1911 committed suicide. You couldn't change these poets, Harris remarked; he'd tried, but there it was. Others suggested that Middleton's life might have been different if he had had a new set of teeth; as it was, he suffered a great deal from pain and melancholia.

[5] Other articles Harris published in the *English Review* were: "Renan: The Romance of Religion" (March 1911); "The King of the Jews" (April 1911).

Miss Cot had dispatched on April 4 one of their purple-lettered crea-
tions to Austin Harrison. They began the letter in a way of which
Harris was to grow increasingly fond. "Dear Austin Harrison, With the
sad superiority of the senior I am going to drop that Mr., which is no
distinction to either of us. . . . You ask me very courteously, for any suggestions in the editorial business. I am no editor as I have said, or
rather I was an editor in spite of Frank Harris, in spite that is of the
best in him and not because of it." But who in the name of heaven was
Mrs. Belloc Lowndes, he wondered, and why did Austin Harrison publish her work? A grisly story of a creature decapitated by most im-
probable chance, discovered by a maniac, dished up on a cheap platter,
garnished with parsley, flavored with the good and high English sauce
of adultery with home comforts. . . . "I have never laughed over anything for a long time as I laughed over it. There is no country in the
world where serious things are put to such shame and silly, light and
casual ephemeridae are treated so seriously as in yon foggy isle."

Perhaps it was Mrs. Belloc Lowndes who stirred Harris to write
his "Thoughts on Morals," which appeared in the *English Review* in
June 1911. Morals, Harris declared, were rules of health; as such they
should be remolded each generation. The Ten Commandments were
obsolete, and "Be yourself," "Be wilful" and "Never conform" were
more to the point, for there was no one in the world like yourself, nor
ever had been. Boys should be taught to question everything. Furthermore, a little excess in youth, gratifying natural desire, was less harmful than the abstinence generally recommended in England—indeed,
temporary excesses, far from being harmful, were positively beneficial.
And this tolerance, far from being afforded only to boys, should include
both sexes, for "were it not for the inconvenience of maternity it would
hardly be denied that love, passion and the myriad consequences of
love were the more natural in women than in men and should be regarded with even greater leniency." All his frustrations about the
"idiot prejudice" of English education materialize: by which system it
was "bad form" to write well or to speak foreign languages or to differ
in any way from mediocrity; by which boys were encouraged to develop their muscles rather than their intellect.

"Thoughts on Morals" resulted in an uproar in various correspondence columns, particularly between the respectable covers of the
Spectator. Matters were aggravated further by the *English Review*'s advertising policy. A pamphlet, headed "The Great Adult Review," was

widely circulated by post; following the heading was the question "Why Adult?," which was followed in turn by a list of reasons:

BECAUSE

Our standard is NOT that of the "young person," either the callow lad or raw school-girl.

Our aim is NOT to be the Review of unsophisticated youth or of the baby's nursery.

The Editor does not use the blue pencil on what the magazines call "naughty words."

Authors are not *requested* to write down to the mob public.

We recognize no self-appointed censor, but only the censorship of public decency and the morality of truth.

We feel it a duty to maintain a platform for literary expression that shall be free and unfettered.

We oppose Mrs Grundy and all self-righteous societies.

We stand for courage, originality, progress, truth and literature.

On June 10 St. Loe Strachey, editor of the *Spectator*, launched his attack on "The Great Adult Review" as a whole and Harris' article in particular. The propagation of such views, he said, was harmful to the state in the highest degree. Particularly hung up on display were Harris' remarks on the passion of women; such a sentence could well be described in the words of the eighteenth-century poet Green "as a receipt to make a harlot," spluttered St. Loe Strachey. As a result he refused that month to include any notice of the *English Review* in his account of the magazines, "nor do we intend to do so for the future, unless the tone of the magazine becomes very different from what it has been of late . . . we condemn the tone and the tendency of the *English Review* on moral questions, and we do not desire to be parties to giving the *Review* in question a wider influence." Newspapers were the watchdogs of the state, he concluded, and "they should certainly give a warning when they see garbage being dumped on the nation's doorstep."

Correspondence raged. St. Loe Strachey had roused the deep resentment of the literary authors of the country, Arnold Bennett wrote to tell him; of this fact he had personal knowledge. The *English Review* published its reply by listing ninety-five writers, including Tolstoi, Gorki, Henry James, John Masefield and Harris' friend Mrs. Belloc Lowndes, all of whom had contributed recently to dumping garbage on the nation's doorstep.

Harris was deeply wounded both by this storm and the one that was now raging over his "Talks with Carlyle"—for it seems that the holocaust over "Thoughts on Morals" had spurred on Alexander Carlyle to the attack. (Six months after "Talks with Carlyle" had appeared, Alexander Carlyle published, in the August number of the *English Review*, "Frank Harris and His [Imaginary] Talks with Carlyle," to which Harris had replied in the same number.) Harris now hated Strachey with venom. "The very type of a muddle-headed, half-educated, self-important and silly creature who probably by purchase has got hold of a weapon too sharp and too heavy for his feeble-foolish hands," he roared in his reply. He saw the whole thing as an act of persecution directed toward his own ruin. He added a new word to his vocabulary, which he assumed would pass into the English language—"Strachery,"[6] meaning dishonest appeal to mob morality. His answer—which when published covered two and a half columns—caused him difficulty. "I have never had anything I found so hard to do," he wrote to Austin Harrison with rare humility and detachment. "It has stopped all my work and spoiled my temper a dozen times which only proves how conceited I'm getting. His Highness doesn't think he ought to be slanged and jeered at which only shows that he's not fit yet for the Crown of Thorns."

He seemed thoroughly shaken. Harrison and he were to lunch at the Savoy, where Harrison would read the reply: "Be punctual dear," the letter finished, "Yours sincerely Frank." Certainly the furore clinched his paranoia.

In his reply his disappointments and blighted hopes once more break surface—his despair over unfairness shown to women, the unjust libel laws. He rides his old horse: English juries were accustomed to giving fantastic and ridiculous sums for mere errors that deserved no punishment at all; if one was a writer wishing to discuss the English view of morality and sex, one was outlawed—any paper could and would single one out, hold one up to ridicule and contempt, set out deliberately, with malice, to ruin one. Week after week, Harris said, the *Spectator* had attacked him in the form of answers to correspondents, posing as moral censors.

> You, St Loe Strachey, take me to task and read moral lectures, with all the authority of your Punch and Judy show. Do you know what the *Spectator* is and what English morality really looks like

[6] Lytton eclipsed St. Loe, and the word "strachery" passed into oblivion.

to dispassionate eyes? Thirty odd years ago the *Spectator* published some of the unnaturally vicious verses of Swinburne while condemning young Thomas Hardy, today it boycotts and befouls honest intellectual discussion in a half-crown review, while not daring to say a word against the perpetual lewd suggestiveness of this and that weekly journal.

Woe unto you, Scribes and Pharisees, hypocrites! Woe unto you who strain at a gnat and swallow a camel, who permit *Salome* on condition that no head, but only the painted simulacrum of the prophet's head, shall be seen on the stage.

English morality indeed: Piccadilly Circus at night and the *Spectator* as censor. There is a pit fouler than any imagined by Dante, a cesspool bubbling and steaming with corruption and all shining with putrid iridescence of hypocrisy—that pool is English morality, and one of the foul bubbles on it is the *Spectator*.

To this torrent of words, St. Loe Strachey remarked, readers of the *Spectator* were exposed "with the utmost reluctance."

It was two months after this scene that Harris, somewhat bruised and battered, first met Hugh Kingsmill Lunn. Once, in the pages of *Vanity Fair*, Harris had described the life of man being like a catherine wheel: starting with a small noise, dancing round and round, throwing off sparks, shining with a circle of magic white light, radiating energy to the audience, then gradually slowing, the sparks dying, the radiance fading, rocking back and forth, and stopping, a burned-out ember in the dark night. Now, in 1911, the nights were beginning to draw in, the shadows to lengthen, but there was still some heat in the sun; Harris retained some of his magic, some sparks did fly. For a young, inexperienced man such as Kingsmill, Harris' appeal lay as a (self-confessed) great lover—he was attracted by Frank's enthusiasm for literature, impressed by his air of superiority toward it; his admiration was deepened by his sympathy. Harris seemed to be the master of life, but while the Shaws and the Wells were honored, he was ignored and reviled. "It was a singular privilege, we felt, to witness this Calvary of a great soul," Kingsmill wrote in his *Frank Harris*.

The meeting and subsequent friendship of Hugh Kingsmill and Harris are also reported in the fragmented memoirs of Nellie. This section is dated July 11, 1932, and, like Augustus John's visit, is supposed to be a corrective to Kingsmill's *Frank Harris*, published that year. Underneath there is one of her notes: "I do know Lunn. I also know how small and mean and what a cad he is." Although Kingsmill suspected Harris' secret wretchedness and lack of confidence and detected his uneasiness and tenderness, although he had a relish for him, Frank emerges from *Frank Harris* the rascal and rogue, bristling, bellowing, dubious and comic. In fact, Kingsmill had been more impressed and influenced by Harris than he afterward cared to admit; he had taken him for his father figure, thereby liberating himself from the puritanism so closely associated with his own father. Later he was ashamed of himself; his shame and horror of sentimentality he turned to irony, and he made an extremely funny and brilliant caricature—one for which Frank himself would not at all have cared. Poor Nellie's gasping, sprawling prose is no match for his tight, concentrated stuff, charged with energy and humor. Conspicuously lacking in literary talent or knowledge of punctuation, she relies for attack mainly on unflattering descriptions. "A young man had been writing to Frank saying how much he admired him and his work and begging him for a meeting." The meeting, she said, duly took place in a tea shop.

Lunn was full of praise and hero worship, we were obliged to leave for they were preparing the tables for dinner. Lunn insisted on accompanying us to Roehampton in fact it was almost impossible to get rid of him. We had to go somewhere to dinner I remember. We all stood outside the door talking. I had with me a little dog. Lunn was one of those people who always has to pretend he is doing something—like playing tennis or golf—this night it was golf. So he was swinging his stick. The result was my poor little dog got in the way and was nearly killed by his stick—of course he was all apologies—Well that was my first meeting, he was he said 24 or 25, he was about 5ft 8. Broadly built, his head was rather round, his hair scant—and of dirty light brown colour—his mouth was wide and very thin lipped and his eyes were the smallest I have ever seen in a human head—they were neither kind nor frank, just shifty—small beads—Frank spoke of them and said later at dinner the man has no kindness for the eyes are the window of the soul. Well days went on and Lunn continued to write—and meetings took place between Frank and Lunn, it was as tho' Lunn had fallen in love with Frank. Lunn was always on the job—letters daily or himself. I never in anyway interfered in this friendship in fact knowing how much Frank needed help and friendship I was glad.

"Frank's Glory"

Kingsmill, in *Frank Harris*, records how he met Harris on August 28. He had been fascinated the previous year by *The Man Shakespeare* and had written several letters to various countries which had not reached their destination. After Kingsmill's puritanical childhood and a schooling with the stress on developing muscles rather than intellect (the system that Harris was so strongly against), Frank with his defiance seemed like a breath of fresh air. Harris was at the time preparing a lecture on Jesus—"The greatest wonder of all, the best that ever wore flesh"; however, he left it to meet Kingsmill at the Café Royal.

He was standing inside the entrance, a few yards from the street, peering short-sightedly at the persons coming in, a man below middle height, as I had guessed from his work, but much broader and stronger than I had pictured him. He was wearing a bowler hat and a braided overcoat. As he smiled hesitatingly at me he was so unlike my idea of a bitter, impoverished genius, and so near the conventional notion of a Jew financier, that I walked past him. But no one else seemed to be looking out for me, so I turned back and asked, "Mr Frank Harris?" His diffident air vanished. Shaking my hand he said, "There is an excellent wine at the Savoy I want you to taste"; and a few minutes later we were seating ourselves at a table overlooking the Embankment, when he leaned forward and rumbled in a deep whisper: "Would you change places with me? There's a South African millionaire behind you who I whipped once in one of my papers, I can't enjoy my lunch if I have to look at him."[7]

Having been attracted to Harris by his praise of poets as the greatest of the sons of men, and by his contempt for politicians and practical activities in general, I was puzzled and rather disconcerted by his telling me, as soon as he had settled himself with his back to the offending financier, that in his youth he had joined a gang of labourers and had soon been picked out by the foreman as the smartest of the lot. A little later, he continued, he was employed in

[7] This was the first of many lunches. Kingsmill remembers one taking place again at the Savoy in November 1911 (Kingsmill to Hesketh Pearson, May 20, 1926). Arnold Bennett came in with the actress Gertrude Kingston. "My God," said Harris, "the woman's got a cunt like a horse collar," "by which figure he meant, I believe, to express dislike in general rather than physical disapprobation. . . . I happened to be carrying a Pearson's magazine. A.B. glanced at it (having just clapped a white bowler on his head) 'reading that for pleasure or for pain' he asked in his high-pitched voice." Kingsmill was far too disconcerted to do anything, while Harris remonstrated in a large human way with Arnold Bennett—a general improvisation on the theme "Boys will be boys."

281

a bookshop and presently all the clients were insisting that he must attend to them. He not only knew where every book was, he knew its contents as well. He had worked on a railway, too, mastered the whole problem of signals, and wanted to better the prevailing system, but the other employees banded themselves against him in jealousy and blocked his endeavours. As a waiter he had astonished everyone. . . . But suddenly he was quoting Gretchen's appeal to the Virgin in *Faust*, his fine eyes cast up to heaven, and his rich voice trembling with agony of the dishonoured girl.[8]

They left the Savoy, went to Dan Rider's bookshop in St. Martin's Lane, where Kingsmill heard Rider's[9] famous laugh, then to Stewart's, where "Mrs. Harris" was having tea. "A lovely woman," he recorded in his diary. "She was more than twenty years younger than he, with Titian-colored hair, very white skin and large brown eyes, and was always beautifully dressed. A general impression of velvet and satin draped round a tall supple figure remains in my memory."

We drove out to Roehampton, where Harris was then living. . . . After dinner we walked down Putney Hill. It was a warm evening, the deep blue sky of late summer above us. In my exhilaration I was swinging my stick, and it struck Mrs Harris's lap-dog, who was taking the air with us. The poor brute suffered for forty-eight hours as a result of this blow, which was typical of the clumsiness I always displayed in everything which concerned Mrs Harris.

A month later I went out to Roehampton again. Richard Middleton was there, and after lunch we walked over Wimbledon Common. Middleton in a low sad voice, paid tribute to the Common as a good hunting-ground for young girls. . . . Two girls of sixteen or so were standing on the edge of the Common as we approached Wimbledon. Harris raised his hat and in an earnest voice expressed the hope that they would be at the same place, at the same hour, on the following afternoon. He would, he said, bring

[8] Kingsmill has also this to say about Harris' rendering of Gretchen's appeal to the Virgin (Harris had been giving his performance at lunch with Adela Schuster): "I think that is so effective, Mr. Harris," she observed, "the way you get tears into your eyes. Please tell me, is it difficult to manage?" "Tears? . . . I didn't know. . . . I assure you. . . . I was not aware. . . ." When they returned to the office—Harris was editing *Hearth and Home* at the time—he roared round the building looking for someone to bully.

[9] Dan Rider, according to Laurence Gomme, always looked like a butcher, with a very clean white shirt and rolled-up sleeves. More incompetent than crook, rather an indifferent man as far as money was concerned, in Gomme's view.

his car along and give them a drive. They tittered at first, but his solemnity awed them and they promised to be there.

That evening, as Kingsmill walked down Putney Hill with Harris and Richard Middleton, he had a sense of life opening out for him with infinite richness, he told Elmer Gertz years later. Another, quite different young man, earnest and without humor, who was equally impressed by Frank when he met him this year was John Middleton Murry. He told Elmer Gertz that he had fallen under his spell for a time. Though Harris was past his zenith and smacked of tragedy, the glamor of past glories hung about him still; one felt that he was a great man, who moved in a great world and did great things. Murry, in *Between Two Worlds*, tells how in the early autumn of 1911 he began to frequent Dan Rider's bookshop, and, with his usual adaptability, he absorbed the faith that Frank Harris was the greatest master of the short story in English and the greatest critic of Shakespeare. "Life" was his specialty and consisted essentially of love affairs—on these Frank Harris was a connoisseur and an authority. One of the habitués of the shop was "Mr. Hugh Kingsmill," a cheerful, hilarious, breezy and altogether disarming fellow. Then one day he met Harris, who came striding into the shop "with his great moustache," his shining emerald stud, his brown-strapped buckskin shoes, his straw hat and his gray raincoat over his arm, referred to Middleton Murry's "little magazine" (*Rhythm*), and hinted that he might not be unwilling to write something for it. Next day Murry was whirled off to lunch at the Café Royal to be a rapt audience for his talk and an admiring witness to his imperial manner with waiters and managers. A few days later he was speaking of him as Frankie—as he was known in the bookshop circle —and listening spellbound to a plan for making *Rhythm* the rival of the *English Review*, the principal feature necessary for this being the addition of some financial pages. His intoxicating talk was like, Murry said, building castles in the air.[10] Murry during this time was financially in a bad way and Harris gave him ten pounds without his asking for it.

> And if I am told that this was done simply to impress me I must answer that I do not altogether believe it. Harris could have im-

[10] Kingsmill likens Harris' talk to a strong man raising enormous dumbbells, one after the other. The spectacle is magnificent—the torso, the stomach, the muscles— "Ah, ah!" the audience sighs. Then a prodigiously small boy hops onto the stage and carries the half dozen dumbbells away.

pressed me at a cheaper rate. My finding is that there was a genuine streak of kindliness in Harris's nature . . . that this impression is a different one from that formed and conveyed by Mr. Hugh Kingsmill . . . is mainly due . . . to the fact that Mr. Kingsmill's father was a relatively wealthy man. All wealthy fathers were legitimate prey to Harris, according to his queer moral code. But at no time did Harris conceal the nature of his code: to get by any means the money of the rich bourgeois and employ a little of it to help the poor artist. I think, too, that Mr. Hugh Kingsmill's clever book about Harris would have been a better one if it had been warmed with a little more sympathy. It exhibits Harris but it does not understand him.

Kingsmill began his "clever book" with a story of Harris and Middleton Murry in Dan Rider's shop the following June. One day, about half a dozen Harris worshipers were waiting in Dan's inner room for Frank, who had just arrived from Nice. Murry had brought Katherine Mansfield with him to introduce her to Harris, whose books they had been reading together during the spring. Murry was publishing a eulogistic article about Harris in the July number of *Rhythm*. To recreate the soul of Shakespeare was one of the highest tasks that a great artist could undertake, it said; to achieve where Coleridge and Goethe had failed needed a man on a spiritual equality with Shakespeare himself. "Who is the man who has done this thing? This man is Frank Harris, acknowledged by all the great men of letters of his time to be greater than they; accepted by artists as their superior, unknown to the vast British public, greater than his contemporaries because he is a master of life."

Their talk as they waited in the inner room was desultory, said Kingsmill, like the talk on the battlements of Elsinore before the arrival of Hamlet's full-throated father. "A stir in the outer room of the shop, a movement of the air such as precedes an avalanche, and Frank Harris was with us." He brandished the June number of *Rhythm*. "Good God, Murry!" he roared. "What have you done here?" Murry rose to his feet very pale. It was an article claiming James Stephens to be the greatest poet of the day, standing with Sappho, Catullus and Shakespeare, that had taken Harris' displeasure. "Pah!" he shouted. "Drivel!" Everyone in Dan's shop knew that the next number held Murry's comparison of Harris and Shakespeare. They were moved by pity at the terrible situation.

"On the table lay the contents bill of the July number of *Rhythm* headed by the article on Harris: 'Who Is the Man?' Harris picked it up and read out the first three items.

"Who Is the Man?

"Drawing.

"The Shirt.

" 'The Shirt!' he repeated, and threw the bill down with a laugh. 'Drawing of a man in a shirt, eh? By God, Murry'—and he was beginning to improvise in Rabelaisian vein on the man in a shirt when Murry burst into tears and ran out of the shop. 'Good God!' Harris stared round in amazement. He was even more astonished to hear that the girl who had rushed out after Murry was Katherine Mansfield. Why had no one told him?" There was a long silence and then Kingsmill remembers Harris and himself outside the shop. " 'Go and bring them back, Lunn,' he was saying. 'Tell them I am infinitely sorry, I would not have had this happen for worlds.' His hand went to his waistcoat pocket. 'Take a taxi both ways.' He pressed two coins into my hand—pennies, but the moment was too tense for trivial adjustments. 'Both ways, Lunn,' he repeated, and went back to Dan's. Katherine Mansfield and Murry were sitting opposite one another on either side of the fireplace in their Gray's Inn Road flat. They had been crying, but were now composed.

" 'Harris is awfully sorry,' I said. 'It was just his . . . you know. He wants you to come back. He sent me in a taxi.' They shook their heads. 'He's wonderful, wonderful!' Murry sighed. 'But . . . No, not just yet. Not today.'

" 'Not today,' Katherine Mansfield echoed."

Shortly after this Murry's love affair with Harris ended. W. H. Smith, he said, had refused to circulate a number of the *English Review* containing one of Harris' stories, "An English Saint." Everyone at Dan Rider's, it went without saying, knew the story was a masterpiece, that W. H. Smith's attempted suppression was iniquity. Murry meanwhile, at Harris' instigation, was reading a volume of Stendhal's works, and there he came upon the original of "An English Saint." He felt horribly hurt at the toppling of his idol.

A few months before this incident Kingsmill had spent some time with Harris in Nice. Just as they were preparing to leave, according to Nellie, Lunn turned up to stay with them. Leaving God and his disciple together, she departed for London to find yet more furnished accommodations, this time in Lexham Gardens. As usual, money was in short supply, but Harris refused to be deterred. "Let me know how we stand at the bank, my heart sinks at the thought but don't mind. I've one or two ideas which should put us right," he wrote in his usual vein. One of these was to edit the Labour *Daily Herald* with Ben Tillett, another to buy the *World* with the financial help of the father of Lovat Fraser, the latter being another member of the admiring bookshop circle. In the meantime he supervised packing up the old flat and arranging for the sale of the curtains, found a fresh place, which required new wallpaper, sofa- and chair-covers, and stayed up late talking to Kingsmill. "I'm wearing out, sleep is the most necessary thing in life . . . alas! I talk too much," he wrote to Nellie.

Yet, Kingsmill observed, he was far quieter in Nice than in London. They would go for long drives into the mountains, visit the roller-skating rink and walk down the Promenade des Anglais. Often Harris would be content to let others talk while he sat in abstracted silence. His group of acquaintances was not a stimulating one: a chauffeur, whose wife was the disinherited daughter of a millionaire, and a German who claimed to have twenty-five local ladies at his disposal and who appeared one evening with a collection of dirty postcards, anxious to know which was most likely to titillate a lady. One day they motored to a castle where "a nephew of a famous Victorian poet lived"— an Englishman of about sixty, who had left England in some haste many years before. (This was undoubtedly Harris' friend Alfred Tennyson, whom he had in mind as a potential buyer of various busts and paintings.) Kingsmill gives an extraordinary picture of the outing.

> The castle was in disrepair; on the floor of the dining-room sat a baby of two, pensive and unwashed; an Italian boy, one of the staff, lounged about in sulky indifference, and a fat cook bustled to and fro preparing and serving refreshments. Our host, an enormous man with fists like hams, was courteous but seemed remote, a little dazed. "An astonishing man," Harris said to me later. "Of an insatiable appetite." The baby, it seemed, was his by the cook, but in the pressure of his ceaseless activities, which had comprised the Italian boy, he had, I gathered, forgotten about the cook except as cook, and had hardly had time as yet to notice the baby. "I wouldn't leave my grandmother alone with him for five minutes," Harris said, "if I prized the old lady."

Kingsmill duly departed to England by train, and Harris, who was to return by car with two Americans, stayed on, trying to settle his affairs at Monte Carlo, which still hung over him after all those years.

In Monaco he discovered that five judgments amounting to 50,000 francs had been made against him, and he was obliged to mortgage the piece of land he still held at Eze. It is clear from his letters to Nellie that his nerve was beginning to crack. "I'm very tired and very depressed," he told her; he wished she was there, he was a little scared of the lectures he was preparing and wanted to get on to a lighter novel. By the end of May[11] he was on the road with the Americans, a journey that was depressing and disagreeable but one that was probably the inspiration of the novel *Morning,* or *Love in Youth.* "Oh Nell," he wrote again, "I want you so much: I'm tired to death of wandering about without you to talk to and share my impressions, and I'm beginning to feel very old. . . . I tell you there is no chance except through America and these people show me how hopeless America is. If you say a word the man looks grave and the wife sick; it's too terrible. One would think they were not human. I'm tired of this whole crew."

In Paris he met some admirers, Leonard Merrick and his wife. "He's fine—frank and eager but very poor: she's rather pretty and good to him I think: but they are *poor.* . . . I'll write about him, give him a *boost* up." To be poor, or to give the impression of being poor, was to Harris an admission of defeat. Money was as essential to Harris' life as the air he breathed, enabling him to live in a proper way; petty economies were bourgeois, as we know, and Harris, at any cost, refused to be bourgeois. About this he was now quite ruthless. From Paris he hurried on to Haut-Buisson to see if he could recruit any of the princess' funds. Whatever his feelings for her may once have been, it is clear he was now interested in Alice—as in most people—for any use to

---

11 The new flat was lent during the rest of 1912 to J. D. Fergusson, the painter, who was house-hunting. Eventually Fergusson discovered "La petite Faroundelle," a small, two-up, two-down house in Cap d'Antibes. "My Gahd," Harris said when he saw it. "That's the hen house." Fergusson, his wife, Margaret Morris, recalls, liked Harris very much; he looked upon him as a modern Robin Hood, robbing the rich to pay the poor. Harris admired very much a certain painting by Fergusson and wanted to buy it. Fergusson, however, did not care to sell to people he liked. Harris took it on the understanding that if ever Fergusson was in need he would ask for payment. A little while later a bill came from Bourlet for paint, canvas and so forth. Could Harris pay the debt? Harris did so, by return mail.

which he could put her and anything he could extract from her. Among the undulating paths and long hedges covered with sweet peas Harris became once more depressed and obsessed by Nellie and the lack of her letters. "Not a word from you yet Nellie, not a word of encouragement —silence to make me anxious and nervous and weaken me." The place was beautiful, a perfection of comfort, but the cooking was too rich, and "Madam" pressed him to eat, saying that he was too thin. Melo-dramatically he saw himself on a desperate and lonely mission to raise funds for his distressed lady, but he was doubtful that he would suc-ceed. "She has built some new cottages here as fine as villas, said they had cost too much, had made her poor. I have no hold on her: still she's kind and I'll do my best. . . . I have a sort of desperate courage in me: win or lose. . . . I'm nervous and excited. Oh Nellie I wish you had written: it seems like an ill omen. It's not like you either and it hurts terribly: still it can't be helped now and I mean to do my best. I feel deserted: you're not ill, I pray. I'm making mountains I suppose."

The outcome of his visit to Haut-Buisson remains unrecorded. Ultimately Lovat Fraser's father did not purchase the *World*, but he did buy *Hearth and Home*. Harris himself supplied none of the money, but promised at intervals that soon he would be producing his £500— which resulted in board meetings that were occasions of bitterness. His new admirers were enthusiastic. "Our heartiest congratulations," Leonard Merrick wrote on August 6. "For a moment I tell you hon-estly I found it difficult to see what Frank Harris was going to do with *Hearth and Home*: but before I had read the paragraph through I was a convert. You write about it so breezily and vigorously that I be-lieve you'll show London that you can run a ladies' paper as brilliantly as a *Saturday Review*. You are really a most amazing personality—the more I see and hear from you, the more different you are from what I had imagined."

Hearth and Home was staffed from the enthusiasts at Dan Rider's bookshop, all conversation having hitherto been centered on "when Frankie got a paper." According to Kingsmill, Harris began by picking a quarrel with the retiring editor and insulting a fat regular contribu-tor, to whom he had to pay £50 for breach of contract. Kenneth Hare was appointed drama critic, and immediately there was a terrible scene with someone he thought was called Welland to whom he went for advice. On hearing Hare's news of his appointment Welland leaped to his feet, seized his hat and stick and shot off, never falling below a ploughman's trot, to the office of *Hearth and Home* in Fetter Lane. Frank Harris, *"only yesterday at teatime,"* had asked Welland to be drama critic. "By George . . . *He shan't play hanky-panky with me!"* Through the closed door of Harris' office came a voice, said Kenneth Hare,[12] of the vitality of the minotaur, blended with the disillusionment of the ghost in Hamlet, kettledrums and skylarks' trills. And Welland backed down. Hare was beckoned into the office, and the kettledrum was stopped by the telephone. Some offer was being made that Harris did not find alluring. "No bun—no bear," he roared, replacing the receiver. He could not understand how Hare had been foolish enough to go to a *rival* for advice.

At 11 o'clock to 11:30 every morning Harris crossed the threshold into the office, his personality penetrating the thick walls. Once, when business was slack, Harris narrated the long story of the poor commercial traveler, the farmer's wife, the enraged farmer, the Bible and the dog, "details of which I refrain from recording," wrote Hare, "because I understand they have since appeared in a 'printed book' "— where it is Harris himself who is seducing the farmer's wife. Once Kingsmill, Rider, Harris and Hare all went for "a spin" on Hampstead Heath in Harris' car. They went either to the Spaniard's or Jack Straw's Castle wanting tea, and within a few minutes a dispute had arisen. Harris wished for tea in the garden, but the landlord insisted that it should be indoors. "There," cried Harris, shaking his finger in the face of the fat, florid man, "there you may read the Saxon soul. There you may see all England in a microcosm. A symbol! Beef, brawn, beer, belly—but NO BRAIN." As they dashed home across the heath in the twilight a reclining lady, her dress in sweet disorder, smiled broadly at Frank from a rustic bench. "Legs!" bellowed Harris, from the joy of living. "Legs!"

Hearth and Home's two most regular contributors, according to themselves, were Kingsmill and Enid Bagnold, who had been introduced to the circle by Lovat Fraser. Between them they interviewed various telephone operators, authors, dressmakers and pupils of Cheltenham Ladies' College. Once, Kingsmill says, he pleaded in an interview for a bolder attitude to love, which brought one of the readers to the office armed with an umbrella; and Enid Bagnold visited Annie Besant in Esher, where she was giving two Indian boys—one of whom she believed to be the Theosophist Messiah—bread and milk.

[12] Kenneth Hare and Dorothea St. J. George, *London's Latin Quarter*.

The regular readers still had their *Hearth and Home* Guild of Aid for Gentlepeople; Mrs. Talbot Coke, Mrs. Langton Bayly and Betty Modish (an Indian army officer's widow who worked in the same room as the bookkeeper and Kingsmill) still advised on dress, beauty and furnishings and addressed cozy letters to people with names like "Les Lunettes," "Espoir" and "The Boatswain." But these standbys were supplemented by all the features that went to make a Harrisian magazine—investment columns, obsessions with South Africa, articles on Lord Grimthorpe's villa, Cimbroni, explaining that it was built out of stolen antiquities from Paestum, and a love-at-first-sight column, inspired by a contemporary discussion in the American papers, "Will Our Readers Help Us to Say Which Forms They Believe In." The readers declined.

After the first few numbers Harris wrote very little. To restore his nerves and his confidence he was indulging in an affair into which he was putting all his sophisticated technique. "So you want to be a journalist?" Harris had asked Enid Bagnold, looking her up and down and practically lifting off her skin. The second day he had met her he had taken her to lunch at the Savoy, a lunch that was to Enid Bagnold both shaming and fascinating.

> Not yet in love with him [she writes in her autobiography], his faults of taste came out on my forehead like a cold sweat. He talked loudly of his three companions, Christ, Shakespeare and Wilde. The name of Jesus went round the tables like a bell of bronze and heads were raised to listen. Dishes were sent back as uneatable. . . . Waiters were recompensed with half-crowns built in silver castles. I was ashamed. But soon I grew ashamed of being ashamed.[13]

[13] Kingsmill says that after the war he met a woman who had been in love with Harris. He talked always, said the woman, as if he held the key of life. "As if only with his help would one pass into the kingdom of experience. What nonsense all that was—about Passion and Freedom! And how it impressed one! And one was sorry for him, too. He seemed stronger somehow than so many of the smug people who had won in life. One thought of him as a rebel who had refused success in disgust at the price one has to pay for it. Yet there *was* something there—a tangled, troubled light. . . . I still see the horizon of his eyes and talk flaming like a sunset. . . . And yet it's gone—how it's gone! I suppose because it was all so unreal. I thought it was real enough then—but there was too much 'Love,' and too little natural affection."

Alec Waugh has a sympathetic and delightful sketch, *The Woman Who Knew Frank Harris*. Here she is fiction, a colonel's widow living in the Seychelles. She turned books she disapproved of into spills, i.e., *The Struggle for World Power* by John Strachey, which was a book she had borrowed from the club, and one she declared should be kept under lock and key—who was *that silly old fool* to decide what they would read and what they

For let me do justice to myself and my thraldom. And justice to him. He *was* an extraordinary man. He had an appetite for great things and could transmit the sense of them. He was more like a great actor than a man of heart. He could simulate everything. While he felt admiration he could act it, and while he acted it he felt it. And greatness being his big part he hunted the centuries for it, spotting it in literature, in passion, in action.

If anyone could have got her to laugh at Harris it would have been Kingsmill, but, she said, nobody could. "I was sliding into madness." As she slid she did most of the work on *Hearth and Home.* Hugh, she said, was a glorious friend, but lazy, with too much time spent on gossip. Besides, he was studying Harris—not to mention her affair with him, which was to become the subject of his novel *The Will to Love*[14]—and not the paper. So, busily, she rewrote stories from

wouldn't? She had, she said, sent poetry to Frank when he was editor of *Vanity Fair*; she had been a big wholesome young girl. Frank did not hurry to seduce her—he had plenty of time. They met nine times; there were lunches in the Café Royal, in the Domino Room, with its red plush banquettes, its mirrors, its gilt columns, faded panels and frescoed ceilings. Frank dazzled the girl with his power and importance, now and then playing his other role of unappreciated genius ranting against the tycoons of Fleet Street, the Penguin professors who had no fire in their veins, who would never understand out of what dark forests of the tortured soul the sacred fires of art are lit: "I can speak of all this to you, you will understand I can tell it from your poems." He knew everything and everyone. He was wonderful company. . . .

[14] Kingsmill's *The Will to Love*, published in 1919, portrays Harris as Ralph Parker and Enid Bagnold as Barbara. In many ways his portrait of Ralph Parker is more perceptive and sympathetic than his *Frank Harris*, while his views on Mrs. Parker and the marriage are useful and enlightening. Ralph has a bullet head, square hands and large, sticking-out ears. He booms at the waiters in deep, rich tones, and the menu inspires disgust and loathing. Parker is heavy, not corpulent, naturally under middle height, scrupulous about personal appearance—very manicured and barbered, with rich garnet buttons on the waistcoat, and heavy rings. His eyes are amazingly expressive, large, and varying with his emotions from blue to black. The artist is chief of the sons of man, and the writer the chief of the artists, bringing the universe to self-consciousness, persecuted, derided and crucified by the eyeless, envious mob. Mrs. Parker is lovely but fretful. Ralph Parker is a man of the world, steering Barbara through the Café Royal swiftly with a light touch on the arm to a reserved table, and illustrating his speech with many forthright examples of unconstrained utterance. His speech is apparently a deliberate protest against English hypocrisy and mealymouthedness, a crusade for the freedom of speech. One of his theories is that the best brains are crippled by the academic system and that the heart is the only teacher. "Wrong, dead wrong," he would shout, cleaving the air with his fist. A blow to his vanity filled him with panic. His favorite theory is that the key to a man's character is supplied by the nature of the woman he loved. If the woman is ingenuous, sincere and loving, then these are the qualities of her lover. She is the reflection of him. Praising her, he praises himself. To condemn her would be self-condemnation. His worst fear is a fear of madness, and Kingsmill portrays an incident happening when, dining out one night, he fails to remember his own name. His appearance deepens his suffering and the world's contempt. To be loved by women appeases

Maupassant, signing them herself, drew or traced girls from *La Vie Parisienne*, lifted cookery articles from foreign papers. She had no conscience, she says; she obeyed her chief. One night she spotted a seedy-looking fellow lurking about and asked him what he wanted. He explained that he was the man who spent his nights posting letters into various letter boxes. "Mr. Harris's lottery, miss." It seemed that the police noticed when too many letters went into one box. Enid Bagnold was only partially aware of the famous people she was meeting. Once it was Max Beerbohm, with his new wife, who was wearing bracelets outside her black net gloves. Once Harris pushed her behind a pillar in the Café Royal when a small man with fiery eyes sprang up in a fury and tipped over a marble table; it was Lord Alfred Douglas making his scene. Gradually the circle of admirers that had been united under the spell of "Frankie" dispersed; Enid Bagnold hardly noticed that she was the only one left. She was being courted by this ugly, famous and glamorously misunderstood man. To follow him was to follow a detonating trail, hand grenades exploding. Some of her friends refused to speak to her while it was going on. She did not care. He made everything glorious. "He could pull the stars out of the sky, but he flushed them down the drain. Yet what a talker. What an alchemist in drama —what a storyteller." With him one felt one was standing in the prison with Wilde, that one was at the Last Supper. Everything was fascinating—even his ugliness. "Sex," he said, "is the gateway to life." "So I went through the gateway in an upper room in the Café Royal."

On November 16 Harris went to America. He was to give a series of lectures through the agency of Mitchell Kennerley, he hoped to sell his books, and generally, by hook or by crook, raise as much money as possible. Kingsmill's father had secured for him a free passage on a German boat. "Your father really is a brick," Harris exclaimed to Kingsmill, who adds that it may have been in absentminded recognition of this service that Harris eventually dispatched to him the first volume of *My Life and Loves*, with its designs of naked women, inscribed "To Henry Lunn from his friend Frank Harris." The service, however, on the boat was not so good. "A horrible passage," he wrote

momentarily his starved hunger for power and influence. There is nothing he dreads more than violent or malicious scenes with his wife. There is one scene in the railway station, and then they enter a taxicab and drive round and round until the matter is resolved. His wife's affection responds very sensitively to her husband's bank balance.

Kingsmill wrote a third essay on Harris, which was perhaps the deepest and most serious of all—"Frank Harris," in *After Puritanism*.

to Nellie in his best depressed hand. "Heavy swell. The food atrocious—butter in everything and scented tea." The wind and sea had got up, water had entered the cabin, he was prey to the blackest depression. Nellie clearly had discovered about Enid Bagnold. The affair, which Frank needed for reassurance, in no way affected his obsession and fantasies built round Nellie—no less did he need her undivided devotion and attention. Nellie, however, did not see it this way. As Kingsmill wrote to Hesketh Pearson on March 26, 1932, she was a vain woman with, he said, as diseased a vanity as Harris himself possessed; she would take his infidelities as a slur on herself. She would resent Frank because he found her unsatisfactory, because he needed to look elsewhere; and gradually she built up a vast reservoir of poison. For the last three months she had become increasingly distant toward him. No doubt his affair with Enid Bagnold aggravated her sense of insecurity. She was, after all, not in a good position; in spite of his promises Frank remained firmly married to Emily, and she remained firmly a kept woman, not accepted in certain circles. One of his reasons, however, for going to America was to investigate the possibility of his becoming an American citizen, which would, he hoped, improve his chances under different laws of getting a divorce and remarrying. Meanwhile, the further away Nellie drew, the more necessary she seemed to Frank.

I'm going to do my best in New York: but everything seems against me: still the strong make the obstacles into footstools. I can learn all the poetry I'm going to need now when I'm sick, for I am very sick. . . . I don't know why you are so dear to me; but lately since you've been drawing away from me I've lost heart and hope. Of course other men make up to you; but if you yield to any of them I shall go under. Not that that ought to stop you if the affection's dead. My life passes before me as I write: a great effort to understand everything, to learn much, to grow and one great affection, a passion and tenderness for you. And looking back on it I see the life may close now at any moment. The original impulse is nearly exhausted. I am not strong, only my brain indeed and heart seem to live more strongly than ever: but the body's nearly worthless—a rag. How fleeting the life, how little I have done who started out so sure to do so much. This letter's very sad and I don't want to make you sad. At bottom I'm resolved to do my best, to the end. But since you've altered to me I've lost heart. I find it difficult to make any real effort: I don't care to go on. There I had to say it. Now you know. The waters of bitterness go over my head. I will not write like this: I'll leave this letter till tomorrow—a new day. I've been all day in bed loving the rest in spite of the vile sick-feeling and sketching out two more lectures: especially the Great One on religion. I've just drunk some scented tea and it has made me sick. . . . Don't listen Nellie to what the fools say about me: the world is v. jealous of our love and of our continual happiness . . . we are outside its conventions, men and women alike leagued against us, our supposed friends the worst of all. . . . It will be better when I get back: I'll try to put myself in your place more and be better company to you. . . . I love you Nellie: my affection is as strong as I am and will be yours always . . . it has grown into an Epistle and yet it doesn't tell you how I love you and adore you and how I long for you and I wish you were with me here. I ache for you and miss you at every moment. If you were here I could win I think as it is, it is only a desperate effort. My God how I miss you.

Laurence Gomme remembers Harris' lectures as brilliant. There were twelve of them, delivered at the St. Regis Hotel and organized by Mitchell Kennerley.[15] Engraved invitations and tickets were sent round to every prominent person in social and literary circles. Mr. Frank Harris' Lectures were the matured expressions of a profound and earnest study of life, the advertisements read. Mr. Harris was a man of the world as well as a man of letters, and what he had to say belonged to the "real events of our every day political, social and individual welfare." Out of the study of life Mr. Harris had made his own discoveries, rare treasures of experience; the lectures were the settings for these treasures. They were one of New York's social events of the year.

Laurence Gomme had first met Harris in 1911, in the admiring circle of Dan Rider's bookshop, while he was in London finding ma-

---

[15] Mitchell Kennerley had sailed from Liverpool in August 1896, with John Lane of The Bodley Head, to manage the New York office. He started a new regime of personal publishing, operating until 1912 from the Little Shop Around the Corner, a cozy spot with ivy-clad buildings, old family houses and the Little Shop built in quartered-oak style, with a fine prospect over the well-treed churchyard of the Little Church Around the Corner. Kennerley was reckless, according to Laurence Gomme, who reorganized his business, and not a good payer of royalties. Years later he committed suicide because he became involved with a young girl.

terial for Mitchell Kennerley.[16] When Harris saw him he told him he was the one person he wanted to meet in the world, since he had a story he wanted to send to Mitchell Kennerley, and he narrated it right away. It was a wonderful experience, said Laurence Gomme, to hear him tell it—he had heard of his reputation as a raconteur—and he said he would buy it. "Ha, ha!" laughed Harris—it had not been written yet. It arrived duly in Mitchell Kennerley's office, and Laurence Gomme could swear that there was not a word changed or a possible comma omitted from the way Harris had originally told the story. It was "The Miracle of the Stigmata."[17]

On December 6 Kennerley promised to pay £1,000 for Harris' books. Then gradually, it seemed, he backed down, and Harris wrote furiously to Nellie that he was swindling him. First Kennerley promised to keep the original contract and give him £800; next he tried to withdraw because of not having the money, saying that the most Harris could get was £300 to £400. "All my high hopes are foundering; but my courage doesn't go down. Dear, I'm afraid I've failed—not in lectures; but the rest still I've a week and may yet win. Distance," he concluded, "is like a wind that puts out little fires and affections and increases great ones. I miss you every hour and long for you." Adding to his bad news were the tidings that he could not become an American citizen for another year; but then at any time he could get a divorce and be married again.

Mitchell Kennerley had arranged for Edwin Björkman to meet Harris, hoping that Björkman would write about him. He went to his hotel room and knocked. "Come in," he heard, but the door was locked; this happened several times. At last Harris appeared at the door shouting, "Why don't you come in? The door was not locked." "It was," Björkman insisted. "It was not," Harris yelled back, "and I didn't want to get out of bed." He was in his pyjamas, and as he turned his back to close the door, Björkman could see that a square of about one foot had been cut out of the seat of his trousers, revealing two very pink

---

[16] Laurence Gomme had lunched with Harris at the Savoy. Nellie was there, "a very gracious lady," Laurence Gomme said, "but rather timid." Harris was not all that nice to her. There was a great performance at lunch, with Harris roaring for more wine, the waiter pouring it into the old glasses and Harris bellowing for the head waiter to empty them, and so on. All, said Laurence Gomme, to impress some Jew who was there.

[17] "The Miracle of the Stigmata" had been published in the *English Review* in April 1910 and was widely held to be blasphemous.

buttocks. Björkman found the arrangement so startling that his head was filled with thoughts of Wilde. Harris got back into bed, overflowing with Jesus. Anyone who thought Jesus was not a real person was a stupid ass, he shouted. Björkman heard him lecture in one of the smaller halls; he thought him dull. Kennerley explained that he had had a bad case of indigestion and just before the lecture had resorted to the stomach pump.

Laurence Gomme said that he and Mitchell Kennerley had arranged to see Harris off when the time came for his return to England. He arrived by taxi to collect them, his luggage consisting of one small bag and a pile of newspaper packages, which he had piled up against the taxi door. At the pier the stevedores rushed up and opened the door and all the packages fell out into the gutter, which was rushing with water. At last someone found a big box, piled them all soggily in and put them in the cabin. Suddenly Harris discovered that he had lost one of his gloves. Nothing threw him into a worse state than to lose something, and he wanted to hurry back to the gutter and make a search. Mitchell Kennerley tore the other glove off Harris' left hand and threw it overboard. "Now you've got nothing to worry about," he told Harris, who was black with fury.

Back home in Lexham Gardens the same winds that blew out little fires and affections were causing a nasty draft. There had been a scene between Nellie and Kingsmill, a scene of which both rendered accounts, which did not reveal by any means what really happened. Harris for the rest of his life was to blame Kingsmill for ruining his relations with Nellie. Later Louis Wilkinson told Kingsmill, "I think you behaved worse than a third rate whore," and Kingsmill himself told Hesketh Pearson in 1932 that a letter of Nellie's written to someone in America brought back the way in which she had screamed at him in the hall at 67 Lexham Gardens. "She is the vulgar, malignant type, and is restrained by neither decency nor intelligence." Bearing all the screaming and emotion in mind, it is hard to see that there is anything contained in any of the available accounts that would whip up a reaction stronger than mild irritation. "During his [Harris'] absence I went to Lexham Gardens to interview for *Hearth and Home* a girl-composer who was staying with Mrs. Harris," wrote Kingsmill, "and at dinner offended Mrs. Harris by hotly disputing her contention that Shaw, Wells and Bennett would have written better had they travelled more in their young days. [This was straight from the mouth of Harris, who often ventilated his views on this subject, calling it "rubbing shoulders in the market place."] 'What about Shakespeare and Rembrandt?' I asked. They had done pretty well, hadn't they, in spite of staying at home? 'You wouldn't talk like that if Frank were here,' said Mrs. Harris. The truth in this annoyed me and I replied that I hoped she would not send him a garbled report of what I had said. Harris on his return gave me a kindly lecture on my youthful ineptitude. 'You are,' said he, quoting from Wordsworth's *Odes,* 'moving about in worlds not realised.' "

A week or so later, apparently Harris refused through Dan Rider to pay Kingsmill for book reviews, following this up with an odd communication that Kingsmill was not to sell the books he had reviewed, although he was expected to go to board meetings and vote for Harris. Finally four pages of verbal abuse followed Kingsmill's resignation, and they did not meet again for fourteen years. Nellie has her own version, noted in her diary after a visit in Nice from Louis Wilkinson.

> Frank said I was obliged to get rid of Lunn—to get him out of the office—for he made mischief with everyone. One day Frank said I called the office boy and said to him to go and do something. I noticed the boy looking nasty and I pulled him up—all at once he stood still glared at me and said I know you don't like me etc. Frank said he was dumb with astonishment and said what gives you such an idea. The boy said Mr. Lunn told me you didn't like me, you meant getting rid of me etc. Frank said that was the finishing point. He called Lunn and told him and asked him what object he could have in upsetting that poor boy, whom Frank thought really good and liked. Lunn quietly said Oh I always tell people that one doesn't like them; then you find out their real opinion of the people: I still think of Lunn as a pathological case— like a very vindictive and evil minded woman.

In what was to be the biography of Frank, Nellie gives us her version of the actual scene. Lunn had brought a friend, who had written a comedy and was anxious to produce it, to Lexham Gardens. Nellie had arranged the dinner so that Lunn's friend could meet one of her girl friends—who was a musical genius. In the middle Lunn said, "Now don't go and write lies to Frank in America." Nellie said that she was quite astonished. Next morning he called at 11:30 to apologize for being such a cad. "I tried to do you a kindness and you insulted me at my own table," Nellie tells us that she informed him. "Now Mr. Lunn I never want to see you again and I will never speak to you again . . . please remember we are strangers if we meet in the street for I will never know you again under any circumstances. There's the door—good day." And after that tantrum she said she forgot all about him until 1924.

Clearly something traumatic lies, invisible, between the lines. There are two immediate possibilities. Very probably Nellie had been going on about Frank's devotion to her, and Kingsmill, knowing the details of the affair with Enid Bagnold, had been unable to stomach her sentimentality and had told her one or two home truths. Possibly Kingsmill, who was susceptible to beautiful women, was greatly attracted to her, and wishing to identify with Frank, desired to make love to her while Frank was away—which would account for the deep hurt that Harris always told everyone Kingsmill had caused him. Possibly it was a combination of these two things. Michael Holroyd, biographer of Kingsmill and Augustus John, points out that both men's accounts carry something similar in them as regards Nellie. He suggests that Nellie, trying to act in the gracious, sincere way that Frank would wish, flirted. She was a cock-tease. This would explain why neither man mentioned what really happened, having believed that they were being led on; both men's vanity would have been piqued at being refused and they would not care to repeat the story. Hesketh Pearson says, in "Rebel Artist," that from something that Nellie said to him in the 1920s he gathered that she had repulsed John's advances. Kingsmill goes so far as to turn the tables and accuse Nellie of vanity—diseased vanity at that.

In one of her corrective fragments Nellie gives a story that would certainly accord with the first theory. Lunn, she said, who called frequently at Lexham Gardens and always seemed antagonistic not only to Nellie but to anyone else Harris seemed to like—more like a mean, peculiar and jealous woman than a young man—arrived one day just as Nellie was setting out for Victoria to collect Frank, who was returning home from some trip. He hung about, said Nellie, waiting and waiting and then jumped at the idea of joining Nellie on the underground to collect Frank. As they went along Nellie told him how happy she was to be meeting Frank, how he longed to be home and how he was counting the hours. This, in light of his obsessed, depressed letters, certainly rings true. Lunn leaned back in his seat and yelled with laughter. "The wretch," he shouted. "You don't think it true?" asked Nellie. "You think he's humbugging?" "Of course," said Lunn. Nellie said that she felt awful, terribly hurt.

Financially and temperamentally Harris was not in a good way when he returned. In the office at *Hearth and Home* it was rumored that he had suffered a reversal in love and that he had offended his well-wishers by telling them at the end of a dinner given in his honor that he had never encountered newer wines or older jokes. *Hearth and Home* lasted only a matter of five or six months. In 1913, having finally got rid of it and scattered most of the staff, he bought what Enid Bagnold called a "tainted little property," *Modern Society*, complete with its beauty and financial talks and its scandal page. Now, said Enid Bagnold, who, unlike the rest of Harris' staff had remained faithfully at his side, now she was really and truly a journalist. She was up to her neck in it. The first issue appeared in August 1913. "Great improvements are being made in *Modern Society*," it was announced to would-be advertisers. "This journal will be found an excellent medium for reaching people with money." For the next seven months people with money were introduced to all the familiar faces and haunts: Alice of Monaco, Grimthorpe, the Bank of Monte Carlo . . .

Harris, in spite of all his resolutions to try to make Nellie happier, was still pursuing his affair with Enid Bagnold;[18] and Nellie, fortified no doubt by the home truths from Kingsmill, was growing increasingly cool and would sometimes go away and leave Frank alone—something that he hated. "What an evening, Nellie," he wrote in December; "the mere fact that you are not in the house, not in the next room makes *all* the difference. You have drawn away from me now for more than a year: in these last two days you seem to try to come back nearer: do you want to? really want to. I'm not sure. The house is empty and I'm restless: I wanted to work at my Manchester lecture: I've not done much."

18 Harris' nerve was growing increasingly poor; he was desperate about Nellie, his life and his financial situation. It would have been valuable to the understanding of Harris and Nellie to know if Enid Bagnold had detected any of this: whether she had met Nellie, whether Frank ever confided in her and whether he wrote desperate letters to her too from America. Unfortunately, once she had published her account, nothing could be added. She had nothing more to say. Nobody, she felt, could have disposed of a first seduction so elegantly and briefly as she did in her autobiography. Her husband admired it. It was stated without emphasis—like the account of a vaccination—and then left. She so admired it herself that anything further (as contributed by her) would be an inelegance. It is sad that possibly a deeper understanding of a desperate, vain man and an insecure, vain woman should be forfeited for elegance.

Gerald Cumberland met him for the first time when he arrived in Manchester to deliver the lecture. Sometime that year, Cumberland says, Harris had expressed a wish to see examples of his verse. He dispatched some forthwith. Harris replied that one poem was not sensual enough; Cumberland was never able to understand what he meant, since the poem had described seven naked ladies swimming in a pool. They met in the Midland Hotel. Harris talked all the time he was changing from his traveling to his evening clothes and beseeched him to stay. He'd had a rotten journey, he said, and felt unutterably bored. He was to deliver a lecture on Shakespeare to the local dramatic society—an assembly of earnest, pale men and spectacled women. Before his audience he was fiery and provocative, throwing out daring theories, upholding with unparalleled fierceness a wonderful ideal of chivalry and nobility. Then he started on Professor H. C. Herford, who had called *The Man Shakespeare* a disgrace to British scholarship. Professor Herford was, said Harris, a semi-invalid, asthmatic and bloodless. The audience were stirred by Harris' eloquence and anger. At dinner he was delighted that the headwaiter said, "Very good, Mr. Harris." When he asked how he knew him, the headwaiter said that he had had the pleasure of seeing him in Monte Carlo and New York. At dinner he performed, giving Gerald Cumberland and "The Beautiful Lady" who was also having dinner the full benefit of his performance. They were amazed at his discussion of cookery, of what was wrong and what was right with the menu; they were spellbound by his storytelling— the faint gestures that served for a sentence, a momentary silence for innuendo, a dropping of the voice, a lift of the eyebrows—he was at his best when sinister and menacing. Cumberland added that Harris was helpful to him. He drew up a list of people who might be of assistance to him, and in London they got into a taxi and went round to see people. For the next few months, from time to time, good things would come Cumberland's way that could be traced to Harris.

But for Harris the next few months brought nothing but bad. He was up to his neck in debt, with various writs out against him, concerning both money owed and money borrowed. The end came in February 1914. Sarah Bernhardt was coming to London and Harris, it appeared, was to give a great luncheon in her honor at the Savoy (afterward Enid Bagnold discovered that he was going as a guest not as host) and had arranged that Enid Bagnold should go too. She was excited at the prospect and took some trouble with her dress. On the day of the lunch she had bought a hat costing three or four guineas, a white hat with a gull's feather—a negotiation of considerable difficulty, since in her pocket she had only five shillings and in the bank one pound. She had pointed to her father's name in the telephone directory as guarantor, and established her own identity by wriggling about and exposing to view the name tape attached to a school vest she was wearing.

Harris meanwhile had been obliged to appear in court before Mr. Justice Horridge, having commented in the "What the Little Bird Knows" column on the Fitzwilliam divorce case. It would not take long, Harris had assured her—he would collect her at one from the office. She waited in her new hat until half past two, hungry and in despair. Eventually the girl who saw to the advertisements told her that Harris had been sent to prison for contempt of court—"cheeking" Mr. Justice Horridge. Enid Bagnold's reaction was one of fury. The hero worship broke for a moment; she was furious at his conceit and loud mouth that now deprived her of her lunch.

Nellie received a letter written from the court. "I am attacked and shall be sent to Brixton. . . . I want you to come to Brixton and see me and bring my instruments and small bottle of carbolic oils—my pencils and pad and French bread. Don't be nervous dear. I'm amused by the new experience. I told you long ago that Englishmen would have their revenge for truth." Neither Frank nor Nellie was to remain amused for very long. The "barred solitude and ordered ways" did not suit Harris at all; without audiences or anesthetics of any sort he was subject to his worst depressions, anxieties and hypochondria. "The courage to bear is so different from the courage to dare or to do. . . . I bear badly but am learning. . . . Oh Nellie blythe, shall I ever value you as you deserve: every trial puts you higher and higher in my love and reverence. As soon as I think I can't think more of you up you go again you dear sky-rocket." "The dear sky-rocket" soon had a totally white face from the exhausting time it was having rushing about on errands. She had to dash off to Ruggles-Brise. "Say I always speak so well of him for his splendid humanity to O. Wilde and ask him to let you see me each day. He might allow me to have my own lunch sent in to the hospital. I can have it in the ordinary cell but that's too cold: I shiver all day in it. Here in the infirmary I can work a little by sitting wrapped up in furs all day long: but I have indigestion here all the time from the bread I'm forced to eat."[19] In between visits to Ruggles-Brise, Nellie had to pack up all the valuables—statues, pictures, rugs, a painting of Rhodes and his death mask—and get them sent to Nice. She had to take away all his best clothes, in which he had been dressed ready for lunch at the Savoy and Sarah Bernhardt, which in his cell he could not even hang up, then go running back again with his old fur driving coat, toothpicks, and new collars "not peaked up in front and not rough at edge." And she had to run round to the bank and change the hundred pounds that they had managed to get hold of into gold. "Oh darling it was all bound to come: but they shan't beat me: their blows can be turned into boomerangs to dash brains into their silly heads and that's how I'll use 'em." It would all be all right as soon as he could get out of prison. . . .

Meanwhile the bailiffs had arrived at the offices of *Modern Society* and clattered upstairs while the office staff lowered his cherished possessions—his Beerbohm cartoons, an "Indian thing" and a bookcase—on a rope to safety. From within the gray walls of Brixton came the familiar refrain: "My love we'll begin again after this if you'll give me another chance. . . . Oh I want to kiss you and be petted. Don't grieve dear it doesn't matter." But Nellie of course not only was grieving, she was frightened out of her wits. "I want to get away with you out of this inhuman country and never see again the brute people who reward high work with prison," wrote the crucified prisoner. "If I don't write a bitterer satire than Swift it's because I'm what Shakespeare called a 'peasant slave that lacks gall to make oppression bitter.' "

While Harris was interned Enid Bagnold was in charge at *Modern Society*. If it missed one week on the bookstalls the magazine would lose its license at Stationers' Hall. She planned that instead of the usual contributors the pages should be filled by men of some standing. Shaw refused, Joseph Simpson sent a drawing, and Max Beerbohm gave the famous cartoon of himself and Harris sitting at a restaurant table: "The Best Talker in London with One of His Best Listeners." A solemn promise was extracted from Enid Bagnold that it should be used neither as a cover nor exhibited as a poster. Through the solicitor Cecil Hayes she obtained permission to visit Harris as a "business associate." In her gull hat she passed through the arched prison doors and down a

---

[19] Norman Douglas, in *Looking Back* (Chatto and Windus, London, 1933), remembers Harris complaining to him that he was accustomed to wearing bed socks and in Brixton they would not allow him to wear them.

windy brick tunnel, receiving as she went wolf whistles from warders. She was put in a room made chiefly of glass. Across the courtyard she could see Harris, very short without his usual heels, being hurried—"almost scrambling"—by a warder. He was not pleased to hear Beerbohm's stipulation. Nevertheless he promised. Within twenty-four hours the advertising girl had received instructions to "go it strong on publishing" Beerbohm's drawing and "damnation take those fancy promises."

A day or two later a man from Odham's delivered a heavy roll of posters made from the drawing. Enid Bagnold hurried round to Beerbohm, who was elegant in his dressing-gown but angry enough to dress at once, drive round to the office, collect the roll of posters, hurry on to the printers and collect the block, take the lot to the river and, apart from one poster for Enid Bagnold, throw the whole lot in. The block disappeared at once, but the posters unrolled and floated down on the tide.

Harris, according to Enid Bagnold, came out of prison "dismal, empty and needing a shave. . . . He hardly spoke. I hardly saw him again."

CHAPTER 16

"We'll Have the Time of Our Lives . . ."

I am very nearly dead," Harris wrote on March 17 to Austin Harrison, "and shall have to go abroad at the end of the week. Brixton has finished me off." With precarious health and bankruptcy pending he set off alone for Nice, where he was beset with ills. "My hand breaks down even over these letters," he wailed to Nellie. After a "little exercise" he had fainted one morning, and the doctor had said his heart was badly strained and dilated. "I'm in trouble again with waterworks. . . . My shoulder won't get well. It keeps me awake." But everything would be all right when Nellie came. The Easter sky was purple, lowering and gloomy, and against it he built wild dreams: he'd "try to build a castle for us both in Mexico City when this book *Morning* has been a great success. We'll have the time of our lives and you'll love the new strange beautiful country and the . . . patient Indian servants." Meanwhile the paper in the new flat's drawing room was "shocking," and he was working like a beaver to get some books ready for sale. He'd finished correcting *Great Days*. "It's not bad; but it'll never be one of my successes, indeed it's my first failure I think; it can't be helped." (Soon after this he received a condemnation from John Lane, "who's an ass.") The Oscar Wilde book was nearly all subscribed at three guineas, and "I've begun a little portrait of John Davidson for my contemporary portraits: should I tell how his wife snored when he read his poetry?"

But Nellie, in London, was in no mood to be dreaming of castles in Mexico or listening to Mrs. Davidson snoring. She was very shaken by the financial situation—exactly the sort of thing she hated most of all—and she was suffering from sleeplessness. She dashed round pawning pieces of jewelry and generally gathering money together to send out busts and paintings that Harris was hoping Tennyson might buy. One way and another they managed to scrape up £500. "You needn't be anxious now," Harris reassured her, "we've £500 and I'm able to work better than ever. Oh you make me so anxious."

Nellie duly arrived in Nice; and then in April, with the bankruptcy hanging over them, it suddenly seemed that something remarkable was going to happen which might solve their problems. Out of the blue from York Terrace, Lady Warwick wrote a letter. According to Theo Lang, she informed du Cros that it was Edward VII, when still Prince of Wales, who had introduced Frank Harris to her at Lady Dorothy Nevill's house; but on April 5, 1914, she wrote that although they were personally unacquainted, there was no "greater delighter" in Harris' literary work than herself, though this might not provide her with sufficient excuse for thrusting herself upon him. "The fact is I want to see you very much on a matter of great interest regarding certain letters and to consult you. . . . I want to lose no time in approaching you." Could anything be arranged today? she wanted to know. Lady Warwick was herself in a desperate financial position: she was in debt to the sum of approximately £68,000. An existing letter from Ernest Hooley shows that he had tried to engage her in some scheme in 1909 which he was certain could have made £50,000, but nothing came of it. Now, supported by Grant Richards, a congenital bankrupt, she planned that Harris should edit her Life, which would be well fortified by her love letters from the Prince of Wales. Theo Lang has written a book on this subject called *My Darling Daisy*, presenting both Frances Warwick and Harris remarkably unsympathetically. Their desperation for money has obliterated his compassion. Anita Leslie, in *Edwardians in Love* (Hutchinson, London, 1972), on the other hand, gives a delightful and affectionate portrait of Lady Warwick. She was beautiful, she cared deeply about people and she was what Anita Leslie's relations called very naughty indeed. "Very fast—very fast," was Queen Victoria's comment. "You never saw a more perfect *grande dame* at the head of her dinner table," said Anita Leslie's great-aunt Olive. No one who knew her could help loving her. Caring deeply about poverty, she organized a room at Easton Lodge where delicate village girls could learn needlework, and this soon became so popular that the needlework overflowed into a shop in Bond Street—described in *The Candid Friend*: Lady Brooke's (Lady Brooke became Lady Warwick on the death of her father-in-law, Earl of Warwick, in 1893) depot for the Easton School of Needle-work, a depot that unfortunately provoked mockery and contempt in some circles and one that ran at considerable expense to herself, since she had little business head or experience.

Her entertaining was also expensive. Rooms at Easton Lodge were full of flowers, "the servants charmed, the cook excelled himself," Anita Leslie tells us. There was riding or driving, hunting or shooting, "returning to the long gold and white drawing-room for tea, while the ladies would be fluttering like butterflies in gorgeous long-sleeved tea-gowns before the ascent to large chintz-curtained bedrooms where the books had been specially chosen by the hostess for a quiet hour of reading. Then came the great dress-up in tight-waisted gowns for dinner." She was extravagant and spontaneous. Once, Theo Lang tells us, she bought a baby elephant, brought to the door by a traveling salesman; it was sent to Warwick Castle, where later it was joined by two emus, which were seen one morning chasing one of the guests—a gaitered bishop—through the shrubbery. The Prince of Wales went often to Easton, and since the railway station was quite far away, a special station was built for the royal train. Soon after the Earl of Warwick died, Lady Warwick gave a fancy dress ball at Warwick Castle. Guests were summoned to a banquet by trumpeters dressed in cloth of gold. There were minuets, waltzes and champagnes. Frances Warwick went as Marie Antoinette, and thought (she was incapable of hypocrisy, Anita Leslie tells us) how lucky for everyone that she was giving the ball, as it gave employment.

The Labour journal, the *Clarion*, thought otherwise and attacked her: "Thousands of pounds spent on a few hours' silly masquerade, men and women strutting before each other's envious eyes, in mad rivalry of wanton dissipation . . . other men and women and children the while huddling in their ragged hovels." At this Lady Warwick took the first train to London, "dazed by such a version of her glamor-ous ball, trembling with indignation at what she felt to be the injustice of these accusations." She discovered Robert Blatchford, the editor, in a dilapidated office. He was astonished at this vision sweeping in and demanding, "How could you be so unfair?" Mr. Blatchford, who, Anita Leslie explains, had at first been a badly treated brush maker, related carefully the difference between productive economics and such a ball as hers. Dressing up as Marie Antoinette was unproductive, while making pots, pans, houses and bread was productive.

Now, in 1914, Lady Warwick was badly in debt, her creditors were crowding in on her, she had suffered an unhappy love affair and her health was not good. She needed money as desperately as Harris did, and she reasoned that it was, after all, "dear Edward" and entertaining him in the way to which he was accustomed that had landed her in this unfortunate financial state. Why should she not sell his letters and her memories of him, thereby recouping some of her losses? Was this not after all a just payment?

Nellie, in her memoirs, comes up with her version of the business. Frank, she says, was obsessed with the way in which England had treated him—nothing would ever induce him to go there again—an obsession that she considered was absurd. (Here we have an example of Nellie giving only half the truth. Frank was indeed obsessed with the way in which England had treated him, but also, because of the pending bankruptcy case filed against him on May 13, 1914,[1] he could not go to England.) Since he would not—and could not—go to her, as she had hoped, Lady Warwick was obliged to come to him. Toward the end of April, she telegraphed that she had left London and was arriving at a hotel in Nice. Here she proposed that she would pay

---

[1] The final list filed on December 31, 1915.

Brandon & Nicholson (Solicitor)	£149 11 7
[fees for work done and moneys expended between October 3, 1913 and May 3, 1914]	
Oscar Scholzig, Charles Samuel & Barnett	546 6 6
[Merchant and agent for paper deliveries to *Modern Society* trading as B. S. Thomas]	
Leslie, Melville & Fitzwilliam	129 3 8
[cost of damages in "What the Little Bird Knows"]	
Gerald Watson	87 10 8
Henry Hess	81 0 0
[for contributions to *Modern Society*]	
Woollands	4 3 9
[tweed coat; tinsel gauze; satin brilliant; white jap silk gown; green sunshade]	
Harrods	2 10 0
[1 doz. collars: postage to Paris; 3 shirts; 3 pairs cuffs]	

Harris £10,000 to write her life. There is in existence an agreement dated May 1, 1914, which confirms an earlier, verbal agreement made between the Countess of Warwick and Frank Harris:

> Whereas Lady Warwick of Easton wishes to write and publish some *Memoirs* of her life and wishes the book to be well-composed and written and whereas Lady Warwick believes Frank Harris to be an experienced man of letters and able to help her with the said book, Lady Warwick hereby engages Frank Harris to edit her *Memoirs* for the sum of £5,000 to be deducted from the first monies received by the Countess of Warwick for the said book.
>
> Whereas also the Countess of Warwick regards Frank Harris as a capable man of business and desires his help and cooperation in selling her *Memoirs,* the Countess of Warwick hereby agrees in addition to the £5,000 mentioned above to give to Frank Harris ten percent on the sum obtained for her *Memoirs* up to one hundred thousand pounds and five percent on any further sum above £100,000.
>
> In case however that the Countess of Warwick for some reason or other decides later that she will not publish the said *Memoirs* she hereby agrees in any case to pay Frank Harris the first £5,000 for his literary work and advice and 10% more on any offer or offers that he may obtain for the said *Memoirs.*
>
> Frank Harris on his part hereby undertakes to give the Countess of Warwick whatever help she may need and to do his best for her both as literary man and man of business on the conditions above set forth and Lady Warwick finally agrees to let Frank Harris have the rough sketch of the book and the necessary papers.

At the beginning of June Harris left Nice for Paris to look for jobs, once more in the offices of the *World* and the *New York Herald,* and Nellie departed for London, where she had some bits and pieces to tie together, and to gather up monies owing to her for such miscellaneous articles as furniture and armor. Their belongings were spread between various people's London flats, Nice, Paris and the pawnshop. "We are dreadfully hard up—near the bone—eh?" Harris asked her. The silver had gone into pawn, Nellie's jewelry was about to follow it. "You poor dear! I'm very sorry but I see no other way. We must not be caught here without money as there's practically no credit yet . . . get every penny you can!"

With his unsuccessful search for jobs, and his proofs of the first series of Contemporary Portraits, *Morning*[2] and *Oscar Wilde* arriving for correction, he was so hard at work that he could not even read the papers, he told Nellie, and he was not helped by his secretary, who required, it seemed, a servant to accompany her on the street. " 'A man spoke to me,' she minced, and when I said 'Damn' to something her face was a study." It was all very unsatisfactory. And there was no news from Lady Warwick—"the selfish cat"—and Nellie's letters were, as usual, not too good: "no hint of whom you have met or seen; *nothing* personal in your letters: nothing from the heart or to it."

Nellie was not in a good frame of mind; rumors and stories were abroad, and she lost no time in informing Frank. "Your letter makes me despair," he wrote on June 30. "Eve Balfour has no letter of mine that could not be published. . . . I never took her to lunch in a private room: I don't believe I ever had her alone to lunch at all, with her husband it's possible. . . . Eve Balfour is just one of the cases in which I didn't yield a little bit and now she comes to annoy you who did all she could to get me."

On June 25 Lady Warwick once more girded herself into action; she rushed up to London to see one of her creditors, who had been wanting to know why the interest had not been paid on a sum of money he had lent her two years before. Her creditor was Arthur du Cros. Theo Lang gives details of the business. She had precipitated her visit by a letter: could she come and see him about a sensational literary project she was planning from which she believed she would make £100,000? She arrived at Eaton Terrace all charm and friendly ease bearing with her an envelope of letters. She had written her memoirs, she told du Cros. To du Cros, concerned about his interest, the news came as something of an anticlimax. He tried hard to insinuate warm pleasure at her news, then broke off and cast around for words that would frame his thoughts in a kindly fashion. One hundred thousand pounds? He honestly could not see her memoirs making as much as that. Mr. Harris had told her so, Lady Warwick said. That made du Cros furious. Understandably, he did not care for Harris and referred to him as "that poisonous person." He was even more furious when she revealed to him the financial details of the contract and said that the envelope contained letters from Edward. Did Lady Warwick wish that he should keep the matter confidential, du

[2] To be published as *Love in Youth*.

Cros wanted to know. That was a matter of total indifference to her—after all, the book would soon be on the market. Arthur du Cros said that he hoped this would not be, not only for the sake of Lady Warwick herself but for her family—and what about consideration for the royal family? Yes, Lady Warwick had considered that very carefully, but, after all, she would not be in such a desperate financial position if it were not for "dear Edward." If she did make some profit out of the letters it was only a payment for all the money she had spent on entertaining him; and she departed, leaving one of the letters in his care. Arthur du Cros had been drawn irretrievably into the intrigue. Five days later he placed the letter in the hands of the Earl of Albemarle and told him of Frances Warwick's plan to reveal everything. For the next few months he spent much time and energy shuttling between Lady Warwick and various representatives of the palace relaying what turned out to be dummy offers to buy the letters. Lady Warwick would, in fact, have preferred to sell the letters for £100,000 rather than publish them, although all the while she was adamant; to publish the letters and reveal the love affair could be no greater disgrace than bankruptcy.

Arthur du Cros became so caught up in the affair that he decided that he should accompany Frances Warwick to Paris and be present at the meeting with Harris, at which it was proposed the deal would be clinched, and which duly took place on July 14 at the Ritz. Du Cros reported the scene word for word in his diary, and most of the words concerning Harris were exceedingly unflattering. He arrived at the Ritz just after eleven o'clock and refused to go upstairs, suspicious, du Cros explained, lest there be a private witness secreted in the cupboard. Harris was standing at a window, his back to the room, staring out into the Place Vendôme, his body braced, his legs straddled in the Napoleonic stance that he customarily adopted, to compensate apparently for his lack of height. Lady Warwick was not yet there. Why not? du Cros wanted to know. At this, he said, Harris laughed suggestively, as though she had passed a long and amorous night in his company. When she did appear she was greeted by Harris as "Frances darling," and he then got down to business. The book, he estimated, could earn as much as £125,000, and that was a conservative guess. Mr. du Cros must realize that it was not merely a matter of royalties on the book; there would be serial rights from newspapers and magazines, foreign rights—all kinds of possibilities. Du Cros agreed that indeed there were all kinds of possibilities: the possibilities of harm that the book could do, for instance, and the disgrace that Lady Warwick would call down on herself by putting her name to it.

At this Harris taxed du Cros with first threatening Lady Warwick with bankruptcy, then warning her of what she would suffer in attempts to avoid it. No, said du Cros, this was not so. Lady Warwick stood in no fear of bankruptcy if she took advantage of a likely opportunity to dispose of the letters. How much would such people be prepared to pay? Harris wanted to know, in his best agent's style. Du Cros said that Lady Warwick had £85,000 in mind, that this was too much but would be all right for a kicking-off point. Harris dismissed that contemptuously. Frances, he said, had been foolish to talk in such terms without asking his advice. The only compensation he and she would accept for not publishing the letters was the amount they could earn by publishing them: £125,000. Out of the question, du Cros said. Well, Harris must now advise Frances to hold out for £125,000, and he repeated his terms: £5,000 if the letters were published, plus 10 percent of the royalties; and £10,000 if the letters were not included—plus royalties. Without those letters, Harris said, the book would not sell half so well and he must protect his interest. Well, du Cros must advise Lady Warwick not to publish anything at all. In that case, Harris said, Frances would have to pay him £15,000. Lady Warwick nodded. Could a compromise be reached that Lady Warwick would publish her memoirs without the letters, for whose loss she would be compensated by the considerable sum she would get by selling the letters? What about, say, £75,000? No, Lady Warwick considered that too little. Besides, the £85,000 that she had suggested the previous Thursday had not included the fee she must pay Mr. Harris for his work. For his part, Harris pointed out that they were talking about a business proposition—the letters and the memoirs had a market value. He was so confident that they would prove a great scoop that he turned to Lady Warwick and said that if she would agree then and there to include the letters he would cut his fee by half. She need pay him only £2,000. He was sure that the royalties would repay him. Lady Warwick, however, preferred to sell the letters —£85,000 for herself, £15,000 for Mr. Harris—a suggestion that drew a storm of protest from Harris. This was throwing money away, he roared. Du Cros refused to commit himself, but promised to get in touch with Lady Warwick after further consultation in London.

They met, however, before that—on the boat crossing the Channel. On the other side of her hotel bill Lady Warwick drew up a list of her debts and issued an ultimatum. Frank Harris would be leaving shortly for New York, taking with him her autobiography and the letters. In all, she confided, it was now reckoned that they stood to earn £200,000 in the transaction. After all—she repeated it—even £100,000 was far less than the sum she had spent during her association with "dear Edward." Du Cros expressed his opinion that it was sordid to count the cost of a friendship in terms of thousands of pounds; she replied that, unfortunately, one did get sordid when up to the ears in debt.

At this juncture everyone, according to Theo Lang, played a double game, except for Harris. And it was the palace that played the deepest double game of all. At all costs the king's advisers were going to keep the royal scandal a secret. At the end of July Lady Warwick brought into play another pawn, Mr. Bruce Logan, and into his hands she placed the letters for safekeeping. Soon he and his partner, Clarence Hatry, noticed that they were both being followed by solid-looking persons in bowler hats. Then an injunction was served upon them claiming copyright of the papers resting in their safe—and for a while there was silence.

Nellie, however, while she had been in London, had not been silent at all. She had been spreading dark stories abroad as regards Frank's health and finance. Many of his friends did not realize how serious his situation was and believed that his obsession never to return to England rested entirely in pique at unjust imprisonment. "Now look here," Austin Harrison wrote,

> I feel I must just say what seems obvious to all except your self. It is that your vexation is quite unlogical. What happened over that wretched paper of yours is utterly beneath your position. You had no right to have such a paper. You offend your own sense of dignity in belonging to it. You write down yourself. To complain, however if having such a paper you get swiped at by one . . . of the victims . . . is really too funny. In you, it is simply screamingly droll, you who go about talking of Jesus—but Jesus never ran a "Jerusalem Funny-bits" to publish anonymous show ups of the girls the apostles had, the bottoms the Romans kicked and those the Gentile dancing-girls licked. . . . If he had we should have been spared the Christianity of the Churches and you, with no Jesus to

talk about, might have been revealed as a man of humour . . . if you want to be a blackguard journalist of the Crosland type, well tis your affair; but then don't come out, when hurt, and say you are badly treated. You *know* perfectly well that Fitzwilliam merely acted in self-defence: the awful part of it all is that you one of our greatest men should be making mudpies of that sort. . . . Now I want you to "give over" being a mad hatter, come back here. Nothing has happened really. But do for God's sake cease being a child and be the man some of us believe you to be. All that is needed is a sense of humour, a little humility. Look here, try christian science. Don't laugh it is a wonderful thing for the nerves.

But because of the bankruptcy Harris was doing his best to convince himself and the British authorities that he had nothing at all to do with England. "Ever since the Boer war I have not felt any sympathy with the English or English methods of action," he wrote in answer to Austin Harrison. "For the past twelve years I have lived there as little as I could. The whole English spirit is alien to me and has been doing me harm, making me bitter and contemptuous. . . . The moral atmosphere of England is deleterious to my spiritual well-being and accordingly I propose to keep out of it if I can."

He made a further—and substantially erroneous—statement to the British authorities on July 11, 1914.

> I, Frank Harris, of Villa Vittoria, Chemin de Fabron, Nice, Alpes Maritimes in Republic of France, Author
> 1. I oppose the petition presented to the Honorable Court on the ground that I am a foreigner that I have not committed an act of bankruptcy as alleged in the said petition and was at the date of the bankruptcy notice and have since remained out of the jurisdiction of the court.
> 2. I was born in Galway in 1855 but settled in America at the age of 14 years in 1869 where I lived until 1878. After I had attained my majority in 1876 I renounced my allegiance to any sovereign or state other than the U.S.A. and became an American citizen. I have maintained my American citizenship and have been called to the American bar. About 1887 I was compelled for reasons of health to establish a permanent residence on the French Riviera which I have maintained up to the present time. For the last few years I have in the summer months spent some weeks in this country except as in the next paragraph mentioned. I have however never exercised any rights of citizenship.

Whilst in England in or about September last I acquired an interest in a weekly periodical called *Modern Society* for a short time until the end of December, I undertook all the duties of editorship, which kept me in England until the beginning of 1914. In January of 1914 proceedings were taken against me in connection with an article appearing in the paper and I was committed to prison for contempt of Court. Immediately after my release at the beginning of March viz the 20th day of March, 1914, I returned to my residence in Nice and have since then not been out of France.

That summer in Paris money was extremely tight; there was no credit to be had. With great difficulty, Nellie says, they managed to move into their new flat in the Avenue du Bois. All the men who were supposed to be decorating and setting it in order disappeared. Meanwhile Lady Warwick had apparently begged them to go to Easton. On August 2 Paris was declared to be in a state of siege. A broad river of people flowed down the streets and pavements shouting, "Vive la France," and "La Marseillaise" was taken up by thousands of voices, rising and falling on waves of sound. On August 4 Britain declared war on Germany, and Harris had to take his English secretary to the Gare du Nord. It was blocked by immense crowds of people leaving; it was not possible, he was told, to buy a ticket. He managed to bribe someone to let them through to the back of the station, where two trains awaited, already crammed. As Nellie and the secretary waited outside the station during his negotiations, a large lorry drew up with a dozen English soldiers all dressed in odds and ends. The crowd handed them bottles of wine, accusing them at the same time of having run away from the front. This annoyed Nellie, she wrote in her diary. She told the taxi driver to drive as near the lorry as possible, and then just as a soldier was putting some wine in his mouth she told him what the crowd was saying. The soldier glared and said they'd been reconnoitering and resting under some trees when they had been surrounded by Germans and had just managed to save themselves. He stood up on the lorry and yelled the "Marseillaise." The whole of the front of the Gare du Nord was a mass of people, you could have walked over their heads, said Nellie. Every man stood up with his hat off, officers and soldiers to attention. In the middle of all this Frank appeared from the station waving and looking distractedly about—it took him ten minutes to reach them. Eventually the secretary was squeezed into the train. Next day the city was almost empty except for detachments of soldiers marching. It was nearly impossible, Harris found, to get money; the banks were virtually closed up. He was allowed 250 francs, that was all. There was no credit anywhere. It was an appalling situation: everyone must pay cash, yet it was almost impossible to extract it from the bank. Food shot up in price, nearly three times as expensive. Harris set out one day, intending to stock up on rice, and found he could buy only small quantities. There were no trains for civilians on the metro—all were taken for the troops. Shops were sacked, hotels closed, restaurants shut, theaters stopped. It was altogether very dull. Nellie was dispatched to Dieppe and England, and arrived having had to stand all the way in a crowded third-class carriage and allowed only hand luggage. Harris said that he intended to stay and see the Germans enter Paris. Everyone waited; stories abounded of how silver had been buried, houses abandoned. Meanwhile Harris dashed off to review the front. "This war of nations is going to test every man," he pronounced on August 29 to Gerald Cumberland. "The question for you is have I quickened you to be a brave soldier in the Liberation War of Humanity? Did virtue come out of me? or discouragement?" He concluded with some of his favorite words of Joubert, words that he was to use more and more to conclude his letters. "There is no such sure sign of mediocrity as constant moderation in praise. Ha! Ha! Ha!"

Thereupon he set out for Essex. To foil the officers of the bankruptcy court, Frank traveled to Easton, under the pseudonym of Frank Vernon, and stayed as a guest of Lady Warwick at the home farm until the middle of October—"but we paid," added Nellie, "4 guineas a week for our rooms and board."

Every morning Lady Warwick went along and told Frank part of her life, according to Nellie, and every afternoon Frank dictated it to a stenographer. About thirty chapters were written when, said Nellie, Lady Warwick got cold feet. The letters from which they worked, she added, were photographs, not originals. Harris worked so hard "that I got rather queer this afternoon and had to wash away all my lunch and then go for a walk," he wrote to Nellie, who had gone on financial business to London. He had completed "the Astor episode . . . tomorrow I tackle the Prince business. . . . Lady Warwick goes to town tomorrow . . . she was most charming today when I told her how mean I have to be in U.S.A. She told me to try to borrow money saying she'd give her name too as security so that I might get £1,000 or so to go to New York with, and is to see Logan tonight about it." Nellie, from London, posted to him packages of cake, socks and cider. And then Logan gave the show away, Harris told her on September 29. "Her solicitors and Russell are meeting today to offer her £50,000: no wonder she talked of £1,000 to me but that's not right: she promised me out of the first lot £5,000 for the writing and I think I've deserved it. . . . We shall have a wonderful time in old New York."

Before he set sail he and Nellie had dinner with H. G. Wells at the Dower House. That this was a meeting of some friction is indicated by Nellie's memoirs. She started her Lady Warwick episode by somewhat irrelevantly sniping at Wells. Since this was dated June 26, 1936, her ill humor could have been stimulated by reading Wells's *Experiment in Autobiography*, which contained several unflattering references to Harris and which had been published two years earlier, in 1934. "About Wells," she had scribbled, "I can only say as I have said about others—Frank hurt Wells' vanity terribly. He used to call him Kipps, and always imitated a Cockney accent that Wells had early in life. When Frank had to follow a speech [Wells's] given at the Ritz Hotel to Robby Ross for Oscar Wilde, Frank imitated Wells as only Frank could with a sarcasm that was pointed and terrible. Therefore perhaps Wells never got over that." Not only does she start her episode with Wells, but she also ends it with Wells. One day, she wrote, Lady Warwick said that Wells was coming to call. Next day they were invited to supper at the Dower House—where the Wellses were living. Mrs. Wells was kind-looking but thin, very much wrinkled and unusually quiet. They were all in the sitting room when suddenly she went off into hysterical cackles of laughter. In the usual English way, everyone pretended not to notice and talked away as if nothing had happened.

Before Harris' departure from Glasgow on the R.M.S. *Olympic*, Lady Warwick wrote him a bread-and-butter letter, as it were.

> I cannot let you go away without *trying* to tell you all my gratitude for your wonderful and immense interest in my life and in the description thereof. The *only* way in which it can be of value was to be taken in hand by your magic pen and your incomparable genius. That in time to come it will be valuable I have no doubt— but it will be entirely owing to you—I realize absolutely—besides all this, I have grown, with deeper knowledge of yourself all these weeks to value, even more than I did before, your friendship and

confidence—and if mine, in return, are of any use to you, you have them for life—and your charming wife also—These are not banal words but I have a feeling that our meeting and allegiance are for good, and that the day will not be far distant when *your own* personality and talent will be recognized generally by all nations: both East and West, Europe and America—as they deserve to be. I want you—for my sake, to cultivate a kindlier feeling towards the world at large—to believe there is more good than evil in every human being—and that such things as persecution from the jealous and even prison-experience don't really count . . . as against the wonderful "inside" soul and spirit that are yours and that *no one can* take from you. Kindly thoughts attract *good* cycles—and your *good* times are coming—be patient, for I know you will *win*.

I am installing a little shrine in my sitting room here, dear friend—a picture of yourself, on the wall . . . beneath a bookshelf dedicated entirely to your books. Everyone of them together—a "Frank Harris" corner in my room as in my heart. . . . Take *great* care of yourself! I believe that the sun is rising for you and believe in the entire friendship and gratitude of F. E. Warwick.

By the middle of October Harris was once more at sea. The waters were rolling and his head was sick, but again he was filled with optimism and was singing a familiar tune: "I do believe I'll win this time and pretty soon: I love you my darling Nellie, take care of yourself and don't flirt!"

CHAPTER 17

America

O N arriving in New York Harris set himself up at his favorite St. Regis Hotel and immediately dispatched to Nellie a tiresome diary of his life: how he had unpacked, slept and breakfasted. Although Wells claims that Harris' ship had been twice under threat of torpedo attacks, this is not mentioned; either this was dull stuff compared with details of unpacking and breakfasting or the letter is not in existence. The first few days he sent out his letters of introduction, hurried off to various newspaper offices, saw Pulitzer and sold him an article about explosives that he had written on board ship, found Hearst's managing director was "a poopstick," wrote an article on war, and received Madame Strindberg, who appeared immense, ill-dressed, with no money but full of suggestions.[1] Nellie should go along and see Tree and get him to send Frank introductions to some "society-swells" like Mrs. Belmont who would allow him to lecture on the war in her drawing room. "Everyone hard up and pro-British," he told her. "I will not kick against the pricks for it might

[1] She had arrived in New York fresh from running a cabaret club in a Soho cellar, The Cave of the Golden Calf, where, wrapped in a fur coat, she reigned over couples enjoying the bunny hug and the turkey trot. As war advanced she had stripped the cellar of everything she could carry and sailed for New York. Before this, in spite of attempting suicide several times, she had survived a tumultuous affair with Augustus John, whom she had pursued across Europe carrying a revolver.

mean starvation. I've had enough: I won't lie: but won't tell all the truth."

Soon the St. Regis proved too expensive and Harris moved to 244 Riverside Drive, overlooking the Hudson. All day long the sun shone as hot as July in Paris. Aleister Crowley appeared at the St. Regis with phlebitis, "more like an Egyptian than ever, yet he has a certain cunning which I'll try to turn to my advantage"; and Madame Strindberg, whom Harris had seen too much of—she was getting him talked about—was enthusiastically suggesting that she and Nellie should go into a millinery and dressmaking business together. "I think it would be a hit: but it would take some capital and we are as poor as church mice." The food was bad and expensive, the streets infernal, the theaters worse than in London, and he and Madame Strindberg were depressed together.

Matters concerning Lady Warwick's memoirs were not progressing. Harris had visited a friend of hers called Marsh, who was of the opinion that nothing could be done about the sale of the letters in wartime. In peace, yes, it would be easy to get £100,000. For a wild moment Harris wondered if, instead, Lady Warwick would consider selling all the Vandykes and other paintings out of Warwick Castle "for a mint of money." She would say they were heirlooms, he supposed, "although I don't know what that means exactly." He knew a man in Paris who would copy any one of them so you could not tell the difference between the copy and the original. "I want you to propose it to her," he urged Nellie, conjuring a singular picture of Lady Warwick and Nellie, fretful but gracious in her tinsel gauze and satin from Woollands, struggling clandestinely out of Warwick Castle with huge packages. Meanwhile Harris was all set to publish the Astor story. Lady Warwick had cabled her assent to this, "but could she give me this *in writing* for really her letters are so contradictory that I hesitate to act without her special written authority. . . . I'm afraid I'll lose a good market through delay and she may be sure I shan't give away more of the letters than I can help." And then would Nellie just go along to Peter Robinson and find for his landlady, Mrs. Meek—"a nice little woman, tiny, a head shorter than you"—a rubber coat that she had seen there last summer for £2? From a course of lectures and his war articles Harris managed to scrape up enough money to cable some for dresses and for Nellie's passage. "I just set my teeth each morning," he wrote on October 29, "and go on smilingly certain even when I'm most doubtful or depressed!" Everyone in New York, he wrote, was asking after her. If only he could get that advance of £1,000—and he meant to get it—then he was sure that she'd have a good time. If only he could get it he'd save the flats in Nice and Paris, and then in May, when the chestnuts were out, they would be back in Paris with a fortune, the war would end and they would bask happily in the Indian summer of his life before the winter, but meanwhile he must work on. . . . "I've really worked like a dog at these war articles to get £50 to send you," he wrote on October 31, "this next week I shall write *three* stories just to get the cash for you. . . . Believe me your situation worries me a thousand times more than my own. Your dear sad letter came this evening and brought tears to my eyes. I'll give you no more cause for sorrow dear, and let us love each other more and more—then the poverty won't matter so much."

Back in England, Lady Warwick went to see du Cros on November 19. She agreed she could not publish the letters, but what she could publish was the account of the palace's intrigue over the whole affair. She was planning to ridicule all the people involved. Could such a clever businessman and friend as du Cros give her advice? She had heard stories about du Cros himself, she added, which laid him open to criticism. This threat, Theo Lang tells us, disturbed du Cros hugely; he suggested that she should legitimately earn money by obtaining contracts for war material from the French, Belgian and Russian governments. She left behind her a chapter dealing with Astor—one of King Edward's favorite millionaires. Next day du Cros earnestly implored her not to publish the piece. Then follows, according to Theo Lang, a mysterious story. A week later du Cros received a visitor, Mr. Marsh, who asked the value of the Warwick estates. Two hundred and fifty thousand pounds, said du Cros. An American friend of Marsh's, British-born, had a wife with £500,000 of her own who was willing to gamble this sum to achieve the common American ambition of establishing herself at the top of the social ladder in England. A condition of purchase of the Warwick estate would be that Lady Warwick should surrender certain letters known to be in her possession. Lady Warwick's explanation was that Mr. Marsh's friend was really a German with ulterior political motives. Du Cros rushed off to Lord Albemarle, and nothing more was heard of Mr. Marsh.

In New York the general opinion of Harris was rapidly descending. Shortly after his arrival, Kate Stephens says, the National Arts Club gave a dinner—a feast, she calls it. Among the group of first-table guests was Frank, whom the toastmaster invited to speak. Harris rose and began on the porcinity of the American people, the poverty of letters, the stupidity, the lack of liberal culture. A lady leaned over and warned him to take care or the National Arts Club would not be inviting him to another dinner. Frank's voice was loud: "I don't care whether the National Arts Club invites me to another dinner or not."

It was his war articles that really harmed him. They began that autumn in the Sunday edition of the New York *Sun*, and in January 1915 were published in book form under the title *England or Germany?*[2] It caused an international furore. Under the title of "The Adventures of Frank Harris" the *New Statesman*, on June 19, 1915, launched an attack both on Harris and on his mischievous anti-British articles. First it reviewed the decline in Harris' career as a literary editor, his fall from the heights of the *Saturday Review* to *Modern Society*; between Shakespearean and short-story enterprises, appearances in court in connection with curiously shady cases, and closing his career with a short spell in prison. Next it examined Harris' qualifications as editor of the *Saturday*. They were not apparent. He had no sense of politics and no affiliation with the peculiar brand of Toryism for which the old *Saturday* stood. Under Harris the *Saturday* had taken an independent line in foreign and imperial affairs: it was against aggression on the Indian frontier and unorthodox—from the Conservative view—on South Africa. As an influence in domestic politics it was almost nonexistent, but in literary, artistic and musical matters it was the most vital and stimulating weekly journal in the English-speaking world. "Now here," claimed the *New Statesman*, "is the circumstance that gives the *Saturday* a particular importance in the modern history of Europe, and Frank Harris a place amongst the sinister figures connecting the age of Bismarck with the cataclysm of last August. The *Saturday Review* of 1895–9 started in the English Press the cry that Germany was the enemy and would have to be destroyed."

[2] *England or Germany?* systematically attacked all Harris' *bêtes noires*: the English oligarchy, so-called justice, savage laws, prisons, snobbishness and hypocrisy. It attacked America, which, said Harris, was with England against Germany on immoral grounds; it was a stupid, senseless, unnecessary war. What it all amounted to was that England was envious of Germany, of her efficiency and her trade. War had been declared to crush her trade rival, a war on which millions were being spent in a country that Mr. Booth of the Salvation Army declared had a third of its population on the verge of starvation.

Abuse of the Kaiser (who was referred to as William the Witless) was coupled with a denunciation of Germany's policies and aims. The *Saturday Review* was filed in Berlin. Prince von Bülow when writing *Imperial Germany*, a widely read book, quoted a passage from the *Saturday* saying that if Germany were extinguished tomorrow there would not be an Englishman in the world who would not be richer. The previous autumn it had been taken out of the file and used by the German press bureau to convince the neutral countries that for a generation England had been planning the annihilation of her rival. Toward America the *Saturday*'s tone had been equally offensive; nothing, it seemed, would suffice but that the *Saturday* would embroil both Germany and America in war with England. The directors of the German press bureau, "conceiving doubtless that it is no part of their business to supply a biographical sketch of their interesting ally," took pains to circulate with one hand Frank Harris' recent articles from the New York *Sun* in order to prove how abominable England was, and with the other distributed from the *Saturday* relevant passages to show that England had willed the war two decades before.

Bernard Shaw jumped to Harris' defense the following week. *England or Germany?* was mainly an attack on English law and English prisons, he said, and English philistines as against English geniuses.

> When Frank Harris really edited a paper, he edited it very well, as the files of the *Fortnightly* and the *Saturday* show. But when, preoccupied by more fascinating activities, he left the office boy to edit it, the results were disastrous. The office boy, plunging recklessly into finance, would express an opinion that such and such a bank was a rotten concern, not knowing how easily a bank and its customers can be ruined by a run provoked by the idlest rumour. Or the boy tried his hand at smart society gossip, and playfully attributed conduct to highly placed and blameless persons, which, if true, would have made them socially and politically impossible for life. Harris was always ready to apologize for these "accidents," as he calls them in his books, in a tone which showed how trifling he thought them; and he could not understand why, in spite of this simple settlement between one gentleman and another, he should be cast in heavy damages, with the judges sternly approving instead of protesting, and even thrown into jail for a perfectly natural (to him) contempt of court.

The book amounted really to a mixture of pique and wish to fight for the underdog. This, said Shaw, was why he was supporting Germany—he was a martyr to pity. The article served Frank right, but he did not like to leave his reputation precisely where the article left it.

On July 17 a letter was published from S. K. Ratcliffe. He explained that it was Dr. P. Chalmers Mitchell who had been behind Harris and the whole *Saturday* policy in respect to America and Germany. He had taught him the theory—which had since been emphatically repudiated—of the biological necessity of warfare between expanding peoples. It came from the so-called Treitschke–Bernhardi theory as to the biological and beneficent necessity of aggressive war. America and Germany were jostling each other, England should be ready to fight both of them when the time came, etc., etc. On July 31 Harris answered. For some years past the story of the Man of Sorrows had taken that place in his life which had been occupied by Shakespeare; now he was called from the work he loved by a virulent attack as one of the vilest of men. There was quite a little in Shaw's letter that he disagreed with, but at least he came nearer to understanding him than most: showing a "wounded concern" for England. Now he was building up, stone by stone, as it were, "a clerestory to the great Temple where unborn generations of men shall worship." Then he hoped to write his own life and tell of varied doings and brave adventures. It would most likely be called *How I Fell Among Thieves*, and would be divided into three stages. The longest would be, How I got on; the most humorous, How I got honor; the shortest and the saddest, How I got honest. This would be followed by an epilogue describing his sufferings and descent into hell, an inferno that Dante himself could not have envisaged: an English law court, an English judge and an English prison. And afterward a brief space of freedom and sunshine and work in the light, and gay adventures—"for as you soar up into the blue pigmies fire at you with paper pellets and friends shout humorous nicknames at your earth-borne shadow, but life is good, and the spaces of air sun-kissed, and some great spirits are with you to cheer and encourage; and in spite of war and disaster, red ruin and broken hearts, the soul takes joy in God as the eye in light." "I don't care what they say," Harris told Nellie, "the thing is to produce masterpieces and let 'em talk." Once, when it was casually observed that Harris could not expect everyone to like his book, he boomed out, "A man may be judged by his disciples: Jesus had Paul, I have Arnold Bennett." But he did not have Arnold Bennett for much longer; even he, loyal supporter that he had been, quarreled with Harris over *England or Germany?*

Loneliness, lack of money and the feeling of persecution were affecting Harris' equilibrium. The war articles, written largely to acquire money for Nellie's passage, had caused a breach with her too. For the most part America had been disappointment upon disappointment, he had written to Austin Harrison, during the early part of the winter. But with the prospect of the war book coming out in January, *The Yellow Ticket* being issued by Grant Richards, and the approach of Nellie on R.M.S. *Lapland*, perhaps he would find New York worth living in; until then it had been like the city on the Dead Sea where the fruit was ashes in the mouth and the kisses without savor. Now he was casting his eyes enviously toward a winter spent in the East Indies.

But the winter was passed firmly in New York, and it passed very badly. Nellie and Frank fought almost constantly. Matters were aggravated by the fact that Nellie's favorite brother was killed at the front. She ranted and raved against the Germans and at Harris for supporting them in his articles. In her memoirs she tells a story of how they went with Louis Sherwin to a party at Carl and Fanya Van Vechten's. Nellie was feeling "v.v. miserable," she says, passionately pro-Allies, and there she was, obliged to meet Baron and Baroness Meyer, who were pro-German and anti-English. Afterward Louis Sherwin claimed that Frank yelled all the time, "Nellie bring the *whiskey*." All Nellie could remember was Sherwin talking to Fanya about highballs, of which Nellie had never heard. This seemed hilarious to them all— except, obviously, to Nellie. She departed in the spring determined to leave Frank forever. "In 1915," she wrote in her memoirs, "I went back to London from America, I had made up my mind never to return again to Frank (many men were exuberant)." But, she says, she looked at all the rich men who could have put her on easy street forever and decided that Frank was better than they were.

The day that she left he mooned about like a hurt dog, the pain of being without her making him gasp, he told her. Moping, he went to Mouquins for lunch, and sat on until they opened the windows and began to sweep up. Then he wandered out to the park and into the Plaza for tea and to talk to the German waiter, and there he stayed until ten o'clock, finally going home, having eaten only a brioche and tea. He felt old and hurt, and the next morning did not care enough even to get up. "Drift, drift, what does it matter! I'm more depressed than ever and it rains, rains, dripping into my life." His "doctor play" would not go, the maid was trying to cheat him, he ought to get up and tidy the Astor papers—a man called Wheeler was coming to see them. "I'm not fit to be left: I'm too heart broken. . . . I had no idea one could get so weary of living. I don't want to depress you. You're young and naturally want to do this and that—and I'll hope you'll succeed. Goodbye dear I wish you all luck!" The following morning matters were worsened by a journalist ringing up to say that someone —he refused to say who—had sent him a story that Nellie had left Harris because of their different opinions on the war and had gone back to England resolved never to see him again, as she had had a brother killed at the front.

In April Lady Warwick wrote; she had discovered that her letters never reached him, so now she was sending them by anyone she knew crossing the Atlantic. Harris was to reply to her by enclosing a letter to Mr. Marsh in New York or sending a letter by anyone he knew sailing for England, addressed to Mrs. Marsh, Ritz Hotel, London. Cables should be signed "Martin." She was delighted that he was writing for a paper, she said—she wished he were editor. For heaven's sake, he should become a naturalized American *at once*. She had been persecuted under the Defence of the Realm Act, and there was nothing to do but temporize, but with Harris as an American she would be able to do anything, since she was in his hands through their literary partnership. She would have to restore the letters, but would do this saying that Harris required a thousand pounds to indemnify him. She had refused all money from the palace, since the *meanest* offers were made to her, but she was trying to get him some money. Did he see the prospect of selling the book before the end of the war? "Mr. M[arsh] told me he was so much impressed by your *greatness* when he saw you in New Y." She was going to send out the whole story of her persecution for his newspaper, and all about the letters; he could publish it "when our Book needs the advertisement."

But after *England or Germany?* and the *New Statesman* article were published, Harris was branded on all sides as a traitor; his correspondence and friends were watched. Lady Warwick sent a careful "message to a friend." She was always the same loyal friend, she assured him, she had no other thoughts, her admiration was as great, she only deplored the loss of prestige of a great man. It was impossible to continue the book as a partnership since now his name banned all enterprise, *but she* held to her contract, and if the book ever saw the light of day, the old arrangement held good as to sharing the profits.

All letters and communication were now impossible, since she valued her position and influence, and "my friend" had cast that to the winds; *all* his correspondence and *friends* were watched, so they must just be patient till something ended the war. "Then I'll come out to the States to see my friend and he *must* regain his old prestige."

All that summer Nellie adopted a policy of writing only intermittently, and when she did write, her letters were cold, hard and short. It was a policy that affected Harris badly. He could not bear being ignored, the coldness, the silence. "Nellie, I love you so that when you are cold to me, it is dreadful." He needed her to belong to, to go home to. He was afraid, he told her, that she'd allowed Hugh Lunn to poison her mind beyond cure. "Then I acted badly and you set your pride and will against me and the evil's done—if so *it would be better to be frank with me*." Again and again he ended his letters as though their relationship was finished forever—"Goodbye Nell, I hope you'll be happy." But then he would not or could not leave it. He would write again: he was near breaking point; he had eaten cold tongue and salad; he had gone to the park and there the three-quarter moon had ridden high, the purple sky had looked as if it had been paved with great fragments of purest white marble and the smell of new-mown hay had brought back to him their first bedroom in Limehurst and the scent of Nellie herself. Did she care or did she not? That was the question that obsessed him that summer. He turned it over and over. For a moment as they said goodbye on the ship he had felt that she did, then he remembered the dreadful scenes and disagreements.

> This last experience with you has been terrible to me; but it has taught me a lot of the differences between men and women. I think I ought to tell you I've often seen you flirting, that is making yourself deliberately attractive to a man trying to make him like you. I've never done this before you. I've not been angry at your doing it. The trifling faithlessness don't matter to me; your coquetry pleases me: it is *pretty*! but lately I've often felt that you have lost all love for me that you felt repulsion even—that's serious, altogether different that kills everything! I've never let anyone speak against you, discuss *you to me*. No one. I'm suffering

horribly, need you dreadfully, am like a chicken whose head is cut off. I flop around mechanically and am bleeding to death.

She *must* care for him, because *he* cared for her. She was under *his* skin, *he* must be under hers. He could not let her go. "I thought yesterday in my disappointment at not hearing from you that I would never write to you again, all was over between us: you had chosen to desert me: you could go. Late last night as I was undressing I thought of you without money undressing too in your tiny room in the d—d hotel full of anxiety as to your future and *alone*: at once I was overwhelmed by the hot rush of blood through me—a warmth of affection, of love: Nellie knows I said to myself, she had only to stretch out her hands and I would come at once to her help: I'd leave everything and everybody for her, she knows that. . . . I *love*, in that high sure way no one but her and never have since first she kissed me."

But she had been gone for a month and she had told him nothing of what she was doing or what she was spending, apart from assuring him "that there's another Mrs. Frank Harris going about London, tall and dark whom I certainly have never seen, your letter does not tell me much."

Nellie had decided to take up singing. For this she needed money. Harris, delighted at receiving a letter with a little more warmth than usual, rushed in with advice and assurances. She was too ambitious, she must perfect her English and her Irish folk songs, particularly the Irish ones; she could always sing an operatic song as an encore. Stick to the folk songs, get them perfect, and he'd send her money for dresses in July. He dreamed that she would return and sing at the Metropolitan and take the lead in some of his plays. "One successful appearance at the Metropolitan Opera and you're made." He was sorry for all the pain and wretchedness he had caused her—wouldn't she forgive and forget? Of course she could have lessons with her *prima donna*, or anyone else for that matter. He'd send the money. He hoped to receive £300 next week, he wrote on May 29, to do "my Oscar book with and I'll send you £120 for Paris and £30 for yourself." Unfortunately, his war book was criticized everywhere and not selling at all well—in his view because it had been issued by an unknown publisher—and the daily papers would not review it.

To save money on living expenses he planned to spend the summer with some friends, the de Rendons, in the Catskill Mountains. Be-

fore he left he lectured at Lawrence, Kansas, and there he saw a portrait of Byron Smith and was reminded of Kate Stephens. He sent her
a letter. They met, they corresponded. Kate Stephens has told her side
of the story in *The Lies and Libels of Frank Harris.* The daily papers
were reporting that Harris was in the pay of the Kaiser's government
and the German press bureau. Kate Stephens went to some lengths to
justify her reason for agreeing to meet him in the first place. He was a
refugee, she told herself, a man at odds with the laws of his country,
broken in his career. They met in the gallery of the New York Public
Library. They laughed and remembered. Harris seemed a pattern of
ingenuous innocence; only now and then a flash of the disappointed,
cynical man rose out of the guise of a joyous-minded child. They almost lost themselves in reminiscences, and then Kate Stephens rose to
go. Without invitation, much to her amazement, Harris went along with
her: "a confiding child seeming loath to leave, clinging in most pathetic wordless appeal." It was a soft afternoon, the sun shone through
a red-gold haze; "we came down the broad marble staircase of the
library and out of the Fifth Avenue door." Struck by the beauty, Kate
Stephens was inspired to point to the tide of moving people: "good
folks hurrying home to rest and dinner," said she. "Swine," spat Harris
with a sneer. "Not a new idea in this country for more than a hundred
years." And then, after a pause, the beseeching child re-established itself, and Kate Stephens was able to explain that Mrs. Margaret Caldwell Smith wished that her son's love letters be published, with certain
names of people and places changed. Soon after this they parted, Harris flattering Kate Stephens by desiring to read a book of hers, *A
Woman's Heart.*

The correspondence continued. Harris was, he said, looking forward very much to reading *A Young Scholar's Letters*,[3] more eagerly
still to Smith's love letters to Kate, "for they were written about the
time I knew him and so might bring half-faded outlines into sharp
distinction. . . . I'm an unhappy prophet," he added, "who has a message to deliver and has not yet found a medium . . . my time is getting
short." He was, he told her, looking for Titans, if not demigods, and
was not interested in well dressed gentlefolk.

Nothing would make Harris rest. He must see the Smith letters.
"Could I not come and just read them some afternoon? They would

---

[3] *A Young Scholar's Letters,* edited by Day Otis Kellogg (G. P. Putnam's Sons, New
York, 1897)—letters written while Smith was studying abroad.

help me I am sure to do a real portrait of him." So in early June he arranged to call and read the freshly typed letters and to borrow *A Young Scholar's Letters*. The typescript carried the change of names —Harris' name being altered to Witley. In *Lies and Libels of Frank Harris* Kate Stephens and the editors state in a footnote: "At the moment June 1915, when Frank was asking to read the letters such was his *volte face* that he would not suffer humiliation if he recognized Witley as himself." The meeting was arranged for June 6 or 8. Harris arranged to call at three o'clock; at twenty minutes past four he rang the bell, laughing, flushed in the face, his breath heavy with wine. He had, he said, been lunching at the Claremont with some young Jewish disciples. Kate Stephens showed him into a carefully prepared room. She had wheeled a table and a chair to an open window overlooking a garden blooming with flaming geraniums, love-lies-bleeding and verbenas, and had laid ready pencils and clean paper. After half an hour she could hear him fidgeting, moving chairs and papers. She went to him, and he settled himself back on the cushions and started talking: how he'd defended Kitty O'Shea and thereby defeated his own ambition to enter Parliament; how Lord Randolph Churchill had come by the disease from which he had died; his own marriage, and how his wife had thought he would be a second Bismarck; his illegitimate children; his adventures with "the only woman he had ever loved"; the sexual abnormalities and aberrations among Londoners; his solitariness and his soul sickness—and he begged that "I would help him live through the summer by writing to him." Daylight had nearly faded when, toward nine o'clock, he left saying he might be too late for dinner with his friends at the St. Regis.

"I've just finished Kellogg's book," he wrote on June 11. "Some of the letters or rather here and there expressions in them recalled him to me vividly but none with that reality of represention which his letters to you evoked." He believed Kellogg to be a dull dog, unfit for the task. "This reading has had a sort of Sabbath influence on me half saddening, half consoling—like the quiet loneliness of a summer. Let us keep in touch with each other—will you? The years vanish when I talk or write to you and I see a slim girl again with the heavy-lidded eyes."

Kate Stephens was clearly delighted with Harris—he brought out her unemployed maternal instinct. There is no doubt she had him in mind to edit Smith's letters. "Dear child," she wrote on June 12, "I

agree with you as to 'the reality of representment' of the manuscript letters. I know them 'by heart.' . . . But apart from what they
told me—what they stamped on my solitary life—I am able to see that
their love is of a very exquisite quality and their lyricism v. beautiful. . . .
These qualities you and I see are one of the great reasons why I
say the letters must be preserved to the world." She was the last to do
such work—emotion might sweep away expressions—but she could bear
a hand in it.

> *You* are the one through sacredness of his memory to you, your gift
> in writing, your Celtic je-ne-sais-quoisity. If such a work should
> finally appeal to your taste and feeling, I will see it set before the
> world in right dress. . . . You should have the "royalties," I only
> the permanent possession of copyright. You say, "let us keep in
> touch with each other." . . . If we ever lose touch it will be by
> your seeking. You are too delightful and delicious a child to suffer
> so far away. Every erring child should have a bit of mother's-apron-
> string tied to him. When you think you need the apron-string
> come. From what you have told me it is clear that you really need
> it all the time and do not think you do—the motherlessness of
> your early years is apparent.

Harris was not overpleased with this little-boy image. He replied
on the same day. "Your charming letter brought back the past to me
vividly." He had tried to paint Smith in "Gulmore, the Boss," but the
portrait had failed because he had tried to paint him without fault. "If
I told the sexual weakness I should make him live but hurt you and
that I won't do. . . . I can't imagine what childishness you detect in me,
unless it is just the mother-instinct speaking in you." Kate Stephens
was shocked by his words "sexual weakness." "How could he?" She
recognized the rumor that Smith had fallen in love with the daughter
of the Greek family with whom he was staying and ever after suffered from wet dreams. A misconception, she wailed. She must put him
right. "Dear Child" turned severely back to "Mr. Harris."

On June 20 he went off to stay with the de Rendons in the Catskill
Mountains. At first all seemed good. "Dear Constancy," he wrote off
to Kate Stephens, "the silence is balm to the soul." Mrs. de Rendon
was a splendid housekeeper; the food was good, the house was comfortable and it was *free*. Onteora Park was in a mountain valley like a
saucer, two thousand feet above the sea, surrounded "with wooded

breasts of hills," orchards, wild strawberries and silence. The park covered three thousand acres and included an inn and a pub. It had been settled by a small company of artists and men of letters who had pledged themselves never to sell their houses to Jews or outsiders. The view was marvelous, he told Kate Stephens on June 30, taking time off from his final corrections on *Oscar Wilde*; one looked from the top of a precipice down the valley of the Hudson. "I must write something but alas I'm unhappy and lonely and adrift."

"I think you should have married some large-waisted, deep-breasted woman in the fold of whose ample arms you, a child, might find cushioned ease and refuge from over-worked nerves," Kate Stephens replied, "a woman who would love to think what kind of puddings you should eat, who, in the absence of a valet, would see that your stockings and necktie . . . [were] laid out for you on Sundays and Thursdays." "It was in this letter, I believe," she continues in *Lies and Libels of Frank Harris*, "that I suggested Frank bring over from England the daughter of his, who, he told me, was then twenty-seven years old. Doubtless, I argued, she would prove a practical comforter in making a home for him." "Dear Diotima," answered Frank on July 5, from the depths of a depression. Her sympathetic, sweet letter had wrung him so that he poured out a synopsis of his life, the first draft of which was mere vanity: "All the falls and stumblings left out—the successes mine, the failures and punishments inflicted on me by vile men. . . . The truth is, I suppose, that my vanity is as abnormally developed as my ambition. . . . And now that circumstances and outside events thwart my ambition and make the pleasant ways of vanity difficult for me or impassable, I rail against Fate and shake angry fists at the sky for all the world like a spiteful child. The only redeeming trait in me is that from time to time I see myself as I am and smile at the extravagance of self-love. . . . Give me as much of your dear self as you can, comrade; for the grasshopper's a burden and the days few and hard."

Harris' life in the Catskills was dreary. He had no time or opportunity for anesthetics. He spent his days between writing, worrying about Nellie, quarreling with the de Rendons and exercising his paranoia. His Oscar Wilde book was under threat of libel; Grant Richards "was as selfish as sin and up to every move in the game but indifferent honest." Rider was an enemy and would pocket any money he could. Every morning Harris was awakened at seven with a cup of tea;

he would have preferred to be up earlier, he says, but he could not get his tea before then. Outside the purple mountains cut across the white-blue sky; he lay in his pyjamas and his "little serge coat," reading and writing as the fit took him. Mostly it took him to write long, melancholic letters to Nellie filled with nostalgia and dreams: "It is plain we really love each other: let us stop tearing each other to pieces. . . . Come dear I kiss your *mouth*. I love you: don't be mean. At this moment I want you and you only and my sex throbs to touch you—and you can make me thrill with pleasure from head to foot if you really give yourself. . . . Now dear, dear Nellie, get me two pairs of *thin short gauze drawers. . . .*"

Nellie's moods changed like April weather. Early that summer she wrote "sweet dear letters." "You say you love me and are sick because I feel miserable and you want to get back to stop me feeling lonely . . . you don't or won't see that those girls' letters are nothing but stimulus to me when *you* treat me badly. Alone I find it hard to live, impossible to do anything. . . . You say stop your writing and I'll alter; I stop; but you don't alter. Then I begin again: after all it's better than flirting here with some new person; but it all means *nothing* if you really love me and are eager to show it—nothing." Would Nellie send him some Dubois powder, he wondered, and *pilules sédatives* from Paris? On July 8 he sent off the first unbound copy of *Contemporary Portraits*.[4] "It is great I'm sure: what do you think of it? Which of them do you like best? Or are you too little interested to read 'em?"

Nellie was more interested in extracting what material benefit she could from the wreck. "You write that you hate to lose your jewellery," Frank replied. "I can save that too but not with your callous indifference. I did think of you when you went: wired you money *a fortnight before you said you'd need it* and you tell me you got ill through being

---

[4] Rebecca West was to review *Contemporary Portraits* in the *Daily News*. First she described how she had heard Harris deliver a lecture in a Soho cellar, also frequented by Spanish dancers, who, when addressed in Spanish, would ask, "Wot's that, dearie?" The night that he appeared, the author of "Montes the Matador" was in a state of unaccountable and violent annoyance. He leaped upon the stage and delivered an address on style that proved to be one of the tragedies of literature. He called on everyone to hate all English critics, and then, for no reason, dropped into a highly articulate account of how Balzac would have treated a certain incident of extravagant indecorum in *Madame Bovary*. The address had the quality of a bad dream, said Rebecca West, since no such incident had occurred in *Madame Bovary*. *Contemporary Portraits* she found horrible, and was visited with a vision of Harris, elderly and cheerful, sitting on the edge of a chair in a respectable drawing room chirping, "I didn't oughter talk like this did I?" But she admitted some parts did have truth.

hungry. If you knew how that hurt me: you'd neither have done it nor written it." By August 6 she had received about £166. Harris' target was to send £500 to redeem the silver and jewelry from pawn, leaving £200 over for Nellie's dresses and passage. The reproaches went on. Nellie never told him what she was spending, never sent him the books or clothes he asked for, or encouragement with his work.

> Ruined love may be rebuilt, I believe; but it takes two to rebuild it: alone I can do nothing except regret the past and cry over lost happiness. And soon it will be too late to rebuild anything—life is jealous of useless regrets, vain attempts to make the dead past live again. You have dwelt on your injuries, brooded over them till you are bitter and hard and I've begun to do much the same. . . . I love you very dearly: I think you are a noble woman full of generosity and affection; but your pride is insane and it is turned against me and I can never take you to my heart again if you are *unwilling as you were in New York.* Your cold indifference has broken me and crushed me.

Nellie's next move was to cable for more money against an "unexpected illness." That sent Harris into a frenzy. He'd sent double the amount of money she'd said she could live on, and then all she could do was to cable for more. Well, he simply did not have it—and he'd asked her not to cable, because of the expense. Now he would have to walk two miles and borrow money from total strangers; the news would be all over the place and would do him infinite damage. It was simply heartbreaking, and she had not even done the one or two little things he'd asked her: she had not sent the Eton ties—not one had arrived, neither had the fifty copies of *Women in Love.* "You simply must be more careful or rather you *must* let me *know how you are spending the money and how much you will want.* . . . I strained everything . . . you hinder me working by this foolish silence and these surprises. Now you'll say another letter of reproaches: I can't help it. Try to behave reasonably and I won't reproach you, *but what am I to do?*" It was too bad, there he was living from week to week on lectures without complaining, working like a dog—with a dog's reception whenever he went in to meals—and Nellie was too careless, too inconsiderate to write him the truth—and worse, she sent him a letter calling on him to recant the beliefs he'd expressed throughout his life.

Relations with his hosts were not good either. Nellie was right, he told her eighteen days after he had arrived, "the de Rendon" woman was a cat, talkative, badly educated, conceited, and ill-tempered to boot. "She has told a story of his [de Rendon's] dreadful disease, told me how the other morning in a rage he bent her thumb back till it was nearly out of joint . . . why does a woman give her husband and *her-self* away like that!" Not only did she gossip but she could do everything, Harris grumbled. She could write novels, she could sing—and did so while he worked—she defiled the King's English, she hummed out of time and out of tune, she bragged about her voice and her training till everyone was sick: "on earth there never was anyone so conceited on so little!!!" Harris could not live with her for an hour, he said. "The other night she had the impudence to say that she had never seen a man who didn't want her! The d—d liar. I wouldn't want her if she were the last woman on earth!" But there it was, he was saving a great deal of money, and if Nellie could write a flattering letter, that would help.

All August he corrected his *Oscar Wilde*. "Don't forget to reply to my long letter asking you to get some honest bookseller to help sell my *Oscar Wilde* book in England: you can sell it @ 25/- a copy and there *are* 300 or 400 orders. Every penny is clear gain and will get your jewellery and my watch and chain from *Suttons* (Victoria Street). . . . We must get it all out here and make a real *splurge* in New York this winter—there's no other way of winning big with these cute snobs or fly rings as they should be called."

On August 23 he had his final scene with Mrs. de Rendon. It had rained all day, and Harris was in the sitting room. Mrs. de Rendon said, "I wish you wouldn't sigh so, it gets on my nerves." "I'm sorry, I didn't know I had sighed." "Yes, you did and it makes me so nervous I can't work." "I'm sorry but you've been humming the whole afternoon so that I couldn't work." "In my own house," the lady replied, "I shall do as I please," and got up and went into her bedroom. So Harris went off to the village and hired a room in the Beech Tree Inn. The worst of it was, as he told Austin Harrison, he was still quite uncertain whether Nellie was going to come back to him or not. "Besides if she comes she will want to sing, sing, sing and that'll disturb me," he added.

Packing to go to New York, naked in the heat, he was beset with melancholia. He ought to have written a play (*The Ten Command-ments*), but he needed joy and hope to make him write. Now he understood Oscar when he used to say, "I can't Frank, I can't," he told Nellie. "You've not sent me one good sweet loving letter, not one . . . my heart's bleeding—I lay awake last night and it seemed to me I could hear the slow heavy drops—the gush is over—the drops even becoming slow. . . . Did anyone ever go to New York before with such leaden hopeless feet? How sick I am of the whole Civilization—the American materialism, rush, gabble and insincere vanities. . . . Goodbye Nell. I hope you'll be happy!"

That September it seemed that at last Harris was ready to rid himself of his obsession. If Nellie were going to fight with him as she had done the previous winter, then it would be better for both of them if she did not come out.

> Please think the matter over ripely. You have changed to me from a loving, sweet-tempered, unselfish woman, into a hard careless defiant selfish woman like . . . Mrs. de Rendon. I'm not as strong as I used to be: mere work has broken me down twice this summer and my position here and power of earning money is more than precarious. It is only the resolve to do my work and give all my message and a little . . . the hope of a happy evening of my toilsome life with you in Nice and Paris that enables me to live at all and struggle. I am fighting for life and *you* fight with me. . . . I try to help you and make arrangements so that you can get money in London and help us both and you pay no attention—but insult me instead in my misery. Well, the debt I owed you is paid; you have given me bitter hours of misery and loneliness. I am still willing to do my best to rebuild our ruined love so that it may shelter us for the rest of our days; but I can't do it alone and I shall not try to, unless I have your *solemn promise* that you are going to do your best . . . but Nellie do not deceive me or yourself: if your love for me is dead, let us bury it decently I will still help you: but don't come out, if your opinions on the war *mean* much to you, or if you want to come in the same temper as last winter. I couldn't stand it. . . .

By October 1 Nellie had finally dismissed easy street; she sent "the first sweet word: you're coming out at once." Not that the sweet word was without its sting, as, to Harris' incomprehension, she was now claiming that he did not understand her: "I wish I could see it." She was in her usual practical and financial muddle. She kept sending cables saying that the pictures and linen were on their way from Paris and she must have some money, when at the same time the American

Express was saying that they were still all packed up in the flat. "I can't make out what you mean," Harris wrote furiously. "I've not got £230." Next she desired to get her diamond ring out of pawn and to bring her singing instructress—a countess, no less—with her. Frank replied, no; they had no house, he had no money, and it would be an added responsibility. The first sweet word was followed by a second: "It was sweet dear of you saying you would love me and make up. I will do all I know: I've had my lesson. . . . I'm only a child who'd rather give up living than try to live without your love."

On November 7 Nellie arrived—accompanied by the Countess Mozzatto. Harris was instantly visited with visions of "scenarios" for the movies and getting Nellie to act in them. "She'd love it too. Why not see her about it?" he asked a new contact, Jay Kaufman.

CHAPTER 18

Parlous Times

THAT autumn of 1915 the two sides of Harris emerge clearly: Harris the melancholic, the hopeless, and Harris the optimist, the paranoiac Christ-genius, rude and aggressive, noisily delivering his message in the teeth of the American people. His was now by no means a case of unfounded paranoia. Mencken reveals that a special meeting of the Academy of Arts and Letters was called. They sang "God Save the King," kissed the Union Jack and put Harris in Coventry. Literary reviews never mentioned him; in polite circles he was spoken of only in whispers relating to the salary he was supposed to be receiving from the Kaiser; and the boycott continued all his time in America. "The *New York Times* refused to mention my books or me," he told Upton Sinclair in February 1917. "Till I got *Pearson's* I was in danger of starving simply because of my socialist propaganda and radical views generally." Poor blind ones, it was they who did not know. "You once said of something of mine that it was very clever and interesting and all the rest of it but I was 'not a Titan,' " he told Michael Monahan. "You are quite right. I am not a Titan, but one of the immortals. Nothing Titanic about me, but Olympian."

"Have you seen the contemptuous brainless notice of *Contemporary Portraits* in the *New York Sun*?" he asked Kate Stephens. "A poor foolishly blind guide who doesn't see that the whole book is the first defence of the artist and seer and prophet which has appeared in literature. . . . The incurable malignity of the mediocratic. . . ." Then "V.O." of the *Post* called him stupid and wrote that he was glad that Harris was not heard. "They don't need to stone the prophets here," he wrote to Kaufman. "They simply leave them alone, or greet 'em with cheap insult."

February came, and at last the Oscar Wilde book was ready. The mess, the untidy proofs, the incompetence and misunderstandings with Dan Rider were over, the book was assembled, correct, in order for the public.[1] It was submitted for inspection to John Sumner,[2] who proclaimed it a disreputable book that could not be published in America. "I am returning herewith the proofs of your proposed publication. . . . I read the matter carefully up to the point where the litigation between Mr. Wilde and the Marquess of Queensberry terminated so abruptly and regret to have to express the opinion that the publication and sale of this work would be a violation of our state laws. . . . I believe that the book in its present form would make an appeal almost entirely on its salacious qualities."

At times like these Harris the prophet disintegrated and Harris the lonely, rootless, broken exile emerged. "Were I given to self-pity," he wrote to one of his admirers, Hesketh Pearson, "I could arrange a moving tale: friends and money lost, health shaken, universal contempt." At times like these his disciples felt most protective toward him.

---

[1] On August 20, 1930, Dan Rider wrote a letter to Mitchell Kennerley explaining his side of the negotiations. His view of the whole thing was that Harris was mad, that no man was ever more justly made bankrupt or committed to prison than he. He was muddled, impatient and paranoid, Rider said. The *Oscar Wilde* had been set up in England; it had been with the greatest difficulty that Rider had found a printer to undertake the job, but at last had got someone in Plymouth. Harris insisted on page proofs, which, said Rider, he immediately started to carve up unmercifully. This annoyed the printer, and there was considerable delay in getting altered proofs from him. Harris, in Paris, was meanwhile growing madder than ever, consigning books to the printer, Rider and the devil. Then the war broke out. At the same moment the Dutch handmade paper arrived from Holland and was lost on the docks. It took Rider months to find it and get it to the printer, who, as soon as he received it, told Rider that he was not allowed by his solicitor to print the book as it stood, on account of certain libelous statements. Before this there had been a long correspondence with Harris suggesting that certain modifications be made. Harris, however, had insisted that every word should stand. Finally the printer refused point-blank to go on—and tried to retain the paper. Forty other printers refused to have anything to do with it. Rider was heartily sick of the whole business and sent the paper and the only copy of corrected page proofs to Mitchell Kennerley.

[2] John Sumner was executive secretary of the Society for the Suppression of Vice, which changed its name in 1947 to the Society to Maintain Public Decency. He died, aged ninety-four, on June 22, 1971, "happily unaware," according to his obituary in *The New York Times*, of "the explicit sexual material in books, plays and films" that surrounded him.

There is no doubt that Pearson's flattering and sometimes adulatory letters helped Frank through America, just as there is no doubt that Hesketh was for several years besotted by him.

"Who is Hesketh Pearson?" Shaw asked Robert Ross that autumn. "He worships Frank." In another letter, to Frank himself, Shaw wrote that he had received a letter from "the enthusiastic Hesketh Pearson, whose general attitude to all men of letters in London who did not instantly throw down their morning's work and devote themselves heart and soul to the modern Christ (alias Frank Harris) is that they are cads, scoundrels and ingrates."

"You seem to be gifted with something very like divine insight," Pearson wrote on October 9 to Harris. "Pray God you will some day be acknowledged for what you are. No one so human, no one as soulful, no intellect so noble and rare and beautiful, has been given to this country. Your whole personality, embracing as it does an unmatched loving-kindness and complete understanding is beyond compare and to consummate everything you have been given the crown of thorns." Harris purred at words such as these. "Don't be afraid of excessive hero-worship," he wrote.

Like Kingsmill, Hesketh had come to Harris through *The Man Shakespeare* and had written to congratulate him; like Kingsmill, he became embarrassed by his infatuation and sought to adjust it. He has written two essays on Harris. The first, while he was still under his spell, was "Frank Harris," in *Modern Men and Mummers*. "A work by most writers is like a manure heap, with a solitary rose-bush in the centre," he said. "A work by Frank Harris is tropical. You don't know how it all grows; you just realize the amazing fact that it has grown and that it is all very much alive and pricking." The second, published in 1965, is "Rebel Artist," contained in the volume *Extraordinary People*, and sets out to correct his first essay. Hesketh was influenced by Kingsmill, with whom he enjoyed a friendship that lasted until Kingsmill's death in 1949—a friendship fortified greatly by Harris, whom they made the butt of their laughter, complaints and criticism. His ironical attitude is very similar to Kingsmill's, although gentler. But again it is the sexy, noisy, public Harris who emerges— generous certainly, but the performing Harris—Harris the genius seen from without.

The first time that Pearson saw a performance was in 1913 at the Petit Cabaret Club in Heddon Street, where Harris was to lecture.

Hesketh, upon his arrival, was shy and without money. He hovered on the stairs, then spotted what he presumed to be the chucker-out, a short surly fellow in evening dress who was twisting his moustaches before a looking glass, patting his hair, wiping his mouth with a red silk handkerchief and making faces at himself. Finally this man fixed a grin on his face and marched onto the stage to give an embarrassing, supposedly humorous speech about the absence of stage furniture. It was so embarrassing that Hesketh left the Petit Cabaret without meeting his idol, and wrote to say that his dislike of parties had prevented him from making his acquaintance. Soon after this he called at 67 Lexham Gardens. Here he was delighted by the way that Harris talked to him man to man, with no sense of one generation to another. At one point in the conversation Harris excused himself, left the room, and returned bearing Nellie upon his arm and handed her into a chair— a performance that did not strike Hesketh as funny until later. From this moment his conversation was no longer peppered with oaths, but was delivered with constrained propriety. Hesketh noticed particularly the facility with which tears sprang to Harris' eyes; at the mention of Oscar Wilde he wept copiously.

At the next visit Hesketh was introduced to the sculptor Gaudier-Brzeska, who had the furtive air of a suspicious man, said Hesketh. All that evening anyone whom they encountered was invited by Harris to contribute to a sum that he was raising for Gaudier-Brzeska. Another collection was also occupying his mind: he was preparing a pen portrait of Whistler, and he asked everyone for memories or stories. From Lexham Gardens they ventured to Jo Davidson's studio, where a bust of Harris was being completed. There was quite a gathering, including Joseph Simpson and a man who worked on the *Times*. While he posed, Harris told the story that Kenneth Hare had heard, only now it was he, Harris, who was engaged as a commercial traveler for a firm distributing Bibles, it was he who called at a remote farmhouse and seduced the farmer's wife, only to be surprised by the farmer, toward whom, while struggling into his trousers, he extended a Bible and proclaimed, "God is between us." What with the details and ironical comments from the company, the story lasted for two hours, and was continued in various pubs and along various streets as the evening progressed. Everyone, as the story and the evening grew longer, became more and more drunk —except Harris. As they staggered into the last pub it was the general opinion that the publican might refuse to serve drinks unless he knew

the names of his distinguished clientele. Accordingly he was introduced to Shakespeare (Harris), Michelangelo (Davidson), Rembrandt
(Simpson), Napoleon (the man from the *Times* who had been fighting a walking-stick duel with Hesketh) and Shells (a mixture of Shaw
and Wells, representing Hesketh). Soon a brawl developed. An iron
pole shattered the back of Hesketh's chair, a spittoon flew through the
air, narrowly missing his head, falling instead onto the foot of a man
seated in the next alcove. It was not long before the police arrived—
"No doubt with the object of questioning Shakespeare, Rembrandt,
Michelangelo and other celebrities"—but the party broke up and
vanished into the night.

All through 1915 and 1916 Hesketh's letters were fine medicine
to Harris, who played his part of sweet, sorrowful genius so hard that
one wonders sometimes if his crucifixion had affected his wits. "I'm
trying to build up another home all to begin over again," he explained
on the arrival of Nellie and the countess, "but a brave heart finds the
toil a new and enchanting adventure. . . . I've learned life's chief lessons very thoroughly and it doesn't frighten me. But that the British
should yell hate and fury at me because I sell myself makes me smile,
even were the accusation true, for they are accustomed to expect it in
their favourites. Why did Winston Churchill cross the floor of the House,
take office under the Liberals and attack the Unionists? Why did
Thingumybob shuffle off his belief in Free Trade and take up the cud-
gels for Protection? Simply for a peerage. And these men had comparatively no temptation. They had not been ruined by illegality, broken
in health by an unjust imprisonment, exiled in poverty and age."

The new adventure turned out to be anything but enchanting. In
November he was appointed advertising manager for the Chesapeake
and Ohio Railroad. The prospect of his salary inspired him with new
vigor. "Do up 3 Washington Square so as to astonish them," he told
Nellie. With the money he speculated that she would be able to get
her things out of pawn, pay the rent for the Paris flat and wait without
hurry or anxiety before making her grand debut as an opera singer. To
sustain them meanwhile he would give lectures in the drawing room,
and he had some plans for free eating. "I'm trying to work out an advertisement scheme which will give us all our meals at a swell hotel
for nothing. I think I've got it! I want to give a series of dinners to
New York editors and music critics here, and have 'em afterwards to
hear you sing and then get a puff of the Hotel in their papers. I'm

sure I can do it. I shall call the dinners 'Octaves' and have wonderful cards designed for it. . . . We shall win in New York this winter, if brains will do it."

Although Nellie had arrived with every resolution to make their life work, peace did not reign for long. "You have told me you love me and wish to make our life together to the end," Harris wrote to her in the middle of November from the Greenbrier Hotel, White Sulphur Springs. "Well, I believe you because I love you and never wanted anyone else. To set your mind and heart completely at rest, I'll stop writing or receiving letters from anyone you object to and *I'll give you proof of this* when I return to New York. You yourself shall *put an end to the whole affair.* I don't really care a cent about anyone but you and I'd rather have my Nellie back as she was before that snake Lunn came into our lives than all the women in the world." And when she came to see him she was to bring a gallon of Chablis with her, his instruments, dress clothes and pencils.

Harris' time was spent between West Virginia, Chicago and Washington Square worrying about his finances and the dull, uninspiring booklets and folders he had contracted to write. It was an arrangement that suited no one. "I've never worked so hard," he assured Nellie, "I'm at it fourteen hours out of twenty-four." In Chicago he worked hard in another way—by making possibly useful contacts both for him and Nellie. There was George Arliss, and Harrison Parker, president of Hearst's *Chicago American,* who was, according to Harris, all enthusiasm over his talk. Ideas flew like dust in the sun. Would he live in Chicago for a big sum and three years? He would—but the idea came to nothing. For Nellie there was Miss Meredith, "who is an actress with Mr. Bat Andrews, one of the *most powerful* journalists in the country. He would give you puffs as a singer and beauty in *Vogue* and *Vanity Fair* which would set all America agog to see you and hear you and besides he could give me a series of articles to do." To accomplish this coup Nellie should invite Miss Meredith to tea and compliment her on her talent and beauty. "Then we may get her friend Andrews who really is both rich and important. Mr. Clark is coming at three with the best non-puncturable pneumatic tyres I have ever seen—perfect." At Washington Square he dreamed, quarreled with Nellie, gazed out at the arch in the middle of the square, festooned with snow and gleaming with icicles, and wrote long, complaining letters to Hesketh Pearson about New York, which was as hard and shallow and greedy as an old whore—"the most terrible city in the world for the weakling or artist or scientist, or indeed, any man of genius or distinction. This people loves education and endows it with an incomparable munificence, but it cares nothing for the flower and fruit and object of education— men and women of talent. Americans are appallingly purblind and self-satisfied."

By the end of March 1916 all the fine plans and contacts had come to nothing and relations with the officers at the Chesapeake and Ohio Railroad were poor; they were, said Harris, writing insulting letters, wanting to be rid of his services by April 1. Relations were also poor with Nellie. Her music was a great source of trouble, and Harris resented it, although he did his best to be reasonable. Later A. I. Tobin told Elmer Gertz that he was always rushing in and interrupting Nellie at her lessons. She had been all too ready to astonish everyone with Washington Square. Not only were the decorations astonishing but so were the bills. On all sides firms were demanding their money. It had been hoped that John Quinn would buy several of the paintings and sculptures that had been brought over from Paris. In this Mitchell Kennerley had acted as go-between. "Now is your chance to get a Gaudier-Brzeska," he had told Quinn in 1914. "I think that when Harris returns to New York I shall be able to arrange with him to bring over everything in his apartment, including a dozen Conder fans, a Rodin bust etc." "Phone Kennerley every day about Quinn," Frank urged Nellie. "We really must have some money." Nellie replied with curt little notes, and then, the last straw, refused to kiss him goodbye, sulking at their uncomfortable living conditions. "Now, my dear, dear girl let us try to get on with more sympathy: we both hate the conditions: they are dreadful for me and unpleasant for you, but if you'll try, I will. . . . Then I knew I'd have a dreadful time with the bank and had looked forward to your kiss on parting as a sort of reward for getting the credit as I had no time to run about and hunt for money as I had promised. . . . When I got to the bank the cashier said before everyone 'this is the man who overdraws twice in a month.' I had to turn the rudeness to fun so I said 'well, any sort of drawers are better than none at all' which made them all laugh."

Matters were not helped by the threatened arrival of one of Harris' illegitimate daughters. The incident shows his nervousness at Nellie's tantrums. Paddy Burgess was over thirty, very plain and in a bad way financially, unable to get any secretarial work. Presumably this is the daughter who is mentioned by Kate Stephens, and presumably the previous year, while he was despairing of Nellie, he had written and suggested that she might come to America. Harris had arranged that Slocum, the manager at the Greenbrier Hotel, should employ her as his English secretary, but she had delayed so long that the post was filled. Now he wondered if she could work for him and had sent her money for her passage. "Our whole life seems to be Pain," he wrote to Nellie. "I don't know how to help it: I seem to be always giving you pain: I can't discuss it. . . . I don't know why it should hurt you: but I'm afraid it may: I'd help anyone belonging to you; but I'm afraid you'll dislike this and make it hard for me—still there it is—I couldn't leave her to starve—Can't you like her? . . . I'm miserable having to tell you. I wrote it last night. I'd rather write it than tell you. I thought of calling her my niece if I had to explain her. But, I can't be unkind to her. It's not her fault and I would not wish you to be unkind. . . . Now be kind to me, if you can. If I didn't love you, it would all be easy, but I can't bear to give you pain. . . ."

The letter was obviously not a success. Attached to it was Nellie's comment: "This refers to a woman called Paddy Burgess. I have a photo of her. Any way she did not come to America. She came to Nice one day."

Sometime while Harris was living in Washington Square, Henry Miller met him and was greatly impressed; Miller was about fifteen and interested in reading and lectures. At this time his father was a Fifth Avenue tailor, and among his clientele was Guido Bruno,[3] an eccentric literary fellow, Henry Miller's father thought, from Greenwich Village. One day Bruno brought along Frank Harris, rough and tough as a favorite prizefighter, whom he introduced as a famous

---

[3] Guido Bruno was arrested in the streets in 1917 for selling a book containing a story "Edna, A Girl of the Streets"—the only thing that Harris could see was that Edna spoke once of a "big soft beddie"—and came up for trial under Magistrate Murphy, who was contemptuous, vindictive and insulting. Harris was there as a defending witness. In the court John Sumner asked him one question: "Have you an ordinary mind?" "Thank God, no," Harris replied.

While Guido Bruno saw Harris as the New Messiah, and wrote *The Wisdom of Frank Harris*, published in 1919, he also saw him as a means for getting money. Every time he visited him Harris believed something went missing. Certainly he took Harris' 1917 diary. "What is there lacking in me that I find it so hard to keep a diary?" Harris had asked himself between the pages. "A dozen times I've tried in vain, but this time I hope to succeed." Bruno had shown the whole diary intact to Tobin and had hoped to sell it to him, but for such a sum as was quite beyond Tobin's means. So Bruno sold it bit by bit in batches and torn-out pages.

author who desired to go to a yachting party. Henry Miller's father had no respect for artists at all—he was used to having only respectable people in his shop and viewed Bruno and Harris with grave doubts. He thought they were jokes and accordingly brought out a wide-blue-striped flannel. What should they have for trousers? Harris wondered, believing that Miller was talking about a blazer. The same, Miller assured him. "I'm not appearing in a minstrel show," Harris boomed ironically. And then in the next second he was defending Oscar Wilde. For fittings he had to go to the dressing room at the back of the shop. Nearby, Henry Miller and the staff sat on benches and altered clothes. There were three or four men, Jewish, as well as Henry, all supposed to be learning about cutting clothes; but what they really talked about was Russian and Yiddish literature. One had a voice like Caruso, and he would sing when Henry Miller's father went out to get drunk. While he was having his trousers fitted Harris would talk of Shakespeare, Jesus, Oscar Wilde. Who is that man? the men wanted to know. In that dressing room he seemed like God. He had a magic, magnetic personality that flew out into the cutting room. He was always at ease, always interested in what everyone was doing. When the suit was ready, Henry Miller had to deliver it to Washington Square. He rang the bell. "Let him in," cried a voice from the bedroom, and Harris jumped out of bed—in which he had been with a woman—quite naked and unembarrassed. Miller read his work and was deeply impressed by *The Bomb, The Man Shakespeare* and *Oscar Wilde*.

The publication of *Oscar Wilde* had caused Harris nothing but bother. Because of the "prudery of New England Philistinism" he had had eventually to publish it himself. He sent out various copies, hoping for reviews and huge orders, and a prospectus, part of which read: "The Crucifixion of the Guilty is still more awe-inspiring than the crucifixion of the innocent. What do we know of innocence?" "I wanted to make this life of Wilde the best biography extant," he told Mencken on June 9, 1916. "Have I done it? Who shall say! . . . When are you going to review it?" "By the way," he wrote again on August 5, "I have to thank you for your review of the Wilde book, which I should have enjoyed more if it had not been for certain imaginary statements in it that seemed to me derogatory." In England the faithful Hesketh was recruited as agent. Besides getting for Harris a dozen colored or striped shirts ("a pair of buckskin braces, too, would be a Godsend") he sent round copies of *Oscar Wilde*. Some were returned with terse comments. Conrad wrote in the third person saying that he was out of sympathy with the writer over both his subject and more serious matters; Kipling said that he disliked both the writer and the subject; Bennett that Harris had put himself out of court and he refused to discuss his work; Wells said that he was a liar; and Galsworthy that he would rather not give his opinion. Shaw, however, wrote a long letter to Harris giving his views on Wilde and an account of all the meetings he had had with him. This later was added to the book as an introduction. To Robert Ross, Shaw wrote that Frank's samples of Oscar's conversations were like translations from Tacitus and Thucydides, with no trace of the impressive levity that was Wilde's great quality, but, all in all, the book said what needed saying better than any other.[4]

Harris dictated his letters to a series of illiterate secretaries who typed so wildly, so erratically, that the end results have strange messages from Harris scribbled all over them. "Oh these typists," he scratched on one. "By the bye," he dictated in a letter to John Quinn on July 1, "I wonder would you consider writing for me little personal sketches of the Irish revolutionaries. I am about to have an organ and I would very much like to give ten portraits of these victims of what Kipling calls Pestis Teutonicus"—or it should have been "Pestis Teutonicus," but the secretary had typed "Prestis Teutonius." A wonderful scene arises: Harris in bed, dressed in his long socks, his pyjamas and tie, important: "I want to write something strong on the matter," he rumbles, rolling his r-r-r's, "and your complete knowledge and impartial presentation of the personalities would be of infinite value to me"; the typist, pink and nervous, crosses her fingers, and the letter results in invariable disorder.

Harris had decided to turn his series of articles "On the Trail"

---

[4] Lord Harberton too liked *Oscar Wilde*. "I should say it was the best thing you've done," he wrote on August 6 (year not given), "and it makes me absolutely love him." He had always said that Harris was one of the best journalists ever born, and the two trials could not have been better done. "You are a very peculiar person: some great merits, but many failings (or worse) and some conventional poses and assumptions that are unpardonable." Anyway, Harris had made Harberton love Wilde, but often he had made him dislike Harris himself. And then he had overdone Jesus. Had he ever read:

This Jesus is a sloppy word
Mainly a sponge to wipe the tiresome eyes of stupid people?[5]

[5] Ernest Arthur George Pomeroy Harberton (1867–1944) was author of *How to Lengthen Our Ears*, 1917.

into a novel and had submitted some to George Brett of Macmillan. "I have written two gorgeous chapters of the new book *On the Trail*," he told him, "really humorous." Brett, however, did not think them gorgeous at all. "The character of your hero is insufficiently developed . . . ," he told him, "he is not so indelibly impressed upon the readers as to make the reader in sympathy with him and his aims."

In July Harris got his organ. "I've got a magazine at last," he told Hesketh Pearson on July 1, 1916. "I'm going to fight for Peace and Goodwill to men and fair play to all and truth."

"Unluckily Frank has been made editor of the American *Pearson's*," Shaw told Robert Ross, "and he has sent a budget of his first number for distribution here. . . . They will infuriate everyone, as they consist of accounts of how he rescued from neglect and starvation those obscure and reviled geniuses Kipling, Wells, Conrad, myself and perhaps later on Meredith, Hardy and Swinburne."

Harris felt better once more. When Theodore Dreiser's *The Genius* was held up by the censor he was quick to rush to the fight. "I wanted to meet you over the Dreiser case which I think should be fought," he wrote to Mencken on August 15, 1916. "If you find you have any time, if you would phone me I would be glad to have you at lunch or dinner and talk over ways of discomfiting the enemy." The Authors' League should not be content with merely signing a protest, they should ask for subscriptions; they should inform Mr. Dreiser that they would defend his book and pay all expenses for his defense; afterward they should pursue Mr. Sumner and his society for malicious prosecution. The Authors' League did none of this. Harris resigned, and the enemy remained undiscomfited.

The first Harrisian issue of *Pearson's* appeared in October 1916 and contained among other features a piece called "Our Pork Barrel," contemporary portraits of generals Joffre and Haig, by the editor, and "The Love Stories of Edward VII"—the results or part of the results of his work among the manuscripts of Lady Warwick, who is referred to throughout as "the lady." Set out, like most of Harris' work, as an interview and chat show, it begins with the start of the royal romance and Prince Edward throwing a bottle of ink at the head of "the lady's" previous lover Lord Charles Beresford. There is a vignette of Lady Charles Beresford, known as Piggy, who was hairless and whose hat and wig blew off one day while driving with "the lady" in a coach-and-four, leaving her with only a bald head shining in the sun.

Wasn't the prince rather boring? wondered the interviewer. No reading? No ideas? Ah! murmured the lady, but he had manners, he was remarkably constant and admired her exceedingly. Some incidents, explained the interviewer, were of such a décolleté nature that he declined to include them; many turned up later in the interviewer's autobiography.

During the six years in which he edited *Pearson's* everything and everybody was material to be used, particularly Bernard Shaw, as he himself had remarked. Again and again Harris returned to him. "I have already told in print how I harnessed Bernard Shaw to the *Saturday Review* in London and how we worked together in perfect amity year in and year out." He published his "gorgeous" chapters of *On the Trail.* He published his *Contemporary Portraits.* Even Nellie appeared in print, writing articles about fashion and the theater under titles such as "Hot New York." A special number was devoted entirely to Abram's Electronic Treatment—one of the first of those black boxes that periodically crop up. "Poppycock" was what Bell called it in "Oscar Wilde Without Whitewash." The instrument was supposed to diagnose a disease with a single drop of blood; generally, Bell said, the trouble was diagnosed as congenital syphilis. Harris' main contribution was his fight against the legal system and puritanical climate that allowed the censor to ban books on the slightest pretext, and the post office to ransack the mails and confiscate books and magazines. "I intend to go about New York with a lantern so to speak and turn on the light in many obscure corners," he told his readers. "The underworld of poverty and suffering in this capital of Christendom is simply appalling and should be known."

The women's night court was the first institution to receive illumination. In this court women criminals were supposed to enjoy special and sympathetic treatment. In reality, proceedings were corrupt and unjust: prostitutes were subjected to rigged trials and sentences and third-degree prisoners were kept for days without sleep, bullied, beaten and questioned by police officers. "My experiences here of the Night Court . . . are incredibly horrible," he told Upton Sinclair on March 27, 1917. "Justice that should protect the weak, hounds them down, and the prostitute is persecuted in a so-called democracy by patrolmen, decoys and judges. When shall we have a minimum wage . . . ? Oh I do want to see something done before I disappear from the scene."

His activities did not pass unnoticed, either by the authorities or by the victims themselves. The May 1917 number contained details of the Betsy Meyers case. She was a young crippled Jewish girl accused of an indecent act, and condemned, in spite of two doctors testifying that the girl was constantly in such pain that intercourse would be impossible. John Sumner moved into action and seized hundreds of copies of *Pearson's*. Already the February issue had been ordered off the subway stands; and the month before, the Chief Press Censor prohibited the magazine from entering Canada because of the communications and reports it contained "concerning the operations of the present war and the movements of the forces of His Majesty and His Majesty's allies." "We have published no such communications or reports," blustered Harris.

Betsy Meyers wrote saying what joy and courage the exposé had given her, and John Sumner applied for a warrant for Harris' arrest. This inspired him to a further fit of rage: "I intend in future to draw attention to the worst cases of . . . entry on the part of the police," he spluttered before rushing off to Washington to ward off imprisonment. "I shall, too, from time to time expose the intolerable evils inherent in the infamous decoy system. . . . I intend to force him [Sumner] to confine his activities to his own like, the people he can measure."

He returned from Washington mortified, indignant, and $300 the poorer. The judges, he said, were cruel and stupid; moreover he caught a chill. Hypochondria set in. He fasted four days, had a bath, stood near a window, which brought on a fit of ague, took quinine, and called the doctor, who diagnosed "pleurisy with effusion." Weak and wheezing, he tottered off to the trial of the anarchists Emma Goldman and Berkman in July; and a "grotesque caricature of a trial" it was, he recorded in his diary. All anarchists were excluded from the court. At the close of the trial Miss Goldman wanted to consult Berkman on the appeal. "Certainly," the judge replied. "You will have ample opportunity." They were immediately separated and dispatched within the hour, Berkman to Atlanta and "the Goldman woman," as the New York *Herald* called her, to the women's prison in Jefferson. It was said, Harris concluded, that the Russian envoy of the revolutionary government would ask the authorities at Washington for a retrial on the grounds of unfair decision, extravagant sentence and the fact that the pair were Russian citizens. "This is the line I shall help."

Harris was now aggressively socialist, pacifist and highly impressed with communist ideals.[6] "I am not pacifist without qualification," he explained to Upton Sinclair; "but nine times out of ten the gentle, truthful, dignified answer does turn away wrath. . . . You think I am biassed against England. I studied that oligarchy for twenty-five years. It is a capitalistic despotism and almost the same despotism is fastening its claws on the throat of American labor." He believed that America had gone into the war because the capitalists feared for their investments. Being an idealist, he considered that the war was mere stupidity. Man had the key to the universe, he told Hesketh Pearson, he could make airships rise from the ground, submarines pass under the sea. "And instead of realizing the vision splendid, he is intent now on murdering his fellow man and stealing his territory and trade . . . he is making the fairest of lands, a butcher's shop, where human beings are being carved and killed by the thousand. The silly little brute."

He carried on long correspondences with the American socialists Theodore Dreiser, Eugene Debs and Upton Sinclair. His correspondence with Sinclair is long and often quarrelsome, touching on the war, politics, literature and Sinclair's sex life. Harris was obliged to take him to task over Europe, a subject on which Sinclair considered himself an authority. "You could not put Alsace-Lorraine under international control," he scolded him. "It is babyish to talk like that." Then Sinclair praised Jack London, at which he was treated to full details of *The Iron Heel* affair. "Jack London it seems to me might have thought but didn't; he was evidently too greedy for money and enjoyment to give himself time to do his best work. . . . The more I read of your praise of Jack London the more I wonder."

"Do for God's sake leave off throwing your weight where it is not

[6] The Russian Bolshevist movement he saw as an idealistic attempt to end, or at least mend, the dreadful competitive society organized for individual greed. "Americans care for nothing except getting rich," he ranted to Hesketh Pearson on September 5, 1919; "a pretty wife and new motor car are all they think of. I want to get away from the thin mouths and heavy jaws and brainless greed of the Common."

Harris had a high opinion of Trotsky, with whom he had spent two hours. They conversed through a translator who did not know French very well, thus Harris' views were not too clear. Later he wrote to Upton Sinclair that he had heard Trotsky was "turning out to be a military genius. He has got they say nearly a million men under arms. If the Bolshevik government under Lenine and Trotzky can sustain itself for another year, it may weather the storm and prove the greatest experiment in recorded time. Fancy what a difference it would make if there were one really social republic in the world."

wanted in favor of militarism and put it where it is wanted, in favor of a minimum wage," Harris urged him. "By the way what are your ideas about sex, marriage etc.?" But Sinclair, apart from fancying cooperative homes and community care for children, was not overkeen to divulge them. "You have told me nothing of your views on sex," Harris wrote, planning his portrait. "I cannot make bricks without straw." And again, in June: "Send me your sex stuff . . . any incident that counted in your development or any early love episodes from even fifteen. . . . I still do not know whether you were tormented from thirteen to twenty by sex as I was."

It emerged finally that Sinclair's main view was that sex was conditioned by venereal disease. This was far too unromantic for Harris, who concluded his portrait of him by saying that he wished he would fall in love desperately, as one falls in love at forty in the heat of the summer: "I want him intoxicated with the heady fragrance of love." Upton Sinclair objected strenuously to the suggestion that he needed a love affair to make him into an author. It was in his view as close to rubbish as a literary critic could write.

In 1917 the Harris household moved to 29 Waverly Place, where they were joined by Harris' niece Gwladys Price Williams. It was a "sumptuous apartment," according to Harris' lawyer, Frederick Hackenburg, furnished with works of art and "with very impressive antiques" that Hackenburg rather suspected of being clever imitations. Gwladys Price Williams told Elmer Gertz—when at last he had managed to catch her in 1931 to interview her—that the house was busy from morning to night with luncheon and dinner guests; that Nellie would run up bills even when Frank was having an awful time trying to pay them; that unpunctual as he was, he never kept Nellie waiting for a moment, he would leave important engagements to meet her and accompany her for interviews with music teachers. She observed that he was careful never to make Nellie jealous over his affairs, but he did not like it when other men admired her. She in return disliked female admirers' referring to him as "Master." He always kissed Nellie good night, never forced himself on her, said Gwladys, who slept in the same room as Nellie. Dressed in a nightdress, with her long braids hanging down over her bare shoulders, Nellie could look like Desdemona. "I remember how I loved to have you play and sing for me and how wonderfully sweet your voice was," Gwladys wrote to Nellie in 1928. "You used to sing Ave Maria as no one else has ever done for me. I wish I could hear it again: it was beautiful."

> You ask me details of my daily life [Harris wrote to Hesketh Pearson on April 30, 1918, dispatching to him a suitably edited itinerary]. I wake at about eight in the morning, get a grapefruit and a couple of cups of tea and write or dictate till twelve-thirty; then I get up and dress. I try to go out for five or ten minutes' walk or run before my lunch at one-thirty; from two-thirty to three-thirty I snoozle; at three-thirty I go to the office to see people, deal with correspondence, calls etc; six to seven-thirty I take a walk if I can; then I come in have a cup of soup, no bread; afterwards I either read or correct manuscript till one o'clock. Then I am supposed to go to bed; but if I have taken any coffee during the day, and it is a perpetual temptation to me, I probably do not sleep till three or four and pay for it by feeling tired and worn out next morning.

It was not only coffee that was a temptation. Claude McKay gives a very different description of his visit to Waverly Place in *A Long Way from Home*. To McKay, who was at the time working as a waiter on a train, Frank Harris appeared as "the embodiment of my idea of a romantic luminary of the writing world." On McKay's arrival at Waverly Place, Harris' voice roared out like a great lion's, with strength and dignity. Nellie, with equal strength and dignity, floated down in a rose-colored opera cloak and out of the door to the theater. "Of all the arts," Harris growled, "the theatre is the tinseliest of them all— mainly for women." And he went off to fetch some white Rhine wine. "Pour me a glass of any real Rhine wine," he said, "and I can tell you exactly from where it came without seeing the label." The evening passed in a series of explosions. He exploded over Herbert Spencer, so hard that it frightened McKay. "I knew him well," shouted Harris, describing him as a narrow, bigoted, self-opinionated and John Bullish unscientific Englishman, self-righteous and a smug philosopher of British philistinism. He thundered, roared, boomed and trumpeted, striding across the floor, creating action to match the color and vigor of his words. To Claude McKay it seemed that he talked like a god; like a wizard, he evoked his contemporaries, gesturing and posturing like the waxworks in Madame Tussaud's. In the middle of it all Nellie returned in her rose-colored cloak, Harris descended for more wine and Nellie went upstairs. When he recited, his voice came out like a rich refrain, a fugue pouring through the pipes of a great organ. As the wine fell in the bottle it seemed to McKay that Harris was intoxicated more from his memories and the words, like jewels, that flew from his mouth than by the wine. It was not the meaning so much as the sound; it seemed that Harris' voice was like a waterfall, roaring inside McKay's head, a disembodied element. What an evening! Harris talking for the beauty of talking, talking exquisitely, the conversation of extraordinary spontaneity and length. McKay returned to his train feeling that he could do the work of five waiters. After a while, agitated to action by that voice, he took Harris some prose. Harris' forehead grew wrinkles, he shook his head. What McKay had written, he announced, was like a boat full and sinking with water; when it was bailed out it would sail well enough. With a red pencil he underlined. On this occasion McKay met his secretary, a little blonde from a western town who had written and implored that she should come to New York and serve the Master—in any capacity. Every week it seemed he received dozens of such letters, which he was obliged to ignore. Toward 1920 McKay went off to England, and among other people met Shaw, through Harris' introduction. When he returned he found Harris less poised. *Pearson's* was losing money and was hounded by the post office. Claude McKay meanwhile had published a volume of poems in London, but one entitled "If We Must Die" had not been included, as McKay had been advised that it would be wiser to omit it. Harris roared and shouted: he was a bloody traitor to his race, Sir. Civilization and the English had emasculated people, depriving them of their guts. It would be better if McKay were a headhunting cannibal in the jungle than a civilized coward.

The finances of *Pearson's* were certainly poor. Through various begging letters and schemes Harris just managed to keep the magazine going, but again and again he was obliged to travel to Washington to fight the censor and the post office. "I have been so worried by the post office people that I cannot describe the incidents to you," he wrote to Upton Sinclair. "In England at least when they worry you they give you men of position and brains to fight but here one is persecuted by people who do not understand simple English."

Again, in August, the issue was pronounced unmailable, costing the magazine $3,000. "By the way would it not be possible for you to send me a list of say five thousand subscribers to whom I might appeal for subscriptions to *Pearson's*," he asked Upton Sinclair in December 1918. To S. N. Behrman: "I have read your story 'Hope Macomber' and like it. I could use it I think but the main difficulty is a financial one. *Pearson's* is not rich as you probably know and just at present I am having a particularly hard time of it. I wonder if you would care to let us print your story without payment." Behrman's reply is not available.

In *A Solitary Parade* Frederick Hackenburg describes the scene at the magazine offices in Union Square. Seven or eight employees were preparing circulars, signed by the magazine's business manager A. W. Ricker, for mailing to stockholders and subscribers offering for sale stock in the Dixie Oil Company of Kentucky. Here, Hackenburg discovered, was a scheme to use the magazine's mailing list for oil-stock promotion, a promotion with which, he pointed out, Harris had refused to have anything to do and which ended in disaster. Ultimately Hackenburg appointed a receiver and a settlement was effected; but in spite of there being little publicity, *Pearson's* reputation was impaired. Harris was, in Hackenburg's view, the most genial individual he had ever met. In a room full of strangers he would almost immediately be at the center of an admiring circle. One night he and Harris dined in the main dining room of the Vanderbilt Hotel. The headwaiter mentioned that some years before he had had the privilege of serving Harris and a party of distinguished gentlemen on the Riviera. Harris was delighted and bristled with wit for the rest of the evening, and the waiter was given an enormous tip. Once they went together to interview Brentano, the New York publisher. Harris said, "I have had legal troubles in Asia Minor, in Spain, in Morocco. . . . I want you to meet my present lawyer Mr. Hackenburg. He is the only barrister I have ever had in whose case I had no regrets when I paid the bill." Hackenburg was very flattered, and it was only after he had disengaged himself from the magic of Harris' company that he realized that there was a large bill overdue.

Despite the difficulties, *Pearson's* had its admirers. "In point of editorial ability, literary quality and moral leadership and force there is not another magazine in the country that begins to compare with *Pearson's*," Eugene Debs had written on January 28, 1918.

Your splendid editorials, reviews and portraits are in a class
of their own, and it is anything but a flattering commentary on

American intelligence and culture, to say nothing of its vaunted ideals of democracy and freedom, that *Pearson's* has to battle continuously for its very existence. But that very fact, disagreeable and disheartening as it may appear, is *Pearson's* chief glory and the reason for the remarkable fidelity and devotion of its patrons and supporters. . . .

You have gone far beyond the ordinary bounds of magazine literature in attacking governmental corruption and social abuses. Your attack upon and exposure of the iniquities of the night court and the preying upon innocent unfortunates by the very ones who are paid to protect them was a great piece of work in the public interest and will result in incalculable benefit in the future. . . . You are of course besieged by enemies, the enemies of truth and justice, the arch-exploiters and oppressors of the people, but you have also the most ardent of admirers, the truest of friends and the staunchest of supporters. . . . You are waging a heroic battle for the people in their greatest crisis and if they fail to sustain you it will be to the utter prostitution of magazine literature and to their own disaster and shame. But I shall believe that they will sustain you and that *Pearson's* shall triumph gloriously in the struggle for a higher and happier humanity and a freer and better world. . . .

Charlie Chaplin writes in his autobiography that every other week it had seemed that *Pearson's* was going to fold. He had read Harris' books and admired him. After one of the many appeals, he sent off a contribution, and Harris sent back two volumes of his *Oscar Wilde* and a note saying that he was one of the few who had helped him without even knowing him. When they met, he says, he found Harris' handlebar moustache a little disconcerting. He adds that Harris had a beautiful young wife with red hair "who was devoted to him," summoning the image of Nellie the gracious hostess, the affectionate, attentive wife, the part that involved being shown into the room on the arm of Harris and helped in and out of chairs. The evening lasted until four in the morning, drinking and talking—with Harris doing most of the talking. Then Chaplin decided to go off for the remainder of the night to a different hotel. This, Nellie explains (she has an account of the evening in her memoirs), was because his wife, Mildred (née Harris), was trying to serve a writ on him and he used to leave the Carlton Hotel by the kitchen entrance dressed as a woman. Later he gave them the benefit of the performance. What a treat it was, said Nellie, to see him flinging his head on one side, putting his hand on his hip and flaunting. By the time that he left, all the hotels were full, and eventually the taximan invited him for the night to his own place in the Bronx, where Charlie Chaplin shared a bed with the taximan's son and never slept a wink all night.

By December 1919 Harris had fallen out not only with polite American society but with at least one of his admirers—Kate Stephens. In 1916 he had sent to her the October and November numbers of *Pearson's*. "I find myself here torn up by the roots and bleeding from a hundred tendrils," he told her, "and the ground in which they have thrust me is not pleasant to me and I shall not take root. This American climate I find harsh and unfriendly to an extraordinary degree." Kate Stephens replied that as a sort of quasi mother of his, "who thinks a child needs a good deal of spanking and a little petting," she did hope he was physically well and happier than his letter would show. When she'd seen his activities and interests advertised, she had thought he was coming to an understanding of "our life and its magnificent idealism." The mixture of Kate Stephens' patriotism and motherliness roused Harris to fury on October 17. She accused him of not understanding *"the magnificent idealism of Americans"*—well, she was right. He saw no signs of it. He saw that 2 percent of the population owned 65 percent of the wealth. He saw twenty families living in nine rooms, with one water tap between sixty-nine; he saw child labor, girls working in department stores for five dollars a week, all liable to be discharged at a moment's notice. Magnificent idealism! He saw a government that cost two billions a year, but no municipal theaters, opera houses, art galleries or pensions for artists. Not a thinker in the country, not an original thought to have come out of it since Emerson. "Savage individual greed run mad is what I see and nothing else. A country where every friendship is difficult and love rare. *Debtors' prisons in the twentieth century!* Man a chattel. Ferocious sentences for every offence against poverty. A poor imitation of English civilization which at its best is a hundred years behind the times. Magnificent idealism! How can you write such nonsense I can not imagine. A cheap surface optimism of the well-to-do, a thin superficial culture without morals or even manners that's what I can see but idealism!" Poor ingrate, Kate Stephens said later in *Lies and Libels of Frank Harris*. Poor swollen fool. So shallow that he could not see that sneers at his refuge made him absurd. To Harris himself, on October 18, she had written, "Dear Jimmie Harris, I had a rather amazing letter from you tonight. Don't send another like it, dear boy." She feared he was not well, that he lacked lightness and brightness in his life. He must have been tired out, his judgment nodding. She spoke of a friend who had seen him with a blonde in a picture hat; she hoped that Mrs. Harris or some other member of his family had come to bear him company and cheer his solitariness. He should now be the beautiful, lovable laddie he could be and drop all hyperbole and exaggeration. Harris replied briefly that the friend who saw him one evening with a blonde in a picture hat probably saw him with his wife. "He or she certainly did not see me with any other man's wife." Then there were three years' strained silence.

Now, in November 1919, Kate Stephens feared that he would add to his list of contemporary portraits one on Smith. She wrote that from what she had learned of his activities she knew very clearly that he had no real comprehension of Professor Smith, and that what he might write would be a terrible travesty of his spirit. Would he very kindly never at any time write of Professor Smith or make any reference either to him or to her? "Dear Lady," replied Harris on December 4 from a new address, 8 East 15th Street. He was sorry that after a silence of three years she should write such a spiteful letter—a hotchpotch of material absurdities and fictions written apparently to provoke him. Well, he was far too busy and hopeless to correct her misstatements and perverse imaginings, but as regards her chief trouble, she could set her mind at rest; he wrote portraits only of persons of original genius, so she was therefore perfectly safe. In his autobiography, however, he had to mention his debt to Smith.

He had been painting his "portraits" steadily, and in 1920 published his third volume. No one, in his view, was going to be able to study anyone in the future "without bottoming himself on my work."[7] On the publication of his first volume he had told Kate Stephens: "I am primarily now an artist—having given myself to this one mistress for more than thirty years. There is nothing sacred to me now for I am a reporter in the great sense, one of God's spies as Shakespeare called himself."

> What a gorgeous undertaking it is to try and report the soul
> of a man [he wrote in his introduction to the third series]. Great

---

[7] To judge from the difficulty I had in 1973–74 in getting the first and third series (particularly the third) from the London Library, apparently numerous people are doing exactly that—bottoming themselves.

men are to us the ladder Jacob dreamed of reaching from earth to Heaven; they show us the way to climb, the heights to be reached are so to speak the altar-stones of our achievement; the love of them is a vital part of natural religion, their words our authentic inspiration and Gospel. . . . To know their sex obsessions by their works is not enough, we want the personal touch of intimate knowledge. . . . I have tried to paint no one whom I have not loved at some time or other and had the Age been less mealy-mouthed I should have liked to block in the outlines with heavier shadows and so reach in a more vivid verisimilitude. In my Autobiography, however I intend to be franker than the world will allow me in these "Portraits."

To Harris admirers, Leo Rosten[8] said, the *Contemporary Portraits* were like an introduction to the great salons of the world. One lady wrote that when her daughter had finished either the first or second volume she sighed and said, "I want to marry Frank Harris." "My dear," her mother murmured, "perhaps he has children as old as you." "Oh no," the child disagreed, "he's young, can't you tell he's young?"

Shaw was not so impressed. Harris was always writing about people, he told him, and usually literary people, but he didn't unmask them, rather he transfigured them with a thick *maquillage*—very striking, skillfully laid on, romantically effective, but still *maquillage*. Whenever possible Harris submitted his subjects to a sort of questionnaire; some wrote substantial portions of their portraits themselves. "I have not completed your sketch," Frank had written to Theodore Dreiser on June 10, 1918, "so I am only sending you a page which I want you to fill out about the treatment accorded to *Sister Carrie* by the publishers and the public, and I want you also to fill in for me or to expand the two pages that I have written about your belief on the deepest subjects. You seemed more pessimistic the other day and I did not quite get your complete drift. . . . Have you been in France, and if so, when and why and how long; do you know French? Have you been to London and what did you get out of it? Have you been in Germany, Spain or Italy?"

Continually Harris was obliged to convince himself of the quality of his work. "I want you to ask yourself if any one has ever done a better portrait than I have done of Dowson or even of Thomson," he asked Mencken. "And I like my George Moore." His methods of bookselling,

8 Best known perhaps for *The Education of H*y*m*a*n K*a*p*l*a*n*, 1937.

due partly to his own incompetence and partly to bad luck and the censor, were not profitable. He would keep all volumes and dispatch them as soon as he received orders. "I have got hundreds of copies of the Oscar Wilde book here," he wrote to Christopher Millard on March 20, 1919, "and with Shaw's addition it is really good. . . . The book retails at $5 and the cheapest I have sold copies here for is $3 and then only for orders of 50 or 100. . . . I wish you would take hundreds of sets, and I'd give them to you at half price: could you . . . ?"

In April 1920 he was inspired to open a bookshop at 57 Fifth Avenue for which he would pay an enormous rent. "I am going to sell pictures there and works of art, and give lectures," he told Max Beerbohm. "I want to talk say on a man called Max and I want a likeness of him to put in my window, and two or three of his books of caricatures. . . . I'll pay for 'em willingly! . . . especially an original of Frank Harris if he has done a good one of that fellow's mug." He would lecture on Aubrey Beardsley and show his illustrations from the *Yellow Book*; on Rothenstein, Brzeska, Wyndham Lewis, Lionel Johnson, Davidson, Arthur Machen. Not least of his works of art was to be a complete edition of his own works in fifteen or sixteen volumes.

And then Robert D. Towne appeared on Harris' muddled financial scene and began negotiations to buy *Pearson's*. Typically, it all began with marvelous promises, dragged on, and ended with Harris believing that everyone was in a conspiracy to swindle him. It seemed marvelous. Harris was to be retained as contributing editor, correspondent and European representative of *Pearson's*, with his headquarters in Paris, at a salary of £100 a month. He was to be paid $25,000 for *Pearson's* to put him on his feet. The money did not materialize. Harris meanwhile trailed round in the wind and snow in Chicago lecturing. He spent most of his time in bed with flu; whenever he got out he had to clutch the radiator for support, since the ceiling flew round his head. Buckland Plummer, who helped to run *Pearson's* during the last years and who disliked Harris—much to Kingsmill's amusement—sent with his wife an account to Kingsmill of Harris' visit to Chicago.[9]

[9] There were several people in Chicago who found Harris dislikable. One story here is of interest since it illustrates how in 1974 the legendary "bad" Harris has almost entirely eclipsed the real person. The niece of a lady whom Harris knew in Chicago met a friend of mine recently at a dinner party. During dinner she apparently told him various stories. "What an extremely nasty person Harris was," this friend said to me at our next meeting. He would tell me no more than that Harris was extremely nasty—or something of that sort—and it was agreed that the best thing to do was to get in touch

Mr. and Mrs. Buckland Plummer went to the hotel to call for him. On knocking at his door they were asked to go away, since he had not finished dressing. Half an hour later a terrible bass voice boomed out like a thunderclap. "Plummer, where are you?" On entering the room Mrs. Buckland Plummer was presented with a pin and asked to fix Harris' collar so that it would not slip. The maid, he explained, had stolen his two gold clips. Mrs. Buckland Plummer could not get the pin through his stiff collar and Harris was furious: "My wife can do it"—a remark that convinced Mrs. Buckland Plummer that he had no gold clips. He complained of a very sore throat and for an hour gave them a detailed account of his sufferings. He was fidgety, anything but a good companion. His lecture was supposed to begin at seven; they reached the hall at ten minutes to nine. They could easily have got there before, Mrs. Buckland Plummer said, but Harris fumed and delayed and fidgeted for the express purpose of making them late.

The hall was in East Chicago, in a very disreputable neighborhood, half-filled with evil-smelling foreigners. On entering, Harris, who had hitherto ignored Mrs. Buckland Plummer, affectionately took her arm, and with him continually patting her hand they walked down the center aisle like a bridal couple. Every now and again Harris would bend toward her and smile into her face, moving his lips as though whispering sweet messages but in reality saying nothing, while Mrs. Buckland Plummer marched bravely forward with a face devoid of emotion. When eventually they made the platform, Harris turned to Buckland Plummer and said in a distressingly audible voice, "What a disgusting crowd of people: I have never spoken before such filth in my life and how dreadfully cold the place is!" The chairman was ready to die, and after explaining there was no way of heating the hall, and after he had sent to a neighboring hotel (four blocks away) for a glass of water—which Frank did not drink—Harris began by telling the audience he intended lecturing on Shakespeare, since Bernard Shaw was not sufficiently important for him to talk about. At the end two girls and a young man sent up to the platform to complain

---

with the aunt via the niece and collect the facts and letters. But when approached, the aunt was very sorry, she felt unable to give any details about Harris' trips to Chicago; and her niece now gathered that some aspects of the stories with which she had regaled this friend of mine were not "entirely correct." The aunt was now "quite elderly," and no useful purpose could be served by trying to question her further. . . .

that they had come to hear about Bernard Shaw, whom they loved. Harris deplored their lack of taste, asked them for subscriptions to *Pearson's*, and made appointments for lunch with them—which he did not keep since they did not subscribe. Harris and Mrs. Buckland Plummer did their bridal walk out again. At the exit Dr. Ben Reitman, a prominent Chicago socialist, barred the way and told Harris that he had not heard a word of the lecture and that it was damned rotten. Harris turned purple with rage, mustered his dignity and walked away.

Often his lectures were his only source of income; he dealt them out like a pack of cards. Percy Ward could have Bernard Shaw and Jesus if he liked, while Mendelssohn could have Shakespeare and prohibition. In April 1921, the money still not having appeared from Robert Towne, Harris organized one of his begging schemes. He asked, "HAVE I A HUNDRED FRIENDS?"

To My Friends,
The troubles of *Pearson's* struck me at the wrong moment.

About a year ago I made an arrangement to bring out one thousand sets of my works in fifteen volumes, you may have seen that they were advertised some six or eight months ago at $40 the set. I had made an estimate for the printing and for the paper. I gave the order to begin printing the books. Within a month printing went up 33% and within another month paper went up from five cents to twelve a lb.

I saw at once that I would have to buy the whole stock of paper immediately if I were not to be swamped, so I bought it all and paid for it cash at twelve cents. It afterwards went to nearly twenty. The price of printing also increased again.

The consequence is that the capital I had put aside for the thousand sets of my work was insufficient. I have paid the printer $3,000 and still owe him $5,000. I have paid for all the paper. In other words I have paid about $10,000 and have about $5,000 still to pay. I cannot get my books till I pay this money. Then there is the binding.

Have I a hundred friends who will find me $40 apiece? If I have I will give each of them a set of my books, autographed, and I will give them besides $20 back out of the $40 within a year, that is they will get my books at cost price and autographed.

Roll up and let me have your checks and your names and

addresses. I shall acknowledge personally each contribution in *Pearson's*. Within three months you shall have the books.
Yours sincerely,
FRANK HARRIS

One of those to roll up was Quinn, who preferred not to have his "participation" acknowledged in *Pearson's*, since it would mean a flood of letters from artists, writers and other persons. As it was, he complained, everyone seemed to see him as a sort of performing Buddhistic figure with seven heads, fourteen eyes and ears, seven tongues, seventy-seven hands and forty-seven feet, all bestirring themselves to act in the interest of the dear friends he had befriended so often in the past.

Harris when at the height of his financial anxieties still took time and trouble to help artists in need. "Do you know Zorach?" he asked Quinn. "He has done some beautiful modern things and I want you to know him." "No," replied Quinn. "I know his work, it's a feeble little talent . . . so as your friend Hamlet would say 'the man's work delights me not, nor the woman's either.'" "Your letter is a masterpiece of discernment," replied Harris without rancor. "Against my will I agree with every word of it; but Zorach is a likeable fellow and he begged me to help if I could so I did."

May 1921 saw the birth of another wild scheme. If Shaw's permission could be obtained to use his name on the Oscar Wilde book and his praise of *The Man Shakespeare*, Harris was promised $50,000 "for the movie rights." Accordingly Nellie was sent to England in June and Harris was left minding her rather seedy, neurotic little dog—a job at which he would have been appallingly bad. "Cappie has been a dreadful plague," he wrote crossly to Nellie. "He wakes me a dozen times a night." For two days after her departure he did nothing but cry and snap; gradually he began to "dance," Harris told her, and "make fun," but by that time Frank was too ill from want of sleep and worrying about money to derive any amusement.

A new name had filtered through the financial net—Weir, who, with promises of $25,000, had gone off to fetch it from Washington. The scheme involving Weir seems to have been madder than ever, including Lady Warwick once more, the Kaiser and the Queen of Romania—all of whom, it appears, had a fine Hollywood future in store for them. "Weir swears by all his Gods he'll come back with a pile and let me have five thou for Lady Warwick and at least a thou for you," Harris wrote to Nellie at the Savoy. Cables followed. "Promise Lady W. 5,000 extra for getting Queen Roumania, ten thousand if Queen will come America, let Daisy make terms with Queen cabling proposal up to half profits. We make heroic scenario secure Queen's signature to draft agreement made by Stanley Parker." The money did not materialize. "At any rate," Harris assured Nellie, "if he [Weir] does not turn up with the money you may be quite sure that I will get to work and get you $500 or $600 more for your passage. . . . Take care and eat beef steaks and remember I love you always with all my heart."

In order to make money he wrote a story about prizefighting. "I've just written the best prize-fighting story that was ever written," he explained to Mencken. He needed the money to get Nellie back from England. "That's why I sat down to write this story . . . it should kick up a real sensation. I want you to make the best offer you can for it for I really want the coin for my wife and you are the only editor and almost the only man in U.S.A. to whom I tell that."

Nellie meanwhile was having a lovely time in the Savoy, and wrote descriptions of the velvety service that made Harris' mouth water. Shaw had apparently advised her to get an American millionaire and say that she'd marry him if he would give Frank fifty thousand dollars. Nellie tells us in her memoirs that she protested that American millionaires were not interesting. Shaw said that that didn't matter, while the money did. At Frank's request, Hesketh Pearson was piloting her round London. About ten years later, on March 16, 1932, he wrote to Kingsmill saying that she had taken him up to her bedroom and showed him her bed, implying that it was rather large for one person. Meanwhile, it seems, she had set spies in America to watch what Frank was up to in her absence. There exists an obscure letter referring to obscure people headed "Overlook Mountain, Woodstock, N.Y., 6 P.M.," and signed "Claire." "An hour ago I was sitting at my window. . . . Frank came down the hill with Mabel and told her *he did not want to see me.* She offered to call me, but he asked that I *not be told of his having been here.* Now, he may not have cared for me to have known of the dark-haired Jewish looking young girl with him, *or* he may be upset over the Weir matter which could it be? The girl asked *who* 'Claire' was and Frank replied: 'I do not want you to meet her.'

When she insisted he grew angry and said: shut up. . . . So Nellie, puzzle it out and tell me what to do in this matter."

Nellie's negotiations came to nothing, but the *Pearson's* affair resolved itself sufficiently well for Frank and Nellie to return to Nice at the end of 1921, both of them American citizens at last, having been naturalized that April.

CHAPTER 19

The Curse of Poverty

IN about 1920, Harris tells us in
My Life and Loves, a terrible thing happened. A fairly pretty girl called
on him, wanting to know whether he required a secretary. He was, he
said, not moved. "Suddenly I realized the wretchedness of my condition
in an overwhelming suffocating wave of bitterness." Before he had had
only to look at a young girl—to catch a glimpse of alabaster limbs
shining under black silk—for his mouth to parch and his mind to move
automatically into gear toward her conquest. This was the end; desire
was there, but not the driving power. Impotence meant, he said, the
end of hope. Optimism had been a cocktail stimulating wild schemes
that would make his fortune, romantic adventures that would conclude
in the private velvet-hung apartments of the Café Royal and other
establishments. Now, he said, the loss of virility meant that all glamour
and excitement were gone, and because he was no longer interested in
new adventures he was no longer interested in new plays and reviews.

For Harris to be physically impotent was to frustrate him to the
point of madness. Instead of lessening his sexual activities he increased
them—antics which in turn drove Nellie mad. In August 1924 she had
been sitting up late discussing Frank with a friend, Louise Hamilton;
she has the following garbled fragment noted in her diary:

> ... we drifted on to people we had known in New York. I told her
> that the Lund girl was in Europe. She then told me about some of
> her talks with Frank last year in Paris and said really I saved him

from being shot by Mrs. Lund, I asked how, she said Mrs. Lund had said he was going about with her daughter etc. and she was willing to arrange a marriage if they wished but unless she would shoot. Louise was amazed when Frank responded but the girl isn't a virgin, she said how do you know, he said I've looked. I am so surprised I have not slept all night, I am now waiting for developments for the girl is over here and probably with Lord Alfred Douglas, who she says is wonderful. Louise said to Mrs. Lund but how can he marry when he has a wife already—one whom he seems to be satisfied with etc. I'll get some more light on this—only it has made me fight for myself and that is a good thing. Frank is really sexually mad, perhaps it takes men like that when they can't do any more anyway it's hell for the looker on if they care and I am helpless. So I must look after myself whilst I have time.

As Frank's sexual competence diminished, so he became more obsessed with other men's sexual weaknesses—especially in those men whom he had admired and who had been superior to him intellectually or physically. For a long time other men's sexuality had interested him in a critical sense, since he believed that sex was the key to the character, that no study could be properly balanced unless it took a man's sexuality—or the lack of it—into account. He was fond of saying, as we know, that the joys and satisfactions of a full sex life awakened in a man an appreciation of beauty: here was the reason that Carlyle had never responded to beauty—he was impotent. Why did Maupassant go mad? Because he had syphilis. Filling in sexual misadventures—syphilis, impotence, wet dreams—was what he called filling in the shade of a portrait. It balanced the light. Years before, he remembered discussing an essay of George Moore's on Verlaine with its author. Verlaine's genius, he believed, would be appreciated better if one knew that he wore no linen and how dirty he was, going about with strange venereal diseases. "Then," Harris had told George Moore, "picture him in a mood of absolute humility on his knees before Jesus . . . or half drunk, sobbing psalms and you will have done something." In his *Contemporary Portraits* he had already done a lot of shading, much to the irritation of many people,[1] and what he could not finish

---

[1] His Wagner portrait was included in *Contemporary Portraits*, fourth series, published in 1923, and was written simultaneously with his account in *My Life and Loves* of student days in Germany. Poor Ernest Newman, Wagner's biographer, took endless trouble and scholarly energy pointing out Harris' inaccuracies in three successive articles in the *Sunday Times*, June 1924.

he was going to ink in, in his autobiography. His portraits, complete with their shade, emerge like seamy tea-table gossip. When it came to writing fiction and trying to present passion, Harris was so busy idealizing sex—larding it with reverence, nobility of body and spirit—that the result was grand sentimentality. When was he going to drop those dreary people who lived for love, died for love, but never existed? Shaw wanted to know. It was time he dropped the cabaret; he used the love business just as he used pen and ink, as part of the materials of writing.

As Frank's physical and intellectual incompetence grew, so did his preoccupation with Jesus. "I have always wanted to make a study of him in some story," he had told Augustus John in February 1910, "to show how Renan missed him, made him too goody-goody. The man who said 'much shall be forgiven her for she loved much' had surely been in the stews. If he did not love some Mary Magdalen beyond all bounds then I'm a Dutchman. His horror of the *bourgeoisie* and their petty thefts, comes out in every word he says. . . . Jesus, when he went to Jerusalem to be crucified, must have been crucified in life again and again before that. All the noble spirits have been crucified." "I am at my greatest task," he told Quinn eight years later, "but making progress in a Life of the Man Jesus." What emerged over the years were several short stories: "St. Peter's Difficulty," "The Miracle of the Stigmata," "The Holy Man," "The King of the Jews."[2] In 1915 *The Man Jesus*, by Mary Austin,[3] had been published. Later, after Harris' death,

[2] Published in paperback in 1919 by Pearson's library.

[3] In her autobiography, *Earth Horizon*, Mary Austin tells how she had an argument with Harris at the Arts Club. Harris had been invited to discuss the artistic temperament. She was sitting next to him, and soon they got into a discussion about David Graham Phillips. Harris thought him the most promising of "our younger novelists." Mary Austin disagreed. Harris was exceedingly vexed and said that she had no right to question his judgment. He'd had a drink or two, added Mary Austin. When he was called upon to answer the speaker he replied in considerable dudgeon. He said the Arts Club had no right to ask him to reply to a man who knew nothing of his subject, kicked his chair and sat down. Mary Austin was called to speak instead. She did not agree with the speaker, she did not agree with Harris either, but she did speak, taking care to say things that were pacifying. Then Harris got up and told them all about his own short stories and their surpassing qualities. Gradually he talked himself into a good humor, kicked his chair two or three times and sat down. Harris has his own version of this. He says Mr. Wheeler, the president of the Poetry Society of America, gave a speech that meandered on and on about how the poet generally found it difficult to pay his debts and what a pity it was that he often evaded the ordinary laws of morality. Harris could not contain himself—dense, arrogant philistinism, which he had never met in England and which was to be found in full cloddishness only in America. Much to his surprise, Mary Austin ended her colorless speech (he had excused himself, as he could not possibly follow such talk) by saying that she was sure the audience would like to hear what Mr. Harris had to say. Mr. Harris said that he rose and told the Arts Club that he knew poetry societies in London, Paris and

Elmer Gertz acquired his copy—along with two other volumes, one of which contained a number of photographs of naked ladies, names and addresses stuck inside. It is clear that Harris had read Mary Austin with care and had spent time and energy in underlining her text and making remarks in the margin. The two of them make illuminating reading. Not only is Harris preoccupied by "The Man of Sorrows" but he is identifying with him also. They were together in their isolation, their unappreciated teachings, their hatred of the bourgeoisie. In parts he appears to have become confused and seems to believe that Mary Austin is writing *his* autobiography. "She is speaking of me. A true prophet and I too believe in repentance and peace and in love," he wrote once; and again, when Jesus "comes filled with the sense of divine kinship": "She is speaking of *me*." "*All through his career*," he underlined, "he displayed in the use of his extraordinary gifts a reticence and sense of proportion, *unequalled among men of genius*." "Except me," he adds. He did not agree with some of Mary Austin's descriptions. Her Christ strode out a little way ahead of his companions, bronzed, hardy, his turban off to catch the mountain coolness, his long hair blown backward from his "rapt countenance." "Fundamental error," scribbles Harris. "Weak he was." "Why tall?" he asks elsewhere in the margin. Jews were short usually. As he underlined he corrected her prose, sometimes questioning her essays in the *mot juste*. At one point he queried "the soil as red as a heifer," then took exception to the "terrible blank treeless land" being "spined" with low shrubs. "Mary sees nothing," he complained once. "Bosh, she lies": "*boh! frew frew!*" When she observed that "incalculable harmonies" came when a man "loves greatly, when he finishes a great work or *when a son is born*" he is reduced to whistling: "whew!"

Nevertheless over this red-heifer soil, this spined terrain, he saw that he and Christ had walked together into the desert to find the true way. Was it not exactly the same? Christ had gone a carpenter, been tempted by the devil, triumphed and emerged a teacher and prophet, to be crucified; while Harris, the man of letters, had entered and been hounded by a Satan metamorphosed into frightful forms: Arthur du

---

Berlin, and if anyone had dared to make such a speech he would have good reason to regret it. The poet and artist had taken the place of the prophet and guide. As for debts, had the world ever paid its debts to its "poets"? In fifty to a hundred years, he told the audience, they would all be turned to dust, and nothing would be known of them, their names would be forgotten.

Cros, Lord Justice Horridge, John Sumner, for three. He too had emerged, he too would teach, he too was being crucified. His autobiography would be his bible. He would be the Christ of love—love, that is to say, in every meaning—Christ of sex and food and drink. He would enjoy all the hallucinations of a desert father without all the inconveniences. Like the desert fathers', his hallucinations would be confused with reality; as the desert fathers passed over land, fire and water on the backs of crocodiles and tigers, so Harris traveled, famous, over the continents of America and Europe on expensive horses and motor cars, his disappointments turned to triumphs, distinguished comrade of the most illustrious men, glorious lover of the most tender virgins. With that autobiography he was going to make a fortune; with the ghosts of past seductions, hope visited him again. He was going at last to buy a house in Nice, and then he and Nellie would go round the world—it would be their honeymoon.

By the end of 1921 he was in Nice to begin his Life, pausing now and then, dressed smartly in fresh Eton ties—supplied by Hesketh Pearson—tied in a sailor's knot, to deliver a series of lectures. At the end of one, he told Hesketh, a man jumped up and asked Harris to explain how New York had treated him "as an old prostitute." "I said I couldn't understand the question." Had Harris not written of New York as an old whore? No, said Harris, he had not. Whereupon the man proceeded to read out passages from "Frank Harris," in *Modern Men and Mummers*, wherein Hesketh had published some of Harris' letters. At least a dozen people left, indignant.

That winter was a sickly one. Nellie had prickly heat on her chest and Harris felt ill, weak and old. *"Desire faileth and the voice of the grasshopper's loud in the land,"* he complained to Hesketh Pearson. However, one of his daughters appeared, at least on paper, to cheer him and correspond with him. Gradually Frances Congden took over from Hesketh, who was corresponding now with Hugh Kingsmill and falling under his influence and out of Harris' favor. Frank was a demanding father—a mixture of voyeur and parent. Frances acted as his agent, rushed off to publishers, round to Hesketh Pearson himself to collect copies of books that he had not sold, supplied introductions and, above all, an audience. "The 'Autobiography' is the main thing," he told her in April. "Now it will be in 4 or 5 vols if I live; but the first *vol* is already a third done and void of offence save to the Puritan, and really I have had joy in writing it. Casanova is a *gourmand*, not to say *goinfre;* he eats and eats and eats, kisses and kisses and kisses and all his kissings are the same: the girls are hardly differenced. . . . But I am a *gourmet*: from hors-d'oeuvres to the savouries, from the first sip of a fine Château vintage with the soup to the last drop of dry Comet port I've enjoyed the best." There he was, her father, sixty-six, and he could run a hundred yards very nearly as fast as he could at sixteen— and did, every morning of his life. "And a word to you," he added. "I want little girl-figures let into the text, just seductive outlines here and there. I'd get Augustus John to do me some: but fear he's too well off now, still I'm going to write to him and ask for White Magic in black outlines from his pencil."

Meanwhile he pressed his daughter to tell of her "love experiences," and when eventually she did, they saddened him. "I wish you had told me all about it: I might have helped tho' advice I always say is like an old suit of clothes and suits no one but the wearer." He was still anxiously running round to see anyone who might be good for a contemporary portrait. He called on Picasso, who refused to see him. "Picasso denying himself to me is worse than silly," he complained to Frances. "I can do him an infinite amount of good and wished to."

At the beginning of June he returned once more to the Benighted States, as he now called America, making his way by Montreal. As usual, his voyage was a trial; his letters to Nellie are the usual medical itinerary, how many degrees of fever he had, how his cough rasped his chest, how he had a bad headache on waking. The steward had failed to put him at the captain's table, he felt old, the price of wine was so high because of the poor rate of exchange for francs that he drank cider with meals that were atrocious. And what a dull lot the other passengers were, all playing bridge and talking about money. And then he ruminated in his usual way over their life, their rows, their unhappiness. The difficulty of sex now was added to that of money; but as soon as he had made a fortune, it would be all right, he knew he would make love to her once more. "You don't know how I've been blaming myself since I came away for not making love to you: I wasn't sure you loved me and so did not show you how dearly I care for you . . . we must begin to show each other how much we care . . . if you respond to this appeal, I'll try to be your lover again. I want to be Nellie dear! and you must try to have confidence in me and my affection and love for you, which is very deep. Nell I'm getting old: I feel it dreadfully. I want you at every minute, and I'm lonely sad! I don't want to sadden you; but I'm desperate at times still I know a brave heart can win even now with my brains so I'll do my best." On and on he brooded. He meant even to come to terms with Nellie's singing. "I've been very foolish: I thought you took up singing to make yourself independent and get away from me; latterly I've seen that you were willing to give it up if I really wished it."

Taller and taller he built his dream castles, fuller and fuller he crammed Nellie's dream wardrobes—the way to her heart was through rich velvets, satins, diamonds and gold. "The first thing is to get you clothes," he told her. "You agreed that 3,500 francs or $300 would do that or nearly then I have 4,500 francs to repay . . . and I propose to get out your jewellery—all in a month if possible." His fevered brain whizzed on with plans. He would run an advertising paper both in New York and Chicago; hard work and "a good tongue" should do a lot, and he might even find a Jew "Angel." And then, as if for the first time, he told her that what he really wanted was to get her to forgive him all his sins and follies, "and above all show me more love and let us try to have the end better than the beginning."

He arrived in Montreal so short of money that he was unable to engage in any therapeutic tipping. He had to avoid his cabin steward, and dash down the railway platform just as the train was pulling out so that he had no time to tip the porters. In the train there was a nasty scene in front of a "carful" of waiting passengers: the berth cost $4.25, and he had only $4.00 in his pocket—much to the disbelief of the ticket collector. In New York he had to borrow money from the taxi driver to pay the porters, and then he had to wait inside the taxi for one and a half hours before Mrs. Stahl, his supporter at *Pearson's*, turned up and was able to pay for him. What a day! Never mind, the autobiography was the thing; with that and various speculations in gold and platinum up his sleeve he would be sure to be buying that house in Nice—he saw it all, "and my love beautifully gowned quite soon."

He set off once more for the Catskills to finish his volume of autobiography, visions of the dream house in the pinewoods, Nellie's dresses and the honeymoon trip round the world wafting before him. His letters are filled with wildly optimistic calculations of the huge amounts of dollars he would soon be wiring her from the proceeds of *Pearson's* and his books. "The bad time is nearly over."

But true to form, nothing turned out right. He was in arrears at the Beech Tree Inn; Marky, who eventually was buying *Pearson's*, was not sending the payments; and his Matisse article was rejected by Hearst "as not suiting their editorial policy"—though what "editorial policy" had to do with rejecting a great human story the editor would be puzzled to say, snorted Harris. There was little amusement or adventure at the Beech Tree Inn; the ghosts of his past, together with his sciatica, prickly heat and bleeding chest, shut him into his obsession with Nellie. The formula was by now well worn. He meant to make her happy; he would; but could she love him when he returned to Paris with money in his pocket and his autobiography, which would prove a second gold mine? He'd bring all the furniture, books and paintings from store, "and we'll set up our own home for good and for all . . . we'll have an auto too and make life pleasant and gay." And Nellie would have a proper wedding ring. But Nellie, in Nice, was more interested in the present; she wrote that she had only three hundred francs left. "Don't think I am careless of your need of clothes," Harris wrote on July 29. "I'm not and shall do my very best as soon as I can dear. Don't talk of ill-luck please for as it is I'm terribly depressed." And the food was worse than ever, but he had to stick it out until September 10 and finish the "gold mine." On top of this he had "to do the whole magazine"—twenty-odd pages to write in four days— then he would have eighteen days clear for his autobiography. By July 1923, he calculated, his life story should have brought in at least $40,000: "I want you to own it all." . . . "Here on the Trail the 'Autobiography' is very hard to do: the novel confuses me. Still I have today done the VI chapter."

He worked through August, eighteen hours on end, reporting his progress to Nellie, who wrote back, sometimes lovingly, sometimes complaining. By August 14 he had written 90,000 words—being particularly delighted with his chapter on Smith. By August 30 he had finished. "I'm a long step nearer to you and our honeymoon." Now the printing remained and a settlement with *Pearson's*. And then he believed there was $50,000 to be made. How lovely that house was going to be, and how lovely Nellie was going to make it—"with rose-gardens and bowers." And he would bring back with him a Buick Sedan and take Nellie to Venice in it by road. "I want my laughter loving Nellie of twenty years ago back again." He painted the future like a boy, he knew that, "but always with you, Nell dearest, and if work'll bring the dreams to pass, it'll all be as rose-coloured as you deserve."

By September 16, having had two rows with Marky and called him a slick Jew, Harris had settled to sell *Pearson's* for $2,000 and to contribute once a month for a year. One of Harris' admirers from Chicago, R. H. A. Schofen, said that he walked the streets of Chicago when the last number appeared with "his goodbye." Frank planned to come to France by way of Germany, in order to get his book printed, hoping to arrive in Paris by November 5. This was an arrangement not much to Nellie's liking; she was lonely and wished that Frank would go to Paris first. He did not, and indeed was so delayed by financial wrangles with Mitchell Kennerley, Haldeman-Julius and Brentano over the copyright of *Contemporary Portraits* that he did not arrive in Berlin until November.

It was bitterly cold, with snow, as he struggled to the printers. Nevertheless he was quick to reassure the restless Nellie that he was going straight off to buy her silk stockings, "a white costume" and a wonderful white ermine collar two feet broad and very long that was "given by the Tzar to an Archduchess"; meanwhile he had already posted some black silk stockings and crêpe de chine. His disciples waiting anxiously in America he informed that he was nearly dead. But the first volume, he told Schofen, should "flatten all dovecotes": it was the naughtiest—or the only naughty—book ever written, nicely illustrated with nude girls "with hair wherever hair grows and excellently bound." In spite of having to send to Nellie for envelopes full of indigestion powder and *pilules sédatives*, along with some *pommade hongroise*, he was having a good time; the theaters, art and music, he wrote, were the best in the world, and people were giving him gala dinners and complimenting him on his accent. Would Nellie consider living in Germany? he wondered. What with its cheapness, good wine, well warmed rooms and lovely walks in Baden-Baden and the Black Forest, there was a lot to commend it. Nellie replied crossly that she would rather return to the United States than spend even a year in Germany, and as the time drew on became increasingly restless. Harris' finances meanwhile worsened. Ten thousand copies cost him $3,000 to print, and then he found there was a heavy tax on all goods leaving Germany. He swallowed more packets of *pilules sédatives* sent by Nellie and more indigestion powders, but was still optimistic. "That honeymoon of ours is going to be *some* festival. Yes Sir."

But Christmas that year was certainly no festival, not at least for Nellie. Sometime just before it or just after, her debut as a singer had taken place; it was apparently an unremarkable event. Frank alluded to it once and then remained silent. Nellie, however, wrote a disagreeable letter. "Why write me such a letter!" exploded Harris on December 29. "God knows I'm depressed enough. I don't know how to get my books out of the d—d country and you say you won't wait; you'll go back to England. I was so broken that I left my umbrella in the cursed cab—the first I've taken in a week and lost that too. . . . Already they are packing the books and any day I may get the permission to take 'em out—24 hours later I'll be on my way to you; but please don't make my burden heavier. I'm nearly played out and Marky demanding 6 articles by the fifth and Filson Young asking me for one for the *Saturday Review* and Austin Harrison not answering me about the Matisse Renoir article I sent him."

Nellie's letter, it transpired, not only had made him lose his umbrella but it made him lose his temper with an official and so get his case postponed. His worse fault, he told Nellie, was impatience, and if she showed impatience too, "we shall come to grief." He had bought her a present for every week that he had stayed away. Soon he was off to Leipzig, the fur center, "to get your skunk"; he was looking at coffee cups—should he get table knives? Last week he had bought "a silver scorpion 3 inches square with barbaric opals: really a remarkable artistic clasp for gown or wrap" and this week the "prettiest hand-embroidered blouse I've ever seen." To these he added "a beautiful tortoiseshell bag," and according to an account book, "a morning descente du lit," a green-embroidered evening dress, a gray coat and a bead bag, which, at 420 francs, was the most expensive item on the list. "But O God! I'm tired of living here and living on the tiles without a bath even and without you." His suffering was terrible, he told her: if he took salts every day he succumbed to lumbago, and as soon as he stopped them he got piles. He spent his time sending off his inscribed copies. Unfortunately, several went astray, in spite of his dedications, inscriptions and addresses, "written in my best schrift," and in spite of largesse distributed in many thousands of marks; Mencken's copy arrived just south of Paris, at the address of an English gentleman called Mr. Vivian, who was most surprised. At last, on January 19, his permits were granted—at a cost of a million marks.

After a "painfully prolonged" journey he arrived back in Paris on January 28. His books traveled in batches, and as soon as they arrived in France they were seized at every point—borders, the Gare du Nord —by the French customs. One lot Harris managed to divert to Italy;

the Italian authorities, having been informed that the books were pornographic, arrested them at the frontier and proposed burning them. Another lot was held up in the Ruhr disturbances. "Fancy the French and Italian authorities prohibiting it [Volume I of *My Life and Loves*]," he wrote to Mencken. "Do they want nothing but the *filth* of Rabelais and Aretino. After all mine is pure fucking, as Maupassant used to call it, the first of the fine arts." Harris, who by now was running very short of money, rushed off to Cologne, and on the advice of Shaw, cut out the illustrations and returned with 200 copies. The authorities stopped him again. That spring was spent chasing here and there trying to save cases of books. A crew of people, some of them incompetent, drove books round Paris and over the United States border. The situation was becoming desperate. There was nothing for it, Harris decided, but to borrow money from his friends.

"Here I am in a cheap little hotel, Hotel Haussmann, with £10 and no more," he told Shaw. He needed a loan dreadfully; his wife was in a little hotel in Nice and he must go to her help as soon as he could. All his friends, he said, who would have helped him were dead, he had no one to turn to but Shaw. It was impossible to write well, or even do one's best, when one was half crazed with doubt and anxiety as to next week's food. If Shaw decided to give him another chance he was to cable the money. If he only knew what this confession cost him, "but help from you will give me new courage: to be thought worth saving by Shaw is worth half the battle. I should like to save my conceit by telling you how many I helped in my good days and how willing I was always to help every artist or man of letters worth helping . . . help me this once Shaw and I'll never ask again." Shaw did not help him— disliking, as he called it, "begging letters"—much to the chagrin of Harris, who was quick to assure him that his luck had turned anyway; several large debts that *he* had been generous enough to lend had been repaid. In any case, under the circumstances, he had been intending to repay Shaw's kind loan as soon as he had received it.

What with the confiscation of books and Marky not keeping up proper payments, prospects for the future seemed as disappointing as ever and relations with Nellie as precarious. However, they scraped themselves together and installed themselves in a large and airy flat in Villa Édouard VII. The summer was spent in chasing frustratedly after the authorities and making plans that came to nothing: a Who's Who for the Riviera and a trip to the northwest frontier of Canada, where

FRANK HARRIS

Harris told Mencken he was thinking of going to take up some mining leases.

In spite of his disappointment with the first volume, whose bad reception only confirmed the more his crucified Christlike attitude, Frank was now thinking of his second and third.

> I am going to see how interesting I can make the next two volumes [he told Mencken on March 24, 1923]. I shall tell how Maupassant went mad with syphilis and how English leaders of the House of Commons were tarred with the same brush. And I shall tell it all with loving kindness and sympathy and with no desire to "knock" misfortune that might have happened to me. . . . My book is a sign of the times: we've had enough of lies and concealments; now we'll try the naked truth and see how far that will bring us. . . . I want to sit on my behind in Nice and write the greatest Memoirs that have ever been written . . . and if my health holds you'll yet cherish the six or seven volumes of your friend and admirer.

For the next few months, however, his health was not good. "Life is like dust in my mouth," he wrote to Upton Sinclair. "I've been ill here for some weeks and terribly depressed for a long time." At the end of June he brightened up. He'd seen, he told Nellie, a wonderful film about animals and children. He was going to buy the option—there was a fortune in it. It was a sentimental story of a chimpanzee called August stealing a baby and hiding it in a cave, feeding it on goat's milk and teaching it to suck eggs. There was a great deal of carrying the baby over crumbling stone bridges and wobbling about at the edge of yawning precipices while pursued by athletic girls and the mother. "Thrilling," Harris described it; it brought tears to his eyes to see the chimpanzee trying to imitate the child washing—"pure revelation." He was off to Canada to sell it, a fortune in his pocket. "Hurra!" It seemed, however, that he would probably be arrested if he set foot either in Canada or New York, and Nellie, to whom he referred sickeningly as "wifie," went to New York in his stead to enlist the aid of Charlie Chaplin. "If she succeeds and I believe she will, my chief trouble will be at an end, for I'll be able to buy a little house and the naughty 'Life and Loves' will give us enough to live on moderately." Unfortunately, Chaplin would have nothing to do with the scheme, apparently because of *My Life and Loves*. "Film buyers are *Jews* in name and nature," complained Harris.

376

In January 1924 Aleister Crowley,[4] who was about as badly off financially as Harris, appeared in Nice hoping for a loan. There was a spare room, ready and "yawning" for him, Harris said. But by the time he had appeared, Nellie's sister Aggie had arrived to fill it. Harris had seen Crowley quite often in New York—he would drop in for a "petite verre of brandy" and a talk. Then he disappeared, and a number of people had come round to Harris at 40 Seventh Avenue—one of his numerous changes of addresses—asking for him; he had been writing checks, and there was no account at the bank to meet them. Now Harris was delighted to see him, and, filled with good humor, promised gaily to lend him 500 francs. Next morning he did not feel so good. "You must have hypnotized me yesterday," he wrote on January 3, "for on going to the Bank I find I have overdrawn my account and can't help you as I had hoped. I'm sorry but I'm going out now to see if it's possible to get some oof. I shall do my best . . . but I'm not hopeful." But he did get it, and he did lend it. Two weeks later he was wondering if Crowley could raise some money so that they could buy the *Paris Evening Telegram*, which was for sale. If he could find "just 200,000 francs," he would "stand it even." A more incompetent partnership could not be imagined. "Tomorrow I'm to see the Prince," wrote Harris on January 17, failing to reveal who or what prince, "and I'll know more: of course I'll give you time over the miserable 500 francs. I wish I could say 'forget it.' " Two weeks later he was "keeping things simmering" and had the money promised "from one source" on or before the first of March. "Get what you can on your side and we'll all stand in together." Meanwhile, perhaps Crowley could sell his memories of John Ruskin for him: just take it round to Hearst's man. But now the paper was the thing; it would bring in $1,000; it would be crammed with facts that would make Britons stand up. February dawned, no money had materialized. "I do hope you will get a letter or two to your important people pretty soon," Harris wrote on February 9, "for my big people are delayed through the vagaries of sovereignty." However, his prospective partner was outdoing him now with hypochondria and financial impotence. "Your letter is like a moan," Harris told him. By March, Crowley was prostrated by ill

---

[4] Crowley mainly admired Harris' voice; never had he heard one capable of such power and passion, combined with perfect control and delicacy of expression. Once at the Hôtel Meurice, he remembered, they actually stopped the band in the Great Hall to allow him to tell a story.

health and Harris was desperate. Without funds, he rushed in and took over the paper.

Harris was now out for any credit he could get. To this end he had two main possibilities. There was his nephew Tom Harris, the son of William: "If I can borrow $6,000 from him we'll be free of anxiety whatever happens." Nellie was to send a letter to Harris saying: "Ask Tom for $6,000 for the house—Les Ravinelles—the exchange has made it so cheap and add we can save easily enough to pay him back in 2 years; but you're sure he's kind and likes us as we like him—I want to show him the letter. You say you like him so much or you wouldn't ask. I'll only use the letter if I must. P.S. The chief word in the letter should be at the end thus—'get Tom to lend us the money Frank; I want a house of my own and will pay him back: every *dollar counts double now*. Your Nellie.' " Then there was a shrouded negotiation involving Gerald Hamilton[5] and some resources in Cairo. If neither of these worked, Harris proposed to write a mystery book "that would cause a sensation"—*An American in Paris*, which would involve various scandals, including Dreyfus, the Panama swindle, the Daudier scandal, to say nothing of the war.

By March 12 he had the paper—"then if Egypt pays we'll be well off pretty soon and if Egypt doesn't pay, I'll be in a pretty mess." The worst of it was that he had hurried Tom out to lunch and asked him for $2,000, "and he refused the mean hound: he had just told me that he had $50,000 still to spend on his house, 'I wish I could Uncle Frank, but I can't' . . . if that d—d Gerald would go to Egypt as he promised we'd win big and I'd get you on the stage and give your lovely voice a chance—why won't he go? Tell him he endangers his 100,000 franc promissory note if he doesn't go for Cohn won't give it up and if he goes and succeeds we'll make a lot—It's true."

By March 14 he had wired Gerald Hamilton, telling him plainly that he would lose his 100,000 francs unless he cabled 400,000 from Cairo. He had learned all about the paper; he could make it pay, but it would be hard, pettifogging, constant work and not any money to speak of in it. "If I get the money we'll keep it—that's my resolve," he told Nellie. Meanwhile she had to arrange legal documents to transfer the lease of the flat, furniture and works of art and silver over to her.

---

[5] Author of *The Norris and I*, Allan Wingate, 1956.

The Curse of Poverty

Then, if and when the money comes I'll hasten to you and we'll go where they won't easily find us. Not that they'll look: I shall write at once the articles I promised in favor of Egypt: what more can they want. I'm past incessant work, Nellie, there's no sense in blinding oneself: I've taken all pains but this cold has struck me down because I was tired out—and all in. Where shall we go? is the question: I thought of Italy or Spain first or the U.S. entering not by New York but by Boston or by Canada? Think it all ripely over: you know I'll do what you wish. But I think we ought to take most of the best furniture and books etc. into Italy saying we are going to Spain for the summer. We can then let the apartment for next winter and sell the lease and the rest of the furniture. . . . We must not be so poor again. My books and writing will give us a fair living and we shall have $20,000 behind us for eventualities and so can make our peace with Fortune. . . . Again I repeat get Gerald to go to Cairo and cable me the money here before the first: that's the centre of our success. . . . Now I've written for hours it's all love for you and a hope yet to be happy together.

In the middle of March he and two others—"Hunt and Paterson"—took command of the paper.

I contribute a first col each day with stories like Brisbane in New York: then a story by O. Henry and by Maupassant then a gossip col about the king of Bulgaria. Paterson is the American journalist who started the paper and was my rival in buying it: he can and will better the business side of it and increase the "ads" we are a very strong team. At any rate I'm aboard and it would be difficult to dispossess me: suppose I make it pay at once and tell Cohn I'll pay him gradually: all I want is the credit he can give me: I believe he'll do it for he has nothing else to do. It's a bold, a desperate game if you like especially as I shall have to pay expenses; but nothing venture nothing have. . . . Trust me Nellie I'm going the right way for fortune, tho' the bluff is difficult, I'll bring it off. . . . Tell Gerald if his note has been discounted, the cash on it paid so if it is not met he'll be sued for it immediately; *but first get out of him the address of his rooms in Paris*; then scare him off to Cairo—there's fortune there for him and me. . . . *I'm in the saddle*; on false pretences if you like, but I'm there with spurs on.

By March 25 the whole thing had come to grief. "Partly because of Cohn's lies, partly owing to definite promises of monies not being

379

realized I had to come away and leave the *Paris Evening Telegram* as a derelict. I've seen Cohn twice—in Cannes and he says he'll ruin me and cash the promissory note of a friend which I backed for 100,000 francs and gave him. . . . Now I must write to Hunt at all costs and ask him to begin an action for obtaining money under false pretences against Cohn," he told Crowley. What had happened was that the owner, Cohn, had apparently promised Harris that he should take over the paper in installments, but before this arrangement could be put through, Cohn was persuaded that Harris was pro-German, whereupon he changed his conditions and demanded 100,000 francs.

Broken, Harris returned to his books. There he was, just on seventy, he wrote off to his disciples and admirers, praised by Shaw, Meredith, Wells and Bennett, fifteen to twenty books to his name, and he was unknown and positively disliked. "There is no such parallel for such ostracism."

By July 5 he had finished Volume II of *My Life and Loves*, "after a month of travail." If the wolf came to the door, he told Mencken, he'd read a chapter to it—that should scare it away. "The last three chapters are wonderful," he told Ben Rebhuhn, "and the *last* chapter all love, not passion merely or sex-urge but love that forgives all and more than all a great climax. . . . They can all say what they please: this book will put me with Shakespeare when I've finished. Don't laugh, for I'm crying I've been a year over it and the end felt bad." He was resolved to lead English literature out of "the prison of puritanism" and into the tradition of Chaucer and Shakespeare and so give it a chance of becoming the world literature, he wrote round to numerous people.[6] There were naughty stories and witty stories, stories of the court and the cesspool, gluttony, high thoughts and divine poetry, side by side with bawdy tales and smutty verses. It was the most sensational book he'd yet written, containing the intimate sex history of a dozen of his most famous contemporaries, describing sex thrills that he thought would make all other books appear dull, stale and flat. "Forgive the self-praise; it's genuine!"

Volume I, besides being seized by the censor, was now being pirated in various lands. "I have just read your life lent to me by a friend," wrote Austin Harrison, "and the only expression I can find is Gee!" And why in the name of Ireland, he wondered, those pictures

---

[6] Quinn replied dryly that he feared that Harris would find it even beyond his strength and willpower to lead English literature out "of the prison of puritanism."

of nude females? "Your book is so brutally candid that one is afraid to be seen with it," Francis Clark told him. Did Harris see the white hands of his "loves" stretched out to him when they touched him? How full of ghosts his life must be. The general opinion of the book, as voiced by Louise Hamilton, via Nellie, was that it was written by "an old man etc. and she was tired of defending him and his attitude." Gwladys Price Williams told Elmer Gertz that Nellie had read the manuscript of Volume I, chapter by chapter, and threatened to do everything under the sun if it were published. Just then she was spending a substantial amount of time away from Frank: "I must look for myself whilst I have time."

While she was away Aleister Crowley reappeared, in a worse state than ever. He was struggling with his own memoirs; he was short of money, with nothing left to pawn, and the hotel was just about to throw him out. As soon as he had the required funds he was going off to England to attack the *Sunday Express*. He had, he explained to Harris, been chosen by the gods to bring to earth the basic formula on which mankind would work for the next two thousand years; the Word had been dictated to him by an unseen personage in Cairo twenty years ago. Unfortunately, both he and Harris had made the mistake of trying to live the regular life of English gentlemen. This the gods would not allow, and were energetic in foiling all their plans with increasing severity—to wit, the recent fiasco with the *Paris Evening Telegram*. What Harris should do was to take Crowley's mission seriously and lend all his energies—which would then be renewed like the eagles—to establishing the Law of Thelma. Capitalism was heading down the cataract; the only alternative at present was bolshevism; the Law of Thelma would provide the third way. For the last years Crowley had been training various people to act as a brain for the human race; already he had a number of people, of some importance, interested. The whole idea of this proposed suit with the *Sunday Express* was to give the opportunity of proclaiming this law in such a way that it would attract all those who were ready to cut the painter and come out of the raving herd—a herd which, he explained under an asterisk, was comprised of the Elder Conklin's cows. He could assure Harris that the world was ready for this move; even the "successful" were sick to the heart of the hollowness of everything. The lawsuit would provide the necessary publicity, his opening and closing speeches would be prophetic, and Harris could make practical use of the situation and organize everything. "Do this and we shall not have lived in vain! . . . Please don't think my troubles have turned my brain," he added. "*Love* is the law." Up the side of the paper he appended lines of a sacred verse: "Come up through the creeks to the fresh water. I shall be waiting for you with my kisses."

"I need hardly assure you of my wish to help you," Harris replied carefully, "but I'm nearly powerless." It was his opinion that if Lord Beaverbrook had tried to bring such a libel against himself he would have found some powerful solicitor, who would go halves with him and make Beaverbrook pay; there should be $20,000 in such a libel action. As it was, he was biting his nails and correcting Volume II of his Life, which no one wanted; and he couldn't get it printed until he'd sold the German rights of his Shakespeare book. But he still had half a dozen American gargoyles up his sleeve and one or two "great portraits." Would he ever live to finish them?

CHAPTER 20

The Crucifixion

THE flat at Villa Édouard VII was arranged in a style to suit a messiah busy spreading his message. It was furnished with every sort of prop—statues, books, photographs, letters —so that Harris at any moment in any room might stretch out his hand and summon the ghosts from the past, crowding them round his visitors. Francis Dickie, who had written an article mentioning Harris favorably, has a fine description. The flat was entered by a long hall whose walls were lined with a wealth of literary treasures: etchings by Whistler, photographs of Shaw, Tolstoi and Maeterlinck, and autographed letters from Pater, Wilde, Carlyle and Emerson. The first night Dickie had met Harris was at the Villa Nell, where they were both guests at a dinner party. Harris quoted whole acts of Shakespeare, to the point of boredom. On the strength of his article Dickie was invited to dinner at the Villa Édouard VII. The library exuded a monastic air, with white walls and high ceiling, a huge crucifix and statues of six saints, four in marble and two in wood, which Harris explained were relics from the time of the *Expulsion de l'église*; he had managed to pick them up for very little in the houses of peasants.

His bedroom was something else again. Very large, with the walls gleaming white, covered with paintings of women in the nude arranged so that each was visible from the bed. Upon Francis Dickie's expressed admiration, his host moved to a drawer in the tallboy, and with the expression of a naughty boy, extracted an envelope. Here were photographs, each beautifully executed but very little different from any standard "dirty picture." Just before dinner the doorbell rang. A man was at the door to see Frank, who returned after ten minutes with a small canvas, a nude of a girl reclining provocatively on a cheap sofa—nice flesh tones, competently executed, but no masterpiece. Harris viewed it greedily, his "little eyes" burning. The artist, he explained, was a young painter friend of his—poor devil, desperately hard up, couldn't sell anything. "I just couldn't refuse to buy it when he had to have money to eat." When the bell had been answered Nellie turned to Dickie and confided to him disconsolately, "Another artist to borrow money, Frank gives away an awful lot of money." All evening, Francis Dickie said, Harris postured, thumbs in vest, throwing out his chest and arms, achieving height, reciting and telling again and again those stories he had written in his autobiography. Nellie again and again expressed concern that he was overworking. It was a fine performance by them both. "Do you think I have ever written a poor book?" Frank asked once with amazing fearfulness.

Back at the bank, funds were dwindling. Volume II, with its sex thrills and intimate stories of Harris' contemporaries, was seized at all frontiers and pronounced vile by the critics. "All the idiots condemn me," complained Harris. The book-packing industry continued disconsolately at Nice, he and his secretary, Miss Krim, parceling and camouflaging packets. Frantic letters sailed round the world to his agents and disciples by way of Germany and Canada, a bewildering complex of initials. To his team at the Frank Harris Publishing Company in New York, Einar Lyngklip and Ben Rebhuhn—who signed their letters among themselves "Your friend in Harris"—he would write letters like "My dear R. I cabled Miss T. not to send any more books to Mrs. M—: she sends me no money. . . . Please tell me how many copies you or L. have sent her to date. S. is selling his through Miss G." All the worry, he added, was making his digestion crack up; and he followed with intricate details of the greasy soup he had eaten and the amount of blood he had washed out. But India and China were beginning to order, he told his admirers, and friends wrote from Montreal suggesting they had found a way to smuggle the goods through a remote frontier post. At headquarters in New York, letters flowed in confirming all the obscene things their writers saw every day in the streets that endorsed the Master's words. If John Sumner could see some of the "many interesting letters" he would call the mounted police, Raymond Thomson told Elmer Gertz. One young man assured the members of the Frank Harris Publishing Company that if they would accompany him he could point out girls and women "frigging" themselves in public. It was, he declared, a common sight. Unfortunately, he lived too far away for them to avail themselves of the offer.

From France, Harris carried on his never-ending task of obtaining money. Matters were not resolved over the manuscript Harris had written for Lady Warwick, which he still held together with the typed copies of the Prince of Wales's letters. He had communicated with her none too politely in 1921 over the matter—at the same time as the wild plans involving the Queen of Romania were hatching—and Lady Warwick had been hurt by his tone. That *he* should think she had gone back on a friendship after all she had suffered because of it! *She* who all her life had been exploited and wrung dry by those she trusted—to be accused of spite and moneymaking. . . . She had *no* money; he had known she was poor six years ago, now she was absolutely finished. She had asked for the manuscript back because she wanted to reread it, erase half and renew their partnership. . . . She wanted to ponder over it and make suggestions; her copy was burned, as were all her letters and copies. He could have the lot back; he would see that they were valueless to her. She had a lot to add and a lot to suggest. When could they meet? She felt so bad over his letters she had no heart to write more. Nothing had materialized and now, through Grant Richards, it was agreed that while the £5,000—as stated in the contract—was not possible, he should receive £1,000. Even this apparently simple transaction could not be completed without a furore, with Harris informing everyone that Grant Richards and Lady Warwick together were out to swindle him. He had a book just coming out, he told Lady Warwick, on April 23, 1925, "to which I could easily add the whole story."

> I've just been swindled by **Grant Richards the English monocl'd publisher** in the most brazen way [he told Reggie Turner on May 10]. In 1914 I wrote with Lady Warwick her life with Prince (afterwards King) Edward: she promised me £5,000 for it but the war broke out and she could not pay. I could have sold the book plus the King's letters and letters from **W. W. Astor** again and again but Lady W. begged me not to so I refrained.

The other day she sent Grant Richards to get the book and letters from me: she gave me her acceptances spread over a year for £1,000 and he endorsed them. . . . When he returned to London he bargained with me for immediate cash; he promised me £750 down if I would send the bills. I sent them and he sent me £400 supplement. When I threatened him, a measly £50 more: meanwhile Lady Warwick assures me she gave him £750 to send to me 6 weeks ago so Grant Richards has come down to embezzling money.

Lady Warwick was not pleased by Harris' tone. "I really truly can't have letters of abuse from you," she wrote. She had written to him as she thought charmingly, but he couldn't think that she could allude happily to their unlucky enterprise. Promises of £5,000 could never materialize in 1925, and nobody cared for those Victorian experiences, nor did anyone have the money for such things. The world, she said, was saner and better and moving more quickly to the socialist state than either he or she had ever dreamed. "Your letter is hopelessly raging against me—an innocent person. Your friend and business adviser Mr. Grant Richards stated your terms and received the cheque from Mr. Payton and me . . . the cheque for £750 was handed to Mr. Grant Richards in *one* payment . . . at once. . . . What possible excuse have you to write to me as you have done?" She had matured, she said, during the tragedies of the past years: "Let us call Peace to the Past." The £750 that she had managed with great difficulty to raise amounted, she told him, to one-third of her whole personal income, and for a year she would have to exercise great restriction.

There was a second negotiation that year to end in bad feeling and discredit. Harris was anxious to publish his *Oscar Wilde* in England. Before he could do so matters had to be straightened out with Alfred Douglas, who, as the text stood, emerged the villain of the piece and would in all probability take legal proceedings. Harris proposed therefore to write a new preface, and correct the text by way of footnotes. First he needed to negotiate with Douglas, who was staying that summer in Nice with the Dayang of Sarawak, who describes her view of the affair in her book *Relations and Complications*. (Nellie in her turn describes the Dayang of Sarawak in her memoirs as a notoriously mean lady, providing a bar for the purpose of entertaining, but making people, especially men, pay for their drinks. That this is jotted down out of the blue, filed between an inventory comprising among other items "Louis XIV blankets," boot cupboards, tea tables, mosquito nets and works by Augustus John, Rowlandson, and Rothenstein, suggests that she had read *Relations and Complications* and did not care for it.)

Douglas had just served six months in Wormwood Scrubs, having libeled Winston Churchill. The food had been uneatable, the early hours and work intolerable. The whole experience had aged him ten years. The first night Douglas and the Dayang stayed up talking until three o'clock. The Dayang had seen Harris a number of times, she said; he had told her how anxious he was to repair some of the stories which he had believed from Robert Ross to have been true. Douglas jumped out of his chair and declared he would never see Harris, that he had used those lies against him, knowing just as well as he did that they were untrue, in order to sell the book. Harris began to storm the flat; the fortress however was impregnable. He asked the Dayang's cousin, Archie Craig, to lunch; he buttonholed her acquaintances, telling them how he had been misled, that what he had believed to be facts were lies. All this filtered in to the Dayang and Douglas as they sat in their fortress. Eventually Douglas agreed to meet Harris at the Negresco Hotel. At 2:00 P.M., said the Dayang, she passed through the lounge to call upon Isadora Duncan. Through some glass doors she beheld Douglas and Harris opposite each other speechless and bright red. Ultimately, however, it was agreed that they should carefully analyze the book and delete the untrue statements. Together they should write a preface, to bear a double signature, that would deal with each corrected point. For this purpose Douglas went off to stay at the Villa Édouard VII.

As a guest he failed to act in the manner to which his hosts were accustomed. He failed to appreciate the drives on which he was conducted, to recite poetry or to listen to Harris, to admire the views and the scenery. "I have honestly never passed such a day in my life," Nellie complained to her diary on May 9. "I am a wreck. I want to go to sleep and never see him again." That day there had been a long drive planned over some gorge to show the guest "what a heavenly place this is." The guest, however, was afraid to look into the gorge and made a great fuss. Nellie told her diary that she was dumbfounded—he took not a bit of notice of the scenery. Then the lunch was bad—"we couldn't help it we went to the best inn in the ville"—and Douglas chose the way home, a "Cook's route," very soothing, with every dangerous point protected. "The moment we began to go up my trouble began: Frank sat outside with the driver, Douglas sat inside, he raged, he stormed and swore that Frank and the driver wanted to drive him mad. I said 'Oh please don't this was especially arranged as a treat for you.' He kept on by the hour 'they want to drive me mad' and at length he said I prefer to go to prison for another 6 months, I came to the conclusion that I really was in a closed car with a lunatic and it continued for 6 hours. . . . When I tried to steal a look [at the scenery] he yelled, so I had to be sympathetic."

There is no doubt that Harris genuinely believed that he had maligned Douglas. "I've had Bosie Douglas staying with me for the last 3 weeks," he told Reggie Turner, "and he has fairly convinced me that Oscar lied about him even after he came out of prison and Robbie Ross whom I regarded as trustworthy confirmed Wilde's malicious lies." In another letter he wrote, "Robbie Ross was an ingenious liar for I never even suspected him of such an imaginative gift, and Oscar must have lied, with malice persistently for Bosie D. has proved large monetary gifts to him which he always denied."

Douglas, to begin with, seemed to have been reasonably happy about Harris' intentions and informed the Dayang of Sarawak that he thought he meant to do him justice; he also informed her, erroneously, that Harris had now married Nellie. Relations did not remain cordial for long. Harris sent the agreed-upon preface to Douglas in London, but it appeared to be quite different from what he had sanctioned in Nice. Harris was a beast, he told the Dayang; he had double-crossed him; he had done everything in his power to injure him and had repeated all the lies after apologizing for them. And Douglas published the preface as it had originally been written under the title, "The New Preface to *Oscar Wilde*."

> I want you to believe me when I tell you that Lord Alfred Douglas has behaved most shamefully to me [Harris told Esar Levine]. He got [me] to write a preface intended for my Oscar Wilde book, promised if I would publish it he would let me sell a few hundreds of copies, that I have on hand of the Oscar Wilde book already printed without interference. When I came to investigate I found out that several of his statements to me were false accordingly I rewrote the preface and sent him a copy explaining my alterations. He pretended to be furious with me, published the original false preface of mine without my permission while taking

back his promise to let the books go through. On this I wrote to him declaring that he was a "sneak-thief of the worst."

Meanwhile, the new preface was selling well, Douglas boasted. He had received a letter of frantic and comic abuse from Harris,[1] he told A. J. A. Symons, "which really caused me great amusement. He gives himself away so completely in his letter that it might have been dictated to him by his worst enemy. . . . I have had every copy of his book *The Life and Confessions of Oscar Wilde* cleared out of the country. In a few days more I would have been able to get them seized by the Police and destroyed, but as it is they have been sent back by his own agents to him in Nice."

Harris and Douglas were never reconciled, the row lasting until Harris' death—when Douglas had a mass said for him. Altogether, the saga of *Oscar Wilde: His Life and Confessions* is an ironic one. First it was Alfred Douglas who appeared to be the villain and liar; next it was Robbie Ross and the martyr Wilde himself; finally the author was to be accused of being a liar and villain by Sherard, and the whole book denigrated.

Now there was yet another row raging, this time over the car in which they had all driven out on that unhappy outing on May 9, 1925. It had been purchased apparently with money that had been borrowed from Alfred Tennyson, who was growing increasingly restive at financing the pleasure jaunts of Harris and his houseguests; "a fearful scene with Tennyson," Harris wrote in September to Nellie, who was, with Cappie, pursuing her singing career in Paris. Harris had invited him to lunch and given him a check for 2,100 francs, which was the interest on 30,000 francs. "On that he began about the motor car, said I was living on his money, shouted and went on like a maniac; till the Concierge came up—then he tore up the cheque and said I had lived off him, robbed him and he'd . . . I could not but laugh at him which made him wilder than ever. I never heard a man shout so, for nothing. . . . He's mad! But is there a method in this madness to

---

[1] Douglas apparently received one letter from Harris around the beginning of September 1925 that did not cause him amusement in the very least. Harris was so infuriated at the outcome of his preface maneuvers that he threatened to publish a letter that Douglas had sent him concerning his relations with Wilde during the three years before his conviction. He would be interested, he said, to see the effect that the letter would produce before a jury.

quarrel with me in order to get the 45,000 for which I gave him the note? I rather think that's the truth. . . . It was the car . . . that enraged him. What right had I to buy a car? With his money! He was disgusting and his teeth fell half out—never was there such a sight! I think he's going crazy!"

The next year or so passed in sickness, in suffering and in exercising the stomach pump. Volume II had been finished by his birthday, on February 14, 1925, which he informed everyone mistakenly was his seventieth. He was, he boasted, in perfect health—owing to his stomach pump—and celebrated his birth by running a hundred yards in fourteen seconds. By August, John Sumner had seized a thousand volumes at a New York bindery, while Volume I had been taken by the customs at Chicago, because of one of his helpers—"the Margolis woman"—bungling the business. This was doubly annoying; she was supposed to have been well used to smuggling, since her husband trafficked in illegal drugs. Some copies were burned, but some were sold by the customs at a profit, and they kept on turning up under counters at $10. Everyone, Harris believed, was in league to rob him. And then his "perfect health" failed him in Paris, and a bad attack of Parisian bronchitis coupled with anxiety left his hand very shaky—an affliction from which he never recovered. In the mornings he could hardly write, his hand trembled so. Nevertheless he started on Volume III, interrupting it to write his play on Joan of Arc.

Nellie spent much of that time away, singing, with Cappie, while her sister Aggie stayed with Frank, who was toying with the idea of bringing one of his daughters, Norah Stack, over to Paris to live with him. His letters, as Norah told Kingsmill years later, were more like a lover's than a father's. "Dear, dear Norah, little one mine" and "in Paris I'll make a place to meet worthy of you. I'm very proud of you, you dear sweet woman. Ever your tenderly affectionate and loving Frank." Meanwhile he and Aggie did not stint themselves. The wolf may have been at the door, but had he come in he would have dined off partridge—for there they were, Frank told Nellie, depressed, it was true, but eating partridges off two fine Empire plates and wishing that Nellie could have been with them. Nellie, however, stayed away and wrote that in her dreams the wart on Frank's eyebrow had turned bright red—a dream for which Frank did not care. For a short time he diverted his attention to nursing an ill dog that he called Bobbie. "I've seldom been more hurt for I found him in the garden and took him up to the flat and Aggie and I did our best with him but in vain: he whimpered pitifully and next day went the way of all flesh—poor neglected starved little brute!"

The future seemed darker and darker, he told Aleister Crowley with his shaking pen. He found it more and more difficult to write, plagued as he was by the anxiety about money. Yet admitting to poverty was a different matter when those abroad picked up rumors and wrote to sympathize. "Mr. Thomas is drawing on his imagination when he thinks I am suffering extreme poverty in Paris," he told Theodore Fraser on April 1, 1926. "I have never suffered poverty in my life, but I am harder up today than I have been since I was twenty, but still I have just done a new play on Joan La Romée which Max Reinhardt has asked for and which I think will give me a tidy capital."

Unfortunately, *Joan La Romée* too met rejection. There was nothing for it, Shaw believed, but for him to drop it into the wastepaper basket with a good-humored laugh and apologize to posterity for the surviving copies—although he did qualify his opinion by explaining that his health had cracked and he was a ruin.[2] Others believed it to be anti-English. "They lie," spluttered Harris. "It is written with the absolute reverence of the greatest human figure since Jesus the Christ. If that is anti-English so much the worse for the English."

To crown matters, the French were preparing to prosecute Harris and the second volume on a charge of corrupting public morals. The first volume was safe, since it had been printed in Germany, but, encouraged by the British government, which had taken exception to the account of the Lord Mayor's banquet and Fowler's evacuations, the French authorities drew up the case. Winston Churchill too, it appeared, objected to the revelation of his father's syphilis. "He seems to have forgotten altogether that I asked him whether he knew this and whether I might mention it and got his permission. . . . I take myself to be one of God's spies, and mean to tell the truth as I see it."

2 On May 20, 1926, Shaw wrote to Harris. Frank's making a drama of Joan had outraged his instinct, Shaw told him. He felt he must do something quite different, but he did not understand that the something was a short story and not another drama. The result was a shocking hybrid; why did he not throw it into the fire and write his story? He had emptied out the middle ages and the church and the Inquisition and the feudal system, reduced the subject to the story of a young Virginian female, a few dullards and a very modern American executive cheeking an English lord and snapping his fingers at the Holy Office—just like O. Henry, with the Harrisian style superimposed. Anatole France's had been the most absurd *gaffe* in modern literature until Harris had come along with his idiotic La Romée.

Several times "God's spy" had the doubtful pleasure of visits from the police, who appeared, armed with rifles, and had to be given drinks and a hundred francs.

The pending trial was a source of great entertainment to Hugh Kingsmill and Hesketh Pearson, who were amusing themselves by writing to each other about "Frankie" and trying to get him to write once more to Kingsmill. "I'm really too busy to waste more time on Hugh Lunn," Harris replied to Hesketh, much to his and Kingsmill's delight, "he hurt me so I cannot think of him with patience." To add to their pleasure, a lady from Ramsgate, Florence Smith, was writing to Kingsmill proposing that Harris should be smuggled out of Nice until the agitation had died down. Hesketh and Kingsmill waved their pens, wildly imagining Florence Smith in an enormous crinoline walking with stiff circumspection along the Promenade des Anglais with "Frankie" under the crinoline, "trying not to disconcert his accomplice by following the sweet way of love according to routine."

His disciples in America saw the trial as being of "deep significance." It dealt with a great book, they said, and a great man. They saw themselves defending freedom of speech. The Christ had come and had found the Way through flesh. Raymond Thomson wrote Elmer Gertz on October 27, 1926:

> The Master is surely the best guide through our modern life that we have, and we believe firmly, with you, that it is our generation and the generation before ours, that must be enabled to hear and learn of him, rather than the men and women of the older generation whose characters are formed and whose minds are made up. As lovers he puts most of us to shame. His genius is the genius of love, as it was of Jesus. It seems that Jesus matured in his mother's womb and was born with a spirit already in the heights. . . . For this reason it must have been that he gave so little importance to sensual life. . . . But the Master supplies the missing chapters. He was endowed with the ordinary human nature in an extraordinary degree, with the added power of a quite infallible and instinctive sense of direction towards the comparatively better; the sense which has been poetically called "the finger of an on-ward pointing God" . . . he has won and made plain the wisdom and the way; that through the body lies the way to the spirit that was Jesus. The delightful extract from a letter that the young woman sent to you seems to show, as one would expect, that women are quicker to recognize the truth about the Master's example than men.

Harris himself was busy receiving a substantial postbag.[3] People wrote to him of their marriages, their gluttony for women, their self-hatred, their homosexual leanings; lesbians wrote about their friends. One lady called Ruth carried on a bedroom correspondence, of which several pages are missing. She imagined "Boy dear" just getting into bed, she felt his warm body pressing against her—"and at that moment you'll make me yours forever"; her body would grow hot, she would become mad with desire. "I'll want to touch your sex with my hand to see if it is stiff with desire and then I'll want to touch your body with my lips—but first your mouth." The letter continued in this vein: the whole body was visited, each orifice investigated and lubricated in the proper Harrisian manner, while the pleasure mounted and kisses crisscrossed the paper.

More and more Harris' life was a paper one. His health deteriorated, he became shakier, his body was racked with convulsive hiccups, his memory for names departed completely, and as a final straw, the car burst a pipe on an uneven paving stone and let out all the petrol.

The silver went in and out of pawn as regularly as clockwork,[4] and the grippe and phlebitis continued into 1927. "It is strange that when I heard from you last you had been ill and I was well," he told Shaw on April 3. "Since then I have come to grief. I caught grippe early in December and had convulsive hiccoughings with it. As soon as I got well, I went out for walks and took my usual exercise and was soon astonished by the swelling of the veins of my right leg which

[3] Nellie records in her diary that some time after Harris' death she enjoyed cocktails and lunch with Frieda Lawrence. She told her how the girls worried Frank, because they expected him to live up to the reputation he had given himself. Nellie used to go off shopping and leave Frank with all the adoring females. She would return after about an hour and a half, and Frank would rush out the moment he heard the door open and say, almost in tears, according to her: "Why did you leave me with that awful bitch? For God's sake come in and get rid of her." "Frank, you love it," Nellie would say; then he would go up to the ceiling. Nellie and Frieda Lawrence nodded together over their sexy husbands. Mrs. Lawrence said she had suffered similarly over the publication of *Lady Chatterley's Lover*, saw herself besieged by an army of Ruths, Peggies and Bessies, with their filthy letters—far filthier than anything either Frank or D. H. Lawrence had ever written. It was particularly the virgins, they agreed; and Frieda Lawrence and she also agreed that they should write an article for the *Ladies' Home Journal* giving their version of what they had suffered in trying to save their poor men.

[4] Mappin and Webb had a case of silver deposited with them by Nellie on July 26, 1927, which came out again on February 18, 1929; it comprised silver teapots, sugar basins, dented cream jugs, bottle stands, jam-pot mounts, pepper pourers, ashtrays, inkstands, crumb scoops, asparagus scoops and an electroplate cake service.

turned out to be phlebitis. So I am for the last 3 months compelled to keep my leg supported high up, and to pass all my time in bed or on a sofa. . . . You are honoured and famous and rich—I lie here crippled and contemned and poor." Even Shaw's writing had stood up, while Harris' wobbled across the page like an old man on sticks.

In spite of his infirmity, his wild plans would never cease—wild plans to rush off to the Rio Grande with a thousand copies of his autobiography, meet Ben Rebhuhn "and get them in"; to travel to Windsor, Canada, with three hundred, then on to Detroit. "You have no idea how we've suffered: my wife has pawned everything even her watch to keep us going"; he was bent, if not broken. But to straighten him, there were plans to lecture on "great personalities," in Chicago, New York and Philadelphia. He was going to put a politician, a prose writer and a poet in each lecture and throw in for good measure a few worthies—King Edward, Queen Victoria and President Wilson—"to bring the audience from heaven to earth." He hoped that Einar Lyngklip might accompany him as a sort of businessman. By the end of March, Esar Levine had been imprisoned for trafficking in obscene books, and Harris was accusing everyone of muddling the editions and refusing to send him any money, and the disciples were telling themselves that it was unlikely that the Master would come—he was still sofa-ridden—and it seemed likely too that he would be imprisoned on landing. When someone called Frankel wrote telling him that his goose was cooked in America until the smell of his autobiography died out he was furious. "Disgraceful," he blustered; there was no more smell about his autobiography than there was about *Hamlet*. However, although the prosecution had been dropped in France—mainly because of petitions both in England and France signed by numerous men of letters—the English were opening his letters, photographing them and sending police inspectors round to all his friends, forcing them to give up the books he had sent them.

In the middle of April, Harris received an unexpected visit from Kingsmill, who was determined that Frankie should not die without his catching another glimpse of him. He related the episode with relish to Hesketh.[5] It was a bright, sunny day as he set out with his friend John Holms from Menton. "Have in mind the blue Mediter-

[5] Michael Holroyd is anxious that it should be pointed out that Kingsmill did not go to visit Harris solely in order to write funny letters to Hesketh. He was at the time making his final notes for his good essay "Frank Harris," in *After Puritanism*.

ranean, the blue sky, palms, barren mountains, pleasure palaces and all the other things which make the Riviera so unspeakably repulsive." In Nice they took a taxi to the Villa Édouard VII, where they saw a car about to leave. Therein sat Frank Harris and Mrs. Harris. Kingsmill confessed that his nerve failed for a few minutes. Both the Harrises had noticed him, and Holms, who had been observing Harris closely, said that his face became tense. As Kingsmill advanced, the car began to move. Kingsmill held up his hand; it stopped, and he wondered if the Harrises might have any objection to his calling some time that day. Harris looked bemused and said "surely," at five o'clock. Mrs. Harris said that Frank would not be back at five o'clock. Frank said that he would; Mrs. Harris that he wouldn't; Frank that he would. Five o'clock was decided upon. The car moved on and there seemed to Kingsmill that there came from it an explosion of hate. He ran after it, and Harris told him that he hadn't recognized him, partly owing to his having aged and partly because of his own failing memory. Mrs. Harris again expressed her certainty that he wouldn't be back at five o'clock; no one took any notice.

At five o'clock he returned to the villa and was at once admitted to the sitting room, where he and Harris grasped each other by the hand; Mrs. Harris was there and endeavored to convey a mixture of remorse and incipient desire in her gaze. There too was a man from Liverpool called Hooton, whose soul was just beginning to ferment, "who was fain to pasture on Harrisian meads" and who had apparently traveled to Nice only to see Harris. Frank moved over to sit by Kingsmill, at which Mrs. Harris immediately ordered him back to his own chair and told him to put his legs up; he obeyed and his legs were covered with rugs. He then discussed at reasonable length his phlebitis, inscribed volumes of autobiography and *Contemporary Portraits* for Hooton and settled down to a two-hour monologue on Bottomley, Churchill, Hooley, Shaw, Bennett and Wells. "It was very pleasant to see the old villain again, but it all seemed unreal," Kingsmill concluded.

Four months later Harris had started work on another volume of autobiography, and, between pages, got busy dyeing his moustache, which was, he told Nellie, *fiercely black*: "I laugh at myself." On September 22, aged eighty-eight, Emily Harris died. Three weeks later, on October 15, Frank married Nellie in the American Church. At the age of seventy-one he was a bridegroom for the third time. The belief that he was Jesus was by now so embedded that he recorded in the register that his mother's name was Mary Vernon, confused no doubt with Mary the Virgin.

A month later he was in Berlin lecturing on Shaw, Shakespeare and Frank Harris. The newspapers for November 8 and 9 were full of praise for him. People were not bored during the evening, reported the *Tägliche Rundschau*—they passed most interesting hours with this "tall, skinny man" with drawling speech and demeanor. He was well received, especially when he chose to get his own back on Shaw for being celebrated and in good health, while he was rejected, infirm and crippled with disappointment. There was much talk of Wilde's incomparable wit and Shaw's total lack of any. Shaw had only appearance and affectation, Harris assured his audience; he had come to London at nineteen, and for years had not fallen in love—"*he is no poet whose soul is silent.*" The Berliners were delighted. Shaky and half-blind as he was, the papers reported, he had the freshness of youth. To mark the German translation of his books there was a reception given at the Lessing Hochschule. All "the best-known personalities of public and official life" stood to receive him. Over all these attentions, a spokesman from the office of the Lessing Schule told Elmer Gertz, Mr. Harris became most astounded and overjoyed. To brace himself "he allowed alcohol—which during this entire time he had been imbibing in no mean amounts—to be served." For luncheon two bottles of heavy twenty-one-year-old Rhine wine were drunk by him, and before the lectures, during the lectures, and after the lectures he was accustomed to brace himself with straight whisky from his silver flask. He did not, Elmer Gertz's correspondent told him, "ordinarily allow the other pleasures of the Big City to pass by unenjoyed." One of the pleasures of the "Big City" was a girl called Erika Lorenz, with whom he corresponded on his return to Nice and whom he eventually persuaded to come and be his secretary—much to the anger of Nellie.

His letters to Rita—as he called Erika—written partly in German and partly in English, show how Harris lived through other people. This affair, feeble as it was, sparked off a momentary flash of life; a letter meant hope, silence meant death. "Wretched, lonely, sorrowful and deserted," he wrote on his return to Nice,

> I went in today to the Express Co and got your wire. Straightway the clouds lifted, the sun shone and my heart came into my mouth:

I was myself again: but you mustn't do this Rita, it's wrong of you, and one of these days, you'll be sorry for it. Love, as I told you is a plant of tenderest growth; treat it well, take thought for it and it may grow strong and perfume your whole life. But treat it carelessly, leave it a whole week without a word and suddenly when you want it, you'll not find it. I've had four dreadful days: when you did **not** write, I turned again to my work, and lost my loneliness in labor; but even now I can't forgive you entirely: I had put you on a pedestal—high above ordinary woman: but now I'm no longer so sure of you. Yes, you've big . . . passion in you and a love of truth; but you can't love me as I thought you did, or you would not have left me 8 days without a word. There's something in you I don't understand and cannot make out. . . . There are some men that neglect or coldness seem to excite; but I have always been made much of, always had the desire of perfection in me—in my work and my life. I was so proud of you and your self-sacrificing devotion; but now you've made me doubt. Quick, quick, I want your explanation and can only pray it may be completely satisfying. Already I excuse you: you are so young and you push me from you: you will not give yourself completely to me—you child! But Rita mine, you must never make me suffer as I've suffered in this last week: I'm too proud, too old to endure it. I've made all sorts of blunders in these 8 days: I've offended old and tried friends, could not listen to them or show interest in their troubles; I was wounded to the soul, what did their petty troubles matter to me wounded to the soul. No letter yet. Wednesday 14th. None since 4th ! ! ! ! ! ! ! Mean child.

For Christmas she sent him a photograph, but still no letter. He continued the fuss. She had given so freely, so nobly in Berlin; now there was nothing. There he was, reading about the love of Wagner that had inspired the music of *Tristan*; he could beat Wagner's "word expressions," Harris said, but not the lyrical passion of the music. But the next volume of his life would hold the eternal image of Rita's love in "its boldness and its strange modesty." "The boldness of my passion shall be there too: I want it to be a monument to you so that people a hundred years hence will write of you." He was dreadfully frightened that she wouldn't like this " 'Life' of mine," that the amorous incidents would shock her. "They seem so numerous, but if you think that the half dozen in the first volume are spread over 12 and 14 years they will not seem so frequent. And of all of them there is not one that counts and means so much as my meeting with you and your love beautifies and ennobles my life as nothing else has ever done. . . . It is for this reason partly that I beg you to write oftener and more from your heart."

By February 6 she had arranged the date of her arrival in Nice— to coincide with Nellie's April business trip to New York. She was not to be frightened, Frank told her in German. She could count on him and his love, of course. He was hers body and soul, and even if it would cost his life he would be willing to die for her. If only he were ten years younger—Oh God! how he wished he were! She had no idea how he loved her. She was his only possession, his treasure. She was so brave, he longed for her, her presence was essential. "Tell me all your business affairs," he urged her. "I only wish I could help you in every way . . . the money to come to Nice naturally I will send you but if you want more, let me know please. I want to make you happy, soul-contented and joyful. Can I do that? I'm going to try my best. . . . I want to enrich your life, *to be a blessing to you as you have been to me.*"

Leaving Frank, Aggie and Cappie all with nasty coughs, Nellie arrived in America on April 17, 1928, and stayed in the Woodstock Hotel. She felt lonely and terribly sad, she told her diary, much as she loved New York and was glad to see it all again; all the time she had a tearing in her heart, worrying how Frank was getting on with his leg. This anxiety is recorded just before she launched into a tremendous dissertation against Erika Lorenz, who had traveled to Nice on April 10. In New York, Nellie says, she received a telegram from Frank telling her that every day was a year long and to hurry home. She worked hard, she says, and visited the Frank Harris Publishing Company, where all were agog to see the Master's wife. Her performance of devoted wife of a crucified genius was clearly impressive, or anyway to Raymond Thomson, who was quick to pass on descriptions and anecdotes both of her and the Master to Elmer Gertz, waiting in Chicago. She had, he said, a sympathetic gaze through confiding large eyes, a beautiful voice, low and clear, full of caressing, appealing modulations. Her face was marked with care and anxiety, and her eyes left a deep impression. After writing a story, she said, Frank was always greatly depressed and felt that he had failed to "transcribe the conception." The act of poetry was an orgasm, Raymond Thomson explained, making the word flesh, and he felt an abrupt letdown. It was not long after this that the entire Frank Harris

Publishing Company felt an abrupt letdown; that April, John Sumner raided five bookshops within a week. Thomson and Ben Reuben were arrested, and the Frank Harris Publishing Company prudently changed its name to The Rare Book Case.

Business matters settled satisfactorily, Nellie set sail for the Villa Édouard VII, which she found "topsy turvy." Aggie had departed, so had Harris' previous secretary, the maid was discharged, and Erika Lorenz was installed. Was such a muddle possible, Nellie asked herself, since she had been away only for a month? After three or four days she told her diary that life under such conditions was not worthwhile—there she was making sacrifices, and they were taken without a thought; "in fact he was so used to it that it counted nothing." And she came to the conclusion that no person, man or woman, however great, was worth sacrificing oneself for.

> I have come to this conclusion after years of trying and hoping, it's like pouring water down a sink. . . . I restored order to the house and then told Frank I would stand no more—I was fed up —He said, I was hoping you would like the woman. She is such a good secretary. I said out of my house she might be all he wished and desired, but in my home nothing doing. . . . He swore—that I was mistaken, he had never met her in Germany, she was not the woman. . . . The funny thing is he is always so terribly exigent for looks. . . . What can it be? She is to say the least very plain, and ordinary looking. She flatters him and his work—it doesn't matter what he writes or has written she ladles in praise, without discrimination, its the greatest stuff that ever was etc. etc. He loves all this and cannot see that its false. She does not understand English enough to tell whether its good or well written, still he always loved flattery and now he's got it.

To Aggie she wrote: "Frank's secretary works hard—Frank wants her back, working after dinner, he asked me what I thought of her; I said she looked like a sack tied up in the centre, he said she is very clever, she's very plain but quiet."

That spring Frank had received two other female visitors—Nan O'Reilly, traveling with Rose Meyers. Encouraged by Nan O'Reilly's husband, Silas Newton, an admirer of Harris', they made an appointment to meet Harris, who had written to say he could spare one and a half hours, four o'clock to five-thirty, at which time he must meet some friends. At nine-thirty that night, Nan O'Reilly told Elmer Gertz, she and her companion finally "prevailed upon him to let us get him some dinner." He was such a wonderful talker, so interesting, that time had flown for all concerned. During his wonderful talk he had said, with tears in his eyes, that his one ambition before he died was to return to America without being imprisoned. He knew this to be impossible; the authorities would have him thrown into Sing Sing on arrival. Nan O'Reilly told him that Silas Newton, a man of influence and wealth and one of his most ardent admirers, would be able to arrange this, and would be even more inclined to do so when he learned that Frank had a lecture tour all lined up in Chicago—thirty lectures at $1,000 each. The money was ready and waiting if only he could land. Mr. Newton was a businessman, Nan O'Reilly told Elmer Gertz; he had figured that Harris had not yet outlived his usefulness. How much would it cost Frank to travel round the world? he wanted to know. Five thousand dollars, Frank thought. Newton said that things had changed, being more expensive than they had been when Frank had been a boy. Frank said $6,000, whereupon Newton proposed to finance him on a trip not to exceed $10,000, after the lecture tour. In return Newton asked that Frank should turn in any writing he did as a result of the tour, and he would print and advertise it.

The summer passed stormily. Frank dictated away to Erika, telling of his fictitious sex experiences in India, China and Japan, but often his fantasies faltered and did not flow easily. And then there were rows with Nellie. "I can't write—another row!" he wrote in a very shaky hand on June 17. "I am unhappy and the money does not come in—I must see you for a long talk one of these afternoons—do forgive me—it is not all my fault—I am working for the future but whether I shall succeed or not I can't say yet! Let us hope—you are so dear and so good! Thanks from my heart. Meanwhile help me to finish my work dear."

There were brief respites when someone would come to lunch or dinner and Harris could forget himself and perform again for his audience. On August 21 Nellie recorded in her diary that Shaw lunched. It was all very gay, full of laughter and salacious stories: "fireworks going all the time, I mean fireworks of wit."

By the middle of the summer Harris was thinking of moving house once more. He wrote off to Newton with this in mind asking for $1,000. Newton replied acidly that he was not interested in Harris' rent; his funds were for the purpose of traveling. Harris replied that he could not get tickets without money; besides, he needed to pay the rent. Newton sent $1,000. On October 22 the Harris household moved from Villa Édouard VII to 9 Rue de la Buffa. The packing had gone on for several months. Harris, with his impatience, his untidiness, his mess of books and papers, made the greatest difficulties, but at last everything was arranged; and without warning he telegraphed to the Newtons that he was arriving on November 10 aboard the *Albert Ballin.*

Newton meanwhile had had an appalling time rushing backward and forward to Washington to obtain special permission to go to the quarantine department and get Harris safely into the country. He also had to rush through the proceedings of buying a new house in order to take care of Frank and Nellie, who, uninvited it seemed, were expecting to stay with them—indeed, Nellie had not expected to make the trip at all. They were treated from the start, said Nan O'Reilly, like royalty. There was a car at their disposal, a visit from the family doctor every day, their laundry and chemist's bills were paid, Christmas presents provided, pocket money supplied, and a bottle of wine a day set on a table where never before had there been served anything at all in the way of alcohol.

Harris had come off the boat in a long sealskin coat, with a healthy, broad smile spread over his face. He nodded slowly round. "Hello everyone," he cried. "Hello." On land he threw his arm round Tobin's shoulders, assured everyone that he thought he'd never get off the boat alive, and, according to Tobin, tipped his steward $5,000. It was clear from the start, said Nan O'Reilly, that Frank was in no condition to make a tour. He was an ill man, unable even to hold a spoon or cup to his mouth.

In spite of this disability he could make his way most days to a speakeasy and have long and vociferous lunches, holding his disciples spellbound; and one, at least—Abe Tobin—ate and drank with one hand while with the other recording faithfully the conversation in shorthand, word for word, all of which is contained in the unpublished volume "Table Talks with Frank Harris." The excitement had been intense among the disciples before the Master had arrived. Tobin had been rushing round in his white dentist's coat, Leo Rosten remembered, beside himself. To him even the air seemed different after Frank had landed, charged with electricity. Newton was not at all keen on Abe Tobin, who kept arriving at the house, secreting forbidden volumes of *My Life and Loves*, which Frank then sold privately. Since at the time Newton was engaged in several lawsuits on Harris' behalf, and was instituting third-party claims against Mitchell Kennerley and Brentano's, he saw no reason why he should have Tobin in the house as well, and he told Frank so. Long before he set sail once more for Nice Harris had fallen out with his hosts. With him Frank had brought a collection of his most valuable letters and manuscripts. On these, Nan O'Reilly said, he demanded a loan of $25,000. Newton, however, declared that the letters were not worth a penny to him. Harris stormed and raved and ranted and refused to speak to Newton for several days—while remaining in the house, eating at his table and spending his money. Furthermore, said Nan O'Reilly, he informed his host that he owed him $10,000, since he had promised him that amount. He was quite incapable of realizing that his failure to go round the world made any difference to the arrangement. It was a misunderstanding all round. Newton believed firmly that the trip was a business matter, while Harris dismissed any question of world tours, and knew himself to be on a pleasure trip to see his disciples and that it was the duty of Newton to support him.

When Tobin was not smuggling in illicit copies of *My Life and Loves* he was hurrying round to the Brevoort Hotel to collect Harris' private postbag—which once fell into Nellie's hands, causing a terrible row—or to dispatch telegrams to Erika Lorenz; then he would conduct him to the speakeasy where the Master delivered what was to be his last public performance before an admiring circle. Tobin noted it all down: the faint gestures that finished what he left unsaid, the dropping of the voice, the look, the lifting of the eyebrows, the amount of sugar he had in his coffee, the alcohol he added from his flask, how he poured wine all over the tablecloth, the terrible time he had spearing his lamb cutlets, how very noisy he was even over such things as opening a cupboard to get out Nellie's hat. Leo Rosten, for his part, had been fascinated by Frank's swarthiness against Nellie's creaminess, his air of a stallion. He seemed incredibly romantic, with his great voice that came out of the bottom of his lungs. At one lunch he told a story of Hardy at a reception given for *Tess of the d'Urbervilles* in which he incorporated one of his favorite *mots*. "My Gahd, Harrrdy," he told them he had said, "that woman must have had a cunt the size of a horse collar." Nellie smiled vaguely round the table looking fey and distant, ignoring such coarseness, Leo Rosten said, very much "the lady." Tobin meanwhile was examining her minutely, noting down the roundness of her bosom. When she used cosmetics, he declared, she did not look more than thirty-five, but her heavy, slow walk, her choice of dark corners in the restaurant betrayed her. She was slim, but not thin. Her arms and the upper part of her body were beautifully molded, the curve of the chin to the throat swanlike. She loved clothes and longed for them. Her sister-in-law worked in a "fancy underwear" factory. Tobin gave her a lovely pair of knickers with a pocket for mad money. She was, in his view, ungrateful—not only about the knickers—and inclined to be surly and sour, and because of *My Life and Loves* was constantly embarrassed by indecent proposals. Harris, said Tobin, had confided his life's motive to him: to satisfy women as much as himself. Thank heavens, he had joked, he did not have lock-jaw.

The first of the lunches had not started well. Harris was hungry and they had to wait until ten to two for three ladies who were late. Harris ranted and raved about how everyone was cheating him. "Just wait until Frank has had some wine and you'll see how nice he can smile," Tobin recorded that Nellie assured the gathered company. Sure enough, upon the appearance of a quart bottle of Chablis, his voice improved, mellowed like a violin, and he was able to kick up his usual scene when the waiter was unwise enough to pour the new bottle into old glasses. When a blonde passed he peered hard. "Is she fair?" he asked Nellie. Nellie assured him that she was not. He was not able even to walk down the road without some mishap. That day his flask dropped through the lining of his pocket. "Oh, oh, oh," yelled Harris. Tobin feared that he had sprained his ankle. They managed to wrestle with the coat and extract the flask. In the bank there was another scene. The man said that he could not change foreign money. At once Harris flew into a rage. "What stupidity," he bellowed. "I think I'll write them up a bit. That will serve them right." Next he disliked the exchange rate. "Robbers," he bellowed. "Bloody robbers." Outside he was all meek and mild again and on another tack, taking Mrs. Tobin's hand and patting it. "Ah! Mrs. Tobin, it has been a pleasure indeed for me to have met you. I must come to your home to see the kiddies," Tobin remembered that he said, and he kissed her hand, took off his hat and bowed like a cavalier.

Harris was clearly delighted and flattered by Tobin. Anyone who thought him wonderful and intelligent had the compliment returned. "I must put in writing what I have told you at our last meeting," he wrote. "There is no one I ever met who understands me and my writings as well as you do and I want to urge upon you now, as I have done before, that you write the book about me and my works."

The Harrises returned to France in the middle of January. For a few days Frank dictated to Erika Lorenz as he had not dictated for a long time, but the excitement and the movement had been too much for him, and he fell seriously ill with influenza and an attack of hiccups that lasted eight days and nights. "My God I hear them in my dreams," Nellie wrote to Tobin. The New York papers carried reports that he was unlikely to recover. While he lay ill Nellie extracted a promise from him that he would do no more work on the autobiography and that he would hand to her all existing typescripts. Miss Lorenz was bundled back to Germany. Before she left she sent a sad little letter to Nellie, who, she said, had accused her of interfering with her life. This she had never done. All the time she had known that "Mr. Harris" had really loved and cared for Nellie. Even when she'd seen him off at the station in Berlin he had jumped, really jumped, when he saw the train and had run down the platform crying, "Oh I am so glad to go home." When poor sacklike Miss Lorenz had seen Nellie for the first time she had gone very quiet and had said to herself, "She knows that she is beautiful and sees that you are ugly." This, she told Nellie, was not flattery, she was far too sad. The sympathy they had had between them was quite apart from "Mr. Harris'" and Nellie's life. "I learned in my life that one is only happy if one can give but happier still if there is somebody who wants to take what one can give." She had never dreamed of inspiring "Mr. Harris" but had recognized that her letters were important to him. If "Mr. Harris" had been able to work better in America than in Nice, Erika Lorenz said, then she was only too glad; he had been in a dreadful state before his departure, unable to dictate one page.

When Frank eventually recovered he was convinced that poor Erika Lorenz too was swindling him. She was one of the worst women in the world, he informed Tobin, had vanished with nine or ten months' work on the fourth volume—nearly a year of his best work hopelessly lost. He wrote abusing her. Her reply was brief and concluded that she was replying, anyway, only on behalf of Mrs. Harris, that she would not answer any other letters from him. Another friendship was finished.

Nan O'Reilly too had fresh cause for complaint. When Frank had been ill Nellie had cabled: "In God's name have pity on me, am desperate." Silas Newton had cabled back $500 and had never received a word of thanks. By June, Harris was convalescent enough to complain that Newton was not selling his letters and was claiming that he owed him money. Poor Nellie was bustled back to New York that autumn to retrieve the letters. Again, Nan O'Reilly reported, she stayed in the house for five or six weeks. This time she had fallen down on the boat and hurt her knee, and the doctor came to attend her. As for the letters, Nan O'Reilly explained, the Newtons kept them so that Nellie would have something to fall back on after Frank's death. Silas Newton had offered at one stage to return them providing Harris would write a book on them. He figured that, since so many people insisted that Frank could not possibly have known all the celebrities to whom he laid claim, he could prove himself by writing a book, reproducing the letters and writing a little sketch concerning each man, how he had met him and the occasion for letter writing. Later the papers, Nan O'Reilly said, were all turned over to Arthur Leonard Ross, Harris' executor, from whose hands they passed to the University of Texas at Austin.

Sometime around 1929 one of Harris' admirers, G. S. Viereck, visited him. They had met and corresponded before Harris had left America for the "Winepots of France," and Viereck's portrait was included in the fourth series of *Contemporary Portraits*. Now Viereck, who would have liked to have lived in a world created by Harris, was sniffing Europe. He describes his visit to the Master in glowing colors in his *Glimpses of the Great*.

He arrived at a party, where Harris was being entertained, at a suitably lush moment. The sun was dipping into the ocean, he said, the hills and water were red, the tide was softly caressing the rocks, and Viereck saluted the sunset with cocktails. Harris was carrying on, in resonant accents, upon the theme of cruelty. Nature had given man over a hundred organs for pain and hardly any for pleasure. Now, had he been God, he would have done just the opposite. He would have given a hundred organs for pleasure and one, or perhaps two, for pain as a warning to protect life. What is the meaning of life? asked Viereck and his young companions, awe-inspired. Harris looked at Nellie. The sea was in her hazel eyes, said Viereck. The sunset endowed her hair with metallic luster. "I am doubtful," Harris pronounced, "whether life has any meaning." "What," asked Viereck, "is the meaning of life after seventy?" "The meaning of life after seventy," responded Harris, apparently in the manner of the catechism, "is to me exactly the same as the meaning up to seventy, except that the pains and disabilities increase and the pleasures diminish." Praise, like food, had always been a help to him, he added; what he loved was ease and a certain dignified luxury.

Harris' health was now poor, he had a moist, vitreous stare, his voice was a muffled whisper, wheezing in his larynx—gone were the bellows of yesteryear. His breath whistled through his throat and his mirth turned into a fit of explosive coughs enough to scare everyone out of the room.

In 1930, as a last coup, Harris contracted to write the biography of Shaw. He busily sent round a circular to friends and critics. "I don't want people saying later when it is published 'But you should have put in my story of Shaw' or 'Why did you leave out this postcard I got from him?' So I am hereby warning all such critics to send me their stories, quips, inscriptions, autographs, photographs, postcards, letters, telegrams, cables, interviews and such now, or forever hold their peace"; and he busily sent off lists of questions to his subject. "You really are a 'daisy,' " Shaw replied on January 18, 1930. He had put six questions to him, replies to which would be a book, about a year's work, which he would then decorate with nonsense about impulses and resolutions and high purposes and all the rest of the literary junk. No. He would not have him write his life on any terms—Nellie would do it better. He had made Shakespeare a cross between a sailor in a melodrama and a French criminal. What he would make of him God knew; he must drop it. Frank was undaunted; he did not drop it, and Shaw continued writing letters, gloomily putting in small pieces of information here and there, all the while assuring Harris that he would make either a ghastly mess of the biography or a conventional affair that would do nothing to his reputation. On September 18 Shaw noticed that Simon and Schuster were advertising that the biography was authorized and contained 15,000 words by him. Shaw had written denying this; furthermore, if Harris published one word of his, he would have the law upon him. That letter threw Harris into a terrible state.

"Think of it, Shaw, and put yourself in my place for a moment. I wrote to you again and again asking for special informations on special points. You sent me those informations. Naturally I incorporated your letter in my book and now you tell me if I use a word of yours you will have the law on me, if you don't, your publishers will. What am I to do? I cannot re-write the whole book. I have received the money for some of it already. . . . Think Shaw, I have never sought to injure or hurt you, on the contrary I have done what I could to show you kindness. Why should you hurt me in this way?" And Shaw relented: he would see him through with plenty to quote, he said.[6]

With Shaw's biography, Frank Scully hobbled onto the scene.

Frank Scully, who died on June 25, 1964, was a journalist who during the last thirty years of his life endured forty operations for heart conditions, cancer, tonsils and shrapnel wounds. His literary works included *Fun in Bed, What Made Alexander Great* and *Behind the Flying Saucers.* The last claimed that flying saucers were real and came from Venus controlled by magnetic force; the critics were not impressed. It was Scully who, being Nice correspondent for a theatrical paper at the time, was responsible for American and London papers printing long tributes on the death of Harris—some years before he died. Not only did Scully claim that he was the literary wizard behind the Shaw biography[7] and the author of Harris' letters to Shaw, which Harris signed, but also that he had written *On the Trail*, telescoping several incidents and sticking on a middle and an end. After this, he said, he started work on the Shaw—which he dedicated to himself—with a view to turning the 10,000-word portrait that appeared in the second series *Contemporary Portraits* into 60,000 words. The two of them made a pretty crew, as described by Scully: Harris groggy with hiccups, a host to phlebitis, neuralgia, rheumatism and bronchial asthma, and himself on what he called "hospital status," with "five suppurating sinuses after an amputation of my right leg." They packed their bags against a journey to Vittel in the Vosges mountains and proceeded thither loaded down with all the stuff ever written about Shaw, the Harrises making a fifteen-hour taxi journey while the

---

6 Although Shaw disliked "begging letters" he was not ungenerous. When Frank died he sent Nellie a check, and he saw her through the proofs of the book, correcting and cutting. Later, in 1938 when she was in a desperate financial state, so that she could get some money for the book, he wrote an introduction to *Oscar Wilde*, in spite of Douglas, Sherard and Kingsmill, who all tried to interfere.

7 *Rogues' Gallery.*

Scullys advanced by train. The hotel that had been selected by Harris' latest secretary was not only on the "wrong side of the tracks" but was situated twenty feet from where all the manure and freight trains backed and pulled all day, starting at six in the morning. To make matters worse, the hotel had the most dreadful ear-splitting gong. The Harrises' taxi arrived in pouring rain, and immediately Frank set to ordering cognacs and soda against his ague. For five days Frank was there shivering, Scully said, and pinching any bottom within his grasp. Then he decided to return by train to Nice. Scully remained in the rain, writing. There in Nice Harris sat peering at badly typed script. His memory was nonexistent. Every time he read something it was new to him. Twenty-five thousand pounds arrived for him, said Scully, in Vittel. Scully forwarded it and received in return £39 rather than the £500 he had expected. However, more interested in art than money, he claimed, he worked on feverishly and eventually reappeared in Nice after a hazardous journey, conveyed by a crazy driver who managed to dislodge the trunk containing all the manuscripts and source books, which, before it could be retrieved, had been hit hard by a car coming the other way. In Nice the working hours left much to be desired. At ten o'clock Frank would still be in bed, his moustaches curling in a paper clip. He slept every night in heavy woolen underclothes and pyjamas which had to be dried each morning on the radiators. His appearance downstairs was the moment for a walk to the Palais de la Méditerranée, taking him to 12:30, which was lunchtime. Then he was gay, shakily conveying hors d'oeuvres variés, onions and Graves into his mouth. Then two small steps to a chaise longue and an open fire-place for a nice sleep until 3:30. Now came the afternoon drive—a two- or three-franc taxi drive round the pine-covered hills until 4:30, when he was impatient for a drink—and it was not, Scully added, usually tea. Then he would wrap himself up in front of the fire and read. So Scully would return to the writing—alone. "I turned out 150,000 words in ten weeks," claimed Scully. "I had spent four months on the book."

This routine was punctuated by Harris' seventy-fifth birthday party. He drank everything and anything, noted Scully, and suddenly his face turned green. He ran for the bathroom. Five minutes later he returned rosy-faced and smiling once more, having "washed out."

It was Scully who gave Nellie the 1931 diary in which she mapped out the last invalid year of Frank's life. Here we can see just the sort of person she is—loving her dog, security, pretty clothes, parties, people and funny stories. She liked to have her nails manicured in her room, to have her hair done and to go on trips to the hills to pick lavender or to Juan les Pins "to see the new pyjamas—really some of the women from the waist up were almost naked"—no backs at all (a feature that Frank enjoyed thoroughly).

On January 4 they visited the cinema, which made Frank sick. On January 6 he had recovered enough to receive Ben Tillett:[8] "Really such an amusing fellow, good hearted, loves a good lunch and a drink." He was just the guest for an invalid. He assured Frank that had he stayed in England he would have been Prime Minister, and made him feel a daredevil, recalling how just before the war he had driven the car down narrow mountain paths at such a rate that the two elderly ladies who were with him had begged to be put out so that they might walk home. Tillett was altogether a popular lunch guest—he could sing comic songs and tell funny stories.[9] Those were the times that Nellie enjoyed, but all too often there is recorded: "Nothing doing," or "Just a rotten worrying day." On January 17 she noted: "Scully wants to employ labour—a competent man who knows how to write because now they have all the 'material.' They or rather Scully has dug out all sorts of things, letter, and scraps of Frank and G.B.S. all Frank's written about G.B.S. in the past and with all this other stuff Frank has got now it will arrive at 100,000 words. The awful thing is money, we are desperately in need of it right now. I cannot make any difference in the house—the moment I try to make an economy Frank goes in for something more luxurious."

On Frank's birthday they went in for a luxurious party. Fifty people appeared. "Perfectly lovely day and all the world seems to be sending telegrams and flowers. I am so glad because Frank seems so cheered." On February 25 she was in her element again giving a party for "Pauline." "What a crowd turned up," and then on March 13: "We had boulebaisse hope its spelt right and nobody will get spots after it." On the 16th they went to "Emma's . . . for a Party she gave

---

[8] Ben Tillett (1860–1943), Secretary of Dock, Wharf, Riverside and General Workers' Union of Great Britain and Ireland, Labour Member of Parliament for North Salford, 1917–24, 1929–31.

[9] Ben Tillett wrote a bread-and-butter letter to the Harrises on January 14, 1931. It had been a "cheerio" to see them both, he said, to find all the bonhomie, and the courage of life, to share in the brightness of conversation, the wit of it all and joyous sense of camaraderie. It gave the vein, the pep, the sap to life itself and completed the joy of an all too short stay in Nice.

for Stella Ballertone . . . she had turkey, chicken, ham, sausages, Paté de Fuge [?], Salad Russe, Salad Francée, Salad goodness knows what. Wines and champagnes. We danced—there was quite a crowd of people —at 11 we wended our way home-wards. We had to walk." March 17 was Nellie's birthday: "(Hell) I would love to forget it." Scully insisted on coming "and taking us to lunch . . . we lunched at Reynard's out of doors it was v. gay." On March 20 Scully and his wife lunched. "Mrs. Baker came in from St. Paul looking very tragic!" It appeared that a scandal was rocking Nice: it was being whispered that Frank could not write any more, that Miss Krim was putting things together and Scully was rewriting, "etc." Even Miss Krim laughed, noted Nellie, "as Frank had completed 60,000 words of sheer matter re this Shaw book and Scully knew at the beginning he was engaged to dig and find data etc. stuff that Frank refused to do."

And so the days passed between lunches, light dinners and sometimes the movies, which never seemed to agree with Frank, giving him attacks of the hiccups. There were drives through fields of yellow jonquils, cherry, apple and peach blossom, the young green spring hills of Vence: "a peep of heaven in beauty" was how Nellie described it. On April 6 that "Bounder Newton" was telling lies again. On April 24 someone had made "an attachment" against Frank's bank account for "some imagined thing that happened 30 years ago." Fortunately, Nellie observed, there were only 200 francs in the account—but suppose they made a claim against "our home . . . Frank could remember nothing about it." On May 1 "at nine thirty Scully and his wife called for Frank's corrected M.S.S. of the typewritten Shaw"; on May 6 Frank had a touch of jaundice and became ill, requiring morphia; by the ninth he was in a state of collapse, but by the twenty-second had recovered enough to walk out and sit on the terrace of the "Grand Bleu." On their return they discovered Scully, who traveled up to the flat in the unreliable lift. The door was opened and the maid said that Lady McCarthy was in the sitting room, whereupon Scully shot down in the lift again. Lady McCarthy was full of news. Scully had written to her, she said, that Harris was so ill he was obliged to be in Saint-Raphaël to see a specialist, and his wife was so ill that she was in bed. "Mon Dieu," said Nellie, "I understood why he fled down in the lift." On June 18 Charlie Chaplin appeared, without his cockney accent. He had been visiting his school, Hanwell, near the Crystal Palace. It had been an emotional and spiritual experience, he said; everything was the same, even the holes in the walls where they stuffed the meat.

The summer straggled on. In July the maid went away for her holiday and Nellie fell down and hurt her leg. On August 13 she had either prickly heat or fish poisoning. On the fourteenth, Pierre Bodin came, bearing more flowers than Nellie had ever seen one person carry before. Frank became so unwell that they were obliged to telegraph Bodin that they were unable to go to Saint-Tropez. On August 17: "Frank seems terrible sad and continued to sit in his chaise longue after the maid had served the lunch. I waited some minutes and said surely you are coming and not going to let me eat alone. He came over v. slowly . . . pulled the chair out. He looked at me very sorrowfully and said 'Nellie how sorry I am to go and leave you.' I said with a lump in my throat what do you mean? Knowing his days of depression. He continued to look at me 'so sorry to leave you alone to fight with all the ghouls that will be after my flesh.' " On August 18 Nellie's face was so swollen that she was unable to go out. Frank took his drive alone, insisting on going out, and returned at 6:30. Nellie was in bed "feeling bad." Frank said pathetically, "I wanted to tell you that I will never go out of the house without you again." Swollen face and all, Nellie got out a bottle of champagne to celebrate. On August 19, breathing with difficulty, Frank took his last drive; on his return he had a heart attack, coupled with asthma.

All the next day he fought for breath, and by the twenty-second his temperature had risen to 101, so that Nellie recorded they would not be able to keep an appointment to go with "Auntie Crotch" to Vence for her birthday. But by the twenty-fourth a big cylinder of oxygen had arrived and Frank seemed to be rallying once more. Nellie went to have her hair done and began thinking once more of "Auntie Crotch" and her party at Vence. Frank lay the next day on his chaise longue in the studio, looking out through open windows to the mountains. His eyes had lost their brightness, he could not eat. Nellie arranged for a nurse to come. She arrived on August 26, "so fresh and clean." Frank had asked for a pad and pencil; he held the pencil but wrote nothing. "Tomorrow I will," he said. At midnight the nurse woke Nellie from what seemed to be the heaviest sleep she had ever been in. The doctor was there in ten minutes. Frank, he said, would get through the night all right. There was a crash.

I rushed to his room. There was Frank sitting up on the edge of the bed. The nurse had given him a glass of champagne, he had dashed it out of her hand. I wiped his hands and his pyjamas, his eyes were wide open and ablaze—as of old—I got him to lie down . . . all at once he called Nellie my Nellie—I'm going. I waited, he fell into a sleep, nurse and I watched. . . . Frank slept peacefully and like a child. At twenty minutes after five nurse said he had gone. I called him and for the first time in all my memory he did not answer me. He was asleep for ever.

The funeral service was held in the American Church, where four years before they had been married. Nellie had no money to pay for a grave—a caveau—and for a little while it seemed she would have to bury him in an ordinary plot—which meant that after a certain time the body would be dug up and the plot used again. For three weeks Frank's body rested in the repository while friends raised the necessary funds. They selected a place in the British Cemetery at Caucade,[10] high up in the aromatic hills, with a view to the sea, shaded by an olive tree. Then "one or two friends saw him placed in the caveau, I saw it bricked over and I came away leaving my real self with my dear company [ion?] to sleep for ever."[11]

Now there were no more rows, no more scenes, and in her nostalgia only the smiles remained, and herself. Nellie traveled soon to England to visit the Shaws for corrections and additions to the biography. On her return:

I looked up and down the platform and it seemed to me that Frank would be waiting, it is the first time I have come back in *years* and not found him—generally he was there, so glad to see me he usually beamed with smiles and laughed his gladness at seeing me, how he kissed me—and told me it is like death to be without you—I have been so lonely—I will never let you out of my

[10] Section G, Row No. 11, Grave No. 1.

[11] Nellie and Miss Krim had a terrible time sorting out the papers. Various daughters wrote claiming money, Norah Stack (now Bradbury) being one. Miss Krim sent her a photograph with a note saying that Mrs. Harris wished her to know that there had been many such claims. There seems also to have been competition to own Frank's bed and the chair from which he did dictation. Mrs. Baker wanted to buy the bed for 500 francs; however, it went "with great pleasure" to a Mr. Gwyn Griffiths, who seemed to be thinking of writing a book on Frank. Nellie hoped that the bed "upon which he always slept in his own room and his chair from which he gave dictation" would help G.G. remember instances in his life while he was doing his book on him.

sight again, oh it's so good you are back damn this poverty that forces me to let you go, etc.—Then generally Frank had a couple of porters to attend him to the waiting taxi and with a flourish we drove off, the porters smiling at their tips—and Frank terribly concerned as to whether the frais and some other delicacy had arrived, he had ordered for my home coming—and then the fuss he made when we got in, he had his darling Nellie again. God was good.

Nellie's last twenty years were spent between America and Nice, struggling with the financial difficulties that she hated. On April 2, 1954, she signed an agreement for the publication of Volume V of *My Life and Loves*—the volume she had asked Frank never to publish. The advance royalties were to be 1,050,000 francs. A. Trocchi edited the book, which was published by the Olympia Press in Paris in 1958, omitting many of the repetitive portraits and stretching, with relish, the Oriental sexual fantasies, in a tone exactly Harris'. Nellie died three years before its publication, on March 25, 1955, from a stroke, in the British-American Hospital in Nice, aged apparently sixty-eight, and was bricked up in the grave beneath the olive tree.

Published Works by Frank Harris

Frank Harris to Arnold Bennett. 58 Letters, 1908–10.

The Bomb. London, John Long, 1908; New York, Kennerley, 1909; Chicago and London, University of Chicago Press, 1963.

Confessional. New York, Panurge Press, 1930.
CONTENTS: Introduction. *Part One: Persons.* Columbus, Joan of Arc, Napoleon, Tolstoy's Last Days. *Part Two: Places.* Great Cities of the World, Seville, Travel in France, Granada and the Alhambra. *Part Three: Principles.* Short Story Writing, The Art of Biography, Thoughts on Morals, Natural Religion. *Part Four: Passions.* An Execution in Paris, A Strange Story of Love.

Contemporary Portraits. First Series (with illustrations). London, Methuen & Co., 1915; New York, Kennerley, 1915; New York, Brentano's, 1920.
CONTENTS: Carlyle. Renan. Whistler: Artist and Fighter. Oscar Wilde. John Davidson: Ad Memoriam. Richard Middleton: Ad Memoriam. Sir Richard Burton. George Meredith. Robert Browning. Swinburne: The Poet of Youth and Revolt. Talks with Matthew Arnold. Guy de Maupassant. Talks with Paul Verlaine. Maurice Maeterlinck. Rodin. Fabre. Anatole France.

Contemporary Portraits. Second Series (with illustrations). New York, the author, 1919.
CONTENTS: George Bernard Shaw. Rudyard Kipling. Ernest Dowson. Theodore Dreiser. George Moore. Lord Dunsany and Sidney

Sime. James Thomson. Lionel Johnson and Hubert Crackanthorpe. Pierre Loti. Walter Pater. Herbert Spencer. The Right Hon. Arthur J. Balfour. The Right Hon. David Lloyd George. Viscount Grey. Georges Clemenceau. Shaw's Portrait by Shaw, or, How Frank ought to have done it.

Contemporary Portraits. Third Series (with illustrations). New York, the author, 1920.
   CONTENTS: Introduction. H. G. Wells. Upton Sinclair. John Galsworthy. Cunninghame Graham. Gilbert K. Chesterton. Arthur Symons. Winston Churchill. Russell Wallace. Thomas Huxley. Louis Wilkinson. W. L. George. Gaudier-Brzeska. Lord St. Aldwyn. Augustus John. Coventry Patmore. Walt Whitman.

Contemporary Portraits. Fourth Series. New York, Brentano's, 1923; London, Richards, 1924.
   CONTENTS: The Admirable Crichton. Wilfred Scawen Blunt and the Right Hon. George Wyndham. Memories of Richard Wagner. Ivan Turgenief, a snapshot. Charlie Chaplin, and a visit to Sing-Sing. John Tyndall. Ernest Haeckel. Grant Allen. Leonard Merrick. Herbert Trench. Max, "the incomparable." Matisse and Renoir. Senator La Follette. Memories of Mark Twain. Meetings with Maxim Gorki. Otto Kahn and Leon Trotzky. The Russian Delegates at Genoa. Emma Goldman, the famous anarchist. Gargoyles: Roosevelt, Wilson, Harding. Jim Larkin. Olive Schreiner: Ad Memoriam. Sarah Bernhardt. Lord Curzon and "The Souls."

Latest Contemporary Portraits. New York, Macaulay, 1927.
   CONTENTS: David Graham Phillips. Eleonora Duse. Henri Barbusse. Lord Bryce. George Russell (A.E.). Mrs. Humphry Ward. Eugene V. Debs. Charles Schwab. Prince Peter Kropotkin. Paul Bourget. Thomas Hardy. Ehrlich of "606." Louis Sullivan. Eugene Fromentin. Sir Herbert Tree. Flaubert and His Letters. Hatred in Art. Leon Bloy. Three Generations of Morgans. The Brothers de Goncourt and Realism. Lord Hartington. Ambassador Bernstorff. A Talk with A. E. Housman. Paul Deschanel. Frederic Harrison. Annie Besant. John Churton Collinns. Hyndman. Horace Traubel. Joseph Caillaux.

Elder Conklin and Other Stories. London, Heinemann, 1895 (1894); New York and London, Macmillan, 1894; London, John Lane, 1930; New York, Frank Harris, 1920. (One edition marked on cover *Elder Conklin and Other Western Stories* and another described as *Definitive Edition*.)

CONTENTS: Elder Conklin. The Sheriff and His Partner. A Modern Idyll. Eatin' Crow. The Best Man in Garotte. Gulmore, the Boss.

England or Germany? New York, Wilmarth Press, 1915.

Frank Harris on Bernard Shaw. New York, Simon and Schuster, 1931; London, Gollancz, 1931.

Great Days. London, John Lane; Toronto, Bell and Cockburn, 1914 (1913); New York, Kennerley, 1914.

How to Beat the Boer, A Conversation in Hades. London, Heinemann, 1900; London, Pearson Ltd., 1900.

Joan La Romée. London, Fortune Press, 1926; New York, Frank Harris Publishing Co.

Love in Youth. New York, Doran, 1916.

A Mad Love: The Strange Story of a Musician. New York, the author, 1920.

The Man Shakespeare and His Tragic Life Story. London, Frank Palmer, 1909; New York, Kennerley, 1909.

Mr. and Mrs. Daventry. A play in four acts. Based on the scenario by Oscar Wilde. Introduction by H. Montgomery Hyde. London, Richards Press, 1956.

Montes the Matador, and Other Stories. London, Grant Richards, 1900; New York, Kennerley, 1910; London, John Lane: The Bodley Head, 1930; London, John Lane, 1952.
CONTENTS: Montes the Matador. First Love: A Confession. Profit and Loss. The Interpreter: A Mere Episode. Sonia.

On the Trail: Being My Reminiscences as a Cowboy. London, John Lane, 1930.

My Reminiscences as a Cowboy. New York, Charles Boni Paper Books, 1930.

Oscar Wilde: His Life and Confessions (two volumes paged continuously). New York, privately published by the author, 1916. With "Memories of Oscar Wilde by G. B. Shaw," the author, New York, 1918.

Oscar Wilde . . . With a Preface by Bernard Shaw. London, Constable & Co., 1938.

Oscar Wilde: His Life and Confessions . . . Including the hitherto unpublished full and final confession by Lord Alfred Douglas and "Memories of Oscar Wilde by G. B. Shaw." New York, Garden City Publishing Co., 1932.

Published Works by Frank Harris

Oscar Wilde: His Life and Confessions. London, Panther Books, 1965.

New Preface to The Life and Confessions of Oscar Wilde. By Frank Harris and Lord Alfred Douglas. London, Fortune Press, 1925; 2d ed., 1927.

Pantopia. New York, Panurge Press, 1930.

Shakespeare and His Love (A Play in Four Acts and Epilogue). London, Frank Palmer, 1910.

Undream'd of Shores. London, Grant Richards, 1924; New York, Brentano's, 1924.
    CONTENTS: A Mad Love. Akbar: "The Mightiest." A Fit of Madness. A Chinese Story. St. Peter's Difficulty. Love is My Sin. As Others See Us. A Lunatic? In Central Africa. The Extra Eight Days. The Great Game. The Temple to the Forgotten Dead. My Last Word.

Unpath'd Waters. London, John Lane, 1913; New York, Kennerley, 1913.
    CONTENTS: The Miracle of the Stigmata. The Holy Man. The King of the Jews. The Irony of Chance. An English Saint. Mr. Jacob's Philosophy. The Ring. The Spider and the Fly. The Magic Glasses.

The Women of Shakespeare (with a frontispiece). London, Methuen & Co., 1911; New York, Kennerley, 1912.

The Yellow Ticket and Other Stories. London, Grant Richards, 1914.
    CONTENTS: The Yellow Ticket. The Veils of Isis. A French Artist. In the Vale of Tears. A Daughter of Eve. A Prostitute. Isaac and Rebecca. A Miracle and No Wonder. A Fool's Paradise. The Ugly Duckling.

THE AUTOBIOGRAPHY

My Life. New York, Frank Harris Publishing Co., 1925.

My Life and Loves. First volume. Paris, the author, 1922. Privately printed.

My Life and Loves. Volume 1. Paris, Obelisk Press (*c.* 1930).

My Life and Loves. 4 vols. Paris (1934?). Privately printed.

My Life and Loves. 4 vols. Paris, Obelisk Press, 1945.

My Life and Loves . . . Edited and with an introduction by John F. Gallagher. London, W. H. Allen, 1964.

My Life and Loves. London, Transworld Publishers, 1966.

FRANK HARRIS

My Life and Loves. Fifth volume. (Purporting to be by Frank Harris. In fact by Alexander Trocchi, based on unpublished material by Frank Harris.) Paris, Olympia Press, 1958.

My Life. Frank Harris. His Life and Adventures. An autobiography. With an introduction by Grant Richards. London, Richards Press, 1947; new edition, reset, 1952.

Frank Harris: My Life and Adventures. An autobiography. London, Paul Elek in association with Elek Books, 1958.

Select Bibliography

Arliss, George: *Up the Years from Bloomsbury*. Boston, Little Brown & Co., 1927.

Austin, Mary Hunter: *Earth Horizon*. Boston and New York, Houghton Mifflin Co., 1932.

Bagnold, Enid: *Autobiography*. London, Heinemann, 1969.

Bell, Thomas B.: "Oscar Wilde Without Whitewash" (unpublished).

Blathwayt, Raymond: *The Tapestry of Life*. London, G. Allen & Unwin; printed in U.S.A., 1924.

Bowen, Frank C.: *His Majesty's Coastguard*. London, Hutchinson & Co., 1928.

Brome, Vincent: *Frank Harris*. London, Cassell, 1959.

Brooks, Van Wyck: *The Confident Years 1885–1915*. London, J. M. Dent & Sons, 1952.

Brown, William Sorley: *The Life and Genius of T. W. H. Crosland*. London, Cecil Palmer, 1928.

Carlyle, Thomas: *Heroes and Hero Worship and the Heroic in History*. London, Cassell, 1908.

Carrel, Frederic: *The Adventures of John Johns*. London, Bliss, Sands & Co., 1897.

Cornwallis-West: *Edwardian Hey-days*. London and New York, Putnam, 1930.

Cumberland, Gerald: *Set Down in Malice*. London, Grant Richards, 1919.

Douglas, Alfred: *Without Apology*. London, Martin Secker, 1938.

Gertz, Elmer, and Tobin, A. I.: *Frank Harris*. Chicago, Madelaine Mendelsohn, 1931.

Goldman, Emma: *Living My Life*. New York, Alfred A. Knopf; London, Duckworth; printed in U.S.A., 1932.

Grosskurth, Phyllis: *John Addington Symonds.* London, Longmans, 1964.

Grossmith, George and Weedon: *Diary of a Nobody.* Bristol, J. W. Arrowsmith, 1892.

Hackenburg, Frederick: *A Solitary Parade.* New York, Thistle Press, 1929.

Hare, Kenneth, and St. J. George, Dorothea: *London's Latin Quarter.* London, John Lane, 1926.

Hart-Davis, Rupert (ed.): *Letters of Oscar Wilde.* London; New York, Harcourt, 1962.

Holroyd, Michael: *Hugh Kingsmill.* London, Unicorn Press, 1964; *Augustus John: The Years of Innocence.* London, Heinemann, 1974.

Hooley, Ernest Terah: *The Hooley Book.* London, John Dicks, 1904.

Huddleston, Sisley: *Bohemian, Literary and Social Life in Paris.* London, G. G. Harrap & Co., 1928.

Hunt, Violet: *The Flurried Years.* London, Hurst & Blackett, 1926.

Hyndman, Henry Mayers: *The Record of an Adventurous Life.* London, Macmillan & Co., 1911.

Jackson, Holbrook: *The Eighteen Nineties.* London, Grant Richards, 1913.

John, Augustus: *Chiaroscuro.* London, Jonathan Cape, 1952.

Johnston, Sir Harry Hamilton: *Story of My Life.* London, Chatto & Windus, 1923.

Kaplan, Justin: *Mr. Clemens and Mark Twain: A Biography.* New York, Simon and Schuster, 1966; London, Jonathan Cape, 1967.

Kingsmill, Hugh: *After Puritanism 1850–1900.* London, Duckworth, 1929; *Frank Harris.* London, Jonathan Cape, 1932.

Lang, Theo: *My Darling Daisy.* London, Joseph, 1966.

Lara, Isidore de: *Many Tales of Many Cities.* London, Hutchinson & Co., 1928.

Linklater, Eric: *The House of Gair.* London, Jonathan Cape, 1953.

Lunn (Kingsmill), Hugh: *The Will to Love.* London, Chapman & Hall, 1919.

McKay, Claude. *A Long Way from Home.* New York, L. Furman Inc., 1937.

Munby, A. J.: "Unpublished Diaries." 1859–98.

Murry, John Middleton: *Between Two Worlds.* London, Jonathan Cape, 1935.

Nemirovitch-Danchenko: *Personal Reminiscences of General Skobeleff.* London, W. H. Allen & Co., 1884.

Nevill, Lady Dorothy: *My Own Times.* London, Methuen & Co., 1912

Novikov, Olga: *Skobeleff and the Slavonic Cause.* London, 1883.

O'Sullivan, Vincent: *Opinions.* London, Unicorn Press, 1959.

Pearson, Hesketh: *Modern Men and Mummers.* London, G. Allen & Unwin, 1921; *Extraordinary People.* London, Heinemann, 1965.

Plomer, W. C.: *Cecil Rhodes.* Peter Davies, 1933.

Richards, Grant: *Author Hunting, by an Old Literary Sportsman*. London, Hamish Hamilton, 1934.

Root, E.: *Frank Harris*. Odyssey Press, 1947.

Roth, Samuel: *The Private Life of Frank Harris*. New York, William Faro, 1931.

Rothenstein, Sir William: *Men and Memories*. London, Faber & Faber, 1931–39.

Sarawak, H. H. the Muda Dayang of: *Relations and Complications*. London, John Lane: The Bodley Head, 1929.

Savage, Henry: *Richard Middleton*. London, Cecil Palmer, 1922.

Scully, Frank: *Rogues' Gallery*. Hollywood, Calif., Murray & Gee, 1943.

Shaw, George Bernard: *The Dark Lady of the Sonnets*. London, Constable & Co., 1914.

Stephens, Kate: *Life at Laurel Town in Anglo-Saxon Kansas*. Lawrence, Kans., Alumni Association of University of Kansas, 1920; *Lies and Libels of Frank Harris*. New York, Antigone Press, 1929.

Stokes, Sewell: *Pilloried!* London, Richards Press, 1928.

Tobin, A. I.: "Table Talks with Frank Harris" (unpublished); *The Love-Life of Byron Caldwell Smith* (introd. by A. I. Tobin). New York, Antigone Press, 1930.

Viereck, George Sylvester, the Elder: *Glimpses of the Great*. London, Duckworth, 1930.

Wells, H. G.: *Experiment in Autobiography*. London, Victor Gollancz; Cresset Press, 1934.

Wyndham, Horace: *The Nineteen Hundreds*. New York, Thomas Seltzer, 1923.

ACKNOWLEDGMENTS

I would like to acknowledge the help not only of my patient editors, Mr. Christopher Sinclair-Stevenson and Mrs. Helen Thomson, but of Miss B. M. Austin, Mr. H. Bilton of the Bradford Central Library, Mr. Philip Burstow, Mrs. J. Chapell, Major Compton, Mrs. Edna C. Davis, Mr. John de Courcy Ireland, the late Dean of Ely, Mrs. Denton, Mr. Eifion Ellis, Mrs. K. Evans, Mr. H. B. Fleming, Mr. James Friend, Mr. Elmer Gertz, Mr. Laurence Gomme, Dr. Teresa Hankey, Sir Rupert Hart-Davis, Mr. F. W. Hardiman, Mr. Keith Harries, Mrs. T. K. Harris, Mr. Austin Harrison, Mrs. Hopkinson, Miss Penelope Jardine, the Reverend J. D. Jones, Mrs. Mary Lago, Mr. Theo Lang, Mrs. Clare Lyon, Miss Anita Leslie, the late Mr. Eric Linklater, Mr. Charles McNeill Caldwell, Professor Gabriel Neale, Mr. Henry Miller, Mrs. Margaret Morris, Mr. Shaun O'Shea, Miss M. Patch, Mr. Hubert E. Parry, Mrs. Hesketh Pearson, Mrs. Jane Price-Williams, Mr. Roger Pugh, Mr. Arthur Leonard Ross, the Honorable Sir Steven Runciman, Mr. Charles Seaton, Librarian of *The Spectator*, London, Mr. Joseph W. Snell of the Kansas State Historical Society, Mr. Camillus Travers, the Reverend Luke Taheney, O.P., Mr. A. I. Tobin, Mr. Sewell Stokes, Dame Rebecca West, Mr. Alwyn Williams of the Rhondda Borough Council, Mr. Gerald Yorke.

I would like also to thank various libraries and universities for their help and cooperation: the Beinecke Rare Book and Manuscript Library; the Bodleian Library; the Boston Public Library; the Bradford City Art Gallery and Museum; the British Museum; the Central Library, Bradford; the City Library, York; Cornell University Library; Dartmouth College Library; Detroit Public Library; Enoch Pratt Free Library; Houghton Library; Harvard University; Humanities Research Center, University of Texas at Austin; Kenneth Spencer Research Library; Library of Congress, Manuscript Division; London Library; Manuscripts Department, Lilly Library, Indiana University, Bloomington; National Library of Wales; New York Public Library; New York University Library; Princeton University Library; Stanford University Library; Warburg Institute; William Andrews Memorial Library, University of California, Los Angeles; University of Pennsylvania; University of Kansas Library; University of Illinois Library; Yale University Library. Finally, I thank Mr. Michael Holroyd for his care and his suggestions.

Thanks are also due to the following for permission to quote passages from published books: The Estate of H. G. Wells for *Experiment in Autobiography* by H. G. Wells; The Society of Authors on behalf of the Bernard Shaw Estate for Preface to *The Dark Lady of the Sonnets* by Bernard Shaw; W. H. Allen & Co. Ltd., for *My Life and Loves* by Frank Harris; Sir Rupert Hart-Davis for *Letters* by Oscar

Wilde; Romilly John for *Chiaroscuro* by Augustus John; Mrs. Dorothy Hopkinson for *Frank Harris* by Hugh Kingsmill.

For unpublished material, I would like to thank Mr. Arthur Leonard Ross for permission to quote from Frank Harris' unpublished papers; The Humanities Research Center, the University of Texas at Austin, for permission to quote from Frank and Nellie Harris' manuscripts; Miss Marion T. Bell for permission to quote from her father's *Oscar Wilde Without Whitewash*; and Mr. Austin Harrison for permission to quote a letter from his father.

Index

Froude, James Anthony, 70, 81, 82, 85
Froude, Margaret, 81

Galsworthy, John, 346
Galway (in mid-19th century), 15–16, 21, 23
"Garden of Sleep, The" (song by de Lara), 93, 95
Garmoyle, Lord, 99–100, 130
Garrick Club, 71, 72, 97
Gaudier-Brzeska, Henri, 340, 343, 359
Gay Dombeys (Johnston), 189
Genius, The (Dreiser), 347
Gentle Shakespeare: A Vindication, The (Yeatman), 192
George, Dorothea St. J., 289fn.
German language, 74–75, 83, 208
Germany, 321–23
Gertz, Elmer, 9, 177, 184, 193, 207, 283, 351, 368, 385, 392, 400
  his sources for FH biography, 24fn., 49–50
  on FH's American experiences, 50, 60
  on FH's alleged blackmail, 190
  on FH's alleged homosexuality, 275fn.
  on FH's days in Germany, 78, 396
  on FH and Nellie, 217–18, 343, 381, 398
Gibbon, Edward, 249
Gilfachgoch, Fishguard, Ireland, 16, 17, 19, 20
Gladstone, Herbert, 257
Gladstone, William Ewart, 106, 149–51, 171
Glasgow, 316
Glass, Hannah, 188
Glimpses of the Great (Viereck), 405
God's spy, 391, 392
Goethe, Johann Wolfgang von, 151–52, 284
Goldman, Emma, 349
Goldsmith, Oliver, 101
Gomme, Lawrence, 282fn., 294–96
Gosse, Edmund, 140, 171, 175
Göttingen, 76–78, 86
  University of, 76

Gourmet, Le, 256
Graham, S. R. G., 230
Granier, Jeanne, 155
Gray's Inn, 125, 126
Great Days (Harris), 304
Greece, 78
Greenbrier Hotel, White Sulphur Springs, 344
Greene, 18th-century poet, 277
Greenwich Village, 344
Gregory, Mrs., 56
Grenfell, Willie, 170
Griffiths, Gwyn, 412fn.
Grigor, J., 71
Grimm's Law, 209
Grimthorpe, Ernest Beckett, Lord, *see* Beckett
Grosskurth, Phyllis, 141
Grossmith, George and Weedon, 100

Hackenburg, Frederick, 351, 354
Hackett, Francis, 172
Hackney *Mercury*, 38, 66, 73, 78, 79, 84, 91, 146–50, 152
Haldeman-Julius, Emanuel, 373
Hales, A. G., 226
Hall, Newman, 163
Hall, Samuel and Anna Maria, 15
Hallett, Col. Hughes, 116
Hallowell, Martha, 49
Hamilton, Duke and Duchess of, 229
Hamilton, Gerald, 378, 379
Hamilton, Louise, 365–66, 381
Hamlet, 200–201, 257
Hampstead Heath, 289
Hankey, Dr. Teresa, 203fn.
Hannaford, Gertrude, 32
Hanwell, 410
Harberton, Lord, 346fn.
Hardwicke, Lord, 202
Hardy, Thomas, 279, 402
Hare, Kenneth, 288–89, 340
Harmsworth, Lord, 117
Harries, Keith, 17fn.
Harries, Thomas, 17
Harries family, 16–17

Wilde, Oscar (cont.)
  homosexuality, 173
  friendship with FH, 177–81, 340, 383
  personality and appearance, 178
  FH's championship of, 178–79, 184,
    229, 292, 340, 345, 383, 396
  court trial and punishment, 178–81,
    190
  blaming of Douglas, 179, 213, 388
  FH's financial support, 180–81, 194–
    199, 203–7, 216, 221–23
  imprisonment, 194–95
  on Riviera, 204–7, 216
  dispute with FH, 221–23
  death of, 223
  FH's biography of, 267; *see also*
    Oscar Wilde (Harris)
Wilkinson, Louis, 296, 297
William II, Kaiser, 322, 362
Williams, Gwladys Price, *see* Price-
  Williams, Gwladys
William Shakespeare: A Critical Study
  (Brandes), 200fn.
Williams Wynn, Lady, 27, 31, 34–36, 125
Williams Wynn, Sir Watkin, 26, 34–36
Williams Wynn family, 33
Wills, Justice, 181
Will to Love, The (Kingsmill), 291
Wilson, Mr., 263
Windsor, Canada, 394
Wisdom of Frank Harris, The (Bruno),
  344fn.
Wolfe, Mrs., 240

Wolseley, Lord, 94, 142–43, 153, 174
Woman's Heart, A (Stephens), 328
Woman Who Knew Frank Harris, The
  (Waugh), 290
women, 118–37, 228
  education of, 119–20
  legal rights of, 112–13, 221
  and prostitution, 112–15
Women in Love, 333
Women of Shakespeare, The (Harris),
  267
Women's Night Court, 348–49
Woodstock, N.Y., 363
Woodstock Hotel, New York, 398
Working Men's Association of Ruabon,
  27, 44
World, 286, 288, 308
World War I, 314–15, 318–23, 350
Wormwood Scrubs, 387
Wrexham Advertiser, 26–28, 34, 36
Wyndham, George, 111
Wyndham, Horace, 115fn., 228
Wynnstay Park, 26, 31

Yeatman, John Pym, 192, 200, 205
Yellow Book (Beardsley), 359
Yellow Ticket, The (Richards), 324
Young, Filson, 374
Young Scholar's Letters, A (Smith),
  328–29

Zorach, William, 363